"Father Paul Mayer's life on this earth was a gift to all who value love and justice. Reading *Wrestling with Angels* is a way to learn about not just Paul's life but also about organized efforts in the twentieth century for peace, justice, and environmental protection and connection. It is a way to understand Paul's call for human beings to 'literally reinvent ourselves through the alchemy of the Spirit or perish, climb another rung on the evolutionary ladder, to another level of human consciousness.'"

—TED GLICK,
author of Burglar for Peace

"Paul Mayer recounts decades of American history from a spiritual perspective, reminding us of the necessity of witnessing, speaking up, and defending the defenseless. It is fair to say that the blood of the prophets ran in his veins."

—JACQUELINE MOSIO,
writer and editor

"Father Paul Mayer was a long-distance runner for justice and a great storyteller."

—CORNELL WEST,
Professor emeritus, Princeton University

"Paul Mayer's spiritual odyssey is a compelling account of a life of service to the planet and of healing the wounds of war and injustice."

—MARTIN SHEEN,
actor and political activist

"Paul Mayer's memoir is a well-told story of recent times by one who lived through the World Wars, the Great Depression, and subsequent American world dominance in economic and political affairs, as well as through the opening years of the twenty-first century. For anyone wishing to understand the problems and possibilities of our own times, this would be an extremely helpful read."

—THOMAS BERRY,
Director, Riverdale Center of Religious Research

"This very readable story of an extraordinary life will absorb you from start to finish."

—PETE SEEGER,
American folk singer and social activist

"Paul Mayer was a great original, and in this potent memoir, he gives us a model of the new man who profoundly makes a difference in world and time. He had many lives—Jewish heritage, Catholic priest, social activist, world server, compassionate caregiver to the poor and the marginalized, and, above all, one who wrestled with meaning and the quest for truth. An extraordinary read, and one that will incite both conscience and commitment."

—JEAN HOUSTON,
author and lecturer

"Paul Mayer was a man of exceptional qualities. . . . His passion for the truth, his commitment to justice, and the history of his long journey in the service of those in social struggle makes him worthy of our attention. I recommend to all who have the opportunity to read this book, that they do so."

—HARRY BELAFONTE,
actor and political activist

"Paul Mayer was a remarkable man with an inspiring story. His memoir not only documents his lifetime of involvement with peace and justice issues but makes a compelling case for caring for our Mother Earth. Like John Muir, Mayer saw clearly how everything connects, and he showed us how to love this world."

NANCY LORD,
Writer Laureate for Alaska from 2008–10

"I think the prose is lively, clear, and appealing—and would appeal to young adults if it fell into their hands. I could imagine reading such a book in my freshman course at Knox, for instance, but I could also imagine it being assigned in high schools."

—NATANIA ROSENFELD,
Professor of English, Knox College

WRESTLING WITH ANGELS

WRESTLING WITH ANGELS

A Spiritual Memoir of a Political Life

PAUL MAYER

RESOURCE *Publications* · Eugene, Oregon

WRESTLING WITH ANGELS
A Spiritual Memoir of a Political Life

Resource Publications
An Imprint of Wipf and Stock Publishers
199 W. 8th Ave., Suite 3
Eugene, OR 97401

www.wipfandstock.com

PAPERBACK ISBN: 978-1-7252-7011-4
HARDCOVER ISBN: 978-1-7252-7012-1
EBOOK ISBN: 978-1-7252-7013-8

.   NOVEMBER 9, 2021 2:29 PM

We move forward in the grand tradition of transformative social movements that have defined American history. We stand on the shoulders of those who have struggled before us, and we pick up where others have left off.

—OCCUPY WALL STREET STATEMENT

TABLE OF CONTENTS

INTRODUCTION | 1

PROLOGUE | 7

CHAPTER 1

THE GATHERING STORM | 9
Born in the Shadow of the Holocaust

CHAPTER 2

AMERIKA, AMERIKA! | 17

CHAPTER 3

AN UNLIKELY CATHOLIC | 24

CHAPTER 4

"COME FOLLOW ME" | 32
The Life of a Monk

CHAPTER 5

UNIVERSITY OF MUNICH | 43
A Bittersweet Return to the Land of My Birth

CHAPTER 6

A MONK IN THE CIVIL RIGHTS MOVEMENT | 52
Encounter with Dr. Martin Luther King Jr.

CHAPTER 7

    THE WAR CLOUDS GATHER | 67
    Vietnam inside the Cloister

CHAPTER 8

    UNDER THE VOLCANO | 74
    Sojourn in Cuernavaca

CHAPTER 9

    LOS POBRES DE LA TIERRA | 84
    Work in San Miguelito, Panama

CHAPTER 10

    THE RELUCTANT BRIDEGROOM | 96

CHAPTER 11

    BLESSED ARE THE PEACEMAKERS | 102
    Vietnam, the Catonsville Nine and the Berrigans

CHAPTER 12

    PASSING ON THE FLAME | 119
    The Peace Underground and New Draft Board Actions

CHAPTER 13

    THE HARRISBURG CONSPIRACY CASE | 126
    Peace Activists as Kidnappers and Bombers

CHAPTER 14

    FBI WET DREAMS | 133
    My Public Information Files

CHAPTER 15

    PROJECT SHARE | 136
    A New Community and Family Life

CHAPTER 16

"You Say You Wanna Revolution?" | 144
The Anti-War Movement, the American Left and the Counterculture

CHAPTER 17

Under the Bombs in Vietnam | 152

CHAPTER 18

USSR: A Peace Journey with Grace Paley | 165
Meetings with Dr. Andrei Sakharov and the Dissenters

CHAPTER 19

A Journey to the Bloody Land of Milk
and Honey | 177
Israel and Palesti; Meetings with Yasser Arafat and Israeli Peacemakers

CHAPTER 20

Interfaith Peace Work | 192
Founding the Religious Task Force

CHAPTER 21

Blessed Are the Feet of Those Who Bring
Good News of Peace | 202
Travel to Japan and Meetings with Atom Bomb Survivors

CHAPTER 22

UN Special Session on Disarmament II | 214
A Season of Hope

CHAPTER 23

"Yo soy un hombre sincero" | 219
Visiting Cuba, Meeting Fidel

CHAPTER 24

    RELIGION IN CUBA, PASTORS FOR PEACE | 230

CHAPTER 25

    JESSE JACKSON'S 1984 PRESIDENTIAL CAMPAIGN
    AND THE RAINBOW COALITION | 239

CHAPTER 26

    "AND A LITTLE CHILD SHALL LEAD THEM" | 263
    Children of War

CHAPTER 27

    A SECOND FAMILY LIFE | 283
    Grandchildren in the Ghetto

CHAPTER 28

    I DO! MARRIAGE AT THE CROSSROADS | 296

CHAPTER 29

    YOGA PRACTITIONER AND TEACHER | 302

CHAPTER 30

    THE MAKING OF AN EARTH GUARDIAN | 310
    Nature, Native American Legacy and Other Influences

CHAPTER 31

    EARTH SUMMITS / GLOBAL MOVEMENTS | 322

CHAPTER 32

    CLIMATE CRISIS COALITION | 333
    Turning to the Future

    EPILOGUE | 343

    List of Images | 347

Introduction

IT WAS ON A COLD day in December 2011, a week before Christmas and a few months before my eighty-first birthday, that I found myself climbing a fifteen-foot linked iron fence along with an Episcopal bishop in his purple robe, a Josephite nun, a handful of other clergy and sixty or so young Occupy Wall Street justice activists. Down below, in their inappropriate Martian riot gear, a group of New York's Finest was waiting to greet us with the traditional plastic handcuffs. We were occupying an unused empty lot in a drab downtown neighborhood, which a wealthy New York Church had denied the newborn movement, in spite of weeks of respectful negotiations. I felt that the time had come in the name of the One for whom "there was no room in the inn" to cast my lot with this visionary youth movement that was sweeping the planet from Cairo to New York.

I had been writing my memoirs for close to ten years and it had always been my hope that my life story—spanning a good part of the fascinating twentieth and now part of the twenty-first century—might be of use, a vision in service to others, especially to our young people for whom I have a particular love and respect. Perhaps it could be a reminder—even occasionally a guide or a handbook—of what even one man can accomplish and change in a lifetime, however imperfectly and unevenly, if he tries to be an instrument of the Divine in service of the common good.

I have much hope that despite all the disasters we presently face in the form of war, economic meltdown and possible climate Armageddon, our youth will have the imagination and pizzazz to turn things around while there is still time. "A little child shall lead them" (Isaiah) is more than poetic rhetoric. They have often been my teachers. The young and courageous leaders of "Children of War" from all over the world turned my life around and are still very much with me. This initiative was a visionary global youth project that I had a hand in launching.

1

I understand the idea of youth leadership as more than a socio-logical concept—almost a spiritual one. In spite of all the protestations of graduation speeches, our young people are still perceived as more of a problem than an asset. It is not sentimental to discover—even sometimes under layers of dysfunction—a certain freshness, aliveness, imaginative power and hope and the ability to create something genuinely new even in dark times.

I realize now as I complete this book in the spring of 2012 that I wrote the previous paragraphs about the power and the imperative of youth vision many years ago when I first put pen to paper. At that time, not in my wildest midnight visions would I have believed the miraculous explosion of youth imagination and initiative that is surging across the planet like a mighty tidal wave. This global youth impetus is driven by an unquenchable thirst for justice, a vision of sharing the earth's riches more equitably and a desire to give voice to the voiceless.

How ironic, almost deliciously inappropriate, that this volcanic eruption should have originated in the Arab world—so often held in contempt and only depicted in caricature—and in the verdant season of spring. The youth of Tunisia and Egypt, with unprecedented courage, used the magic of the Internet and social networks to face the fury and violence of their tyrants. And as an added twist of defying the Western stereotypes of violent Arabs and Muslims, they actually used the inspira-tion of King and Gandhi and circulated the writings of Gene Sharp, per-haps one of the greatest scholars of the history and tactics of non-violent social change.

Now Palestinian villagers, young and old, are defending their water sources and olive groves non-violently every Friday after prayer in the face of brutal repression. And even Israeli youth have pitched their tents for social justice along the elegant avenues of Tel Aviv.

But it came as a greater shock, surprise and thrill when right under my nose in my beloved New York City in the summer of 2011 the Oc-cupy Wall Street movement erupted. In those early days, when very few grasped the historic import of this youth revolt, I intuited that this might be the beginning of something that some of us had been dreaming of for a long time. I decided that this visionary and heroic campaign of our young people deserved at least some sign of support from people of faith and older folks, so I put on my clerical outfit and wandered around Zuc-cotti Park—later baptized Liberty Park. The young people always seemed pleased to see me. At that time I encountered very few other religious types—just a handful of young generous students from Union Seminary acting as "Occupy chaplains." Later I became part of an interfaith clergy group called Occupy Faith under the creative leadership of Judson Memorial Church.

Slowly it began to dawn on me that perhaps I was the one who was being ministered to as, before my unbelieving eyes, a new kind of community was being born. Could this be a contemporary manifestation—perhaps even "secular"— of the *Anawim*, that biblical remnant community of the poor, forgotten and powerless, who, through some divine irony become the vehicles of historical transformation?

Thomas Merton, monk, mystic and social critic and my mentor and lifelong source of inspiration through his writings, had spoken in a similar vein of a new form of youth monasticism in the 1960s in his talk on "Marxism and Monastic Perspectives," delivered to a group of Asian monks and nuns in Thailand just a few hours before his death. At an earlier international conference of student revolutionaries, one of the young participants had challenged him with the assertion "We are the true monks" and Thomas had taken these words seriously. He commented that "the monk is somebody who says, in one way or another, that the claims of the world are fraudulent" and this represented some common bond with the young students of his day—and I believe it still does today.

One of the challenges now confronting the Occupy movement — along with maintaining a courageous spirit of non-violence — is the ancient one of the battle against ego. Like a dark force it lies at the root of divisions, splits, competition (much loved by the imperial state) and all those subtle and not so subtle dynamics that can weaken and even destroy a community. No amount of prescriptions or poring over wisdom texts can heal this malady. Only some form of entering into the depths of the human consciousness itself and going to a place of silence through simple meditation can free us from the grip that ego has on our minds and hearts. One hopes that the creativity that has been the hallmark of Occupy will also be applied to this challenge. These pages will amply illustrate how the wrestling match with ego has marked my life and even as an octogenarian still does on a daily basis.

The ongoing need for such a creative, flexible movement was illustrated by the 100,000 students appearing overnight on the streets of Montréal in June 2012, non-violently protesting educational cut backs.

Then in October the extraordinary Occupy Sandy was another outpouring of youth generosity to face the great hurricane.

I have the shining eyes of all our youth before me as I write—eyes filled with the enthusiasm of their loving and open hearts. In testimony to them, may these pages be not just one more self-serving, narcissistic, pious tome, but rather a word of truth in lying times, to offer some guidance both through my victories and missteps and occasionally provide some entertainment. It has become clearer to me how these pages might serve sometimes as inspiration, sometimes as deterrent, occasionally as an ad hoc guide to young people and their elders.

My early childhood in Nazi Germany had deeply marked me and symbolized for me the first great divine intervention into my destiny, saving me from the fiery fate of millions of my fellow Jews. Perhaps it was this trauma of my early wounding that had given me an instant identification with victims of violence and injustice and the passion for making things right that has followed me all my life. How this skinny little Jewish teenager who lived in Washington Heights, the enclave of German-Jewish refugees in upper Manhattan, made the transition to the Catholic Church and even to monasticism is a riddle, which I hope to unravel more clearly in the following pages.

Quite unexpectedly my eighteen years as a Benedictine monk were also to connect me later to the subterranean revolutionary currents that were stirring within Church and society during the stormy 1960s. These tremors would become the seedbed for a new theology and a radical new cosmology, which would challenge the rigid presupposition of a formalistic, medieval, often cold Catholicism. Within the Church this awakening culminated in the Second Vatican Council where the ancient Church of Rome attempted to open the windows and "let a little fresh air in" (words of the good Pope John XXIII), only to be blown over by a virtual hurricane of dissent and upheaval. This template for renewal and resurrection is as valid today as it was then in spite of the periodic efforts by the Vatican to roll it all back.

Later during my monastic period I was unexpectedly transported to a life-changing encounter with the civil rights movement and Dr. Martin Luther King Jr. in Selma, Alabama. It was here that the profound lesson of the power of non-violent struggle was forever burned into my consciousness by the courageous example of marginalized African American people.

I eventually accepted an invitation to work in Panama at the experimental community of San Miguelito, which helped inspire the *comunidades de base*, those grassroots communities that later became the locus of Liberation Theology. When I returned to the United States as a married priest I began a new life of peace activism during the height of the war in Vietnam by becoming involved in the non-violent destruction of the 1A files in local draft boards, which drafted young men into the dark calling to kill and be killed. This work eventually led to a dramatic visit to devastated North Vietnam, where I experienced living under the fearful explosions of the US bombs. Later I worked with Japanese atom bomb survivors, and eventually co-founded "Children of War," a movement led by courageous teenage youth from conflict zones around the world. I had begun a new career of taking on the invitation of Jesus in the Sermon on the Mount to be blessed as a "peace maker."

About ten years ago the presumptuous idea came to me of putting the story of my checkered career down on paper. I had been gifted with one of the ingredients of an old Chinese curse: "May you have an interesting life." It has been filled with grace, disaster, many missteps as well as moments of achievement.

From the first moment in which I attempted to penetrate the well-insulated obscurity of my birth memory, I realized how so much of my past life felt inaccessible. How can I ever smuggle myself past the forbidding gatekeepers of my memory that seem to jealously guard the well-kept secrets of the past? But when literal memory leaves off, the angel of the imagination takes over as the mysterious guide to one's inner life and serves as the key to those most ancient memories hidden in the subterranean world of the unconscious.

My life has spanned some of the most wonderful as well as some of the most awful moments of the twentieth century and is now shamelessly edging its way into the perhaps even fiercer twenty-first, like the camel pushing his nose under the tent flap. I invite you to join me for the adventure. Climb on board the great cosmic roller coaster and fasten your seat belts. I wish us all the ancient Hebrew blessing: "L'chaim"—to life!

> All of a sudden he discovered, not what he wanted to do but what he just had to do, had to do it whether he wanted to or not, because if he did not do it he knew that he could never live with himself for the rest of his life, never live with what all the men and women that had died to make him had left inside of him for him to pass on; with all the dead ones waiting and watching to

see if he was going to do it right, fix things right so that he would be able to look in the face not only of the old dead ones but all the living ones that would come after him when he would be one of the dead.

— William Faulkner, *Absalom, Absalom*

Prologue

THE DOORBELL RANG INSISTENTLY THAT early Monday morning in June 1972. The caller identified himself as an agent of the Internal Revenue Service (IRS) and this touched on some long-buried fears from my childhood in Nazi Germany. His name was Bob Sullivan, and he had come to discuss my refusal to pay the three percent telephone excise tax, which LBJ, in an act of presidential largesse, had assigned to our apparently undernourished military budget. He was a tall, thin, slightly nervous man with a surprising goatee, and I invited him into our apartment to sit down after the three-story climb. He sat down but declined a cup of herb tea.

I told him that I had recently returned from North Vietnam and had seen with my own eyes how our tax dollars were really being spent. Our Air Force was literally committing war crimes by bombing villages, hospitals, churches and pagodas, and no decent American would want to pay for that, would they? I brought out some grim photographs we had taken of our trip and he got even more nervous, but seemed somewhat interested.

"The bottom line, Mr. Mayer, is that we might have to impound your car or take it out of your salary," was Bob Sullivan's next step in our dialogue. I told him that my car was under someone else's name and I didn't even have a salary. Well, they would find something and he urged me to reconsider, and with that he got up and left.

About a month later the bell rang again and it was Bob Sullivan and the IRS. This time he was taking a different tack. He asked me: "What would it take for you to consider paying your back taxes?" He was now looking for a way for me to get out of my dilemma. I thought for a moment and said, "Maybe if peace candidate McGovern is elected and the war is ended, I might reconsider." It was shortly before the presidential elections. "Also, if they changed the provision about directing the telephone excise tax specifically for military purposes."

He didn't say anything, but it seemed to make him more pensive. In the course of our conversation, he let it slip that the IRS had been secretly auditing my income tax returns. This was, of course, illegal since the law requires that the person being audited be notified. But, of course, we knew that people on Nixon's White House Enemies List and others were under surveillance, having their phones tapped and their mail opened, etc. All of this for being loyal, patriotic citizens and exercising their First Amendment rights and trying to improve their country—but it did evoke some feelings of fear and anger.

He also inquired further about my trip to Vietnam and other peace activities. I told him about various demonstrations and our Fast for Life—a forty-day water fast for peace that I had initiated—and he seemed somewhat impressed.

His last visit came about two weeks later and this time his demeanor was almost furtive. He said that he could not stay too long because his supervisor was waiting for him in the car. Bob said that he had come to tell me that he would shortly resign from the IRS. After our conversations, his conscience would not allow him to continue what he was doing while the war was going on. I was deeply touched and assured him of my good wishes and prayers and gave him a hug for the journey.

He called a week later to inquire whether there were any vacant apartments in our community. There were, and Bob, his wife, and little boy became new members of Project Share. He later became a dedicated peace activist and even ended up hosting a program on the local liberal Pacifica radio station.

It was a heartening reminder of the wisdom of the Quaker adage, "Speak truth to power!"

CHAPTER 1

THE GATHERING STORM

Born in the Shadow of the Holocaust

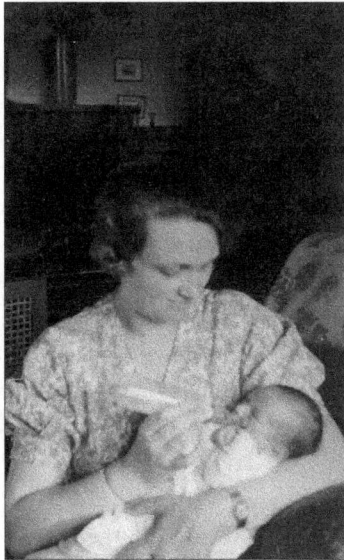

ACCORDING TO MY ALMOST ILLEGIBLE yellowed birth certificate stamped with the imperial eagle of Germany, I was born February 24, 1931 at 4:30 p.m. in the Gagernstrabe Jewish Hospital in Frankfurt am Main. That same year Adolf Hitler laid the groundwork for his Fascist takeover of Germany as newly appointed Reich chancellor. The imperial eagle would soon be replaced by the Nazi swastika.

It was a cold, ruthless world that I was born into, chilling the very bones and heart of me, a coldness that has never been fully assuaged either by human embrace or by sunlight. The cold metal delivery table and the inability of my sick and weak mother to hold and nurse this fragile newborn did not augur a warm welcome for me into this world. Perhaps it was arranged, by some strange coincidence or by the providential dictates of my karmic trajectory, that from my very first breath I would of necessity and by default become a seeker after that other warmth and light of the "Sun of Justice"—of that blazing furnace of which the young Augustine had written: "Thou hast made us for Thyself, O Lord, and our hearts are restless until they rest in Thee."*

Exactly two years later the Reichstag fire provided the excuse for the completion of Hitler's plan to suspend all citizens' rights, including mine. "You are now witnessing the beginning of a great epoch in German history....This fire is the beginning," said Hitler. That infamous fire, which destroyed the German Parliament, gave Hitler a pretext to end all democratic activity. It also signaled the end of my family's history in Germany.

The great, dark clouds of the new state of German politics overshadowed my childhood. Adolf Hitler and his Third Reich were to become the consuming political and cultural passion of the German people. National Socialism with its mythology of the "master race" and its mystical mission of world conquest was fast becoming the new spirituality of Germany.

This was the response of the German Homeland to the humiliations it had received from the political and territorial treaty arrangements of the post–World War I period. Hitler manipulated these feelings of victimhood brilliantly. It was a response that would turn Europe into a flaming inferno and would give birth to some of the most fearsome, demonic inhumanities that the world had ever witnessed.

Hitler and the Nazi leadership saw the opportunity of blaming all of Germany's economic and social woes on the conspiracy of the Jews. This ideology exceeded the parameters of traditional anti-Semitism through the spiritual tenet of the Aryan master race as supreme, with all others perceived to be sub-humans who must be purged. Adolf Eichmann, with the assistance of Heinrich Himmler, conceived of the Final Solution— the extermination of the Jews—carried out through a skillfully organized network of killing camps, supported by an efficient railroad transportation system. These less-than-human creatures, in their eyes, could also

* The Confessions of St. Augustine.

serve the Third Reich as slave laborers. All Jews and other ethnic or political minorities would first have their property confiscated by the State
and then be sent to the labor camps to work themselves to death or to be
killed in the gas chamber, another practical and economic invention of
the Third Reich. Even the teeth and hair of the cadavers would be put to
use.

The Jewish community in Frankfurt was completely unprepared for
this terrifying development, including the study circle led by philosopher
Martin Buber to which my father, belonged. Buber, the great Utopian
thinker, later in his life was to develop a brilliant plan for an Arab-Jewish
bipartisan state in which both peoples could live and thrive together.
Sadly, much to his heartbreak, it was never realized.

Many of the members of the Frankfurt community, even sometimes
the most sophisticated ones, were unwilling to confront the new reality
and its implication for the Jews of Germany. So deep was their identification with German culture that the cresting tidal wave of ideological
anti-Semitism and its systematic plan for the racial cleansing of a country, a continent and ultimately the world, was completely unimaginable.
Their denial was so great that many Jews maintained their disbelief almost right up to the doors of the gas chambers. The statement, "We are
Germans who follow the Law of Moses" reflected the self-understanding
of many German Jews. Of course, we must not discount the pockets of
Jewish resistance organized by Jewish partisans, but they were primarily
in sections of Poland and elsewhere—with almost none in Germany.

My parents represented a well-established part of that assimilated
community. My father, born in Strasbourg (still under German rule),
was a gifted violinist who had performed with Dr. Albert Schweitzer, the
great humanitarian and expert on Bach's organ music, while he was still
preaching at the St. Nicholas Kirche in the Strasbourg beloved by both.
He earned his living as a businessman, the manager of the Kleinling Co.
warehouse, which distributed bicycles, baby carriages and sewing machines. But at heart he was an artist and the live chamber music of Mozart, Beethoven and Hayden always resounded throughout our home.
He was also an aficionado of Goethe and could recite the poetry of the
German bard from memory for hours.

My mother came from a cultivated Orthodox family in Halle on the
river Saale. Her faith was shaken when, as an eighteen-year-old student
nurse, she took care of a gravely ill child who died in her arms. Her decision to become a free-thinking agnostic shook her family to the core. I

always saw her as one of the holiest non-believers I ever knew and she was to devote her life to serving suffering humanity.

Her father, Paul Michael Lehmann, after whom I was named, was a publisher and writer. My great-grandfather, Herman Lehmann, was a well-known philanthropist. Our ancestor Reb Hirsch was a noted hazzan (cantor) who emigrated from Poland in 1815. A moving chapter on his holy life appears in a book on German Judaism.

My father, having grown up in a fairly unobservant home, developed his own religiosity with Sabbath attendance and other observances. Both my parents were independent spirits and my father had little regard for the rigidity and formalism of Jewish Orthodoxy, which he saw as replacing authentic human values. Yet he was an admirer of the devout and opened-minded Orthodox Rabbi Nehemiah Anton Nobel of Frankfurt.

My parents were committed Zionists, regarded by them as a highly idealistic movement. The little tin collection can of the Blau-Weiss (Blue-White) movement was always on the piano to collect money for the Jewish National Fund in support the development of Palestine. There was the hope that we might emigrate there some day as other family members had done.

Although my parents were fully assimilated to German culture, they gradually became uneasy and fearful about remaining in their beloved homeland. What a tremendous teaching this experience of the illusions of assimilation would seem to contain for Jews (and others) in similar circumstances elsewhere. How dependable is the process of assimilation as a wall of protection against the threat of future anti-Semitism and other forms of racism? Here in the US this specter always lurks behind the myth of democracy and equality. (I do not refer here to the occasional confusion between opposition to the uncritical support of Israeli policy and anti-Semitism.) Jews seem to be comfortable and secure with a large middle class as well as high-level positions in academia, the arts, business and politics. In fact, as I write these lines, another Jewish mayor governs New York City.

So the Jews of Nazi Germany could not believe these quite incredible developments. I have repressed so many childhood memories about these terrifying times, yet they still resurface occasionally from the depths of my memory and unconscious. My parents did their best to shield and protect me against the terror of the times, but the reality was too all-pervasive to be kept from my five-year-old inquiring mind and bright curiosity. It would have been difficult not to notice the signs that were beginning to appear outside of restaurants and movie theaters *Juden sind hier unerwünscht!* (Jews are not wanted here!).

In 1935, when I was five, one of the great events in our family occurred—the birth of my brother, Franz Uriel, then Uri and later Frankie. It was a joyful event that made us feel even more vulnerable. He received two powerful names that anticipated his own intense karmic path. He was named for the Archangel Uriel and also quite surprisingly for St. Francis of Assisi. This choice demonstrated how open-minded and free-thinking my parents were. They had great respect and love for the spirit of peace and the connection to all creation manifested by the Little Poor Man of Assisi. This was surely stepping outside of the parameters of the Judaism of their day. Uri's later life would demonstrate with what mysterious prescience he was named.

He was a sweet affectionate child, and everyone fell in love with him. Perhaps he seemed more attractive, especially to his father, than his already slightly pensive older brother, Paul. This family dynamic further contributed to the uncertainty of my early years.

I remember seeing the arrogant school-age Hitler Jugend (Hitler Youth) in their brown uniforms on the street. I experienced intense fear, but even felt jealous and excluded from all these symbols of importance and solidarity. On several occasions I encountered groups of them on the street and they shouted, "dirty Jew" and other epitaphs. They chased me a few times and would probably have beaten me up had I been a little older.

These were frightening experiences and made me feel powerless about my life. The form my quiet resistance took on one occasion was to fearfully stand in front of a Church when no one was looking and spit on the street. It seems that I had already wisely concluded that Christians and their churches were in some kind of complicity with the Nazi oppression. My parents had not taught me this attitude.

I distinctly remember being frightened, revolted and humiliated by the cartoons and caricatures of Jews in *Der Stürmer*, the official newspaper of the S.S., the Storm Troopers who were the elite of the Nazi military forces. These cartoons depicted Jews as ugly with big noses, big teeth and a greedy and gross demeanor.

Strangely enough, I am reminded of all this by the anti-Arab and anti-Muslim caricatures that have become more common today in newspapers and films, sometimes even in the mainstream press.

As the government began to exclude Jewish children from the public schools, my parents enrolled me in the Philantropin, a progressive Jewish school in Frankfurt. Its courageous founder and principal, Dr. Spier, was an enlightened humanitarian and a committed educator. I distinctly remember his kindness to the children, many of whom were having a hard time, and the love of Jewish learning he inspired in us. Towards the end of 1937 the school was closed, and Dr. Spier was eventually sent away to a concentration camp from which he never returned—one more burden of fear and insecurity for me.

Fear permeated the Jewish community like an invisible fog. Rumors about the concentration camps began to spread, but many refused to believe them. Jewish businesses were being boycotted and even closed. Signs were posted outside stores indicating Jewish ownership. My father had a few loyal Gentile employees. One of them, my father's assistant Willie Ungeheuer, remained a friend of the family though many of the other workers left and the company finally closed. Frau Schaeffer, our nursemaid, told us that she could no longer take care of my brother and me.

My parents read the writing on the wall and finally decided to flee. By this time they had concluded that their dream of emigrating to *Eretz Yisroel* (Palestine at the time) was not to be realized. No travel documents were being issued to German Jews. Our good fortune was that my Onkel Robert, my father's brother, was an American citizen who worked for the Voice of America, and through him we qualified for visas. This was indeed a stroke of Providence. Millions of others perished because the US (in spite of the savior image of FDR) contributed to the subsequent mass extermination by its refusal to open its gates to European Jews.

My father immediately laid plans and took the train to Stuttgart in order to acquire his travel documents. After the necessary papers had been issued, he told the Nazi official that he planned to leave in several months. The official, who seemed to have some decency left, said: "Herr Mayer, if I were you, I would leave immediately." He apparently knew that within weeks the Nazis were planning to begin arresting all adult Jewish males.

My father returned to Frankfurt and arranged to depart within the week. My mother, my brother Uri and I planned to follow him later. It was very frightening to see my father walk out of the door carrying his suitcase, stepping into the great unknown. Would we ever see him again? What would happen to us all alone and left behind in such a dangerous place? In fact, a week or two later they began knocking on the doors looking for Jewish males, including my father, deepening my mother's insecurity.

The task of packing together the few belongings that we were allowed to take with us was left to my mother. Most of my parents' financial assets had already been confiscated. The three of us left about a month later. We packed ourselves onto the train to Holland.

I still remember the terror when the German border guards searched our belongings and carefully examined our documents. Their demeanor was arrogant and contemptuous. I was afraid that they would not let us leave. But after what seemed like an interminable time, they stamped the papers and we were on our way to England via Holland to visit my mother's brother, Onkel Hermann, and to connect with my father on our way to America.

My mother departed with a heavy heart and, although I did not yet understand the full implications of our flight from Germany, I knew that we were leaving many relatives and friends behind.

Kristallnacht (the night of the crystals, or the broken glass) took place the night of November 9 to 10 in 1938 when I was seven and we had already fled. It was the darkest night. All throughout Germany, Jewish store windows were smashed and Jewish establishments and organizations were vandalized. Almost five hundred synagogues were burned to the ground. Twenty thousand Jews were arrested and three hundred were killed.

That night signaled the igniting of a diabolical firestorm that would sweep across Germany and much of the rest of Europe. It would unleash a campaign of unprecedented institutionalized racial hatred and extermination. It was one of the first examples of the technology and organizational genius of an industrialized society being placed at the service of mass murder and genocide. Millions of Jews would be killed in the gas chambers and crematoria of the Third Reich, often after indescribable experiences of torture, medical experiments and slave labor. Uncountable numbers of Communists, Gypsies, homosexuals, political dissenters and some Christians were also murdered. The Eichmanns and the Himmlers were among the Nazi technocrats who created one of the most efficient killing machines in history.

Many of my own relatives perished in the killing camps of Dachau, Auschwitz, Theresienstadt, and Sachsenhausen. Most poignant is the memory of Onkel Henri Apelt. He was actually my great-uncle, the youngest brother of my grandmother Bella, my mother's mother. He was a bachelor and he lived with us in Frankfurt for some years prior to our flight from Germany. He was a very tall man, around fifty, balding but with curly red hair and a strong, wiry frame with very big hands. His features were not very typically Jewish. He looked Scandinavian and I wondered about that. Onkel Henri was a devout Jew, prayed with his tefillin (phylacteries) every morning and was a truly holy soul. He was as gentle as he was tall and he became one of my brother Uri's and my primary caretakers while my mother worked at my father's business. I remember him in our kitchen with me on his lap, feeding me breakfast oatmeal with almost maternal affection, spooning the cereal into my mouth with his big hands.

Onkel Henri was one of the fortunate ones who were able to escape Germany to Belgium on his bicycle. It was there he heard the Nazis had arrested his beloved brother, Gustav. He decided to try to rescue him, bicycled back into Germany and was never heard from again.

Even as a child I had a sense of the Divine Presence. On Shabbat my father took me to worship at the Börneplatz Synagogue. It was the holy day of rest when we would put on our best clothes. This coming together of the community took on greater meaning as we experienced the increasing threat of danger, and the greatest fear of all—that of the unknown.

I was always fascinated by the holiness of the Ark of the Covenant where the sacred Torah scrolls were kept. These were only removed on Shabbat for the reading of the selected portion of the five books of Moses or the Prophets, and on Simchas Torah, the feast of the Joy of the Torah, when all the Torah scrolls were carried in an ecstatic dance procession all around the synagogue and were lovingly kissed as they passed through the congregation.

I imagined coming to the shul at night when there would be no one there and secretly opening the door of the Ark and entering it. I was certain that there was a mysterious, illuminated stairway that would lead me directly to the beloved Throne of God. Alas, I was never to realize this holy dream. The venerable Börneplatz Synagogue was burned to the ground by the Nazi vandals, Torah scrolls and all, on Kristallnacht of November 1938.

I would have to seek elsewhere for the face of God.

CHAPTER 2

AMERIKA, AMERIKA!

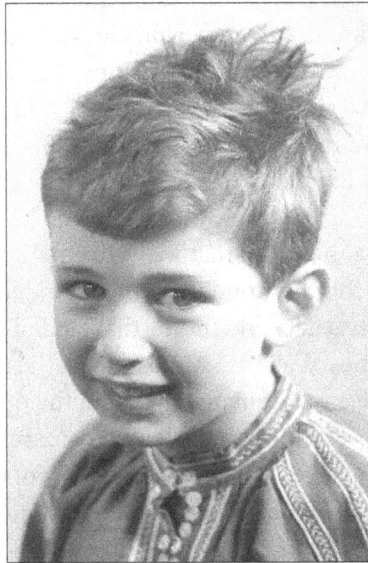

AS MY PARENTS PREPARED TO leave Europe they could not have imagined the indescribable sufferings under which many of their loved ones would perish. The Mayer family boarded the SS *Amsterdam* in Southampton, England, in mid-October 1938, and so began the sea voyage to what we hoped would be the Promised Land. We were among the fortunate few to be snatched from the flames that were about to engulf Europe.

For my parents it was a heart-wrenching separation. They left behind the only life they had ever known. Above all, they had to abandon many family members, dear friends and acquaintances, most of whom they would never see again. They also left behind what they had loved in their homeland: a beautiful country and a rich and ancient culture that had been central to their lives.

Although at the age of seven my whole inner being was in turmoil, I still could not grasp all of the ramifications of our flight. I did experience fear of the unknown that lay ahead along with the loss of everything that had represented childhood stability. My brother Uri at two was already more of a carefree spirit. He charged across the broad deck of our ocean liner and would gladly have leapt into the inviting, foaming green sea if my mother had not restrained him with a harness and leash.

The food was exciting—especially the meat. One of the anti-Jewish regulations of the Nazis was the prohibition of the production of kosher meat of any kind. In the years before our departure the only kosher meat available had to be imported from Holland or Belgium for special occasions, and then gradually even those shipments stopped altogether. I gorged myself on the abundant kosher meat, especially the frankfurters—even to the point of seasickness. Little did this tiny carnivore realize that one day he would sprout into a fervent vegetarian.

On November 9, 1938, after what seemed to be an interminable sea journey, the captain announced that we were entering New York Harbor. Out of the morning fog the wonders of the magnificent skyline and the Statue of Liberty emerged. Could this be that land of new beginnings and freedom that I had heard about? Almost at that very moment Kristallnacht was taking place in Germany, signaling the open persecution and eventual annihilation of the German-Jewish community.

My parents were forced to leave behind most of their financial assets as well as many other material possessions. In fact, they arrived in the US almost penniless.

They spoke very little English, so they could not move into an American counterpart of their prior professions. On almost his first night in his new homeland, my father got a job working in a bakery plant. My mother could not work in her beloved nursing vocation for some time because of language and certification requirements. Imagine how she felt to work now as a masseuse in establishments where overweight Bronx women sought to have their surplus fat sweated and "pounded" off them. It was hard and thankless work.

My mother and father were fortunate to find housing in the apartment of the Flegenheimers, our distant cousins. Unfortunately, they only had room for two adults and barely that. So arrangements had to be made for my brother and I until my parents could establish themselves in a new home.

For my little brother Uri and me it was not to be an easy passage into the land of milk and honey. Uri and I were placed in the Israel Orphan Asylum on East Second Street on the Lower East Side of Manhattan. It was a painful decision for my parents who had so few options at the time. We were to stay there for most of our first year in America.

The Orphan Asylum was not a Dickensian institution and was perhaps even a cut above average. It was funded by the Jewish philanthropist Gustav Hartman and his wife, whom I met there once. She seemed like a decent and humane person, with her beautiful white hair carefully coiffed.

Nevertheless, my stay there represented one more blow on this already painful journey. Separation from my parents—who dutifully visited us on weekends—was frightening in this strange land. I felt keenly responsible for my little brother, Uri, who at two was even more confused than I. Neither of us spoke any English beyond "hello," "thank you," "good-bye" and "ladies and gentlemen," and so it was difficult to communicate with the staff and especially with the other children.

We were not even in the same sleeping area. Now we had to exchange the warm, cozy bedroom we remembered from Frankfurt for a drafty group dormitory.

Thus I was thrown into the icy cold water of my new existence. On practically the next day I was enrolled in the local public school, PS 121, in the first grade under Mrs. Moses. She was an elderly woman with a contracted, unsmiling face who had not imbibed deeply of the milk of human kindness. She was not prepared to give this little refugee boy much leeway, so I was forced to make my way through the maze of foreign culture and incomprehensible language on my own. At the end of my first month, I was awarded an Oreo cookie for reading improvement. I was on my way to becoming an American.

There were some kindly staff people at the Orphan Asylum who took me under their wing. It was a strange culture with bizarre customs. Eating corn flakes for breakfast was incomprehensible and seemed like chewing cardboard. Grapefruit were the sourest of oranges. I did my best to protect and nurture my little brother who, with his innate charm, more easily became a favorite among the children and staff.

After a year of gritting my teeth and crying myself to sleep every night, my parents finally came to us with good news. They had come to take us away with them to our new home at 295 Fort Washington Avenue, apartment 5F on the top floor. It was the unprepossessing building in which my family eventually inhabited three different apartments, one on the third floor and finally on the ground floor where my parents lived right up to my father's death in 1984. Our first apartment was in a five-story walk-up, which charged the lowest rent.

Our new home was located in Washington Heights on West 173rd Street and Fort Washington Avenue, almost in the shadow of the stately George Washington Bridge, which became a symbolic point of reference for my childhood. Washington Heights has since become a dynamic stronghold of the Dominican community. Then it was the community to which the German-Jewish refugee influx gravitated. Sometimes it was ironically titled "the Fourth Reich." On Shabbat, the holy Sabbath day, one would hear mostly German conversation from those taking their Sabbath rest on the benches in Jay Hood Wright Park directly across the street from my house.

I had the good fortune of growing up in a real neighborhood where everyone knew and cared for each other, a form of community, which is rapidly vanishing from the urban scene. My childhood was relatively uneventful. I attended PS 173 directly across from our house on Fort Washington Avenue and later the local Humboldt Junior High School, PS 115 on 178th Street, recently the locus of a wonderful PBS documentary about inner-city kids learning ballroom dancing.

As they learned English, my parents began to assimilate to their new culture. My father became a coffee salesman but continued to pursue his true love—music. My mother finally passed her state board examinations and became a registered nurse again. Many years later at the age of forty she switched to becoming a psychiatric nurse because she felt that her true gifts lay in healing the human soul through psychotherapy rather than merely the body.

At her funeral the crowd almost overflowed onto the street, so renowned was her goodness to those in need. Many of her ex-patients had found their way to the famously hospitable Mayer kitchen table—sometimes to the chagrin of my insecure father, who felt displaced. She had a way of adopting people, patients and others.

One such recipient of her universal generosity was Friedelind Wagner, Richard Wagner's granddaughter. Mausi, as she was called by her friends, had the classical profile of her illustrious grandfather. She was perhaps the only member of the Wagner clan who had consciously separated herself from a family so intertwined with Hitler and the whole mythology of the Aryan master race with its Teutonic Valhalla at Bayreuth. Mausi was bounced on the Fuehrer's knee as a little girl and he was a frequent, enthusiastically welcomed visitor at Bayreuth, the Wagnerian home and shrine.

With the help of the great conductor Arturo Toscanini, Mausi was smuggled out of Germany and cut herself off from her family, especially her mother, Winifred Williams, who is said to have adored Hitler. So when this courageous offspring of the Valkyrian tradition landed in the strangeness of New York, it was my good Jewish mother who befriended and virtually adopted that wandering soul.

About six months after we moved to 295 Fort Washington Avenue, my parents received word from Germany that my paternal grandfather Karl had died of natural causes. Fortunately, my grandmother Klara (Oma, we called her) had received documents—once again through my Uncle Robert's efforts—to travel to the US. She soon joined us in New York, became a member of our household and learned to climb those five flights of stairs.

My mother fostered our Jewish cultural and religious consciousness and a kosher household, just in case some observant surviving relative might come to our table. Each Friday night she lit the candles and recited the ancient blessing, welcoming the Sabbath as a bride. In spite of her own religious skepticism, she wanted us to remain connected to the tradition of our people for which such a bitter price was being paid, and if any family members survived she wanted to welcome them into a Jewish household. We attended Hebrew school faithfully so that we could learn to read the Torah. Who knows, perhaps one day we would even emigrate to *Eretz Yisroel* to be reunited to the rest of our family and to the land of our people.

Even at the tender age of twelve, my religious path began to take a strange turn. I met Rabbi Morris Besdin, a charismatic young religious leader and teacher who loved to work with young people and later became a teacher at Yeshiva University. Much to the shock of my parents, I became an Orthodox Jew. Rabbi Besdin headed Temple Beth Hamedrash Hagadol, an Orthodox congregation of Eastern European Jews on West 175th Street. There has always been a traditional antipathy between the German and Eastern European Jews from Russia, Poland, Latvia, Estonia and the Ukraine. The German Jews considered themselves superior, probably because of their greater degree of assimilation into modern European culture. (A lot of good it did them.)

My parents were always open-minded, liberal and progressive people, but this development was somewhat disconcerting to them. First of all, their "Paulchen" becoming an Orthodox Jew was in itself unexpected and not in keeping with their own values. But to join an Eastern European congregation was a bit too much.

I faithfully attended the Friday night and Shabbat services and became part of a small youth group that spent the Sabbath day with the Rebbe, really a wonderful experience of celebrating the sacred day of rest, joy and reflection in the community. But when I enrolled in the Hebrew school and even chose to celebrate my bar mitzvah there, I broke the barrier of acceptability. My parents to their credit never forbade any of this but privately shook their heads about me in concern. They were to shake them often. The old cantor, Mr. Himmelfarb, who had a long beard and always smelled of garlic, prepared me to chant the Torah texts for my bar mitzvah at the age of thirteen, the day when I passed from childhood to becoming a man of Israel.

In my bar mitzvah speech, I sought to imitate the young King Solomon who did not ask for riches or power but instead prayed for wisdom. I prayed for "a wise and understanding heart so that I may choose a life of virtue and to walk in the path of righteousness. May it be thy will, O Lord, that I bring honor to the name of Israel and to our beloved country, America." There may be those who are skeptical about whether I achieved either one.

My father wanted to pass his passion for music and his gifts as a violinist along to his first born—me. His strategy was to have me learn to play the piano first and then he would himself teach me the violin. So my "career" began at age twelve.

Alas, our complex and sometimes difficult relationship was to sabotage his plans for me. My first piano teacher was Konrad Wolff, a highly regarded concert pianist and teacher and a friend of the family. His students included Leon Fleisher and Abbot Rembert Weakland. In spite of his sweet nature and great patience, my inner resistance to my father and his wishes made me a non-compliant student. Konrad eventually gave up on me.

I was then passed on to Frida Rabinowitch Kahn, the wife of Erich Itor Kahn, also a wonderful concert pianist. The Kahns were close family friends and my father was often page-turner at Erich's concerts. Frida was a striking Russian woman of fiery temperament and a devoted teacher. She was persuaded that she could tame my youthful resistance. Once again my inner conflict prevented me from complying and our musical relationship ended with our throwing piano practice books at each other. Music is one of my life passions, and I have always regretting not playing an instrument.

I was also an ardent Brooklyn Dodgers fan in a neighborhood where this was considered sheer heresy, if not madness, by the "superior" Yankee fans and even by the friends who rooted for the New York Giants. But I was completely devoted to "Dem Bums," who were the underdogs, maybe a little like me. I made regular pilgrimages to Ebbets Field in Brooklyn, often by myself, because fellow Dodger fans in Manhattan were hard to find.

I got to recognize and connect to some of those great players like Peewee Reese, Dixie Walker, Duke Snyder and the rest as I waited, almost adoringly, outside the clubhouse after the game. This was before the day of the incomparable Jackie Robinson, but it was altogether fitting that my Bums should be the first to break the evil color line. I had collected most of their autographs in a precious album and one of the tragedies of my youth was to return from college one summer to learn that my mother had inadvertently thrown it out. But my greatest blow was surely when my Dodgers left Brooklyn. After that, I lost my faith and ceased to be an official baseball fan as I began to realize that baseball had primarily become a business. Of course, I'm still wild about the game.

Baseball and my love for fishing were to prove important in my educational career. In fact, they were one major reason why I did not graduate from George Washington High School with my senior class. I often "played hooky" and missed too many academic obligations to graduate. But in the end, who wanted to be in a confining, boring classroom when I could be whipping that white leather-covered baseball across the green diamond or elegantly casting a Royal Coachman dry fly into a deep pool of the lovely Esopus River in the Catskill Mountains? So much for my academic career.

This was the balm that I applied to the pain of being a troubled, insecure adolescent. I desperately wanted to belong, to be like everybody else. It was precisely this adolescent turmoil that would prove to be the seedbed of the next unexpected turn of my journey.

CHAPTER 3

AN UNLIKELY CATHOLIC

HOW DID A NICE JEWISH boy like me end up becoming a Roman Catholic, of all things, and at the tender age of sixteen? It is a question I am often asked and am still trying to find a satisfying answer to.

One part of the answer must surely be: Blame it on the Irish! In the midst of my stormy adolescence, this was clearly one of the most unexpected developments. I encountered the Irish. There was a large community of Irish Catholics who lived on the east side of Broadway, the other side of the tracks. The west side was almost solidly Jewish, mainly German Jews—and "never the twain shall meet." The only contact with the Irish was when some of these young crusaders would launch forays into our territory in order to intimidate and beat up Jewish youth.

It was my first encounter with the "lay apostolate." They would be wearing their Incarnation parochial school sweatshirts and ask me whether I was Jewish. My mother, who was raising us in the tradition of "children of a martyr race" (from a beautiful, old Channukah hymn), instructed us to always respond with: "Yes, and I'm proud of it!" The young crusaders would then proceed to beat the hell out of us anyway.

Through a strange combination of circumstances some of these Irish lads befriended me, and I actually began to "run" with the enemy in one of the loosely formed Irish gangs. We raised hell, which by contemporary standards would be considered relatively benign activity. There were rare skirmishes with competing gangs, but most of the antisocial activity consisted of hitching rides on the back of trolley cars, shooting craps on the street, hanging out in pool halls and getting drunk illegally on beer. The future vocations of my new companions would range from becoming alumni of Sing Sing State Penitentiary to entering the priesthood.

One of the striking qualities of my Irish comrades, which really impressed me, was their (at least external) loyalty to their religion. No doubt this was a result of their spiritual indoctrination under the Christian Brothers known at that time for their skills in scientifically applied corporal punishment. In any case, these lads took the externals of their faith to heart, even if this was not always reflected in an exemplary moral life, and I found it impressive. I remember one foray into an unfamiliar neighborhood where we entered a local Episcopal Church. Even on this strange but somewhat familiar-looking terrain, I remember how zealously these young ruffians knelt down before a statue of the Blessed Virgin Mary and lit votive candles for their intentions.

In March 1946, during a basketball game, I met Walter Tice, one of my contemporaries, who was a student in Cathedral High School, the minor seminary of the Archdiocese of New York. He was later to become my godfather. Walter was a great athlete and a serious young man with a kind heart. I took note of this and carefully observed him and internally checked him out. My instinctive Jewish self-defense system always assumed that most non-Jews were anti-Semitic and had to prove themselves otherwise. (I think that this is true of many minorities.) He noted my interest in things spiritual and after some time asked me whether I would like to meet a priest friend of his who was a great guy. I can't remember what compelled me to consider this bizarre invitation since

I had no idea what a priest was, but after some hesitation, I agreed to a meeting.

With some reluctance and with my heart in my mouth, we rang the bell of the forbidding granite rectory of the Church of the Incarnation on St. Nicholas Avenue. The receptionist ushered Walter and me into the old-fashioned parlor. After a while the door opened and in strode a slightly built young man with glasses wearing the flowing long black cassock and white collar. He offered me a warm smile, a handshake and a big hello.

This was Father Edwin J. Conlin, who was to be one of the key figures in my spiritual journey. He was a unique phenomenon in the extremely conservative Archdiocese of New York under the ultra reactionary leadership of Francis Cardinal Spellman. One of the first impressions that I gathered from this enthusiastic priest was that he really liked Jews and was quite pleased to get to know me for that reason among others. I did not ever pick up the impression that he had overtly proselytizing designs on this young innocent.

Among his qualities that immediately drew me in was his enormous open-mindedness and open-heartedness. He read progressive Catholic newspapers like *The Catholic Worker* and periodicals like *Commonweal* and *Integrity* and had a fresh approach to Christianity about which I knew very little. We met once a week or so to have freewheeling discussions about life, my adolescent struggles, informally and only occasionally against the background of Jesus and Christian perspectives. I maintained contact with him over the years and, out of respect to him, must add that later in life he has almost proudly become a conservative. He never allowed the non-conventional path that my life would later take affect our friendship or his respect for me. At almost ninety he was still fully alert and a devoted priest. I had the joy of spending a wonderful afternoon with him in a priests' retirement home in the Bronx and he reported his regular visits to the Metropolitan Opera. Shortly after my visit I received the sad news that he had died in his sleep. We shall not soon see his likes again.

When I met Father Conlin at fifteen I was having intense power struggles with my parents, especially my father. I came home late at night and was sometimes inebriated. When they heard about this new-found friendship, they were deeply disturbed. Strangely enough it was my brother, Frankie (or Uri, his Hebrew name, for which he was too often ridiculed in school) who took the initiative on the matter. At the advanced age of eleven he was the first one of the family to audaciously ring that same Incarnation Rectory doorbell to talk to Father Conlin. He proceeded to tell him how upset my parents were and that he must not try to convert his big brother Paul who was not ready for such a step.

Frankie was an amazing child who truly incarnated the spirit and vision of his namesake, Francis of Assisi. He was a true lover of all living beings. He was the one who would often be sent (although I also received this training) to offer money, clothing or food to poor people on the street by my philanthropic mother. I was often too ashamed. Frankie loved and talked to all animals. He was a free spirit and once, at the age of ten, bicycled alone without permission across the George Washington Bridge to New Jersey, fifteen miles away to visit a girl he had met. A New Jersey state police officer, whom he had befriended and charmed, returned him.

So it was my little brother who reported my instability to this possible robber of the Jewish cradle. My parents would follow this up with their own frantic visit. They felt—and probably rightly so—that I was going through a traumatic adolescence and was impressionable, unstable and vulnerable to the spiritual seduction of this young and attractive Savonarola. In fact, Father Conlin agreed with them and said that he would not bring up the issue of "conversion" for at least a year and he held to his promise.

In the meantime my worried parents had discovered Dr. Rudolf Hirschberg, a skilled child psychiatrist. Dr. Hirschberg was the on-campus therapist at Children's Village, a home for troubled adolescents at Dobbs Ferry, New York, a beautiful little town on the Hudson. Dr. Hirschberg, himself a Holocaust survivor who had lost several sisters in the killing camps, was a profoundly kind man, a brilliant therapist and a truly respectful ally to young people.

My parents arranged for me to see him every other weekend as his guest up at Children's Village. It was a great relief to get away from the city, from the tensions of my home environment, and to make friends with the children of the staff and faculty members of the school. I also experienced the joys of a rural childhood, at least momentarily.

Dr. Hirschberg ingeniously found time for us to be together, to talk about my life, and to shed the light of his compassionate wisdom on my troubled adolescence. I began to trust him and to share—as far as my fears allowed me—the shadow life of my inner struggles with him. In the end, after a year, Dr. Hirschberg came to the conclusion, much to my parents' dismay and confusion, that I had enough emotional clarity to become a Catholic, if that was my decision. It was, in fact, a decision I was moving closer to—amidst much inner turmoil. Not only my parents but also many of their friends were distressed and outraged at my decision. One German musician friend actually tried to rip a religious medal from around my neck to express her outrage at my joining the ranks of the persecutors.

Sad to say, about a year later, I received the tragic news that Dr. Hirschberg had committed suicide. Despite his devotion to others, he apparently was not able to heal his own pain and family loss caused by the Holocaust.

In a final attempt to dissuade me from what they saw as a disastrous decision, my poor parents arranged a meeting for me with Rabbi David de Sola Pool, the revered and illustrious spiritual leader of Congregation Shearith Israel, the Spanish and Portuguese Synagogue off Central Park West, where I occasionally sang in the choir. He was the spiritual shepherd of the oldest American synagogue and had been called "something of a rabbinic legend." The rabbi used all of his wisdom and wiles—from my spiritual debt to my people to the sheer foolishness of the ideas of the Trinity and Transubstantiation—against this about-to-apostatize, opinionated adolescent whippersnapper, but all to no avail.

I decided to receive the Sacrament of Baptism and asked Father Conlin to provide me instruction in the Catholic faith. At the same time I developed what would prove to be lifelong friendships with a new set of Irish friends and their families. This was a different group of teenagers, of which most of the boys were preparing for the priesthood at Cathedral High School, the Archdiocese's minor seminary. This did not inhibit their drinking capabilities. Pat Murphy, one of our crowd, worked in the rectory, and through him I acquired a baptismal certificate to use in the local bars stating illegally that I was eighteen.

Pat Ward, also a minor seminarian at the time, and I hit it off immediately. He and his loving family took this unlikely Catholic under their wing. His mother, Mrs. Ward, was one of those simple Irishwomen whose faith is their life. She rose each morning at the crack of dawn for early Mass and lived a life of love and service.

I soon became a fixture in their simple home, especially around their table always groaning under Mrs. Ward's turkey dinners and superb apple pies. Pat's older sister, Grace, now deceased, became my loyal godmother and his other sister, Mary—now Sister Joanne—is still a faithful friend. Similarly the families of Pat McConnell, Eddie Brown and my other buddies showered me with their welcoming kindness. I was also introduced to Irish literature and music, which I have treasured all my life and to which I owe my great love of folk music. It has always struck me as one of the most direct vehicles of a people's struggles, history and dreams. Strangely enough, I think that I had more interest in the Irish music and culture than some of the young Irish Americans who probably wanted to shed their first-generation immigrant identity, somewhat like myself.

I also experienced the richness of community in this warm and connected neighborhood and parish. I fear that very few of our young people growing up in today's typical isolation of suburbia will ever taste this sweet experience of authentic community.

Incarnation Parish is also where I met Father Ivan Illich, who was assigned as a parish priest there. Illich was born in Vienna and had a Jewish mother, so we immediately had some significant things in common. He befriended this skinny Jewish teenager and new convert. At that time the Irish Incarnation Parish was beginning to sprout islands of the Puerto Rican population that was converging on New York City. Through his intimate knowledge of and culturally respectful ministry to the Latino community, he was able to convince the conservative Cardinal Spellman to found an institute in San Juan, Puerto Rico, to sensitize the largely Irish-American New York clergy to the culture, language and beauty of their Puerto Rican parishioners. The institute was a great success and Illich was eventually appointed vice-rector of the Catholic University in Ponce. We formed a friendship that was reinforced by my family and later by my work, Latino culture and a shared vision of the Church.

Ultimately, I have to ask myself—and I am often asked—what were the driving forces that impelled me to this spiritual decision that would change my life forever and cause such pain to my loved ones? It was, it seems to me, a mysterious amalgam of adolescent schizophrenia (or is that a tautology?) and the descent of the Holy Spirit. And who knows in what proportions of each.

First of all was a driving adolescent desire to belong, in this case, to the dominant majority (even the enemy?) as opposed to being part of a persecuted minority. Part of that sense of belonging was a desire not to have parents who spoke with a foreign accent and were not what I considered to be real Americans. I also have to acknowledge elements of a romantic escapist illusion that becoming Catholic would make all things well, would make me acceptable and make life beautiful and easy.

But in the midst of all this confusion, there was also some authentic spiritual power at work that I can only call grace—a divine gift freely given and not earned. There was no blinding flash of light à la my namesake, St. Paul, who was dramatically knocked to the ground on the road to Damascus, was struck blind and was forever transformed into a disciple of Jesus. And yet it seems that God was taking this human, messy situation of my teenage confusion and fear as the stuff out of which the Spirit would shape my own soul transformation and direct my destiny to become an instrument of justice and love and healing in the world. After all, we read in the great creation myth of Genesis how the Creator breathed life into those chunks of ordinary mud. I was a piece of mud being baked in the divine oven.

Through the inventive and humorous teaching of my guide, Father Conlin, I was beginning to go beyond the boredom and deadly formalism of the lifeless Baltimore Catechism used as the instructional text at the time, to allow the figure of the Rabbi of Nazareth to emerge in his power, his luminous—perhaps divine—splendor and his flesh and blood humanity. As I look back on those mysterious, difficult, exciting and destabilizing teenage years, I realize how primitive and imperfect my understanding of the gospels, of authentic Christian life and my love of God were. I also see how my adolescent confusion did not allow me to appreciate the Jewishness of it all, how I did not have to cease being a Jew (as if that were ever possible), how if it had not been for certain anti-Jewish attitudes in Pauline Christianity and anti-Semitism in the early Church, this "conversion" would not have been necessary, and we would all still be members of a radical Jewish sect. Even now I would not have to be a *meshumad* (apostate) to my Jewish friends and critics and have to stop being Jewish any more than any of the gospel narratives indicate that Jesus somehow "resigned" from or was converted from Judaism.

What a roller-coaster ride of the Spirit it was, and I marvel now at how the love of God put up with all of this foolishness, neurosis, pride, self-hate and inner chaos to lead me into what I eventually was to discover, much to my joy and surprise, was the true garden of delight. I tremble in wonder at the exquisite ingenuity of the Holy Spirit, at the remarkable tolerance and patience of the Divine and, above all at the extraordinary, almost voracious sense of humor of the Holy One of Israel.

And so on the evening of February 27, 1947, a few days after my sixteenth birthday, in the cold and beautiful Gothic Church of the Incarnation, Father Conlin poured the saving waters of baptism over my head, and I became even more of a child of God, dying with Christ to darkness and evil, and rising to the new life of light and grace. It could not have been more coincidental that Incarnation Church was only half a city block from Temple Beth Hamedrash Hagadol where I had become a "mature" man of Israel only three years before at my bar mitzvah. I was just being reassured that God really does write straight with crooked lines.

The powerful words of that great hymn, written by the reformed captain of a slave ship during the Middle Passage, now spoke to me: "Amazing grace, how sweet the sound that saved a wretch like me. I once was lost but now I'm found, was blind but now I see."

I was baptized Paul Michael, the beautiful name I inherited from my Orthodox grandfather, who was probably less upset by this development than many of those still on the earth.

CHAPTER 4

"COME FOLLOW ME"
The Life of a Monk

I BARELY GRADUATED FROM GEORGE Washington High School (a few years behind Henry Kissinger, my future nemesis) because of succumbing to the temptations of playing baseball and fly-fishing instead of studying. Then I wrestled with the deep disappointment of being accepted at Champlain College in Plattsburgh, New York, instead of Cornell where I had dreamt of studying aquatic biology.

One of the significant events of this college period was my introduction to the writings of Thomas Merton, the Trappist monk, poet, mystic and courageous social critic. He was to become one of my lifetime mentors, even though I never met him in the flesh. My good Jewish mother, who rarely turned down any request from her firstborn son, sent me Merton's autobiography *The Seven Story Mountain,* which came out that year in 1948. It proved to be one of the most influential spiritual books of its times and was the catalyst of an extraordinary influx of mostly young people into monasteries.

Merton's dramatic spiritual odyssey led him from the life of a self-engrossed bon vivant at Cambridge and Columbia Universities to the baptismal font and service to the poor in Harlem and eventually into the cloistered Cistercian Abbey of Our Lady of Gethsemane in Kentucky, one of the most rigorous orders of the Church. The book had an electrifying impact on my youthful imagination, which had already been toying gingerly with thoughts of becoming a priest.

Now like a lightning flash it became absolutely clear to me that I was to become a monk. If Christ had called me to be one of his followers, why not climb to the mountaintop to dedicate my life to him. It was Merton's moving narration of his personal experience of a divine calling that touched me deeply. Dare I think that the God who made heaven and earth, the stars and planets, the ocean depths and mountain heights was now reaching into my soul to invite me to this new level of divine closeness and service to His world? The radical character of this idea of total dedication spoke to my romantic utopian nature as well as to some place of authentic generosity in my youthful heart.

Surely I understood very little about the concrete details and practical implications of the monastic life. And yet there was a mysterious certainty somewhere deep in my psyche. I had already begun taking a summer refresher Latin course for young men about to enter the seminary. Was it merely coincidence that my Latin teacher Sal DeMucio had once been a seminarian at St. Paul's Abbey, a Benedictine monastery in the lovely hill country of Sussex County, New Jersey? When he heard of my monastic interest, he immediately arranged a weekend visit to the abbey for me.

On that first visit, I was fascinated by the beauty of the liturgy and the unexpected simplicity and warmth of the monks that I met. I had imagined them to be more severe and remote. The silent beauty of the woods and fields surrounding the monastery seemed to call to me. I returned to New York with an application to the college seminary and with a sense of the enormity of the decision that lay before me. But somewhere within me I knew that the decision had already been made by the power of God's love that was ever beckoning me into my greater destiny.

My parents were once again traumatized when I reluctantly shared with them what I was contemplating. As a compromise, I returned to Champlain College to finish the winter semester.

I was studying in my room on a gray cold March afternoon in 1948 when there was a knock on my door. It was the resident advisor who had come to cushion the grim news that my brother, Frankie, had died in an accident. He would have been thirteen that November and was already preparing for his bar mitzvah. He had been playing in an alleyway and his slight frame had fallen through the thin wooden cover of an underground elevator shaft. I called home to speak with my grief-stricken parents and immediately made arrangements to catch the next train back to New York.

My heart was broken at the loss of this dear being who adored his older brother. I felt that I had never given him the attention that his love called for. It was an incomparable loss for my poor parents. They had already lost so much—their homeland, many of their family members and their basic existential security. They had endured the shock of their firstborn son going over to what, for all intents and purposes, was the enemy. And now they had lost their golden child, this rare and magical being who had brought so much light and joy into their difficult lives.

Frankie's frail remains were laid to rest in a Jewish cemetery outside of the city. Strangely enough, he was buried next to Ira Gershwin, the great composer and musician. They were two beings who had brought much beauty and joy into the world.

In retrospect, if I had not been a callous, immature eighteen-year-old still immersed in narcissistic confusion, I might never have taken the next step on my journey. I might have taken into consideration the grief and loss that my parents had already experienced and reconsidered my decision to become a monk. But the wheel of my destiny turned and five months after my eighteenth birthday, I entered the Little Flower Monastery in Newton, New Jersey (named after St. Therese of Lisieux). In retrospect, I wonder whether Frankie's adventurous spirit was not beckoning me forward into the next chapter of my mysterious journey.

I arrived at the seminary for my two-year college course on a brilliant September morning in 1949. My first encounter was with Father Anthony, the seminary rector. He was an interesting mixture of a nurturing father and German shepherd ready to nip at our heels and challenge us in order to sift out those truly qualified for the monastic life from those who were not. Father Anthony was short, a little chubby, with dark hair and yesterday's growth of beard. His twinkling eyes were hidden behind a thick pair of glasses that often slid down his nose. His style was restrained irony and humor as he critiqued and challenged us in this preliminary preparation for monkhood. He seemed genuinely delighted at my Jewishness and actually looked a little Jewish himself.

One of the first things that caught my eye, to my surprise and delight, was a copy of a slender newsprint tabloid called *The Catholic Worker*, published by Dorothy Day, lying on the library table. Little did I know what a powerful influence this eight-page publication would exert on my life and my future. This noble newspaper, which still sells for the outrageous price of "a penny a copy," was to become a beacon and a comfort to me in a Church not readily sympathetic to pacifism, Christian anarchism, racial justice and the primacy of the poor and forgotten.

I quickly seized on this clear understanding of the teachings of Jesus and the Hebrew prophets about peace and social justice with the enthusiasm and (sometimes self-righteous) zeal of an eighteen-year-old born-again radical. It seemed that Father Anthony was himself an admirer of *The Worker* and of Dorothy Day, its remarkable founder. "Dorothy" (as she was affectionately called by all) actually came to give talks to the college seminarians and to the few monks who did not consider her a Communist wolf in Catholic sheep's clothing. She was, in fact, a convert to Catholicism by way of the Communist Party and brought some of its most radical teachings to her understanding of the Gospels.

She established *The Worker* with her co-founder, the great Peter Maurin, who was a simple French peasant with a remarkable vision of a just society based on the authentic principles of Christianity. Together they set up both urban and rural Houses of Hospitality to serve, clothe, feed and shelter the poor and homeless, which also became centers of education, training and organizing in non-violent radical Christianity.

Dorothy exercised a powerful influence on Thomas Merton, the Fathers Daniel and Philip Berrigan and many other key progressive figures in the Catholic Church. She and *The Worker* were to become an essential support and rationale for many of the unacceptable radical causes and ideas that I would espouse over the years. She would also befriend my parents and attempt to comfort my mother over the loss of my brother.

Dorothy would have found it strange, if not hilarious, that her cause for being raised to official sainthood has been accepted by the Vatican.

She and other members of *The Worker* were often arrested in New York City in the 1950s for non-violently refusing, in the spirit of Mahatma Gandhi, to participate in the air raid drills in the subways, much to the chagrin of Cardinal Spellman. Dorothy believed that these drills contributed to the delusion that nuclear weapon attacks could be survived or would even be worth surviving.

When I discovered *The Catholic Worker*, I also discovered to my delight that perhaps I could hold on to some of the political and social values that I had been given by my liberal Jewish parents. My field of action was somewhat limited during my two years in the college seminary, and even later in the monastery, but a clear perspective of the world and of my faith began to emerge. It arose out of the life and teachings of Jesus rooted in the radical social vision of Isaiah, Jeremiah, Amos and the other Hebrew prophets. Justice for the poor, the struggle for the peaceable kingdom and the primacy of the "Anawim" were at the heart of this vision. These chosen ones were the members of the biblical remnant community, poor and often unpopular, if not despised, the bearers of the messianic dream. It was this dream which, like a seed, was being sown in my fertile, young idealistic mind as an integral part of my spiritual path.

The ideas flowing out of my reading of *The Catholic Worker* and other liberal Catholic periodicals, like *Commonweal* and *Integrity* (now defunct), were harbingers for me of new possibilities—perhaps even of a new spring—arising from within that reactionary Church. In the course of time I began to speak out against the US war in Korea, the dangers of the McCarthy anti-Communist witch hunts and the evil of racism and segregation in the South and even within the Church itself.

None of these were popular points of view with most of the other seminarians, nor later with my fellow monks and with my abbot in particular. The Church of those times was the Church of Francis Cardinal Spellman, archbishop of New York and military vicar (chief chaplain) of the US Armed Forces, who was later to become an uncritical supporter of the political status quo and of US foreign and military policies, especially in Vietnam.

The two college years passed quickly and, somewhat to my surprise, I was recommended to be accepted as a novice, the first stage of monastic life. Probably one of the main possible obstacles was my firmly held political and social views. I suppose that the superiors hoped that these were just youthful eccentricities which would be healed by time and the purifying catharsis of the ascetic life of a monk. Alas, this was not to be the case and some of the older monks perhaps lived to regret their decision to accept me.

Sixty or so monks lived a secluded existence at St. Paul's Abbey in bucolic Sussex County, New Jersey, following the venerable Rule of St. Benedict, the oldest rule for monks in the western Church. I would spend eighteen years of my life here amidst the woodlands, meadows, streams and lakes.

As Benedictine monks we followed the ancient monastic motto of *Ora et Labora,* Pray and Work, sometimes interpreted as "To pray is to work and to work is to pray." The daily cycle of common prayer is, in fact, called the *Opus Dei,* the work of God. The Holy Rule even instructs the monk to treat the tools of the workshop and the field "like vessels of the altar." The daily rounds of work and worship are woven into the seamless fabric of the service of God.

On these five hundred acres of verdant beauty we labored to sustain ourselves. The monks raised a large herd of friendly Guernsey dairy cows, well cared for by Brother Leovigild and Brother Beatus, who were among the original founding monks of our monastery from Germany in the 1920s. They were lay brothers and came from rugged Bavarian peasant stock. Brother Beatus was tall and lean with a head of snow-white hair, giving him a distinguished look. Brother Leo was short and as strong as an ox. You could always detect their presence in the choir or refectory (dining room) by the faint earthy odor of the cow barn that never quite left them.

These brothers were actually part of the less-than-democratic two-tiered class structure of the monastic family. The first level was the choir monks who chanted the full Divine Office in Latin and were eventually ordained to the priesthood. They were required to have a formal classical education and study Latin, the language in which we prayed the Psalms. The lay brothers did full-time manual labor (although all the monks did some work with their hands) but were less educated, prayed a shorter office in English and had a respected, benignly regarded but definitely inferior role in the monastery. I was later to object to this system and to urge that we all chant the Office together in English as a way of breaking down the class distinctions, a point of view not well received by those in power.

Benedict, saint, visionary and community innovator that he was, had anticipated the problem of priests in the monastery and of "clericalism" in his Rule, which was obviously based on much practical experience.

He recognized the possible need of a priest to celebrate the Eucharist and the sacraments but was very apprehensive about the proliferation of priests who would throw their clerical weight around. The Rule makes it clear that they should only enjoy monastic seniority based on the time of their entrance into the community and not based on education, class or ordination to Holy Orders—the priesthood.

We also raised chickens, pigs and occasionally rabbits. Then there were the extensive and generous apple and peach orchards. These were tended to lovingly and with great skill and attention by Brother James (Jakob), another of the German monks. Not least of all, I recall with gratitude the wonderful cold hard apple cider (*most* in German), which would quench our thirst during the hot summer days at suppertime. As a young monk it provided a little liquid cheer and uplift to me and the other novices during our time of rugged initiation into monastic life.

Brother Nivard, short, strong and always cheerful, tended the flourishing flower and shrub nurseries and greenhouses that provided the public with the beauty of the earth and the abbey with a source of income. We also prided ourselves on our beehives and large honey harvest. Our laconic and dry-humored Father Augustine tended the hives with great devotion, skill and fearlessness in the face of possible bee attacks that I found daunting. Delicious honey was always in plentiful abundance and very occasionally there appeared a mysterious bottle of mead, a form of honey wine popular in the Middle Ages. Acres of the abbey's renowned Christmas trees surrounded the monastery and we sold them during the holiday season.

> "Listen, my son, to the teachings of your master and incline the ear of your heart."*

This is how the *Holy Rule of St. Benedict* for monks begins. The monk enters a "school of the Lord's service" where he is urged to "truly seek God." The distinctively monastic pillars of his life are the three vows: "Take up the bright, shining weapons of *obedience*" to the abbot, the spiritual father of the monastery who symbolizes Christ himself; "*stability*" or commitment to a specific local monastic family community; and "*conversion of life*," the process of becoming a true man or woman of God—a saint.

We lived a simple and secluded existence spending half of our day chanting the praises of God based primarily on the Psalms of David

---

* *Holy Rule:* Prologue.

from the Hebrew Bible using the ancient mellifluous Gregorian chant. The year-in/year-out chanting of these magnificent melodies and texts seemed to lodge in one's mind and bones. The monk arose with them at dawn and closed his eyes with them at nightfall. We chanted and sang the Divine Office at the appointed times, beginning with the early dark predawn hours, then at dawn, midday, afternoon and nighttime. In this way we sanctified the various times of day, also each season, celebrating the Mystery of Christ's love for creation in his death and resurrection through daily community worship.

The rest of the day was spent in manual labor and the intellectual work of studying and teaching. Our work ranged from baking bread to cutting hair, from caring for the sick to making hay, from feeding horses to picking apples. There was also instruction of the young, aspiring monks in the spiritual life, the Holy Rule, and Sacred Scriptures and the teachings of the early Desert Fathers (scant mention was made of the Desert Mothers back then, although they are recognized now).

We believed that through our daily song of praise and the asceticism of hard work and a simple communal life we were in some mysterious way in solidarity with the needs, hopes and fears of the larger Christian community and of the entire human family before the "throne of God." When we arose each day at 4:20 a.m. to the sound of the bell to chant the Office, we were fulfilling the important role of identifying with the suffering and joys of humanity across the globe. As members of the Mystical Body of Christ, we were the voice and the hands of all humanity raised in praise in the name of the rest of that body in households, prisons, the ghettos, factories, battlefields, picket lines and kindergartens—wherever a human soul was struggling to find peace, joy, fulfillment and justice. This mysterious, energetic interconnection of all human beings and indeed of even the non-human world was what justified and gave meaning to our way of life that some might call foolish or even a waste.

It was into this world that I entered as a novice—a beginner—under the name of Frater (Brother) Elias, to take on the challenge of "truly seeking God" as the Holy Rule states. This was the first of a three-year initiation process. I chose as my patron Elias, the wonder worker and prophet of the Hebrew Bible (I & II Kings), who was carried off at his death in a fiery chariot. He is the precursor of the Messianic Age who is eagerly awaited and given a place of honor through an empty chair at every Jewish Passover table for the Seder meal, and who is also honored in a beautiful evening hymn ("Eliyahu Hanavi") at the closing of each Sabbath and some believe was reincarnated in the precursor of the Christ, John the Baptizer and also venerated among Muslims. He was a kind of fiery hell raiser and wonder worker, and that appealed to me.

The novitiate was a one-year process of initiation to help the monastic family and the novice himself decide whether he was really being called to this vocation. We were an interesting assortment of ten very different people. Frater Reginald (not his real name) made the novitiate year quite a challenge for me. Very early on, he expressed a strong liking and admiration for me and used every opportunity to study, work and be with me, which I found suffocating. I had no reason to understand his feelings in a sexual way (at that point in my naïve development I might not have noticed the difference), but I experienced them as suffocating and isolating from the others. When I expressed my misgivings, he became furious and spent the rest of our novitiate using every opportunity to make my life miserable. I needed no cat-of-nine tails to create a monastic life of penance for me.

St. Benedict was surely speaking from experience when he quoted St. Paul to encourage the monks "To bear one another's burdens and so you will fulfill the law of Christ" (Galatians 6:2). One assumes he was speaking of the law of love that was required in not merely tolerating but actually accepting some of "the brethren" whose quirks and personalities could indeed, at times, be grating. Community life even without any hair shirts could be a daily challenging ascetical practice.

Yet there were others whose presence enriched that year. Frater Ambrose was a Jewish "convert" like myself and refugee from Nazi Germany. He was a gifted concert pianist, a brilliant scholar who was fluent in Latin, Greek and Hebrew and was blessed with a photographic memory. Frater Myles was a slightly older Irishman who had been a printer and who had the charm and wit of the Emerald Isle. There were others, but suffice it to say that we were a diverse group, which is to say novice life was both interesting and difficult.

As novices, we were housed in the unfinished attic dormitory of the handsome old Gothic-style granite monastery constructed in the late 1920s. The ten of us—the babies of the monastic family—began our one-year novitiate in this freezing, unheated dormitory during those fierce Sussex County winters in the northernmost reaches of the New Jersey hill country. The mornings were so cold that sometimes the water in the holy water font was frozen solid as we entered the darkened abbey Church for the 4:45 morning Office. The summers in that non-insulated attic could also be unbearably hot.

At approximately 5:30 each morning the novices ("no vices" we jokingly called ourselves) returned to the novitiate classroom for spiritual reading and silent meditation. It was a difficult time to stay awake and I often found myself with my head facedown on the desk instead of in a state of mystical prayer. But wakefulness against sleep was one of the constant struggles of the monastic life because of our early rising hour. Novices were not granted the mercy of a midday nap, as was occasionally the case for the older monks.

Even at the moment of arising early in the morning before sunrise, the monks are urged to "gently encourage one another so that the drowsy may have no excuse" (HR 28 end). In fact, when the wake-up signal is given, they are to "hasten to be before one another at the Work of God and yet with all gravity and decorum" (HR).

The challenge for the monk to stay awake can be further interpreted as the general state of being a conscious, awake, spiritually alert human being as opposed to the unconsciousness that anesthetizes the majority of humankind. Not even religious people—including monks—are immune to this state of being spiritual sleepwalkers. The Buddha, radiant after his great enlightenment, was asked who he was—a demigod, a prince, a magician? He simply answered: "I am one who is awake."

The early dawn time of prayer and meditation, the central part of a monk's life, was woven into the rest of the day. It took the form of leisurely, meditative spiritual reading called *lectio divina* where one awaits holy inspiration to "taste and see that the Lord is sweet" (Ps. 33:9). *Lectio divina* was the primary form of meditation peculiar to the early monastic tradition. This ancient practice is different from later, more structured and organized—even scientific—forms of meditation such as the Spiritual Exercises of St. Ignatius, the founder of the Jesuit order.

The power of these texts and the Plainsong musical settings throughout the annual cycle of sacred seasons and feasts during the liturgical year were mirrored in the seasonal changes and colors and beauty of the woods and fields of the surrounding natural world. All these inflamed my heart and drew me deeper into the great cosmic reality of the Christ and His Mystical Body, the human community, and suffused my life of prayer and contemplation.

It became clear to me that there was no dualistic split between this spirituality and the world outside but rather that we celebrated a powerful ritual that ineluctably led from the altar to the street. Even from the apparent isolation and solitude of my monastic life, I began to experience the passion of the Hebrew prophets and of Jesus Himself for a world of justice for the poor and powerless. Why should we separate what we did around the altar and in the monastic choir stalls from the Chicano farm workers' picket lines, from the cries of Black children in the inner-city ghettos, or from the growing involvement of the US military in the repression of hungry peasants in the jungles and rice paddies around the world? This awareness was nurtured by my reading, important contact with progressive priests, nuns and laypeople and news my parents sent me.

And so I grew into the day-in/day-out, year-in/year-out rhythm of this simple life lived close to the earth and to one's brothers in community, and through these, in some mysterious way into a very direct connection to God. Sunrise, sunset, the intense dark night of the woods, the brilliance of the starry heavens, the fierce cold winters, the lush spring, the hot hay-making summers, the unbelievably brilliant foliage and apple picking of fall were the glorious tapestry against which we celebrated the mystical seasons and rhythms of divine love and sought to make present the reality of human struggle and suffering everywhere before God's mercy.

Despite my feelings of harmony with the monastic life, it was still somewhat unexpected when after the year of my noviceship, in spite of my sometimes non-conventional views on politics and theology, the community approved me for simple temporary vows. Then after two more years, on August 15, 1954, on the day of the Feast of the Assumption of the Blessed Virgin, I prostrated myself facedown on the cold stone floor of the sanctuary of the abbey Church and made my solemn vows according to the Holy Rule of St. Benedict as a monk of St. Paul's Abbey.

CHAPTER 5

UNIVERSITY OF MUNICH

A Bittersweet Return to the Land of My Birth

ABBOT CHARLES CORISTON, THE LEADER and spiritual father of our monastic family, was a striking figure with blue eyes, a strong square jaw and a full head of silver-gray hair set off against the black abbatial skull cap. He was a talented, if somewhat affected, speaker and was a much sought after preacher and retreat master—especially by the ladies, young and old alike. The abbot was born into an Irish working-class family in Pittsburgh during the Depression years, served as an Air Force chaplain and later studied pedagogy at Fordham University. Consequently, he had not spent a great deal of time in the monastery when he was elected the first abbot of St. Paul's Abbey and this quality of being relatively unknown seemed to make him an attractive candidate. It was a decision that some of the monks would live to regret.

In the monastic tradition the abbot is not merely a religious fig-urehead, but rather, as the Holy Rule prescribes, he "takes the place of Christ" and "is to be obeyed as Christ Himself." Moreover, he is usually elected for life.

So it was often a spiritual dilemma for this young, idealistic monk when Father Abbot seemed to disapprove of many of the political, theo-logical and even monastic views that I held. It seemed that at times the abbot was not sure whether I was more of a Communist or a heretic or some new synthesis of the two.

I thought that, generally speaking, I was an observant monk, zeal-ous for the Holy Rule and the monastic life, always present and a devout participant in chanting the Divine Office—even at the predawn hours— and respectful of the elders in the monastery. And still it was clear fairly early on that I often marched to a different drummer. I naively thought that this drummer was Jesus. Others thought my drummer was Martin Luther, Karl Marx, Che Guevara or Elvis.

The abbot probably did his best within his limitations. It seemed to me that he did not really enjoy being abbot. He was away a great deal, often in his strangely non-monastic green Mercedes-Benz. He was also a skilled pilot and would take every occasion to help Mexican missionaries or do other good works, but far away from the monastery.

In spite of all this, I was somehow approved to move on to Holy Orders and ordination to the priesthood of Jesus Christ on May 25, 1957 during the week preceding the Feast of Pentecost, on which the Church celebrates the descent of the Holy Spirit on the disciples with tongues of fire.

When James McNulty, the conservative but benign Bishop of Pater-son, placed his hands on my head, I experienced those flames of love and union with God and the community as I heard: "You are a priest forever according to the Order of Melchisedech." I celebrated my first Mass the next day in the Church of the Incarnation in Washington Heights, just a few steps away from my former synagogue and some mystical circle was completed—one that I do not yet fully understand. (My parents, to their credit, attended. My, what I put them through.)

It soon became apparent to the community—especially to the ab-bot—that I was looking for ways to take the teachings of Jesus at their word. In 1958 there was a regional boycott of outside scab milk by the local dairy farmers of our then still agricultural Sussex County. These small family farmers were struggling to obtain a just price for their dairy products that they worked so hard to produce. I could attest to this from observing how hard our farm brothers labored. They had to rise even earlier than our 4:20 a.m. waking bell to begin milking and feeding their beloved cows. The local farmers also worked brutal hours and many never had a vacation if there was no one to milk in their absence.

Now the dairy conglomerates refused a price increase and were infiltrating outside cheaper milk into our community. Some of the farmers had even stopped scab trucks and poured the milk out on the highway. I approached Father Abbot and suggested that Christian social justice required that we support and participate in the boycott. He very reluctantly allowed Father Jude and me, one of the senior monks who supervised the farm, to participate.

We must have been a strange sight to these local dairy farmers, who were attired in overalls and boots, when we appeared one bitter cold Sussex County morning on the picket line—one skinny monk and one fat one, in our black monastic habits. These were simple people, largely Protestant, who couldn't figure out yet what those strange guys at St. Paul's Abbey were all about. But they were glad to have our participation and welcomed us into their ranks with hot coffee.

I had also been invited to write a monthly column for the local *Sussex Herald* on contemporary issues such as war and peace, racial justice and Church and society, as well as local issues. Eventually there were complaints from anonymous sources to the abbot about my editorial views.

Even though it must have seemed that way, I truly did not spend my days finding ways to disrupt our peaceful community where the members had come to seek God in an undisturbed monastic life. I was not out to tweak the nose of the establishment (although there may have been a little of that). On the contrary, my basic desire was to be liked, approved and accepted—both as a member of a persecuted people and the child of a father who had often withheld his approval. And yet my life path was to lead me to take decisions and choose causes that would have the diametrically opposite effect.

Ivan Illich continued to support my spiritual journey and to share with me his unique gift of being a friend. He would later write very beautifully about the meaning of friendship. When I entered the monastery, he once came to our abbey to visit me and make a personal spiritual retreat. Both his free-spirited manner of celebrating daily Mass and his vision of the future Church so frightened and threatened Abbot Charles that after a few days of "warnings," he actually asked Illich to leave. This was extremely painful and embarrassing to me, but it did not faze Illich, who thrived on controversy and who urged me not to pay it too much attention.

Up to this point all monks needing to go on unusual trips outside Sussex County (e.g., to New York City for abbey business or even occasional special days off) required Father Abbot's personal blessing before departing, while trips within the county for shopping or medical needs only required the blessing of the prior, who was second in command. However, at that time it was decreed that I would require the abbot's personal blessing for all trips—even local ones—outside the monastery. No doubt, this edict stemmed from the fear that I would espouse some questionable cause or instigate other "troubles" in the community while outside. It felt like modified house arrest.

Work in the monastery was either with our minds or manual labor with our hands. It was a holy task right up there with the life of prayer and contemplation. At first I had been given the job of stonemason and, after laying some crooked sidewalks, I became a house painter. I gradually learned to be an expert in the craft of painting the many rooms of our abbey and even of mastering a big compressor for the more technical spray painting of the exterior of our buildings.

But more was still to come when one morning I was called into the Father Prior Augustine's office (a second-in-command). He had a new assignment for me: taking care of the horses and teaching riding to the summer campers at our beautiful Camp St. Benedict. The monk is called—and challenged by his vow of obedience—to find God's will in the instruction of his religious superiors, for it is written about Jesus that "He was made obedient unto death even to the death of the cross" (Philippians 2:8).

I submitted with some mixed feelings, although I had always had a love for the earth and for all animal life. Father Robert was to be my instructor. Robert came from a Slavic family of farmers and horse breeders in Connecticut and was somewhat gruff and taciturn, down to earth, occasionally given to profanity. He did not have a warm and fuzzy personality but had a good heart somewhere behind his steel-rimmed glasses and severe blue-eyed countenance.

Father Robert, no doubt, wondered what this skinny little intellectual Jew boy from New York City could ever learn about horses. I was appropriately apprehensive and intimidated and a slow learner. He had me begin with riding Katrina, an older horse with one of the most wicked and jarring trots in the world—a choice not made by accident.

And so slowly and sometimes *very painfully* I became a horseman. It was a joy every day, right after the morning Office, to greet the dawn and feed, groom and take care of our horses. The old German monks who ran the farm were at first amused by my new assignment but slowly welcomed me into their ranks. I began to develop an affectionate relationship with our horses—even with a few of the mean ones. This proved to be a blessing in a lifestyle which did not always have sufficient space for human relationship, contact and affection, and so I developed real friendship with these fine animals. Later in the summer months I began my work with the young people as a camp counselor with a special assignment as a riding instructor. It was an unfamiliar context, but I think that I occasionally helped to give some young men a stronger sense of self-confidence through horsemanship.

Then there was always the hard summer work of making hay in the hot sun and picking apples and peaches in the fall. Novices were always assigned to the less attractive job of cleaning toilets and bathrooms. All the monks, priests and brothers took their turn waiting on tables in the refectory and washing dishes. As philosophy and theology students, our primary work was also our studies.

One day, in early 1958, Abbot Charles called me into his office to inform me that Fathers Francis and Myles and I were going to be sent to the University of Munich, Germany, for a year of postgraduate studies. We would live at the House of Studies in Munich attached to the motherhouse of our congregation (a confederation of monasteries), the Archabbey of St. Ottilien in Bavaria.

I received the news with mixed feelings. On the one hand there was surely elation at the prospect of spending a year in Europe in one of its most cosmopolitan cities, München/Munich—"city of the joy of life," as it was called—known for its music, theater, intellectual life and the wild Fasching Beer Festival before Lent.

How could it not also have occurred to me that I would be returning to the land of my birth, which had once expelled me and murdered six million of my fellow Jews as well as millions of others? Even more, it meant living in Bavaria, always a hotbed of enthusiastic support for

Hitler and anti-Semitism and still today a locus of the most reactionary forces in Germany. I wondered whether the abbot might not at least have had the delicacy to think of all this. So much for delicacy.

I slowly began to embrace the idea and prepare myself with growing enthusiasm. I did have an advantage of having had German as my mother tongue, even though it needed freshening up. Even my parents were excited at the idea of getting me out of the narrow (as they saw it) confines of the monastery.

Life at the Uni (as the university was called) did turn out to be an exciting and intellectually stimulating experience. It was my first direct contact with the "new theology" and more radical interpretations of the Bible with which I had already (secretly for the most part) familiarized myself during my more narrow theological studies back in New Jersey.

I was fortunate in being there during the last year of Romano Guardini, the great theologian philosopher and scholar who had spoken out against Hitler and had published his famous "Guilt and Responsibility" as an indictment of German Christian society. He always spoke in the largest aula (lecture hall) where there was standing room only. His lectures were peak experiences delivered with a profound simplicity. One felt oneself to be in the presence of a great teacher, a word that should henceforth not be used too loosely. Many of the other professors were blazing the path for a new understanding of Church and theology.

But amidst all of this beauty and intellectual stimulation, I also brought the burden of my personal history, as well as that of my people, along with me. I had decided that I could not be in Germany (even postwar Germany, 1958) especially as a Jew but also as a priest and monk without exploring the true role of the Catholic Church under Hitler. This issue had always seemed to me somewhat swept under the ecclesiastical rug, and the controversy and apparent cover-up about the role of Pius XII had muddied the waters even more.

I did not have a fully developed investigative strategy, but I felt that my wearing the monk's habit (as we often still did even in public in Germany) and my fluency in German would provide me with a certain cover to explore the issue. Certainly no one would suspect that I was a Jew trying to establish the facts about Nazi Germany.

I began with some formal research and found that the two Catholic bishops (perhaps the only ones) who had really spoken out against the Nazis were Cardinal Faulhaber of Munich and Archbishop von Galen of Münster. They had addressed the issues of euthanasia used against the inmates of psychiatric institutes and the confiscation of Church property under Hitler. This certainly took great courage, but I was deeply troubled by the absence of any significant mention of the deportation and murder of millions of Jews, as well as Gypsies, Communists, homosexuals and other "undesirables." Faulhaber's private correspondence indicated some personal agonizing about the plight of the Jews, but these sentiments were not publicly expressed, as far as I could determine. It seems that he had also minimized the number of Catholic priests who had collaborated with the Nazis. The idea of calling for any form of non-cooperation, never mind resistance, was never raised even when it still might have been possible

My research on von Galen not withstanding, in 2005 the first modern German Pope would "beatify"—a step towards canonization—the archbishop as "the Lion of Münster" in spite of his silence on the Jews and failure to call for even the mildest opposition to the Nazis.

Much of my research was done through informal interviews of priests, many from our own archabbey, whose age would have made them of draft eligibility during World War II (something that no one could have refused without risking arrest, confinement to a concentration camp or worse). I also spoke to lay people of approximately similar ages and occasionally to people on the streets. I practically could not find a single person who admitted to any involvement with or sympathy for National Socialism. One relatively younger woman, a fellow student at the Uni, admitted shame-facedly to membership in the Hitler Youth, but she was the only one.

In light of these experiences, I would experience a respectful skepticism many years later concerning the family history of the then newly elevated German Pope, Benedict XVI. I would, at least, have welcomed an intensive investigation (à la Seymour Hirsch of The New Yorker) and testimony from first-hand witnesses and documentation—as far as possible—about his claims that the Pope's father had left several positions as a policeman in Nazi-infested Bavaria because of his anti-Hitler views, and that the young Josef Ratzinger had been forcibly conscripted into the Hitler Youth—not my childhood impression of the way it went in Frankfurt. These claims may have been authentic, but they deserved a serious investigation based on my experience of general denial in postwar Germany. When I recently tracked down the Pope's biographer, John Allen, he admitted that he had not interviewed any independent contemporary witnesses on these matters. There was one laudatory article about this period in The *New York Times* after Benedict's election in which the reporter had interviewed some local people, but only friends of the Ratzinger family. It also troubled me at the time of his election how enthusiastically and uncritically the international Jewish leadership embraced the new pontiff.

Some of the Pope's later denigrating remarks about Muslims, about indigenous people in Brazil and the inferior status of all religions—even Christian churches—that are not Catholic, made one more than a little uneasy. The return to a Latin liturgy, which included prayers for the conversion of the Jews on Good Friday, was also disturbing: "That the Lord our God may take the veil from their hearts." Then there was the reinstatement of the reactionary British apostate Bishop Williamson who was a Holocaust denier. The Vatican only backpedaled after an outcry from the Jewish community and others. One need not draw any unwarranted conclusions about Pope Benedict's history, but it reminded me of how difficult it was to get to the bottom of this shadowy period of German history and the Church's role in it.

So during my sojourn in Munich I found a society in denial as far as I could discern. Germany, at that time, was celebrating its *Wirtschaftwunder*, its miraculous economic recovery after the devastation of World War II. The nation had suffered enormously, to a great extent because it had embraced (literally) der Führer, and now it was reveling in its Volkswagens, its refrigerators, television sets, stylish clothes, good food and a *Gemütlichkeit*, a comfortable lifestyle.

This was all compliments of the Marshall Plan. Would that the US had had such economic post-war compassion for Vietnam and reconstruction for poor devastated Iraq, in spite of the funds already theoretically allotted and misspent for that purpose.

In the midst of this prosperity, Germany was awash in consumerism with its soul poisoned by moral amnesia, an affliction not unfamiliar to the US after the Vietnam War. A typical response to my inquiries was given by an elderly gentleman with a familiar brush mustache who winked at me knowingly and said that, "Our only mistake at the end was not to have united with the Americans and marched against the Russians together." So much for having learned the moral lessons of Nazism and Hitler.

After my research project, I fell into a mild depression at my failure to discover so few German, and especially Catholic, admissions of responsibility for the horrors of this period. As a result, I also developed serious stomach ulcers, an affliction that I suffered from for many subsequent years. I immediately stopped smoking, a bad habit I had acquired while in Germany. I also had to abandon the unhealthy but interesting Bavarian cuisine. It consisted of greasy, fatty cold cuts and sausage, sharp cheeses, rough but delicious peasant bread and, of course, the omnipresent and wonderful Munich beer.

Almost simultaneously, I received a letter from Father Abbot denying my request to stay on in Munich for another year to work on my doctorate in theology in that intellectually stimulating milieu. Reading between the lines, I detected the abbot's fear that I would be contaminated and seduced by the Teutonic heresies and be led even further astray from the true faith. Instead, I was to be transferred to the University of Ottawa in chilly Canada, where theology, including lectures and examinations, was still being conducted in Medieval Latin to protect the seminary student from developing any original ideas on these matters.

Ironically, after a few months in Canada, Abbot Charles again unexpectedly recalled me to St. Paul's Abbey to become director of our retreat house for lay people. He felt that we had fallen on hard times and that Queen of Peace Retreat could serve the people and also become a more regular source of income—an issue always on his mind. Perhaps he also secretly hoped that my Hebraic ancestry would make me a good financial manager of the enterprise.

No doubt he also felt that greater proximity would keep this potentially straying sheep under his abbatial thumb. This prediction would prove to be only half right. I would create a highly successful project but it was also a case of throwing Br'er Rabbit right into the briar patch.

Queen of Peace Retreat would turn into a center of dynamic Church renewal and would provide me with a bully pulpit for the causes of civil rights, peace and theological renewal. These causes seemed to me to be true to the spirit of Jesus' message, but again troubled the waters of monastic good order. More on that later.

CHAPTER 6

A MONK IN THE CIVIL RIGHTS MOVEMENT

Encounter with Dr. Martin Luther King Jr.

Members of the Sussex County Human Relations Council man a civil rights exhibit at a recent County Fair.

IT WAS ON THE MORNING of March 7, 1965, when Dr. Martin Luther King, Jr., sent out an emergency call from Selma, Alabama, that I heard about the need for clergy and religious people to join him there in the critical struggle for voting rights for Black people. Early that morning, over five hundred activists, including the leaders of the voters' rights campaign, had been brutalized by the billy clubs, bullwhips, rubber tubing wrapped in barbed wire, tear gas and horses of the Alabama State Police and Highway Patrol. The police attacked the little band as it attempted to march non-violently across the Pettus Bridge, which spanned the Chattahoochee River in Selma.

It was then that Dr. King made the simple, almost brutal calculation that the time had come for the white churches and synagogues to put it on the line, even if that meant some white clergy skulls might get cracked and bloodied. He had written in his Letter from Birmingham City Jail that the clergy had "too often been the taillight rather that the headlight" of the struggle for justice.

Now King was stricken with remorse because a preaching commitment in his Atlanta Church had prevented his own presence in Selma on that morning. Hence the passion and outrage in his call for "a ministers' march to Montgomery":

> In the vicious treatment of the defenseless citizens of Selma, where old women and young children were gassed and clubbed at random, we have witnessed an eruption of the disease of racism which seeks to destroy all America. The people of Selma will struggle on for the soul of America, but it is fitting that all Americans help bear the burden.

This emergency call from Selma came to my attention at dawn on Monday, March 8, in a radio bulletin, shortly after the daily morning Mass sung by our community of monks in the ancient Gregorian chant in our peaceful abbey. Mass that day was on Monday of the first week of Lent and the day's Scripture readings were stunningly appropriate: "I will look for those which are lost and bring back those which have strayed, and I will bind up any crippled one, and I will make the weak one strong . . . and I will feed them in justice" (Ezekiel 34:15).

> "Then these in their turn will ask Him: 'Lord, when did we see You hungry or thirsty, a stranger or naked, sick or in prison and did not come to Your help?' Then He will answer them: 'Of a truth I tell you, in so far as you did not do this to one of these least ones, you did not do it to Men.'" (Matthew 25:44–45).

My strong life-long feelings about justice for Black people began with my family's close bond with Ethel Benjamin, our African American cleaning lady, one of the noblest souls I will ever know. In her quiet, dignified way she had shared with me the bitter reality of her family's life in Harlem. More recently Thomas Merton's unsparing *Letter to a White Liberal* had further fueled this passion.

So on that Monday morning, it became absolutely clear to me that I must answer the urgent summons issued by Dr. King. Yet the likelihood of receiving permission from my abbot seemed extremely slim. He had already once denied me permission to attend a simple ecumenical peace retreat.

Nevertheless, in my youthful zeal and with deep feelings for the suffering of Black people in the South, I timidly but determinedly decided to find a way. My first step was to confer with Father Aloysius, the only Black monk of our community (we said "Negro" in those days). Father Aloysius was an altogether delightful character. His skin color was deep brown and he looked very much like an African teacher rather than someone from this continent. Of slight build and medium height, his most striking characteristic was his deep brown eyes made even larger behind thick rimless glasses. Slightly bowed, Father Aloysius (or Allie) was the consummate scholar, always immersed in a theological tome.

He had entered the abbey a few years behind me and we had struck it off right away as the local minorities on the block. Behind his quiet scholarly demeanor there burned a profound commitment to justice, especially for his own people. We often commiserated and joked together about the state of the world, the Church and of our own monastery. It must have been incredibly difficult to be the only Blackman in this all-white world, a feeling I often shared, although there was one other Jewish monk, Father Ambrose. It was always surprising to see Father Aloysius flame out from behind his reserved demeanor when something touched his heart.

He immediately responded with intense enthusiasm to my proposal that we answer Dr. King's call to come to Selma. "By all means, this is something that deserves the old college try," he chortled. He even initiated some fund-raising on his own from a local priest. Needless to say, he shared my profound skepticism about receiving permission from our superiors, but we were determined that the ancient Benedictine motto of PAX would be more than the traditional inscription over the monastery gate.

This would truly be an enterprise guided by the Spirit. The first indication of this providential guidance was the news that Father Abbot Charles was away on a prolonged trip. In fact, he was often away and one suspected that he had some ambivalence about the task of leading, teaching and administering this complex, sometimes difficult group of men. The abbot's absence, however, did not necessarily mean our trip was a shoo-in, since we would now have to deal with the prior, the next in command.

Father Prior Pius was relatively junior in the community in terms of entry date, although chronologically our senior. He had entered the monastery after a stint as a Marine combat pilot, a stockbroker on Wall Street and, briefly, as a Trappist monk at Gethsemane Abbey, Kentucky, which was Thomas Merton's community. Perhaps it was his excessive zeal that may have determined the abbot's choice of him as prior. Abbot Charles wanted someone who would enforce the rules to the letter and Father Pius seemed like the man for the job.

His military-style close-cropped silver hair and rugged hawk-like features were the uniform for his expectation of obedience to the letter of the law. He and I had experienced some run-ins over my pacifist views on war and non-violence, which ran counter to his Marine background. He seemed to regard me as something of a loose cannon and generally as an exponent of the latest dangerous naive idea on either Church or state. (Interestingly, in the course of the years, Father Pius left our monastery for a wonderful experimental monastery in Weston, Vermont. There he has become a warm supporter of his community's involvement in peace and justice issues, and we have become firm friends.)

Hence it must have been through some angelically inspired lapse of memory or perhaps some thus far unsuspected sympathy with the civil rights cause that the prior granted us permission to go. Neither Father Aloysius nor I could quite believe our ears. But our reaction was "Let's get the hell out of here before he changes his mind."

We hastily threw a few things into a bag and changed from our monastic habits into the musty black suits and stiff white Roman collars that were reserved for those rare and dangerous sojourns into what was then known to us as "the world." Our flight from Newark to Montgomery was an adventure in the early 1960s, since air travel was not common, especially for the likes of us.

Some young Black organizers from the Southern Christian Leadership Conference (SCLC) were not the only ones to greet us at the Montgomery Airport. Archbishop Toolan, the local Catholic spiritual shepherd, had stationed a few of his imported Irish priests to discourage priests and nuns in collar and habit who seemed to be joining the campaign in Selma. After all, Dr. King had been accused of being a Communist, a defamation inspired by the smear campaign of FBI Director J. Edgar Hoover. "Sure, Father, and you'd best be returning back home right away. The bishop is warning priests and religious not to get involved in dangerous politics here." All this was not surprising since the bishop had a well-earned reputation for his thunderous silence on segregation in his diocese. Needless to say, we politely but determinedly ignored this episcopal prohibition and piled into the rickety old jalopies that would transport us to Selma and one of the most transformative experiences of our lives.

Within a matter of hours we had been catapulted from the peace and seclusion of our rural monastic solitude into the heat of the civil rights struggle at one of its most historically intense moments. Added to that was the fact that I had never been in the South before and was experiencing culture shock on many levels.

Above all, I experienced intense feelings of euphoria and excitement, and perhaps even a little apprehension. I was deeply moved at the thought of being in the very center of a reality that I had only thought and read about, and in some inner way involved myself in for years—the fight for racial justice in America. It was also the first time that I had been transported from an all-white world into this human mass of predominantly Black folks who were even (presumptuously, it seemed to my still uneducated and somewhat racist consciousness) in the leadership of this movement and making key decisions for all of us.

Here I was in my black suit and clerical Roman collar, my short haircut, still young and inexperienced and wet behind the ears at the age of thirty-four, suddenly surrounded by all of this intensity and life. There was a powerful charge to all this political passion, all this fierce struggle against the status quo, all of this close community, all of this proximity to shared danger and even death that generated unspoken feelings of terror. People close by were being attacked and even killed.

The religious people who arrived in response to Dr. King's emergency call were housed with members of the local Black community. It was Aloysius's and my good fortune to be received by the Simpson family into their modest whitewashed little house. They were an older couple and showered us with simple warm Southern hospitality and treated us like honored guests. They seemed amazed that all these Northerners, especially white people, would come to support them. Little did they realize (and much less ourselves) that it was we who would be enriched beyond our wildest dreams by this experience.

It came as a shock, like a hammer blow to the temple, to realize how poor these generous people were. I could hardly believe my eyes when I opened the refrigerator door looking for a cold drink to discover there one solitary container of milk. It began to dawn on me that my religious vow of poverty was more like a well-intentioned pious charade when compared to the lives of poor Black men and women here and in other parts of the world. This lone container of milk would come to represent the awakening of a new level of consciousness that would stay with me in a haunting way. It shattered the myth of self-satisfied virtue and liberal commitment. It overwhelmed me with a sense of my own privilege and safety in the face of the majority of the people of the world who survived at the edge of misery and existential uncertainty about the next day, the next moment. The memory of this container of milk began the reluctant process of education that would follow me into the barrios of Central America and into the despair of our own urban ghettos and Indian reservations.

Nor was I prepared for the fearsome intensity of the racial hatred that was the lifeblood of the ugly system of segregation and which we had presumptuously come to challenge. It was more than difficult to maintain the biblical perspective of loving one's enemies and turning the other cheek. This would be one of the many lessons that I was to learn from the community of poor and simple "uneducated" people who lived under the terror of this culture of racial segregation and would continue to do so long after we returned to the safety of our white religious institutions.

I can still feel—and almost taste—the bitter animosity and rancor of local whites toward us, since most of us were easily identifiable as the classical Yankee outside agitators. The very fact of Blacks and whites working together to destroy their way of life was an affront and a threatening provocation.

The local and state police represented these attitudes under the guise of law enforcement. It is still hard to imagine how these "peace officers" felt fully justified in treating the Black community with contempt, hatred and brutality. But it was clear that these same attitudes and policies were to apply to "nigger lovers" and other kinds of troublemakers like ourselves.

It was always unsettling to see John Daws of the US Justice Department and a slew of FBI agents consorting and joking with the state and local police. These included County Sheriff Jim Clark, who enjoyed a well-deserved reputation as a racist bigot and was infuriated by this uppity multi-colored resistance movement.

It was truly the Spirit guiding and inspiring this movement as it confronted the ancient institutions and ways of thinking so deeply rooted in the evils of chattel slavery. Nothing brought this home to me like the nightly gatherings in Selma's Brown Chapel. The "chapel" was actually a good-sized brick structure with striking Romanesque towers that had originally been built by freedmen after the Civil War and then served as headquarters for this freedom movement. When the community gathered there at night, the building warmed up and we were very aware of sharing each others' air.

On one of my first nights after the Freedom Rally, I sat towards the front of the sanctuary with Viola Liuzzo, a white woman from Detroit. As we talked she quietly told me why she had left her family to represent the Unitarian community in this historic campaign for freedom. One of their own ministers, Rev. James Reeb, had been clubbed to death a few weeks earlier. I was impressed by her simple modesty in describing her commitment.

These gatherings were a combination of prayer services, extraordinary community gospel singing, and spirit rallies to empower us for the freedom struggle of the next day with its threats and potential for violence, beatings and perhaps even death.

Here was a vibrant form of religiosity, radically different from my past experience. It resembled neither the Jewish rituals of my childhood nor the solemn liturgy of Benedictine monasticism. It was completely new and unfamiliar. This was worship that was warm and alive, traditional and yet spontaneous. It integrated the call and response of slave field songs into memories of ancient African traditional religions. Everybody seemed part of the experience, seemed to own it, even to the point of answering back to the preacher. The prayers came from the heart and the preaching (because the "movement" talks were really preaching) was emotional, loud and often outrageous.

Above all, the music called forth in me a deep feeling of coming home. When the community sang, "I'm Gonna Eat at the Welcome Table," tears welled up from deep within me. When the charismatic Rev. James Bevel spoke, I felt that at last I had found a form of spirituality that integrated politics and religion in an authentic manner. When we sang "I Ain't Gonna Let Nobody Turn Me 'Round" or "I Love Everybody," the non-violent struggle took on both a militancy and a gentleness that I had never experienced before. When the women's choir belted out "Satan, We're Gonna Tear Your Kingdom Down," some deep fearful part of me began to shrink and actually believe that this people's movement could win freedom.

Here was a melding of passion, spirit—even mysticism—and real political struggle that I had been seeking all my life. It was a form of spirituality that led one out onto the street, in particular onto those dusty streets of that once sleepy little Alabama town called Selma.

This was a form of religiosity that I would learn to understand later in greater depth from the brilliant pen of James Baldwin, especially in his essay "Fifth Avenue Uptown." His searing writings about the meaning of the Church to poor Black folks were based on the experience of his own painful childhood in Harlem as the son of a Pentecostal preacher.

I will never forget his stunning description of the weekly metamorphosis of Black maids, cooks and janitors now clothed in beautiful Sunday raiment—the ladies attired in magnificent ostrich-feathered hats, and the gentlemen in elegant pinstripes and spats—all to praise the Lord in His holy place. On this day, the poor appeared in the majesty of God's children to praise, sing and shout, indeed to be transformed by the fire of the Holy Spirit into experiencing themselves as free women and men— God's very own sons and daughters—in their own Church, indeed, with their own unique form of African Christianity.

Thus it came as no surprise that this religious tradition at its best became the source of inspiration and even the home of the Black liberation struggle and that its clergy would often play a leadership role in this revolution. For underneath the issue of voting rights lay the deeper questions of Black rebellion and the uprooting of all those structures and systems that perpetrated oppression in the variety of its economic, social and cultural forms.

After a few days of initiation and indoctrination into this new world of the freedom struggles, the campaign organizers decided that it was time for some of the religious types—often from up North—to join the actual march to Montgomery. A small group of the younger activists had already gone ahead to begin the long march to the Alabama state capitol and to face the insults and abuse and threats of violence from the crowds along the road that the rest of us would soon be exposed to. This was the third attempt within two weeks by this hardy movement to cross the Pettus Bridge. As they crossed it, a cry of jubilation rose from the marchers. It was actually on March 21st, the feast of St. Benedict, our monastic founder, that Aloysius and I set out on this pilgrimage for justice.

National and international press and television exposure as well as the fear of major confrontation and civil unrest had persuaded President Lyndon Johnson to nationalize the Alabama State Guard. The troops lined the road, especially as we marched through more populated areas. None of this seemed to discourage the presence and vociferousness of the white crowds that hurled racist invectives and hateful threats against the marchers. I had feelings of fear that reminded me of my childhood in Germany. Somehow I did not have great confidence in the soldiers' ability (or even sincere desire) to protect us against the members of the Klan and the White Citizens' Council. The armed troops lining the highway appeared steely faced and non-committal, although their very presence created a physical barrier between the marchers and the jeering crowd.

We walked and marched from early in the morning to dusk—seven hot and dusty miles on the first day—with short stops for food and sometimes for common prayer. The marchers knelt on the hard pavement of Highway 80 (also known as the Jefferson Davis Highway) to pray for strength and perseverance and to intercede in a special way for Alabama Governor George Wallace, Sheriff Bull Connor and the sometimes rabidly jeering crowds lining the route of the march. Father Aloysius, more hopefully than I, believed that "our kneeling and praying on that hard concrete and all of us coming together in a peaceful manner must have had an effect even on the police."

It was during one of these rest stops where, as we knelt on the dusty highway for prayer and then nourished ourselves with bologna sandwiches, we were introduced to Dr. Martin Luther King Jr. My recollection is of a surprisingly short and modest man dressed in a business suit and fedora, who had apparently joined the march freshly returned from the airport and a national speaking engagement. His presence was strong and clear and his brown eyes focused and gentle. He warmly greeted and thanked these two young priests who had traveled from the North in response to his call for religious people to come and join the struggle. Tears rolled down my cheeks as I sensed the enormity of the moment.

It was only a brief handshake and I don't even remember the words, but it was one of the encounters that would change my life. Along with Mahatma Gandhi's teaching on non-violence, Martin Luther King's vision and teachings would shape my own involvement and commitment for years to come. It would take many of those years for me to realize how far I still was from the deep inner spiritual and psychological conversion that authentic *Satyagraha* (literally, clinging to the truth) demanded.

This was the radical doctrine that this slight and modest African American minister would use to confront the domestic Pax Romana of the most heavily armed empire in human history. Ironically, his principal teacher in this was a small, gaunt Hindu halfway around the world who had reminded him and all of the Christian West of that central (but well-hidden) teaching of yet another gaunt, brown-skinned prophet named Jesus in his Sermon on the Mount.

When Dr. King was unexpectedly cast on the scene of a bus strike in Birmingham, Alabama, that would prove to be the spark that ignited the civil rights revolution, he did not arrive with the blueprint of a non-violent campaign in his back pocket. In fact, this spark was ignited and its spirit shaped by the quiet but emphatic "no!" of seamstress Rosa Parks who refused to give up her seat to a white passenger and move to the back of the segregated bus as prescribed by a racist city ordinance. As the tribute by the song of the Neville Brothers has it:

> *Thank you, Miss Rosa, you are the spark,*
>
> *That kindled a people's revolution,*
>
> *Thank you, Sister Rosa Parks.*

This theory and methodology, which embodied the invincible power of transcendent love, even of one's enemies, would later be criticized, attacked and forgotten in the controversies involving the younger Black activists of SNCC (Student Non-violent Coordinating Committee), the Black Power Movement, the Black Panthers, and especially the charismatic, and later to be martyred, Malcolm X.

Malcolm did come to Selma where he delivered a radical, fiery speech. Privately he spoke quiet and supportive words to Coretta Scott King, Dr. King's wife: "I am not here to disrupt but to support the struggle of Dr. King. . . . If white people realized what the alternative is, perhaps they would be more willing to hear Dr. King."

Malcolm was assassinated eighteen days later.

It is instructive that the established powers developed a certain strategy of tolerance for Dr. King and his non-violent movement as long as it limited itself to the issues of voting rights and segregated public accommodations in the South. However, on April 4, 1967 (exactly one year before his assassination), he spoke out against the Vietnam War at the historic Riverside Church in New York City. He stepped out beyond the limits of political propriety in criticizing his own government in a time of war. Even some of his close associates counseled him to refrain from this step into the uncharted waters of war and peace. Yet he was steadfast in this decision to expand the spirit of Satyagraha to the bloody Indochina conflict. He declared, "Some of us who have already begun to break the silence of the night have found that the calling to speak is often a vocation of agony, but we must speak."

But it was his leadership of the Poor People's Campaign that began bringing poor African Americans, Latinos and Native Americans and whites together in the quest for economic justice, that would symbolize his radical vision of the "beloved community" and seal his death sentence. It is no coincidence that Dr. King was killed during a strike of garbage collectors in Memphis, Tennessee.

Let all those who have sanitized the life and teaching of Martin Luther King, even by the respectability of a national holiday in his honor, take another look at the life and teachings of this Black martyr and great American leader.

Let them go back to the essential writings and speeches of Dr. King (especially those of his later life) to be reminded of how profound, even radical, was his critique of the political and economic system of this nation and how prophetic was his application of non-violent struggle to the crisis of our times.

One of the best-kept secrets of American history continues to be the truth behind Martin Luther King's execution. At the trial held in Memphis on November 15, 1999 (which was virtually ignored by the media) during the civil suit initiated by the King family, it was determined that the assassination was not the act of an individual racist assassin but a conspiracy of the US government, so hated and feared were the teachings and leadership of this apostle of non-violence. James Earl Ray eventually denied any role in the murderous plot conceived at a meeting in the office of J. Edgar Hoover and carried out by a sharpshooter of US military intelligence.[*]

Dr. King's vision increasingly inflamed my heart and fired my imagination as we marched along that hot and dusty highway on the way to Montgomery and the Alabama state house. Little did I know how profoundly that experience would transform my understanding of Christianity, politics and of life itself.

As we entered the outskirts of the Alabama capital city, the ranks of the marchers began to swell. Hundreds and then thousands from all over the nation joined this sea of humanity as it poured into the metropolis to challenge the centuries-old foundation of slavery and racial segregation.

* *An Act of State* by William F. Pepper (the King family's attorney at the trial), Verso Books, 2003.

Tears ran down my face as we sang the old hymns of a once-slave Church, as we became the new Israel calling on Pharaoh to "Let my people go!" We felt the Spirit come over us as this presumptuous band of "Black and white together" entered the capitol precincts of one of the most segregated states of America. We were already breathing in the unfamiliar fragrance of the sweet winds of freedom. By this time we had been joined by some significant, more respectable, religious, civic, labor and even a few political leaders and the march had grown from 3,200 to close to 30,000. For me, that day represented a fulfillment of the dream that perhaps justice could triumph after all and that the oppressed people of the earth, even the most despised, might have their day in the sun.

We heard Martin Luther King Jr. deliver one of his most eloquent speeches from the steps of the Alabama state house itself. It was as if some huge millstone was lifted from my shoulders as I joined with the children and grandchildren of African slaves in this great triumphant procession. The humiliation and fear that I had carried with me all my life from my childhood days in Nazi Germany no longer seemed so powerful and compelling. My tears were tears of joy and celebration. I felt a little embarrassed at the eruption of such deep emotions. There were many eloquent speeches and moving prayers and songs. But it was the message of Dr. King that illuminated the day. Somehow he represented the pride of our movement, the symbol of his people's long and bloody pilgrimage to the light. Even the Confederate flag flying above the state capitol building seemed pathetic that day in the face of so much courage and dignity.

As the afternoon sun began to set over the crowd, we slowly and somewhat reluctantly began our return journeys back home. Our joy would not be unalloyed for the next days would bring us news of more bloodshed in the name of violent attempts to maintain the racist status quo. The tragic news came that Viola Liuzzo, the white Unitarian from Detroit whom I had gotten to know, had been murdered as she drove a young Black man to the airport. Now she was gone, another corpse in a Southern morgue to remind us of the long, bitter path that still lay ahead. (With all the appropriate mourning for the killings of Viola Liuzzo and Rev. Reeb, I couldn't help noticing how little public attention had been given to the brutal police shooting in broad daylight two weeks earlier of Jimmie Lee Jackson, a young Black man who had died protecting his mother.)

Father Aloysius and I had befriended an African American Baptist Church delegation from Philadelphia and they invited us to join their chartered flight back up north. We gladly accepted, eager to maintain the spirit of community and the protection it afforded as we reentered the Southern society at large. We drove to the airport without any great event.

However, when our chartered Delta flight landed in Atlanta for refueling, the ground crew there refused to service our plane by emptying the waste from the lavatories or providing any food or refreshment. Thus did the fates remind us that racism was alive and well and that our work for a just society had only begun and I experienced fury and humiliation. For years I would have an aversion to flying Delta, unless sheer necessity required it, and even of visiting the South. I was still far from the purity of the non-violent ideal.

We returned to our monastery filled with pride and elation so we were not prepared for a reception, which was mixed and tentative at best. The younger monks received us with unabashed enthusiasm and pride that two of their brothers had represented them in this historic campaign for freedom. At the same time, I could sense the unease among the more conservative brethren who feared that this experience would somehow give us—especially me—license to further disrupt the monastic tranquility and isolation with the noise and unrest of "the world."

Father Kevin was tall, handsome and pure Philadelphia Irish in speech and profile. He looked like he would have done well as a cop or a professional football player. Kevin was balding but always had a little tuft of hair near the front of his head, which gave him the appearance of a fighting gamecock. He had a good heart under his rough exterior and has since passed on to his reward. He was overheard murmuring that these two young upstarts (a Jew and a Negro—or did he use the N word—at that) would cause unrest with these issues which were, after all, "political" and surely tinged with questionable, if not downright Communist influence. He added, "The trouble with Elias is that he's nothing but a liberal Jew."

Their trepidations proved well founded. For from that moment forth my sense of history and of my own vocation as a priest and monk changed profoundly.

My inner life of prayer and contemplation was now inhabited by the faces and lives of those I had left behind in Alabama: the Simpson family who had housed us, the beautiful school children, the many courageous young freedom fighters and the suffering Black communities haunted my thoughts and dreams. All too often the hate-filled faces of the people on the road, the members of the Klan and the White Citizens Council would appear before me as well. In meditation in my monastic cell and in our chanting of the Office, these lives of pain and courage began to represent the leitmotif of my spiritual journey. The suffering of the human family, which we as monks presented before the merciful throne of God for healing and protection each day, now took on the particular qualities and aspirations of this crucified community with all of its fears and hopes.

It seemed that the Spirit had brought me to Selma to become not less but more fully a monk. The abbot must have regretted at times that he had provided me with the bully pulpit of the directorship of the Queen of Peace Retreat House. It was here that I and a few of my younger fellow monks, especially Father Martin, were infusing the up-to-now traditional weekend retreats for laymen and women, married couples and young people with the new excitement of the Church's "opening up the windows and letting fresh air in" that Pope John XXIII had launched through the revolution of Vatican Council II.

It became clear to me that it was my duty as a Christian priest and monk to cry out against this obscenity in its Northern manifestations. Whenever possible I would include the Selma experience and the escalating Vietnam War as examples of the moral implications of the Gospel in retreat lectures and programs.

All of this did not sit well with some members of my monastic community. A few irate, more conservative retreat participants complained that "Father Elias was making the retreats too political." They had come for solace and rest and instead they were given the discomfort of the Gospel. It was painful to live with these daily feelings of rejection from one's own spiritual brothers.

On one of my Sunday-morning parish assignments to celebrate Mass at St. Andrew's parish in Clifton, New Jersey, I mentioned racial justice (and perhaps even the war in Vietnam) in my sermon. I had the audacity to quote some passages from an unusual pastoral letter on war and race by Cardinal Sheehan of Baltimore. On the following Sunday the pastor declared from the pulpit, "The views expounded from this pulpit last Sunday were not the official teaching of the Church." Word was also sent back to the abbot that I was not welcome to return as a Sunday-morning celebrant.

Thus did I begin my activist career with the direct experience that "prophets are not without honor, except in their own country and in their own house" (Mt.13:57). It would not be the last time that I would experience this pain of being attacked or at least not supported by my own community and Church at large. It would be an even longer process—one that is still going on—before I would realize the challenge of forgiving "the enemy within" and seek reconciliation if not agreement with those who were my own.

The words of Dr. Martin Luther King Jr. in his historic address on March 21, 1965 at the Montgomery State House at the end of the Selma march continued to be a challenge to my spiritual and political journey.

The musical cadences of his words will continue to sound within me like a great bell, acting as a powerful antidote to the hopelessness that often lurks at the perimeter of my consciousness. These almost magical sounds still have the power to contradict and heal the despair threatening to invade my soul as I feel overwhelmed by the world's pain and injustice and my own sense of powerlessness:

"Our aim must never be to defeat or humiliate the white man but to win his friendship and understanding. We must come to see that the end we seek is a society at peace with itself, a society that can live with its conscience. That will be a day not of the white man, not of the Black man. That will be the day of man as man.

"I know you are asking today, 'How long will it take?' I come to say to you this afternoon however difficult this moment, however frustrating the hour, it will not be long, because truth pressed to earth will rise again.

"How long? Not long, because no lie can live forever.

"How long? Not long, because you will reap what you sow.

"How long? Not long. Because the arc of the moral universe is long but it bends toward justice.

"How long? Not long, 'cause mine eyes have seen the glory of the coming of the Lord, trampling out the vintage where the grapes of wrath are stored. He has loosed the fateful lightning of His terrible swift sword. His truth is marching on.

"'He has sounded forth the trumpets that shall never call retreat. He is lifting up the hearts of man before His judgment seat. O, be swift, my soul, to answer Him. Be jubilant, my feet. Our God is marching on.'"

CHAPTER 7

THE WAR CLOUDS GATHER
Vietnam inside the Cloister

IN THE MID-1960S, REPORTS OF the early stages of the Vietnam conflict began to seep into our isolated community of monks. We did not have television, but a copy of The *New York Times* appeared in the monastery library each day and a few of the brethren actually looked at it. There was a radio in the priests' recreation room (recreation was one hour after lunch and dinner for conversation), but personal radios in monastic cells were frowned upon, if not forbidden.

So it was something of a surprise when late one night there was a knock on the door of my cell—a small, simple whitewashed room—after Compline, the final Office when the strict Grand Silence reigned. This was a time of sacred quiet dedicated to prayer, contemplation and sleep until after the morning Office of Lauds at 4:20 a.m.

I was surprised to find Father Andrew, one of the senior monks, knocking at my door. Andrew O'Sullivan was a giant of a man in every way—probably six feet, eight inches tall—with blue eyes and a kind, welcoming Irish energy. He was definitely one of the free spirits of our community, a man who read poetry and jogged along our dirt road each day in his habit reciting Shakespeare by heart. He was also one of the few older monks who seemed to respect my views.

Father Andrew appeared agitated and silently waved me into his room—a practice also frowned upon, especially during the Grand

Silence. "Listen to this, Elias, you've got to hear this." Apparently he had a little radio secreted away in his room because he loved to listen to classical music.

He was listening to WBAI, a listener-sponsored New York City station, part of the national Pacifica Network. The program was a news report from the Agence France-Presse, the French news syndicate, broadcasting directly from Hanoi, North Vietnam. This was the first time I ever heard such reliable reporting directly out of North Vietnam. The reportage was astonishing, shocking and far different from the information that mainstream US media provided.

The reporter spoke of having seen the bombing destruction of civilian targets such as schools, hospitals, pagodas and even churches. He had interviewed their leadership and gave quite a different perspective on the war than the familiar White House line.

Good Father Andrew, who was as astonished by the program as I was, knew that I was one of the few monks with whom he could share this discovery. In so doing he not only introduced me to WBAI—the beginning of a lifelong love and sometimes love/hate relationship—but also ignited my passion for ending the US military involvement in Vietnam. I was already critical of US policy in Indochina, but now I knew that I must find a way to become a part of the still nascent peace movement.

A few weeks later I was invited to lead a retreat in Paterson, New Jersey, for the Association for International Development (not the government AID program), a group of Catholic laymen and women working creatively in Latin America, Asia and Africa. They included Pat and Jerry Mische, who later joined our East Orange community, and George Mische, a future peace comrade. These were lay missionaries characterized by a new open-minded, politically sophisticated spirit with great respect for the Third World peoples whom they served.

I was introduced to another priest, ten years older than I, who was co-leading the retreat with me. Daniel Berrigan was an intense young Jesuit, already a recognized poet, who was himself becoming more aware of and involved in the issue of Vietnam. This was to be a life-changing encounter for me, and we very quickly recognized each other as kindred spirits along the peace road and became fast friends.

Dan's friendship, his commitment and his brilliant thinking and writing became a lifeline for me over the years. Our friendship was a great treasure found in a Church that had little room for the likes of us.

The painful lack of acceptance, if not hostility, by our respective religious orders created a bond between us.

Dan was eventually exiled from the country for a year and sent on a pilgrimage through Latin America as a penance ordered by Francis Cardinal Spellman for his views on Vietnam. Spellman was the military vicar, the chief chaplain of the US Armed Forces. He seemed to have some difficulty in distinguishing US foreign and military policy from the teachings of Jesus.

Spellman was, in fact, influential in setting up the repressive President Diem of South Vietnam. Diem came from a devout Catholic Vietnamese family and, while in temporary US exile, was under the wing of the cardinal, who even invited him to stay at Maryknoll Seminary in Ossining, New York.

Dan and I supported each other during these difficult times. On those rare occasions when I could get to New York City, I would visit him at the offices of Jesuit Missions Magazine on the east side in the eighties where he was temporarily housed to keep him out of trouble. He would console me by feeding me good Scotch whisky in milk—out of respect for my stomach ulcers.

One of the additional joys of this friendship was meeting Dan's younger brother, Philip. Phil was another delightful Berrigan, a tall, strapping guy with an even more militant temperament than his brother. He had chosen to enter the Josephite order to serve the African American community as a priest.

He was a prophetic figure of extraordinary courage and originality. He also held on to his ideas with great tenacity—some would say to occasional excess—a quality needed by such a radical dissenter. Instead of settling for conventional ministry to poor Black folks, he joined one of the first freedom bus rides through the South to desegregate lunch counters and other facilities. When the local bishop heard about this, he ordered Phil off the bus and so cut short this brave act. He was to become one of the most committed peace activists of our times and ended up serving more than ten years in prison cumulatively for his non-violent actions. He continued his peace writings and ideas even from his deathbed. (Philip Berrigan died in 2002).

Abbot Charles had organized an opera performance in the local Newton high school as a fund raiser for the monastery. Somehow the opera company fell through, but Father Abbot did not want to lose our deposit for the school auditorium nor the opportunity to create some income, always a concern of his.

In what I can only surmise was an act of desperation, he called in Father Aloysius and myself (as the house liberals, if not worse) to ask us if we would be interested in organizing an evening forum on something like "religion and society." We were, of course, more than interested in doing something creative in this culturally and politically sterile wasteland and were out the door before you could say "Santo Che Guevara."

After a little research on how to put together the most interesting interfaith panel, we came up with Rabbi Israel Dresner, a longtime civil rights advocate from New Jersey; Rev. William Johnson, who was then a Methodist theologian and later became an Episcopalian and for a Catholic—yes, Father Daniel Berrigan, who at that time had not yet attained notoriety as a plainspoken peace radical.

One of the wonderful side effects of this event was that it brought Dan and my parents together, creating a friendship that blossomed over the years. Daniel needed a ride from New York to the event in Newton. He was a devoted non-driver and still is and does not have an answering machine, cell phone or email.

My parents were coming up to see and hopefully take pride in the handiwork of their first-born. Dan reported that the drive up was a sheer joy. My parents, especially my mother, loved to nurture and feed the world. Not surprisingly they stopped for an ample German roadside picnic, which was consummated, much to Dan's delight, with the appearance of a flask of schnapps, probably good French brandy. Thus began a lifelong friendship, especially with my mother for whom he had deep respect and love. When she died, he planted a tree in her memory on Block Island and accompanied it by reading a lovely poem he wrote for her.

The happy group finally arrived at the abbey where we were preparing for the evening's event. The forum was a huge success and played to a packed house. All the speakers were excellent and opened the eyes and minds of this small, somewhat isolated community of Newton to new insights about the true state of the world from an authentic religious perspective.

The star of the evening was our boy Daniel. He had just returned from an amazing journey through Eastern Europe. He reported about Church and society, even Christian-Marxist dialogue from a perspective different than the usual Catholic red baiting and anti-Communist diatribe. In his gentle, restrained and thoughtful way he also gave a biting analysis of the escalating war in Indochina as well as the crisis of poor and Black people at home. Our enthusiasm for Dan was not shared by Father Abbot, and Father Aloysius and I were in the monastic doghouse for some time.

I continued to seek ways to play a quiet role in the movement against the growing American military presence in Vietnam. At that time, I would guess that I was one of a handful of American Catholic priests who publicly opposed the war. Only the bishop of Atlanta had spoken against the war.

I did manage to smuggle myself out of the monastery for a few peace events. One of the highlights was the major peace rally and march organized by the Vietnam Peace Parade Committee in New York. It was a large dramatic march to the UN at which Dr. Martin Luther King Jr. was the principal speaker. I participated with some of the Marymount nuns who were becoming friends and supporters.

Strangely enough, as my image deteriorated at home, my star seemed to be rising in the esteem of the local bishops. It was the time of the Second Vatican Council and of liturgical renewal within the Church. I was developing an appropriate theology of Church renewal—*aggiorniamento*, as it was called at the Council.

Bishop James Navagh of Paterson, who appeared to be a rather stern and conservative man, heard me give a lecture on these ideas and invited me to lead courses and workshops to prepare his priests and communities of nuns (who were always more open) for the renewal of Vatican II. Later he appointed me to the Diocesan Liturgical Commission and invited me to serve as a member of the Priests' Senate of the Diocese.

The next Bishop, Lawrence Casey, had great interest in opening up dialogue with the Jewish community. When he heard of my work and of my Jewish background, he invited me to write several statements and speeches for him on this theme.

This invitation gave me an opportunity to think and write about the new openings that Vatican II was creating towards other communities of faith, especially to my own people. I was also growing in understanding and love for my own Jewish roots and identity. I began to view my Christian faith not as a "conversion" from Judaism any more than Jesus and the early Christian community would have thought of themselves as "converts."

An experience years later was to open up this connection in new, mysterious ways. Somehow Reb (Rabbi) Zalman Schacter-Shalomi had

heard about me, my Jewish roots, my work for peace and—at that time—
for young people. He was coordinating a series of weeklong "Wisdom
Schools" in order to initiate open-minded Jews into the teachings of the
Kabbalah and invited me to participate in one on the "Holiness of the
Earth." When I protested my participation because it might alienate the
Jewish participants he replied: "Father Paul, there are some people who
are born in one tradition or another. Then there are others who are in
between, who are bridge builders. You are a bridge builder. Please come."

Reb Zalman is one of the true visionaries of American Judaism. He
comes from a venerable line of Hassidic Jews and rabbis and as a young
man was already filled with wisdom and scholarship. Early on, he was
designated as the possible future chief Hassidic Lubavitcher rabbi. But
it seems that the Spirit had other designs for this man of God. He was
always a free spirit whose vision transcended the narrow confines of in-
stitutional religious structures. Reb Zalman met and had dialogue with
people like Thomas Merton and the Dalai Lama. He deeply believed that
the Holy One was active in the world in many forms and in many traditions. As a free spirit he also had a number of marriages and divorces and
was in many ways a child of the sixties.

Not only would this week be filled with the spontaneous and joyful
celebrations of the Shabbat by this liberated community of Jews and by
the profound and beautiful teaching of the Kabbalah on the earth, but
also by a powerful revelation of my own identity.

In order to accommodate a Catholic nun, Sister Paula, who was to
be on the Wisdom School faculty, Reb Zalman urged me to celebrate a
Eucharist liturgy on Ascension Thursday. I did so reluctantly for fear of
offending Jewish sensibilities, but the celebration was well received and
enthusiastically attended. I tried to weave the tradition of Passover and
Easter and the Seder Meal—and even some Hebrew—into a sacred unity.
I was deeply moved—sometimes to tears—by the welcoming spirit of
the community, and the good Reb even invited me to wear his gorgeous
rainbow talith (prayer shawl) for the celebration. What joy, what healing!
It was even a certain homecoming for me. Some of the retreatants even
came to receive the Eucharist.

It only dawned on me later that this had been a moment of grace
for this beautiful community as well because the celebration had been
in effect a sacred contradiction to the centuries of hatred and separation
created by Christian anti-Semitism. Many there experienced a profound
healing of the wounding caused by this ancient sin of hatred of Jews

engendered and even justified by Christians and perverted Christian theology.

In any case, Bishop Casey seemed to appreciate my understanding of the common roots of Jews and Christians—both as children of Abraham. Strangely enough, all of this rather official support for my ideas and vision from the local bishop had no impact on my status in the monastery. It seemed to confirm the abbot's—and some of the senior monks'—perception of me as someone out of step with the true faith and the monastic ideal. All of this was very hurtful to me, and sometimes I struggled not to slide into a depressed state.

As the Vietnam War began to escalate, I attempted to find ways of getting involved within the boundaries of my monastic vocation. An opportunity came when the late John Hildebrand of the Fellowship of Reconciliation (FOR), one of the leading interfaith pacifist groups, invited me to participate in a retreat of religious leaders and theologians on the morality of the war.

When I approached the abbot to seek permission, he immediately objected because FOR was not a Catholic organization. As I attempted to explain more in depth, he threw up his arms in desperation and shouted, "Father Elias, don't give me those theological arguments!"

So much for the world of dialogue.

CHAPTER 8

Under the Volcano
Sojourn in Cuernavaca

As THE YEARS PROGRESSED and the country's social and political climate began to disintegrate or be reborn (depending on or how you looked at it) and Vatican II became a reality in the 1960s, my own situation in the monastery became more acute. I increasingly used my work with students, lay people, priests and nuns in the retreat house to focus on the role of Christians in the issues of Church renewal, war and social justice. My message received much acclaim and also some opposition, both within the monastery and without.

A clear split was developing within the abbey with many of the younger monks—and a few older ones—lining up behind me or with me (or with the theological and political *Weltanschaung* I was espousing), even though I was not seeking to be a leader or a source of division. It was becoming more and more apparent that this split would deepen instead of leading to some resolution. The monastery was simply a microcosm of the social, religious and cultural forces that were exploding in the society at large. All of this left me with the dilemma of how to react to this apparently sterile, no-win situation.

The winds of new possibilities, which can often be the breath of the Holy Spirit, suddenly came blowing my way from quite unexpected Southern quarters. The small Christian community of San Miguelito in Panama approached me about joining their exciting experiment in

Central America. Father Mark, one of our young monks who had received permission to work with them some years earlier, was inspired by his experience and had told them about my vision, talents and interests. "Hey, Elias," he wrote, "San Miguelito and you were made for each other." I was intrigued.

This community had been wooing me over the years to consider becoming one of them to perhaps play some role in leadership and spiritual formation and liturgical creativity. I think that they also valued my activist inclinations. So in August of 1966, during our two-week summer vacation, I sneaked off for a two-week visit to Panama. It proved to be one of the great eye- and heart-opening experiences of my life and began a trajectory that would bring profound changes in my life journey.

I went to visit Panama with a very tentative interest, but within the first few days I knew that I was in a place where the ideals of Church and community which I had been dreaming of were actually being realized. It was a warm, loving, welcoming Latino community, very consciously committed to the ideals of the Gospel, but in a way that was not pietistic or self-righteous. There was a quality of high religious and political consciousness among these simple people that was deeply connected to a biblical sense of being the *pueblo de Dios*—the people of God.

San Miguelito had been founded in 1963 by a group of innovative Diocesan priests from the Archdiocese of Chicago led by Father Leo Mahon. When Leo and two other Chicago priests, Jack Greely and Bob McGlinn, first arrived, they encountered the typical Catholic Latin American scene with formalistic cultural Catholicism, which might mean total indifference or consist of sometimes baptizing the babies, occasionally lighting a candle in front of the statue of Our Lady during the annual procession and a clergy who required set fees for every prayer and sacrament. For the rest, cheating at work (if there was any), visiting the local brothels, drunkenness and wife beating were not necessarily seen as being in conflict with the external Catholic practices. All this had little to do with a life of love, of service to the community and of radical personal transformation. Later, many of these same forms of popular religion would be given a deeper authentic meaning.

Providentially, Cardinal Albert Meyer of Chicago, an unusual American bishop, was an open-minded thinker and a real shepherd of his people who had been deeply transformed by his experience of Vatican II, at which he had often served as a voice for the forces of change and renewal. Leo, whom he supported, was now looking for fresh, creative, open-minded priests and nuns to implement this new—perhaps very ancient—vision.

The community of priests and the Maryknoll nuns were a delightful group of dedicated and creative people. They had all to some large extent been attracted by the charismatic Leo Mahon, an articulate, street-wise, cigar-smoking Chicago priest. Someone called him a cross between a French worker priest and a fast-talking Chicago politician—a fascinating mixture. He had a keen analytical mind and a simultaneously pragmatic and utopian vision of building a new kind of Christian community in Latin America.

Instead of implementing the typical North American missionary strategy of preaching Christianity to the benighted natives, the Chicago priests initiated what might appear as a non-strategy, which essentially consisted, at first, of simply "hanging around" and listening, meeting the people—especially the men—through sharing a beer or the national pastime of dominoes. Out of these simple human contacts there evolved informal small group meetings in people's homes that focused on their personal, social and political challenges and problems, and asked what light the Word of God could cast on these. A reading from the Exodus account might evoke questions about what were the spiritual, cultural and political enslavements of the Panamanian people and what would liberation mean today.

This process was largely based on the "Family of God" dialogues, created during Leo's work in his mainly Puerto Rican parish in Chicago. These *Familia de Dios* dialogues recognized the centrality of family in Latino culture and presented God as Father, Christ as brother, and the Church as a community of brothers and sisters united in birth by baptism and gathered around the Eucharist as a family meal. The people, the men in particular, responded to this way of looking at the practicalities of their lives.

It was a process that would later be corroborated by the Brazilian educator Paulo Freire and his brilliant insight in his *Pedagogy of the Oppressed,* that wisdom and consciousness can come *from the people.* It is not only imparted to them. Out of this apparently simple approach a new, remarkable kind of Christian community would be born, one in which these apparently uneducated people assumed ownership and leadership. It was a vision that spoke to my dreams of an authentic People's Church and also would be corroborated by Vatican II and its vision of the Church as a communal circle instead of a hierarchical pyramid.

I returned to the abbey powerfully inspired, shaken and conflicted. Once again I was faced with one of my least favorite but strangely familiar challenges—the hour of decision. I recognized it as an old adversary—I would like to say friend, but that did not apply for me. I knew its smell, its touch, the cold feeling in the pit of my stomach. It was the simple terror of making the wrong choice, messing up my life, and above all, *not doing God's holy will*. As if I should not have known by now that my life was guided every step of the way and the likelihood of my making a major misstep was virtually non-existent. Had I not been snatched right at the beginning from the fiery furnace and protected "like the apple of my eye"? Had I not been lifted up by angelic wings at every moment "lest thou dash thy food against a stone" (Psalms)?

And yet there was a great fear of abandoning my monastic calling and even my particular monastic community. Was this magnetic attraction to Latin America and to the little community of San Miguelito just a romantic temptation? There was also the very Catholic (somewhat Jansenistic and also a little Jewish) unspoken principle that one must always choose the more difficult path. The fork of the road that seems better, sunnier, maybe even a little more pleasurable is probably filled with self-deception, if not downright evil and therefore must be rejected.

These were the conflicting voices careening around my psyche during a retreat at the motherhouse of the Marymount Sisters, who had become great friends and supporters. I still remember walking down a peaceful woodland path with my inner life in noisy conflict as I tried now one, now another solution to my dilemma. Finally, in the face of every argument for my staying at the monastery, it became clear to me that I must go to Panama even though it gave me very little feeling of resolution or peace.

So I returned to my abbey in Newton in a state of great turmoil, facing one more difficult life decision. I had decided to accept the invitation of the community of San Miguelito to go to Panama, a decision that would be the catalyst of more changes in my life than I could imagine.

The regime at the abbey had changed over the years. General dissatisfaction and other internal problems had led to the resignation of Abbot Charles and to the election of Father Augustine as the new abbot. Father Augustine was a short, unimposing simple man with glasses, conservative by nature, with a dry, self-deprecating sense of humor.

As I mentioned earlier, he was our beekeeper and loved his work and the sometimes dangerous population of the beehives. It seemed that this delicate task of relating to his unruly winged charges had given him a certain equanimity of temperament. He was also a deeply religious man who took the monastic life to heart. All this was reflected in the respectful way in which he related to his monks. When I presented him with my request, he simply said, "Father Elias, if that's what you really want, then you can go with my blessing." He dealt with us as mature, grown men instead of as misbehaving little boys as his predecessor had. And so I began to prepare myself for a new life "south of the border."

My admirers and followers at the monastery were sad to see me go and yet were happy for me for finding an appropriate niche in the "new Church" that was being born. My critics were secretly glad to see me go and saw my decision as a confirmation of my unstable nature. My parents were glad to see me move onto a larger playing field but sad to have me move even farther away from them.

Spanish language training was essential, so the first stage of my journey was to be a three-month stopover in Cuernavaca, Mexico, at CIDOC (Centro Intercultural de Documentación), one of the most interesting and exciting centers of its kind in Latin America in the sixties. Priests, religious and laity of all religious and political persuasions were there to learn Spanish and to prepare themselves culturally, historically and politically to work in Latin America.

Cuernavaca is located in the state of Morelos about forty miles west of Mexico City and was well named as "the land of eternal spring." The city is surrounded by stately volcanic mountain ranges and its streets lined with exotic bougainvillea. Its unique flower market was a daily, spectacular display of Mexico's floral beauty and one could carry home an armful of this glory for a handful of coins.

But the most exciting—and sometimes frustrating—thing about CIDOC was its founder, chief intellectual, shaman in residence, and expert provocateur, monsignor Ivan ("the Terrible") Illich—a genius par excellence. Ivan was a longtime friend and mentor from my youth in Washington Heights. He had been one of the supportive Incarnation parish priests during my "conversion" process and later during my sometimes erratic monastic career. He died in 2002 and his myriad obituaries read like a panorama of all that was most luminous, lasting, authentic and of true value in the twentieth (and part of the twenty-first) century. They spoke of his dazzling brilliance and called him "[a] critic of modern institutions that 'create needs faster than they can create satisfaction and in the process of trying to meet the needs they generate, they consume the earth.'"

Or again:

> Ivan Illich was one of the world's great thinkers, a polymath whose output covered vast terrain. He worked in ten languages, he was a jet age ascetic with few possessions, he explored Asia and South America on foot and his obligations to his many collaborators led to a constant crisscrossing of the globe.'*

So it was a mutually joyful coincidence of events when it turned out that I would be spending three months at CIDOC. I arrived in August of 1967 and immediately fell again under his brilliant influence, which some described as hypnotic. Although CIDOC was a noted training place of missionaries of all kinds on their way to work in Latin America, Illich unabashedly admitted that his real aim was to discourage them from going there at all. He said that his work would be successful if many of the priests and others changed their minds at the end of their sojourn to CIDOC and returned to the US.

Essentially, Ivan believed that US missionaries would (even unwittingly) be neo-colonialist emissaries and bring North American values, theology, ideology and politics to the people of Latin America under the guise of preaching the Gospel. I believe that he made some slight exception in my case because of our friendship, and also because I was heading for San Miguelito and he already had some genuine respect for this project, for its founder Father Leo Mahon and for the radical new non-imperialist pastoral approach that had been successfully implemented in Panama. None of this prevented Ivan from giving me the same hard time that was an integral part of a stay at Cuernavaca, especially at some of the intense small group sessions. "Paul," he said (he never used my monastic name), "do you really believe that you're going to do more good than harm to the people of Panama? Did you ever think that the best ministry might be to leave them alone?"

Part of the fascination of CIDOC was the interesting mix of humans brought together in this unique vortex of ideas, faith, experimentation, vision, dialogue and argument. North American priests and nuns, their counterparts from Canada and France, a college class of Quakers spending a semester were joined by a sprinkling of Latinos who came to imbibe that mysterious elixir that gave this place its seductive, magnetic aura.

* *The Guardian*, December 9, 2002.

It was in this adventurous place that I encountered Sister Naomi Lambert, a North American Medical Missionary nun, who had been working in Maracaibo, Venezuela, as a nurse-midwife. She had long black hair (long for nuns, who tend toward something between a crew cut and a bob), deep brown eyes and was beautiful in that simple Black Irish sort of way. I have always been attracted to Celtic women. Our paths would cross again in the most dramatic fashion. Was it the laugh and the twinkle and the teasing irony just this side of sarcasm that made Irish women so appealing?

The CIDOC staff and guest lecturers were consistently interesting and often provocative. Among those, one who sticks firmly in my memory is Padre Alejandro del Corro, an Argentine pre-liberation theologian who I remember especially for his brilliant analysis of a theology of the poor—*los pobres de la tierra*.

He spoke with bitter authority, for he himself had grown up as a street orphan in a Latin American city where he was one of the myriad begging street children who cluster in cathedral squares all throughout Latin America. They implore passersby to buy "Chiclets" (a universal word), matches and sometimes worse.

I was so compelled by his lectures that I did not even notice that he was speaking in Spanish and that I understood almost everything he said. I still remember his exegesis of the role of the poor in the Bible. He said: "The poor are not poor; the poor are the people who are coming; the poor are the people of the future." I think of his words as we increasingly see social movements in various Latin American countries and elsewhere led and inspired by economically marginalized people without arms or money who often are confronting heavily armed military regimes enjoying extensive economic and military support, usually from the US.

Of course, the most exciting gatherings were the ones led by and often convened, usually with very little notice, by Illich himself. These could be either small, intimate gatherings or larger lecture settings. They were both eagerly anticipated and feared by the students. Illich would often use them to confront the participants, especially priests, with what he considered the questionable politics and theology behind their "missionary" endeavors. Although a good-hearted man by temperament, he did not hesitate to resort to ruthlessness in these alleged dialogues.

The teachers at the language school were mainly bright, young Mexicans who were for the most part very skilled and dedicated. They used a simple technique and learning theory perfected, ironically enough, by the US State Department in preparing its diplomats, and, no doubt, CIA agents and other ambassadors of good will for their forays into foreign climes.

One of my adventures there was climbing the legendary Mt. Popocateptl (the Sleeping Warrior), which lies roughly to the south between Cuernavaca and Mexico City. This formidable ice- and snow-covered volcano is the second-highest peak in North America and periodically erupts hot lava into the surrounding valley. It was one of the magnificent adventures of my life but cost me severe frostbite and sun poisoning. I was encouraged to read that a few years ago that Che Guevara had only made it to the peak on his second attempt and considered the great mountain as "the ultimate challenge as a climber and a revolutionary."

Sometimes on weekends we would use our newfound freedom outside the monastery and convent walls for adventurous trips to Mexico City, an hour or so away. We would go in little groups which would often boil down to loosely formed couples. Sister Ursula, one of Naomi's friends, was also developing a growing friendship with Bob, a real farm boy-type priest from the Midwest.

We went to clubs to hear the music of the sixties, which was also popular in Mexico. It was strange but fun to hear the Beatles' music performed in Spanish. One great experience was visiting Garibaldi Square, home of the city's wonderful mariachi bands that play for visiting tourists, as well as for local Mexicans. I grew to love this vibrant music so filled with the exuberant spirit of the Mexican people.

All of this new, exciting experience and time together contributed to an increasingly romantic and, for me, destabilizing relationship. On a vacation period, our little group headed for Acapulco, one of the most popular Mexican seaside resorts. We had a wonderful time swimming, dancing (which I had never done before) and imbibing the romantic tropical aura of this beautiful place.

The combination of being away from the monastic life, being in a cultural setting so radically and exotically different as Mexico, being in a place so intellectually, theologically and spiritually challenging to long-held safe ideas, and finally, being in the presence of that unknown and so entrancing species—women—was almost too much to bear. I could feel myself being swept along as if by some great, gentle and yet very powerful river, not knowing my destination and yet resisting only minimally.

Was it simply my awakening hormones? Or was the stern Saturnian monastic side, which had been predominantly ruling my life until now, surrendering to the romantic side of my personality? Perhaps all of these were conspiring together to lead me ineluctably to a destiny that I had never imagined.

We never consummated our attraction in torrid, tropical (and probably very inexperienced) lovemaking. We nibbled around the edge in what would probably pass for very preliminary adolescent "necking." We did begin to converse openly about our relationship and whether it had a future and even imagined what it would be like to leave our religious orders and unite in marriage. (There was not that much "living in sin" as one sees today, especially in our circles.) It was a time when the very concept of priests "leaving" and getting married was just beginning to be in the air. So far only a handful had notoriously pursued this option in the United States.

In the meantime, my parents had decided to visit Cuernavaca and their first born. My intuitive mother immediately picked up on the incipient chemistry between Naomi and myself. Of course, they secretly loved this idea on many levels, not the least of which was the possibility of their having grandchildren.

Mami and Naomi immediately hit it off like mother and daughter because Naomi was much clearer than I was about the potential of the future relationship. And so these two wise, deep women began to consult, if not conspire, on how to make this happen. I am sure that by now my smart mother/psychiatric nurse had deduced something about my fear of intimacy and of making decisions. Hence I never experienced any pressure from any quarter. My father, of course, was equally enthusiastic, less tactful, and loved Naomi right from the start.

One of the entrancing aspects of my sojourn in Cuernavaca was the simple fact of being in Mexico for a relatively protracted period of time—not just for a quick visit. Querido Mexico, beloved land of such diverse geographical beauty: the sea, las montañas—the magnificent snowcrested mountains—and the tropical rain forests of the Yucatán that won my heart. The greatest treasure was surely the Mexican people— simple, noble, mostly poor and struggling bitterly against an oppressive economic system heavily controlled by the giant from the North. Life is often so hard that these people—men, women and children—are willing to risk death by drowning or exposure and cruel exploitation by "coyotes" who smuggle people across the border to penetrate the United States for some glimmer of hope, for something better. These are the courageous people who are greeted as criminals and interlopers by our government.

Yes, "Give me your tired, your hungry and your poor," as long as they are the right color and they speak the same language. Of course, we could save all this suffering by supporting a just employment policy on both sides of the border.

So the three months of my stay at Cuernavaca flew along. My heart was filled with very mixed feelings: sadness at the thought of parting from Naomi, fear about another huge decision that I saw looming before me on the horizon, excitement and apprehension about moving on to Panama.

In the end, Naomi and I decided to honor the process that had brought us both to Latin America and Cuernavaca. We would go on to our respective places of commitment—to Panama for me and Venezuela for Naomi. While we were there we would stay in touch and pray deeply for guidance for our future together or separately. Only later did I find out that, not surprisingly, in the meantime Naomi and my mother had entered into an intense correspondence and friendship. My mother, wise healer of souls that she was, did not try to influence Naomi or myself to make a decision much as she would have liked to.

And so we left Mexico together and flew on to South and Central America on the same flight. When it came time for me to change plans in Tegucigalpa, Honduras, it was a tearful parting for both of us. But on we went to our separate destinies and into the great unknown.

CHAPTER 9

Los Pobres de la Tierra
Work in San Miguelito, Panama

On November 18, 1967, I stepped out of the plane into the bright blinding Panamanian noon. Father Leo Mahon and few of the Maryknoll sisters were at the airport to greet me. I could sense that they expected great things of me. A better than deserved reputation had preceded me about my creativity and innovative leadership. Here I was with some of that, as well as the unresolved baggage I now carried with me. Moreover, my closest friend and fellow monk at my monastic community and my original contact with San Miguelito, Father Mark Sheenan, had already left Panama. He and Sister Graciela—one of the Maryknoll sisters—had fallen in love and intended to marry. But I decided to throw myself into this new adventure and see what the Spirit had in store for me.

It did not take long for the culture shock to come forward to meet me like a brick wall. First of all, it was the language itself. It was only then that I realized how much I had been spoiled, if not misled, by the beautiful, relatively clear Spanish pronunciation of *los Mexicanos*, in contrast to Panamanian Spanish of the streets where *se comen las palabras*—"they swallow their words." Much of it was incomprehensible to my gringo ear. I had to begin my language training anew.

And so, I fell into a slight depression when I realized how circumscribed my communication skills were. Conrado and Virgilio, the two Panamanian seminarians at the parish, were very sharp young men, both theologically and politically. They were being groomed by Leo and the community to be some of the first Panamanian priests to minister in the new style of San Miguelito. They were looking forward to some intense political and theological dialogues so they sought me out and forced me to speak Spanish, and gradually my ear did become more attuned to the Panamanian rhythms.

Leo had gained his basic experience working in an urban, largely Puerto Rican parish in Chicago. But his larger vision was based on a powerful combination of a radical biblical theology and a sophisticated religio-sociological analysis of the crisis of the Catholic Church in Latin America. His statistical analysis predicted a Church increasingly flooded and overwhelmed, first of all by the astronomical population explosion, and then by the growing masses descending from the countryside into the metropolitan urban cities of the continent.

There they would lose the more positive moral, religious and cultural values of the campesino village to a negative secular materialism, usually in the grips of brutal marginalization, poverty and the accompanying dehumanization. But also the sheer population explosion would so overwhelm the ratio of priest to faithful that the possibility of a community of faith in the midst of the secular masses would virtually disappear or become irrelevant. Leo's original proposal to Cardinal Meyer reads: "If the ratio of one priest to every one thousand faithful is to remain the ideal, Latin America would have to produce six hundred thousand priests in forty years."

Thus the Church of the future would not be a Church that could any longer sustain itself by (even the most ideal) missionary incursions of religious personnel from the US or Spain, all objections to this quasi-colonizing paradigm aside. An entirely new model would have to be created of God's people in Panama or elsewhere in the southern lands. Simply put, this would have to become an authentically Latin American Church led by lay men and women well trained in this new theology, deeply committed to the Gospel vision together with the usually unspoken (but secretly held by some and occasionally explicated) hope of, in the future, having them ordained as deacons and perhaps even eventually as married priests. Such was the dream that inspired Leo Mahon and Gilbert Carroll to present a plan to Cardinal Meyer to set up a model experimental parish community on the outskirts of Panama City, where a small group of US priests and nuns would be the catalyst that could transform Panama City and eventually points south.

Father Don Headly, one of the first Chicago priests to join the experiment in Panama, was a red-headed Irish American, self-confident, smart and articulate and well-trained theologically. Father John Greely (Padre Juan) was an attractive, modest, extremely funny and light-hearted guy, bright and not too attached to his own ideas. Juan served as a perfect counterpoint to Leo's intensity and drive. Father John Enright (Juan Segundo) was a little more slow-moving, but in a quiet, pastoral fashion also strongly committed to the San Miguelito ideal. Father Fred McKiernan, conservative but good-hearted, had arrived from Newark not too long before I did and was still getting his feet wet in the Panamanian reality.

The Maryknoll nuns were a spectacular group of open-minded women who loved the people and already belonged to a missionary order that was beginning to incorporate a new definition of "missionary" influenced by the enlightened principles of Vatican II. Sister Maria de la Cruz was a Chicana, a delicately fine-boned beauty (if one can say that about a nun). Sister Cecilia came from an upper-class Argentine family. As an intellectual community organizer, she was an in-charge powerhouse whose ideas you did not want to cross lightly. She served as Leo's co-pastor. Sister Maura was Hawaiian, warm, outgoing, quietly radical and much beloved by the community. Finally, Sister Beatriz came from an aristocratic Nicaraguan family (her uncle later became a rather conservative president). She may have been somewhat influenced and formed by her class background, but was a hard-working, dedicated community worker.

The greatest treasure of San Miguelito was the people themselves. This self-selected group of Christians had decided to form an authentic Gospel community to strive to be "the light of the world" as Jesus had required from his disciples. He said, "A city on a mountain top cannot be hidden. You are the salt of the earth" (Matthew 5:13–14). "By this everyone will know that you are my disciples, because you love one another" (John 13:35). This would no longer be a statistical Catholicism but a community that had decided to become a community of light even in the midst of much spiritual and political darkness.

The living room "familia de Dios" dialogues took place among these poor, many of whom lived in shanty barrio slums subject to cruel economic exploitation, disease and unemployment for perhaps half of the year, although there was a minority element of a slowly emerging working class. They were overshadowed by the presence of Exxon, Citibank and General Motors, which all had offices on the main avenida. The

United States Canal Zone was omnipresent and represented a major US intrusion into Panamanian territory, society and economy—if not into self-understanding and identity—even while providing employment for many members of the community.

It was an almost surrealistic contrast to see the manicured green lawns, suburban-style houses, golf courses, shopping centers and North American-style churches and schools on the one side of the Avenida John F. Kennedy, and directly on the other side some of the most wretched barrio slums in Panama, if not in Latin America, such as Chorrillo. Here the smell of garbage, bad sanitation and endemic poverty hung over the muddy streets and rickety buildings (constructed on stilts) like a heavy tropical pall. Father Philip Berryman, one of my friends and confidants, ministered wisely to this challenging barrio.

Another challenge facing the people of God in Panama was the presence of the US military. In 1967 it was still "hosting" the School of the Americas (sometimes called the School of the Assassins) near Panama City. It was there that Latin American military personnel, including high-level officers, were trained in the fine arts of war, crowd control, interrogation and what, in a time of a more honest use of language, was called torture techniques. This demonic facility now moved from Panama is still in operation in Ft. Benning, Georgia. There it has faced a large, powerful, popular opposition movement led by the courageous Father Roy Bourgeois, recently unjustly expelled from the allegedly progressive Maryknoll order.

Add to these realities the inequitable distribution of wealth and a general system of economic exploitation. It was always something of a benign mystery to me how each morning the children of the Monte Oscuro barrio where I ministered would emerge for school from shacks built on a sea of mud wearing freshly laundered and starched white shirts and blouses.

These then were the challenges that the community of God's people of San Miguelito faced in the daily Exodus struggle for liberation. It was stunning to hear some of these theological and political themes emerge from the lay leaders of the community, such as Fidel and Severino, during the discussions, training courses, cursillos (lay-led retreats) and liturgical celebrations.

The basic pastoral method developed at San Miguelito started with the family of God dialogues leading to the weekend cursillos. These retreats were moments of deep transformation out of which emerged the *hermanos*—the leadership core, consisting at first of the men who had never been part of any religious community. Women increasingly played a leadership role under the training and inspiration of the nuns, but in the beginning Latin America men were the key because of the ingrained culture of *machismo*. Leo had a great gift for spotting and developing leadership and was a kind of pastoral genius.

The creative, inspired brilliance of this community did not go unnoticed. Hundreds of priests, sisters, bishops, lay leaders and journalists visited San Miguelito every year. Some of them stayed for the dynamic three-month pastoral courses. Thus the San Miguelito model had a broad influence in El Salvador, Nicaragua, Brazil and beyond and would, in many cases, form the seedbed of the later base communities.

The liturgy was seen as the primary locus of teaching, inspiration, transformation, leadership formation and community building as well as a way of touching and evangelizing the growing masses of Latin America. The Sunday celebration of the Misa Típica Panameña was a magnificent experience. It took place in the *centro paroquial* (parish center) of the central parish of Cristo Redentor, which was located in the Paraiso section of larger San Miguelito. The beautiful *centro* was designed like a tent with sides open and was regarded at that time as one of the most modern and architecturally interesting religious structures in Central America.

The brilliant murals around the walls created by Lillian Brule depicted Jesus as a suffering but victorious campesino. The dignified struggle of the Panamanian people showed powerful and sometimes controversial scenes going back to the times of slavery up to the building of a new community and was quite explicit about the oppressive role that the clergy had played.

The Misa Típica itself made use of the traditional music and instruments of the Panamanian culture and was a source of great delight and pride for the people. The beautiful, lively and warm, tropical, indigenous melodies accompanied by the guitar, violin, the local stringed bocona and the singing of the people were inspiring beyond description. These celebrations made my heart sing and leap within me like nothing I had ever experienced since becoming a Catholic, even including some of the gorgeous monastic liturgy with Gregorian chant, which I loved deeply for so many years.

All of this made the Sunday-morning liturgy a powerful and energizing event that everyone looked forward to. Here the powerful homilies—at once deeply theological, political and practical—preached by Padre

Leon or some of the other priests or lay leaders had an extraordinary resonance aimed at psychological and spiritual transformation based on the great Kerygma—the power of the message of God's word. Above all they instilled and deepened the consciousness and self-understanding of the people of being a holy, anointed community of God's people in Panama, the heart of the San Miguelito reality.

From the moment that the opening hymn was intoned—*Vamos, vamos, todos vamos, vamos a la Misa* ("Let's all go to Mass")—the people picked up the lively melody to the rhythm of the drums and the whole community was swept up into a great torrent of music, prayer and the Spirit. Men, women and children danced, swayed and sang like King David before the ark. (Church authorities later condemned this as being too worldly.)

This was the deep, living weekly expression of the sometimes fierce and dangerous, sometimes grinding marginal daily existence for many now transformed into the celebration of the communal Exodus struggle and liberation of God's own people. It was the incarnational theme of God made man among his people woven into the lyrics, ¡*Alelulia, Alelulia! El se hace un campesino para hacernos más divino.* "He made himself a campesino—a poor farmer—so that he could make us more divine."

How mysterious that this extraordinary expression of authentic Christianity should be manifesting itself so brilliantly in this slum corner on the edge of a struggling city in a small Central American country. On the other hand, perhaps it was not so mysterious at all, but rather fitting according to the divine plan that the Hebrew Bible's Anawim (God's little ones) or the community of the mustard seed of the Gospel, God's poor, should be the model for the larger Church community. This would in later years become the true mission and vision of liberation theology and of the so-called *comunidades de base,* the small Christian "ecclesial base communities" (CEBs).

In some mysterious way, the vision and experience of San Miguelito would later evolve in many places into liberation theology and the celebrations of the people's Church. Its seeds were being sown here in Panama. Many of the "graduates" of the Pastoral Institute would develop this model in their communities throughout Latin America.

Douglas Wingeier –the great scholar of CEBs in Latin America—commenting on San Miguelito's basic course of initiation, makes what for me is an historic statement about the significance of San Miguelito:

"This is the first lesson in the first course in the first base community in Central America."

One striking example of the holy influence of San Miguelito was the *comunidad de base* of Managua, Nicaragua. Padré Jose de la Jara, a charismatic Spaniard, had taken three couples to the Pastoral Institute in Panama. When they returned home, Jeny and Luciano played a key role in founding the first CEB there. Father Ernesto Cardenal, later a charismatic leader of the Sandinista revolution of Nicaragua, also studied there and was inspired to found the famous Utopian Christian community of Solentiname.

Cardinal Obando y Bravo of Managua, an outspoken enemy of Liberation Theology, sent priests there on two different occasions to undermine the community. Nevertheless, Father Arnoldo Ventenio, a Mexican Jesuit, without official approval facilitated some twenty CBEs in the Managua area, some of which celebrate the Eucharist without an ordained priest. Through their ministry they also served as a compassionate bulwark against the growing poverty, hunger and disease.

Such a holy impetus, originating from many different theologians and communities, was later to sweep across the small, poor Christian communities of rural and urban Latin America and beyond. This form of Christianity would eventually be considered the most subversive by the ecclesiastical authorities and the Vatican itself and would later be shut down under the pontificate of John Paul II by Cardinal Josef Ratzinger, later Pope Benedict XVI, out of fear of Marxist influence. Some would consider this campaign one of the most pastorally hurtful aspects of the strategy to roll back the vision of Vatican II. The vision would be called "Liberation Theology," as if completely new, although it embodied the most authentic, even ancient interpretation of the Scriptures and the Judeo-Christian tradition.

It seems to me that this particular Church policy was wrong-headed, theologically unsound, repressive, and perhaps even immoral. It appears to have been conceived by people in intellectual ghettoes far removed from the reality of poor people in Latin America and the developing world. Nor could they imagine how much love of God and of each other, genuine community, self-empowerment and a spirit of hope people derived from these intimate ecclesial base communities and their fresh theological perspective.

This policy, based on fear of the unknown, descended on San Miguelito much earlier than the official shutdown of Liberation Theology and had even been anticipated in the prophetic meeting of the Latin American Episcopal Conference in Medellin, Colombia. There in 1968, the Latin American bishops proclaimed their desire to "draw even closer to those who labor in a dedicated apostolate to the poor." Then, quite surprisingly, they read the handwriting on the ecclesiastical wall when they wrote: "We want them to experience our support and to know that *we are not giving our ear to those who seek to destroy their work.*"

As early as 1973, before the sweeping shutdown of Liberation Theology (but after my departure), some of the San Miguelito priests (with a specific focus on Padre Leon) had been brought before an ecclesiastical tribunal on charges tantamount to heresy. The issues at stake were the priesthood of all the faithful, the Real Presence of Christ in the Eucharist and the perpetual virginity of the Mother of Jesus. A panel of theologians had been convened by the Panamanian bishops based on the misinterpreted, if not twisted, minutes of a weeklong retreat of the San Miguelito pastoral team.

The Panama panel eventually praised the San Miguelito priests for their theological brilliance, but Rome reprimanded them and removed one from a seminary post and forced them all to take a humiliating loyalty oath. In the meantime, Leo received a reliable warning from a friend in Rome that a high-level commission consisting of five cardinals and the master general of the Dominican Order was being organized at the Vatican to investigate San Miguelito again. This trial never transpired, in part because of Leo's refusal to hand over documents to the Papal Nuncio but the dark cloud of ecclesiastical repression was gathering over this little community of faith. Although this was before the official pogrom against Liberation Theology, it was a clear example of Rome rolling back the Second Vatican Council.

At one point Leo appeared to have developed a friendly, sometimes even advisory, relationship with General Torrijos, president of Panama who, at that time, may have seemed to offer some advantages to the impoverished Panamanian masses. He embodied some genuinely populist sentiments but was also a military autocrat. When he abrogated some of the civil rights of the local communities (and was later probably involved in the disappearance of a progressive Colombian priest), the Church community inspired the organizing of some non-violent opposition to these measures, which was successful. Leo led a non-violent march carrying the processional cross confronting the Panamanian National Guard. The one-thousand-strong disciplined Christian march impressed

Torrijos and the junta leadership. Torrijos himself expressed grudging admiration for the unity, dignity and commitment of the San Miguelito community:

"If the rest of the common people of the country were as politically conscious and responsible as the people of San Miguelito, then we could move much more swiftly"*

In retrospect, Leo and others may have felt some misgiving about their political involvement distracting from their pastoral ministry. But it seems to this observer—for I had already left Panama at this point—that the struggle against injustice is the cornerstone of a Christian community committed to "the preferential option for the poor." Or as Father Don Headley, one of the pioneering San Miguelito priests, put it: "Isn't it our role to be prophets, exposing injustices when those in power fail to do so?"

One of the things that excited me during my first summer vacation visit to Panama was that the priests and sisters lived in the same simple houses as the people. What a beautiful symbol of identification with the lives and struggles of the community. "The Word was made flesh and pitched His tent among us." (John 1:14)

The new cardinal, John Cody, from the vantage point of his more than comfortable residence in Chicago, decided that this lifestyle with the people was not appropriate. My analysis was that the decision stemmed from a combination of clericalism—God's anointed must live a few notches above the faithful—and the fear of the ever-lurking specter of the possibility of sexual seduction because of the living proximity, perhaps especially from these more "earthy" brown-skinned people. In any case, it was a disappointment upon my arrival in Panama to see us living in a rather nice priests' residence that had been constructed at His Eminence's command.

I was also more than a little taken aback when the Cardinal visited Panama and was hosted for a luncheon at the US Military Officers Club. Then his portly Eminence was even given an official tour of the area on a US naval vessel and all of us priests were invited to accompany him. Most scandalous was the cardinal's failure to defend Leo, one of his own priests and a brilliant theologian, against unfounded charges of heresy and misconduct.

---

* Leo Mahon, *Fire Under My Feet*, p. 131.

In the meantime, my stay in San Miguelito continued to be inspiring in spite of my apprehensions about my future. I celebrated the Sunday Eucharist with the people of the little barrio of Monte Oscuro. Right from the start it was easier to speak and preach there than to understand the tough Panamanian street Spanish. Slowly my listening ability was beginning to improve and it was a great joy to work with the community leaders. They were so caring and accepting of me into the *Familia de Dios*.

This growing closeness made it all the harder to wrestle with the decision that was hovering on the horizon, whether to leave their radiant community and start out a new life with Naomi. It had been such a major step in terms of identity and vocation to leave the monastery and come here and now an even more radical decision lay before me.

I walked the streets of the community in a panic almost every night after dinner, grappling with the pros and cons of a decision. The garbage on the streets and the barking of unfriendly guard dogs accompanied my steps. My deep psychological aversion to making decisions was itself like an attack dog at my throat.

It was then that a letter arrived from Naomi in Venezuela. It simply said: "Is it yes or is it no? I'm moving on." Here was the clear decision of a practical Virgo woman. From my side, one of the most constant struggles in my life journey has been an opposition between the world of love and family and the burdens of duty and obligation. This tension would haunt (or bless) me all of my life and here it was in my face full force.

Needless to say, I went into immediate panic mode and my already existing anxiety escalated to a new level. I took a few of the priests and nuns at San Miguelito into my confidence and they were all very understanding and supportive. It turned out later that several priests and nuns of the community were themselves grappling with similar challenges and decisions and would later end up getting married.

How would such a decision affect the many people back in the States who had looked up to and supported me? What impact would this have on the younger and more liberal monks of the abbey who followed me and my visions of the Gospel and of the Church? What kind of life of uncertainty and challenge lay ahead once I left the relative security that the life of a traditional priest offered me? Finally, was this really the right person with whom to spend the rest of my life? How much of it was about my obsession with beautiful women and the narcotic effect of being loved by such a being?

In the end I followed the intuitive guidance of my heart, not with great certainty or peace of mind. I thought that I really loved Naomi and her coming into my life would be the catalyst of some new and radical change in my life journey. Little did I realize at that time how profound this change would actually be. It would propel me forward into the rough and uncharted waters of a tumultuous, adventurous, exciting and sometimes fearsome sea. She was a person of great quality and we shared the same ideals.

And so I dove off the cliff of uncertainty, hoping that through some divine intervention I would sprout the powerful eagle's wings of clarity and self-assurance. My return letter to Naomi said "yes," since my dominant emotion was love but also with some fear of losing this apparently magical being that was beckoning to me.

In retrospect it has also become clearer to me that for me, and probably for many men, there is often (if not always) the unspoken hope that our relationships with women will give us what we never got from our parents—and from our mothers in particular. It would take me many relationships to learn this teaching. Indeed, I am still far from dealing with this illusion—for illusion it is. And it is usually only through much pain and disappointment that we males might come to enlightenment. The wisdom teaching in this bittersweet healing process is the truth that no one can ever give us what we didn't get from our moms and that somehow we must give it to ourselves.

I began to pursue practicalities of this new decision. It was painful to present my plans to the San Miguelito pastoral team who gave me nothing but support and friendship, although there were feelings of disappointment as well. It was also clearly a disappointment to the people with whom I was beginning to forge close relationships. But in their beautiful warm Latino way they also were loving and supportive. Some even wondered whether it wasn't possible for me to stay on as a married priest, a solution that would have appealed to me for I loved San Miguelito. This would, alas, not have been possible under the present ecclesiastical regime. There were already too many clouds of opposition gathering over the project. The priests and nuns who left to marry would have continued to make a rich contribution to the community—but we'll leave that to another lifetime.

Later in 1975, Leo Mahon himself returned to Chicago and left the community that he had founded and whose people he had loved as the bridegroom loves the bride. The crowning blow was the news from the bishops (and the Vatican) that only a handful of seven men were accepted out of the much larger group that he had trained and presented to be ordained as deacons and in some real sense as the future Panamanian pastors of this community. Leo clearly saw this as a refusal to face the unavoidable reality of the dramatically decreasing numbers of ordained priests, either Panamanian or North American, and as a clear no-confidence vote for his vision that only a growing number of well-trained laymen and women would make the survival of an authentic Latin American Church possible.

Don Headly would stay on to keep the vision alive in a somewhat reduced fashion through a small pastoral ministry that focused on the rural sector together with a conservative Panamanian priest, Padre Pinto, who ministered to the urban areas.

When Don returned to Chicago for a visit to discuss the budget, he received word from Cardinal Cody not to return to Panama, where he had been accused of "being a Communist" and other ideological improprieties. And so a vision for a future Church and a luminous model of authentic community was snuffed out by the blindness, fear and pride of those who had chosen to align themselves with the "principalities and powers" (Eph 6:12), rather than with "the children of light" (Eph 5: 8–9). It is difficult not to see all this leading up to the campaign of the Vatican under JPII and Benedict XVI to cleanse Holy Mother Church of Liberation Theology and the base communities.

I prepared to leave in June of 1968 with a heavy heart. Although my stay at San Miguelito* had been brief, it would have a profound impact on my consciousness. Rarely would I ever have such an experience of authentic Christian community. I was taught more about the powerful role of "the wretched of the earth" in the task of social transformation than any book could have conveyed. Nor would the impact of American imperialism on the life of a poor country ever be an abstraction for me. All these would affect my way of seeing the world and experiencing my life of faith forever.

---

* For those who wish to explore the vision and history of San Miguelito further, *Fire Under My Feet* by Leo Mahon with Nancy Davis (Orbis Books, 2007) is a must-read.

CHAPTER 10

THE RELUCTANT BRIDEGROOM

MY PLANE FROM PANAMA CITY landed at JFK Airport, where I was warmly embraced by my good parents who had never abandoned me for a moment throughout the travails of my crazy life. Old age had not beaten them down. My always unpredictable decisions had put them through their paces. They had experienced the horrors of the Holocaust and the loss of many beloveds, including the death of their dear little son and the apparent loss of their *beni bekhor*—their first born son—me, into the clutches of the enemy.

They had weathered it all with courage, grace and dignity. And now here was the joyful return of the prodigal with the prospect of his marriage to a nice (almost Jewish) girl and the hope of grandchildren. At least her name was Naomi and they loved her like a daughter from the start as she embraced them in place of the parents she had always longed for.

Not so fast! Their returning boy was going to put everybody—parents, Naomi and himself—through one more roller-coaster ride in this human drama. I arrived in New York just in time for my father's seventieth birthday, which was celebrated as only my mother—the consummate party giver—could produce. Our large fold-out living room table was heaped with delicacies: kosher cold cuts, whitefish, many salads and German rye bread. Above all, the *Gewürtztraminer*, the good Alsatian wine from the vineyards of my father's beloved Elsass, flowed like water. Several of my father's musician friends joined him in playing the string quartets of Mozart, Dvorak and Beethoven. Albert Schweitzer had sent a beautifully inscribed photograph of himself. The house was filled with friends rejoicing at my homecoming.

But all was not well with the also celebrated son and bridegroom-to-be. I felt myself falling into a depression of anxiety because I was now facing one of the greatest decisions of my life. I was confronted with the reality of commitment, and I suddenly felt an eruption of panic welling over me in a terribly disabling tidal wave. I had somehow been led to a well-recommended counselor, who also expressed some ambivalence about my decision.

That was all that I needed, given my already ambivalent reaction to practically every major decision making in my decision-riddled life. My fear of commitment hid behind wondering whether the social, cultural and intellectual differences between Naomi and me were too great. Didn't she come from more of an Irish working-class background and I from a more middle-class, intellectual, European Jewish experience? And on and on it went.

So I called poor Naomi in San Francisco where she was staying with her parents. She had already been gifted with a wedding veil from her former religious superior, Sister Patrick, and had bought her ticket to New York. I called to say (believe it or not) that I had changed my mind. To her great credit she replied, "I'm coming anyway. You can tell me to my face!" My parents also encouraged her to come.

And so she did—beautiful, vulnerable with her heart breaking. It was June and our wedding had been scheduled for early October. My parents put her up in the apartment of a friend who was away for the summer. So during those hot unreal New York days of August and September, she spent her time of waiting, feeling isolated in those unfamiliar surroundings. My mother, to her great credit and in her profound wisdom, exerted no pressure on me and even my tactless father managed to keep silent, although it was clear where their sympathies lay.

Naomi and I spent hours and days in discussing, debating and trying to sort out the issues. In the end I came out with what Naomi later described as "a reluctant yes." They always said it would be "for better or for worse." Our future life together would have much of the former and a little of the latter.

I wrote a letter to Father Augustine, the new abbot of St. Paul's Abbey. He was extremely understanding and spontaneously offered to set the wheels in motion for some kind of dispensation from my monastic vows and priestly obligations through our archabbey in Bavaria and then to Rome. I immediately had very mixed feelings about this dubious process of "being reduced to the lay state."

At that time, my specific future plans concerning my priesthood were still in a state of flux. These decisions would soon be clarified. I received a letter from the always intimidating Chancery Office of the Archdiocese of New York under Cardinal Cook, summoning me for an ecclesiastical "interrogation" in connection with a possible dispensation from Rome.

When I arrived at the Chancery Office, I was ushered into a baroque, ecclesiastical courtroom. This had previously been the sumptuous quarters of the Chancery Office. I was intimidated by the marble paneled walls and elegant floors also made of Italian marble. Then monsignor C. appeared attired in monsignorial purple from head to toe. Instead of sitting down with me face-to-face, as would have been a minimal sign of respect for a priest who had honorably served the Church for many years, he had another scenario in mind. He motioned me to a seat behind a defendant's table, and he ascended the stairs to the judge's bench from which he would preside and hold forth behind a tape recorder.

It was all a little ridiculous, considering that we were the only two people in this large and elaborate courtroom where the ecclesiastical tribunal held court. The monsignor sat up there in his celestial heights and began to question me down below as to some psychological or sexual aberrations in my character that would prove that my ordination was a mistake in the first place.

As this humiliating process continued, I decided to inform the monsignor of my true views on the subject. I told him that I did not believe that priestly celibacy was the great burning issue of our times, but that world peace and justice for the poor were. And since this was the ministry that I was called to, I had decided to continue on as a married priest with or without dispensation from Rome. As I spoke, the monsignor's face slowly took on the same color as his purple robe. I was afraid that I might be responsible for a fit of ecclesiastical apoplexy or a heart attack. Consequently, I decided to excuse myself, since I was not experiencing any progress in our non-dialogue.

In recent years there was a public scandal in which the same monsignor was accused of having a long-term lady friend on the side. As for me, after about three years, I received word that I had received a dispensation from Rome and that now I could marry in the Church. As 3rd century Greek philosopher Sextus Empiricus wrote, "The mills of God grind slowly but very, very fine." But by that time I felt that my priesthood, marriage and lifestyle were already approved by God and the community, and so I never accepted the kind offer.

While I was still in Panama, I had written to my friends about my decision because I didn't want to slip away like the proverbial thief in the night, which was how these decisions were often handled. In the States, priests in similar circumstances—and at that time there had only been a few—were shipped out of the parish secretly without even a chance to say farewell to their people.

In my letter I wrote:

> If you are hurt or disappointed by my decision, I can only say that I understand. I am not writing this letter for the sake of seeking approval or disapproval, although I am sure that I can both be helped or hurt by either one of them.
>
> I do not see myself as "leaving the priesthood." While I have no intention of organizing a schismatic Church, I do not eliminate the possibility of some kind of "free- wheeling" spontaneous ministry.
>
> I have always been intrigued by the distinction between renewal and innovation which Bishop Sergio Mendez Arceo makes in his charismatic pastoral letter on the experimental monastery at Cuernavaca, Mexico. After describing renewal as the effort to "renew our structures by discovering their first intentions or by adapting their functions more exactly to our needs and times," he continues: "By innovation, on the other hand, I mean a new spontaneous growth which the Spirit grants us. I mean a search for entirely new ways, new styles of life. I

mean a breakthrough which nothing in custom or convention seemed to prepare for. I mean a new sign offered to new times."

In line with the bishop's vision of innovation, I sense the need for a new kind of Christian presence in the world, the presence of people who experience the Gospel in a completely new life style which incorporates Christian ministry and marriage in a new way of really being "in the world."

Of the many responses which I received, the one that most remains in my memory is the beautiful letter from my old and dear friend Dan Berrigan. I had already informed him of the new developments and my germinating decision while I was still in Mexico. He wrote me:

> Your new development since arriving there is extremely interesting and I am sure valuable. Everything in your life leads to more life. Full speed ahead! Which is not much by way of a map of the seven seas but what else can I offer except the assurance that I understand? No like experience.
>
> If you have come on something frank, warming and liberating, something really reciprocal, you are indeed fortunate and all blessings on you.
>
> "Your life moves as in the case of two young people from sacrament to sacrament. Another way of saying that people await you and will mourn, cheer and take scandal at both ends of the experience. And deserve to be heard. From others a great deal of corrupt expectations and ersatz drooling, a good deal of retardation and pseudo-tragedy and most assuredly, anguish and sacrifice unto blood, whichever outcome—for you.

Then Dan wrote insightfully, as always (mirroring my own inner reflections), about two other priests whose marriage had become a *cause célèbre*:

> Neither man seems ever to have said a word in public about the sufferings of others—they moved (without liberation) from Church-bag to world-bag as though the whole thing was done by theological hocus pocus under klieg lights. But what of the world to which neither seemed ever to have had the remotest vocation?
>
> . . . .If I have not said more of my love for you, my debt to you, please forgive me . . . . Your life is rare and precious to me and many others; out of such a life, only joy and rightness can come. Love me and think of me often, as I do of you.

Among the relatively few letters of support, and a few of criticism and much silence, Dan's letter was truly a cold drink of water in the desert and sustained me by its radiant quality and love. Little did I know then how deeply our life journeys would be intertwined upon my return to the United States.

As I once again sailed forth into the great unknown, I was comforted by the words of the Jesuit theologian Bernard Cooke with which I closed my farewell letter. He was later himself to become a married priest: "Every Christian has to develop a fearless and responsible exercise of his own initiative and until that comes, until people really feel free to go and do what they believe is right—and do so responsibly—until that comes, the mystery of the Church can't be realized because God has made us unique persons so that we might uniquely reflect the Mystery of Christ."

In the meantime on the personal front was my impending wedding to Naomi, scheduled for Saturday, October 5th, the weekend before the notorious Catonsville Nine trial in which I was destined to get involved.

CHAPTER 11

Blessed Are the Peacemakers

Vietnam, the Catonsville Nine and the Berrigans

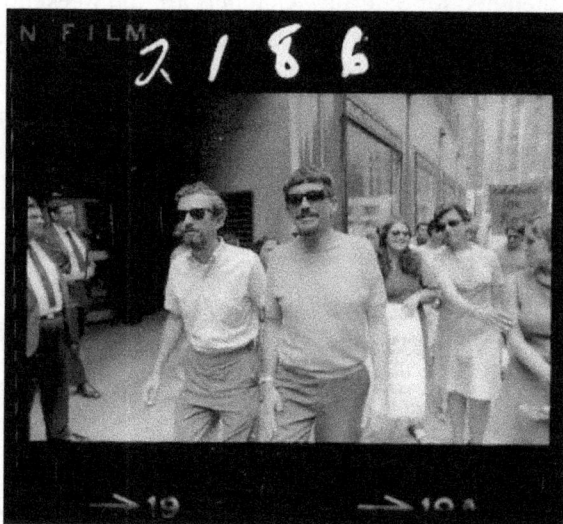

A FEW WEEKS BEFORE MY departure from Panama I had received a dramatic letter from Dan Berrigan written on the night of May 16, 1968. He wanted me to know that on the following day he, his brother Philip and a group of others would commit an act of protest and civil disobedience against the war in Vietnam—one that would entail serious legal risk. He wanted to share these exciting developments with me and asked for my prayers.

In his usual understated manner, Daniel was giving me advance notice of an explosive religious and political action that would send shock waves through elements in the government, through the Catholic Church and even through the mainstream peace movement. A group of nine people, including some priests, were going to up the ante of legal, peaceful, traditional non-violent protest by publicly destroying 1-A draft files. These were considered the hunting licenses that enabled the voracious—and apparently insatiable—war machine to devour the sons of mainly poor and working-class families in order to implement its military policies in the rice paddies of Indochina. These conscripts would also come disproportionately from Black, Latino and Native American communities.

The idea of burning the files first came to George Mische during the earlier trial of the Baltimore Four (Phil Berrigan, Dave Eberhardt, Tom Lewis and Jim Mangel). There the head of the Maryland Selective Service Bureau, a US army colonel, testified that these files were irreplaceable because no duplicates existed. It was then that George turned to Phil and said, "Holy shit! If we burn the files instead of pouring blood on them, they'll never be able to reconstruct them!"

the group that came to be known as the Catonsville Nine consisted of the Berrigan brothers and seven other hardy and courageous souls. At around noon on May 17, 1968 they entered the premises of the local draft board #33 in Catonsville, Maryland, outside of Baltimore, fittingly housed in the headquarters of the local Knights of Columbus. They took the 1-A files of the next 317 young men to be drafted and carried them down to the nearby parking lot and dumped them into a metal trash barrel. There, with the aid of homemade napalm, they set the records on fire and stood joining hands to pray the Our Father. Napalm, a jellied gasoline substance produced by Dow Chemical Company, adheres to and burns human flesh and was being used in bombs in Vietnam by the US military, often against civilian targets.

Contrary to normal expectations, the group did not flee with its job well done, but instead, stayed, prayed and waited for the police and then the FBI to arrive. When the senior FBI agent, a jowly, serious defender of the law, saw that one of the perpetrators was Father Philip Berrigan, he exclaimed, "Oh no, I'm gonna stop going to Church!" He had just arrested Phil and Tom Lewis a few months earlier along with three others for pouring blood on draft files at the Baltimore Customs House. Phil was actually awaiting sentencing for the first act. The nine were arrested, hustled into squad cars and taken off to the Towson County jail.

The other seven "jailbirds for Jesus," besides the Berrigans, were an interesting crew:

- ✤ Tom Lewis was a gifted, young artist.

- ✤ George Mische was a longtime activist and a good friend, a former labor organizer who had also worked in Latin America.

- ✤ Marjorie Bradford Melville, a former Maryknoll nun, had worked in Guatemala with some of the peasant resistance together with Tom Mellville, a former Maryknoll priest and Marjorie's husband.

- ✤ John Hogan, a former Maryknoll brother, had also worked in Guatemala.

- ✤ David Darst, only twenty-six years old, was a Christian brother who had taught in inner-city schools.

- ✤ Mary Moylan, a nurse-midwife, had worked assisting the White Sisters in Uganda and as the director of an organization in Washington that prepared women to work in developing countries.

Daniel Berrigan, a Jesuit priest, was a recognized poet. Philip Berrigan, Dan's younger brother, was at that time a priest of the Society of St. Joseph. Phil was tall, handsome and Irish with a shock of silver-gray hair and the build and self-confident demeanor of a former Army officer and athlete. He seemed to come by resistance naturally—both in terms of keen analysis and gutsy temperament. Phil was clearly one of the leaders and inspirers of the group (although George had been the original catalyst), a role that was sometimes resented by some of the other members who were strong personalities in their own right. Phil was an untiring recruiter of participants for other similar resistance actions, sometimes even to the point of exercising undue pressure on unwilling or ambivalent, weak-willed candidates. When Phil died in 2002 in his Baltimore Jonah House community, deeply mourned by his family and a large community of supporters and admirers, he had spent thirteen years in imprisonment for his work for peace and social justice.

At first, this apparently simple-minded and yet creative action at Catonsville seemed to go unnoticed. There was modest news coverage, although fortunately at least one TV camera captured the dramatic event.

A short article in *The New York Times* and a little press here and were the only attention given to this prophetic action.

It was then that I somehow stumbled onto the scene. I had just returned from Panama in time for my father's seventieth birthday and was living in New York with my parents. It was not at all clear what my next move would be. After some serious soul searching, I had decided to marry Naomi, whom I had met in Mexico. Also, I had very tentatively, and not very enthusiastically, put out some feelers for a teaching or counseling position.

But the God with a sense of humor once again put his hand on me. My old and determined friend George Mische called me with the outrageous idea of being coordinator of something he called "The Catonsville Nine Defense Committee." At first I thought he must be nuts. It did not seem to me that I fit the job description at all.

Then I received a call from Dan that he and Phil wanted to meet with me. They wanted to reinforce the idea that I would be the perfect person to organize activities around their Baltimore trial in October and to generally get the word out on their action. (I can just hear Phil saying, "Let's give Mayer a little friendly pressure.") We met at the office of the Jesuit Missions and drank some good whiskey together, something that the Berrigan boys appreciated. Would I consider being the coordinator of this mysterious defense committee?

I had become increasingly distressed by the escalating war in Vietnam. The peace consciousness that I had been developing during my life in the monastery was sharpened by my time in Panama. Experiencing US foreign policy firsthand in a small, poor Central American country had only awakened me further to the ruthless ambitions of American economic and military imperial strategy. The strong military and corporate presence in Panama and in the Canal Zone left little to the imagination.

Now back in the States I began to agonize over reports of mounting Vietnamese deaths, along with the increasing number of US body bags that brought the war back home. I had been thinking seriously about how to connect with the growing anti-war movement.

Naturally I had been shocked and then inspired by the Catonsville action. This was not a universal reaction even among the close friends of the Nine. Many thought that this was "a little too much." Even Thomas Merton and Dorothy Day—at least for a while—felt that this had gone beyond the bounds of traditional non-violent action. I never felt that way.

In fact, had I been in the States instead of in Panama, it might well have been the Catonsville Ten.

I saw it immediately as an act in the grand tradition of the early Boston revolutionaries who tossed the unjustly taxed British tea into Boston Harbor. And what about Luther's burning of the papal bull and later the whole body of Church canon law? Even Moses, the holy lawgiver, burned the idolatrous golden calf and then made the Israelites eat the bitter ashes.

In any case, after some prayerful deliberation and discussion with Naomi, I decided to accept their invitation. It was a decision that would propel me in a completely new direction into the world of the peace movement, politics and direct action. These were all ideas for which I had always felt great sympathy and support. But the prospect of being directly involved as actor and participant brought profoundly new challenges that both attracted and intimidated me.

From my position of naiveté and inexperience in the ways of the world (having been behind cloistered walls for eighteen years) and much ignorance about political realities, I was supremely unprepared to undertake this more-than-ambitious venture. On the positive side, I brought a genuine passion for peace and against the horrors of the war in Vietnam, good listening skills and ways with people, which helped make me an effective organizer, as well as an ego that was sometimes a burden but also a sustainer in difficult times. I also possessed certain Utopian tendencies that sometimes passed for authentic faith that would occasionally enable me to achieve apparently impossible tasks under adverse circumstances. This latter quality would be greatly needed for the task ahead. Thus I embraced one of the most beautiful of the Gospel Beatitudes of Jesus given in the Sermon on the Mount: "Blessed are the peacemakers, for they shall be called the children of God" (Mt. 5:9).

These luminous words would guide the rest of my life and set a standard that has taken me many decades to try to live up to, however imperfectly. Even as I write, I am struck at how easy it is to take those words for granted—one more job description in the world of the market. I do not reflect often enough on the amazing good fortune of having been called to make this divine ideal of "peacemaker"—the one who creates *shalom* (harmony), in the world and my life vocation. The audacity of Jesus' peace beatitude is all the more remarkable when one considers that hatred, warfare and violence have been the primary vocabulary with which human history has been written.

I had no idea where to start. The Catholic Peace Fellowship, then under the guidance of Jim Forest and Tom Cornell, took me under its wing. At the time they had their offices at the Episcopal Church of Holy Apostles in New York, and I was given a little desk in a corner.

It was not only a new geography on Ninth Avenue and West 28th Street, but even more a matter of being transported into a new geography of the Spirit. It brought me face-to-face—a novice wet behind the ears— with realities I had only read and sometimes prayed about. Here was a radical community of believers who were willing to set aside security, comfort, safety, even physical freedom, in the name of standing at the side of the victims of war and violence. These were all new and strange realities for me: breaking the law of the state in the name of a higher law; questioning whether property that was being put to humanly destructive purposes had a right to exist; confrontation with police agencies regarded by society as the guardians of the common good; and finally, the possibility of prison—the deprivation of one's autonomy and contact with family, community and even sky and earth. All these options were as familiar as being launched in a lunar rocket. So I was scared right down to my boots.

And so with limited resources and with equally modest experience on my part, we sought to prepare ourselves—after consulting with some good organizers in Baltimore—for what would be one of the most significant political trials of the Vietnam War. It was on October 3, two days before the opening of the trial, that I married Naomi Lambert in the lovely garden of our small New Jersey apartment. So as I prepared to cast my lot with those considered renegades by the State, I would also go to Baltimore with solid credentials as a renegade to the Church—a married priest.

During the previous days the defendants had quietly disappeared for fear of being arrested by the Maryland authorities who were afraid that they would not appear at their trial. (They were under double jeopardy, having been indicted by both the federal and state governments.) Actually, they were all "hiding out" at Brendan and Willa Walsh's Viva House, a Catholic Worker community in Baltimore.

It was from there that I received a message from Dan. He had an invitation to address the seminarians and faculty at the Jesuit Major Seminary at Woodstock, Maryland. This was an important opportunity to win over the young members of his own Jesuit order and perhaps mobilize supporters for the trial in Baltimore, so he asked: Would I go and speak in place of the soon-to-be "God's jailbird"? I could not refuse. Thus on the eve of my wedding with classical (and even for me) unbelievable indelicacy, I told Naomi that "I would do my best" to be back by our wedding day the next morning. I spoke at Woodstock that night and my presentation was warmly received by the Jesuit community, although some of the faculty members boycotted my talk as they would have boycotted Dan.

I returned to Edgewater in northern New Jersey (our new home) in the wee hours of the morning, much to the relief of Naomi, who one more time was put through the psychological wringer. Once again, the archetypical opposition and tension between love and family and the demands of duty, vocation and responsibility, so influential in my life journey, would cast their long shadow over my new family. It would do this more than once. It must also be said that Naomi was strongly committed to my (our) peacemaking vocation. Our mutual covenant was that through her midwifery work she would support us financially so that I would be free to serve and work for meager (sometimes no) pay.

Our wedding the next day in the lovely backyard of our little apartment in Edgewater, New Jersey, took place in the shadow of the familiar-since-childhood George Washington Bridge. The wedding was beautifully celebrated by Father Gene Boneski, a priest friend from our Cuernavaca days, who would himself marry later. I wore an elegant blue-green suit made by a tailor in Panama. Naomi was stunning and radiant in a simple wedding dress. We were surrounded by many friends and supporters who had come from the four corners to celebrate. Many of my old monastery friends and supporters came. It was a moment of great joy and consolation for my parents. This was a day that they never dreamt would ever happen.

No honeymoon in the Bahamas for us. I had been recruited to play a coordinating role in the activities surrounding the trial beginning on Monday. After our wedding celebration we loaded our car to drive the next morning to Baltimore and prepare for one of the great political and religious trials of our times. We had no idea what lay ahead.

Our sumptuous honeymoon suite was the cement-floored, basement laundry room of some peace supporters' Baltimore row house. Their contribution to our romance was one rollout single bed for both of us for the coming week. (Many of our comrades slept on the floors of homes and churches in sleeping bags.)

Nor would there be any reports of torrid connubial lovemaking between us. We were so exhausted at the end of each day's courtroom and street activities that we were asleep before our heads even hit the pillows. I was too tired to even feel deprived.

On October 5, thousands (the debated number was between one and five thousand) of supporters from the peace movement's religious community and assorted others descended upon Baltimore. Six hundred students alone came from Cornell, where Dan had served as a peace chaplain of sorts.

Hundreds of police officers with helmets and riot gear guarded the streets and the courthouse, some with dogs. The sound of sirens echoed through the city. Inside the courthouse vigilant federal marshals patrolled the corridors and especially the courtroom, the sacred sanctuary in which infallible and allegedly blind justice was about to be dispensed. The supporters ranged from scruffy, bearded, blue-jeaned hippies to modestly attired, well-scrubbed, cherubic-faced nuns. Above all, Holy Mother State was confounded on how to respond to these nine practitioners of non-violence, albeit in an unexpected form, and their supporters.

Baltimore experienced one of the largest peace marches in its history as two thousand strong marched down Howard Street, chanting: "Free the Nine!" There was a spirit of exhilaration and community rarely experienced at peace—and even religious—events. We all knew in our bones that something very powerful, perhaps even sacred, had transpired compared to which the judicial issues and decisions to be made inside that courtroom were almost irrelevant. It was as if the community had caught the spirit of the words of testimony that would be spoken by Mary Moylan during the trial: "By pouring napalm on draft files I wished to celebrate life, not to engage in a dance of death."

The evening events of St. Ignatius Jesuit Church were, indeed, celebrations of life—with music and poetry and above all the messages of faith and hope. William Stringfellow, Episcopal lay theologian and former attorney in Harlem—described by Dan as "an elegant skeleton"—arrived thin and frail, walking with the help of a cane.

In his inimitable direct style, he carefully mounted the speakers' rostrum and proclaimed with all the energy at his disposal: "Death shall have no dominion!" Then just as carefully he climbed down and returned to his home on Block Island. He would be followed in equal eloquence by the likes of Rabbi Abraham Joshua Heschel, Dorothy Day, Howard Zinn, Harvey Cox and other prophets for peace.

On one evening an outdoor rally took place near the courthouse. I was inspired by the example of some young people and decided to burn my draft card. It had suddenly struck me that we could not leave the burden of the war to our children alone, although up to that time I had enjoyed clergy exemption from the draft.

With trembling hands I took the card out of my wallet and looked around for a light, which was promptly given to me by an accommodating young bystander. I set my card aflame and as it burned brightly in the October night, I held it aloft as if it was a fiery offering to God.

As I was lost in a great admixture of emotion, including a generous helping of fear, I noticed out of the corner of my eye a rather large figure moving in my direction. At first I did not pay it much attention, until I saw that it was a big husky man, dressed in a sports shirt and definitely focused on yours truly, undoubtedly an FBI or police agent. Whereupon as elegantly as possible, I withdrew into the shadows, slowly increasing my pace and my newfound friend did the same. Finally, after an intense chase through the Baltimore back streets and alleys, I managed to lose my pursuer with my heart in my mouth.

Obviously, I had been under some government surveillance all along and this pattern would continue in various forms for much of my future work. It was also clear that intuitively I had chosen not to await capture and pay the penalty. Instead, I had chosen the perhaps less noble hit-and-run strategy and felt pretty good after this first explicit criminal encounter with the powers-that-be.

The morning of October 7, a more elevated drama was taking place inside the Federal Courthouse on Calvert Street in the trial of nine good women and men. Much to the State's surprise, the trial was quite peaceful and only lasted four days.

The combination of a moderately liberal judge, an allegedly antiwar Jewish prosecutor and an African American assistant prosecutor was intended to forestall any charges that this was a "hanging court." The carefully chosen all-white jurors, predominantly government employees, provided the most dependable ingredient for convicting the accused.

Further, all dramatic—if not historic—testimony about the defendants' work for peace and their motivation for going to Catonsville, when permitted, was immediately denigrated as "irrelevant" and the insistently repeated mantra was about the charges as the "destruction of government property" with no regard as to whether said property was an application form for a dog license or legal permit to pursue bloody warfare in Indochina in contravention of the rules of international war. Dan Berrigan later observed that "without our religious beliefs, the action is eviscerated of all meaning." It was like suggesting that the Boston Tea Party was about making a big cup of tea in Boston Harbor and not a revolt against taxation without representation.

The case for the prosecution was neatly summed up by the testimony of Mrs. Murphy, one of the draft board clerks, when asked about the effect of the action of May 17th had on the functioning of local draft board #33. "It has given us a tremendous amount of work, and it certainly has inconvenienced our boys."

And later, when asked about the nature of the files and of her work, she testified:

"Yes, sir . . . I am part of the Army of Defense."

It mattered not to judge or prosecutor whether it was Philip Berrigan testifying to his military service and fruitless meetings with high government officials on the war or the Melvilles about their work with oppressed rural peasants in Guatemala. It mattered not that Brother David Darst spoke about his desire to "raise a cry about the wanton slaughter" or that George Mische referred to the Nuremberg Principles requiring citizens to disobey immoral or illegal commands. The statements of defendants in this Baltimore courtroom were held of no account: not artist Tom Lewis's wisdom that "a person may break a law to save lives," nor carpenter Brother John Hogan's simple teaching, "I want to let people live. That is all." Not even nurse Mary Moylan's sagacious observation, "to pour napalm on pieces of paper is certainly preferable to using napalm on human beings," was heard. Rarely had such profound words of testimony been heard within the precincts of an American courtroom.

The collective wisdom of all the sages, saints and Buddhas would have been to no avail—all would have been dismissed by a soulless gavel rap of "not relevant here!" Until finally, as if in holy despair, Daniel Berrigan in rare clerical garb and appearing more gaunt than usual in this hostile setting, read the poetic meditation which the Nine had issued on that fateful morning of the Catonsville Action:

> Our apologies, good friends,
>
> for the fracture of good order, the burning of paper
>
> instead of children the angering of the orderlies
>
> in the front parlor of the charnel house.
>
> We could not, so help us God, do otherwise.
>
> For we are sick of heart, our hearts

give us no rest for thinking of the Land of Burning Children

and for thinking of that other child of whom

the poet Luke speaks . . .

this child is set for the fall and rise of many in Israel . . .

a child born to make trouble and to die for it

the First Jew (not the last)

to be subject of a "definitive solution."

We think of such men [the resisters]

in the world in our nation in the churches.

And the stone in our breast is dissolved.

Defense attorney Bill Kunstler's eloquent effort to persuade the jury that they had the power to ignore and "nullify" the law governing the destruction of government property as not being applicable to this peace effort was quickly neutralized by the judge. The jury then withdrew to decide the fate of the Nine.

While the jury was out for its one-and-a-half-hour deliberation, Dan asked the judge, "We would like to recite the Our Father with our friends."

The judge, to our surprise, responded, "The Court has no objection and rather welcomes the idea." Theologian Harvey Cox called it a "Pentecostal moment": "Women sobbed, United States marshals bowed their heads and wiped their eyes, jurors and prosecuting attorneys mumbled . . . 'forgive us our trespasses as we forgive those' . . . . City police, bearded peace workers, nuns, and court stenographers prayed together: 'For thine is the Kingdom and the Power and the Glory . . . '"*

When the jury returned, they, one by one, declared the defendants guilty "of the matters whereof they stand indicted." Whereupon a member of the audience—perhaps it was the voice of an archangel—shouted out, "Members of the jury, you have just found Jesus Christ guilty!"

Judge Thomsen responded to the archangelic judgment by threatening to clear the courtroom "if there are any further outbursts."

Phil Berrigan and Tom Lewis received three and a half years, each to run concurrently with their six-year Baltimore sentence. Dan, George Mische and Tom Melville each received three years and David Darst, John Hogan, Marjorie Melville and Mary Moylan two years. Tom and

* Harvey Cox, Jr. "Tongues of Flame: The Trial of the Catonsville Nine" in *The Witness of the Berrigans*, eds. Halpert and Murray, Doubleday, 1972.

Phil were returned to jail in chains until they were granted bail six weeks later. The rest were granted bail. (Much to our sorrow, in 2008 gentle Tom Lewis was taken from us to practice his fine radical art in the heavenly realm where it would be better appreciated, and we also lost the quiet, humble but determined John Hogan.)

Dan stepped out of the musty dark courthouse into the blinding light of day—like Lazarus out of the tomb—and on the courthouse steps announced to a group of supporters and press, "I think that we can agree that this was the greatest day of our lives."

The Trial of the Catonsville Nine, a dramatic rendition of the trial by Daniel Berrigan, was successfully performed off-Broadway and beyond under the brilliant direction of Gordon Davidson and with an eminent cast.

In March of 1970 the Catonsville Nine defendants met in Washington, DC, for a day of reflection, assessment and planning for the future. There were already quiet undercurrents of discontent. Several members of the group resented that it had really become the "Catonsville Two" because of the predictably disproportionate attention given to the Berrigan brothers. They felt that their role was made invisible. (This was true but without the relative notoriety of the two brothers, the action might have remained unnoticed.) They were no longer nine, for Brother David Darst had died in a tragic automobile accident. He was on the way to visit some draft resisters in jail. His terrible death was a hard blow to the community. This sweet young man of high ideals had said that "the way of civil disobedience, the way of suffering love . . . is the only hope left for peace among people."

At that meeting Dan and Phil, George Mische and Mary Moylan all decided against turning themselves in. Mary stayed "under" the longest and actually did not surrender until 1978 when she felt that "there was no sense in being underground anymore." George survived underground for almost a year, during which he refused to surrender while the war was still on. The FBI broke down a door and apprehended him at gunpoint.

Dan was to say later, "I wasn't avoiding punishment, just delaying it and protesting the war." His underground adventures were to become a *cause célèbre* both for the government and for the peace community, and I was to be deeply involved in them.

In early April, the Sisters of St. Joseph of Peace, who lived up to their name, had invited Phil and Dave Eberhardt (one of his co-defendants in the earlier Baltimore Custom House action who was also considering going underground) to visit their beautiful retreat house in Sea Girt, New Jersey. John Grady and I joined them there.

John was a robust, wild, charismatic Irishman and a sociologist who had become co-director with me of the Catonsville Nine Defense Committee and would play a major role in planning future draft board actions. His wife, Theresa, and his beautiful brood of children had been longtime friends of the Berrigans. Several of his daughters and even grandchildren have been involved in many courageous non-violent direct actions carrying on his legacy.

We spent this time together at the retreat house strategizing and writing their press statements and contacting the media about how and why they were turning themselves in after a "Life from Under" rally/religious service to be held at St. Gregory's Church on the Upper West Side of Manhattan.

What happened instead was that the FBI, provoked by the evasive tactics of Dan at Cornell on the previous days (more of that later), had officially decided to renege on a "gentlemen's agreement" for a peaceful process, which had been made with Father Henry Browne, the pastor. At that point Father Browne, a few other priests and some courageous lay employees of the parish then decided to hide Phil and Dave in the parish rectory. But the FBI, now on a massive manhunt, broke into his apartment, from which the two were led away in handcuffs.

A few days before the arrest of his brother and Dave, Daniel had quietly gone underground by disappearing from the Cornell campus and staying at discreet sites in Ithaca and elsewhere. On April 17, he was to join some fifteen thousand peace lovers at the interfaith celebration "America Is Hard to Find," organized in his honor and to celebrate "the spirit of militant non-violence." The festival was held in the huge Barton Hall of Cornell and was visited by a veritable pantheon of political, religious and musical peace luminaries. Musicians included Country Joe and the Fish, Phil Ochs, Barbara Dane, Jerry Jeff Walker and John Cage. Some of the faith leaders were Professor Harvey Cox of Harvard Divinity School and Rabbi Arthur Waskow, who led a Freedom Seder. Historian Howard Zinn, peace leader Dave Dellinger and Paul Goodman, the great counter-culture theorist and writer, were also present.

All had come to celebrate Dan and perhaps witness and support his publicly turning himself in to the authorities. Needless to say, the event was crawling with J. Edgar Hoover's blue meanies. Meanwhile, however,

Dan, inspired by some of his student supporters, had decided not to turn himself in after all.

On the big night, the welcoming words of the traditional Passover Seder had been proclaimed: "Let all who are in need come, let all who are hungry enter." Now the Bread and Puppet group came onstage. That night they were miming a celebration of the Last Supper. The lights dimmed, a rock band began to play and Dan was suddenly hidden under one of the huge puppets of the twelve apostles and just as suddenly was led by some of his student "conspirators," invisible and unseeing—appropriate symbolism for the period ahead—into the darkness outside.

The FBI, who were present in great abundance, for it was rumored that Dan would appear, suddenly realized that their prey had escaped them, and they went wild. Agents began scurrying around, frantically asking, "Where is he?" It was almost a Biblical scene. In the meantime, the darkened hall was lit up by students and others lighting candles and burning their draft cards. Truly "the light was conquering the darkness."

As soon as Dan could throw off his awkward disguise, he was hustled into a waiting panel truck. One of the co-conspirators shouted, "Hit it!" and the vehicle screeched off into the darkness. They drove for a half hour to an uninhabited cabin, and in the ensuing days Dan moved from a farmhouse to the attic of an Ithaca friend.

Finally, by a roundabout route and with a switch in cars, he was transferred to the home of some of my dearest and oldest friends from my monastic days, Frankie and Gordon Smith of Sparta in northwestern New Jersey, who courageously offered their Christian Presbyterian hospitality to Dan. It was at this point that I became more directly involved as one of several key architects of Dan's underground strategy.

During the ensuing months, Dan spoke to an interviewer of what he called "the two responsibilities" of his underground experience: one was his spiritual growth and the other was making a public statement against the war. It was the second of "the two responsibilities" that fell to my and to our collective imaginations. How to keep this adventure of the Spirit alive for as long as possible, how to keep its perpetrator reasonably safe, and yet how to help expose his presence, and the vision and message of our community of resistance to the widest possible public audience? This would be accomplished, as Dan put it later, "by appearing on television, by preaching in churches and by writing furiously for all kinds of publications—in general, by being available in any way that our imaginations could come up with."

Each night he would stay under another roof. From New England to Washington, an ingenious community of havens of safety was created. In the meantime, my telephone was manifestly tapped and the FBI visited and interrogated many of my neighbors. I was often under observation and it required both ingenuity and a certain automotive agility while being followed by "the feds" on the road so that we could accomplish some of the subversive projects with and for our underground adventurer.

The idea came to us of having Dan interviewed by a prominent television journalist. Edwin Newman, the dean of the NBC-TV news world at that time, agreed to be this person and we were delighted. We decided to hold the interview in an out-of-the way motel in Stanford, Connecticut, not exactly the center of the "breaking news" world, but an inconspicuous venue.

With feelings of trepidation, I picked up Newman and his crew at a nearby parking lot and drove them to the motel. There were friendly introductions with Newman and an apparently very sympathetic TV crew. Public sentiment against the war had been growing. The interview that aired the next day was an excellent piece of photojournalism and caused quite a stir.

Next on Sunday, August 2, Dan delivered a dramatic surprise sermon at the Germantown First Congregation, a church near Philadelphia—not too many Catholic churches would have welcomed him. I dropped Dan off two minutes before he was introduced from the pulpit by the pastor, Rev. Robert Raines: "We have a guest preacher this morning who is a fugitive for peace and will deliver God's word unto us, Father Daniel Berrigan." Dan concluded his underground sermon with these words: "There are a hundred ways of non-violent resistance up to now untried or half tried, or hardly tried, but peace will not be won without . . . the moral equivalent of the loss and suffering and separation that the war itself is exacting from many."

Then Dan stepped briskly into the sunlight and jumped into our waiting vehicle and we flew out of the parking lot with one more mission accomplished. Dan took a deep breath and smiled ear to ear with his impish leprechaun smile.

We now set out together on one of the most adventurous legs of Dan's underground pilgrimage. Little did I apprehend what lay ahead. Our destination was Block Island, which sits like a jewel in Block Island Sound off the coast of Rhode Island. It had been chosen after some intense debate among the underground organizers about its suitability in terms of security and some concern about Dan's safety.

After taking many convoluted back roads, we arrived undetected at Point Judith for a beautiful ferry trip to Block Island. In the meantime, we had been joined by Naomi, who had come up separately with our one-year-old son, Peter Daniel. Dan and Naomi boarded the ferry as a couple with Dan carrying Peter in his arms like a dutiful father and me keeping my solitary distance. In this way did we hope to put the always feared FBI off their trail.

Dan's hosts on beautiful Block Island were old and interesting friends. William Stringfellow had been a lawyer in Harlem for many years and had spoken at the Catonsville Nine trial. His *My People Is the Enemy* is a penetrating account of his life and service in the inner-city. Bill was also a devout Episcopalian lay theologian, a man of dry, caustic wit and tongue, a sharp mind and a heart of gold. Always frail of health, his disabilities never stopped his activist life and interests. His partner, Anthony Towne, was of equally good heart, a bearded giant of a man who was a poet and an acute social critic.

We left early the next morning after warm farewells. Little did I know that the next time I would see my dear friend Daniel, it would be in the blue jumpsuit attire of the population of the federal penitentiary at Danbury, Connecticut.

August 11, 1970 seemed like a day like any other on Block Island, with heavy morning fog and mist. There did seem to be an unusual number of birdwatchers in bright ponchos and binoculars in the vicinity, considering that a storm was gathering in the north. Finally, Stringfellow inquired of one of the birdwatchers as to who they were. They responded, "FBI, bird watching, we're looking for Berrigan," and he flashed his ID.

With that, the house was surrounded by agents and several cars suddenly screeched up the long driveway. Dan stepped out of the doorway and calmly announced, "I suppose you're wondering who I am. I am Daniel Berrigan." Then several agents seized him, patted him down and put cuffs on him. One of the arresting agents, in tribute to his college education by the Jesuits (many of Hoover's agents were recruited from Jesuit schools), solemnly murmured *Ad majorem Dei gloriam* (To the greater glory of God), the Jesuit motto. Thus was the mysterious arc completed between Dan's original Catonsville arrest on May 17, 1968, to this Block Island capture of our beloved outlaw on August 11, 1970.

Stringfellow loved to recount the silent but profound commentary of their Knickerbocker terrier, Marmaduke, on these official proceedings. He sought out the newest model FBI vehicle and ceremoniously lifted a leg to piss on one of the tires in contempt for the powers of Holy Mother State.

The next morning every newspaper around the world carried the classic photograph of Daniel in his yellow windbreaker with hands manacled but raised in the V gesture with a victorious, if not gleeful smile, on his Irish face. The news reached all of us very quickly, and I reacted with anger and sadness that this heady period of resistance against illegitimate authority had suddenly been snuffed out by "the Man."

Some of my comrades rightfully (or so they and I thought) concluded that I had messed up a good thing through amateurish ineptitude, which gave away the whereabouts of our fugitive. It was only years later that we discovered that it was actually an inadvertent reference in a clandestine letter written by a prisoner (conveyed by a trusted carrier who was actually a government informer) that in some veiled manner mentioned Block Island as a possible stopover for our favorite fugitive. "And so it goes," as the great Kurt Vonnegut was wont to say.

CHAPTER 12

PASSING ON THE FLAME

*The Peace Underground
and New Draft Board Actions*

BEFORE THE CATONSVILLE TRIAL EVEN took place, practically while the
fires of Catonsville were still smoldering, restless and creative spirits
were already responding to that Biblical mandate of "Go thou and do
likewise!" In August of 1968, almost three months before the Catonsville
trial in October, George Mische suggested that we think about organizing
a retreat to plan future actions. Through some small miracle I was able
to secure the summer camp of my old monastic community. Out of this
small gathering of less than a hundred souls, a flame would be lit that
would blaze across the night sky of the darkness of the war in Vietnam

and ignite a unique campaign of non-violent actions across America far beyond Catonsville or Baltimore.

Our planning retreat quickly began to bear fruit. After an intense weekend of soul searching and political strategizing, an interesting group of fourteen dedicated people began to form who would be known as the Milwaukee Fourteen. They reflected a significant evolution of the original Baltimore and Catonsville model. The validity of the original paradigm of religious resistance would reveal itself in the ability of others to enlarge on the model and find new and even unexpected modalities to make it come alive. The first new development was that such statements of conscience no longer required the participation of celebrities such as the Berrigans. The Fourteen were a feisty collection of priests, one teaching brother, several dedicated young people and one Jewish participant. They were "ordinary men"—if there is such a thing.

On Tuesday evening of September 24, 1968 (just two weeks before the Catonsville trial), the Fourteen walked into the Brumder Building in downtown Milwaukee, which housed several draft boards and, despite the protestations of some cleaning women, removed over ten-thousand files to a nearby grassy spot. There, with the help of homemade napalm, they set the documents on fire, linked arms and, silhouetted against the huge bonfire, sang "We Shall Overcome"—the hymn of the freedom movement.

Their trial, which began on Monday morning, May 12, 1969, was an experience in which I was deeply involved. Even before the draft board action took place, Jim Forest, a navy veteran and a devout convert to the Catholic Worker, in the name of the Fourteen, had invited me to help organize the activities in Milwaukee leading up to and including their dramatic trial. I made frequent trips to Wisconsin and took up residence in Milwaukee for several months preceding the trial and strategized with the defendants and their legal team led by Bill Kunstler.

Perhaps the most dramatic divergence from the Catonsville model would be the conduct of the trial of the Milwaukee Fourteen. If the Catonsville trial was in the style of the judgment of Socrates—serious, rhetorical in the best sense of the word, and dignified—it was perhaps, for all its power, a little predictable. The Milwaukee trial was, on the other hand, more in the spirit of a sacred three-ring circus.

The courtroom of the Milwaukee Fourteen became a veritable psychedelic explosion within the bowels of the beast. In that very place where the state holds the power of life and death, freedom or imprisonment over human lives, these fourteen not only humanized an inhuman place but also took back the power that rightfully belonged to the people.

Very early on, the rather pompous Judge Charles L. Larsen, a presiding judge of the Wisconsin State Court, a devout Catholic and former state commander of the American Legion, set the stage by his declaration that "we are a nation of laws, not of men." The trial would be about "burglary, arson and theft," not about the issues of war and peace that were tearing at the guts of the republic.

The trial began with the defendants discharging their lawyers, including the illustrious Bill Kunstler, because of claims of judicial improprieties and by the announcement that the defendants had decided to defend themselves. Nor did they appoint one spokesperson from their ranks. Rather, each defendant would speak for himself, not hidebound by exaggerated respect for the court.

Jim Forest alluded to the influence of the New Testament in his life and actions "especially Jesus' raid on the Temple grounds." The judge decided that this was "irrelevant, misleading and could lead to confusing the jury." The judge was so concerned about the jurors being influenced at Sunday Mass that he volunteered to call the local parish himself to request that there be no political themes in the Sunday sermon.

Professor John H. E. Fried was allowed to testify. He was an eminent international lawyer and had served as a special expert assisting the judges at the Nuremberg war trials of the key Nazi leaders after World War II. Judge and prosecutor were both duly impressed by his eminent credentials. He made a statement rarely allowed or heard in an American courtroom: "Your Honor, I say with a very grave heart and after very careful study, that the US military intervention in Vietnam does violate those essential and basic provisions of the United Nations Charter."

The eminence of the witness did not prevent the judge from admonishing the jury to ignore his testimony. Moved or not, it took the jury exactly one hour and ten minutes to find the defendants guilty "on all three counts as charged." Whatever misgivings the jurors may have had—and there were none in evidence—were assuaged by the eloquent words of praise by Judge Larsen for duty well done under trying circumstances and in the presence of such difficult spectators. All the defendants were subsequently sentenced to two years in Waupun State Prison with four years probation.

Even as the trial was going on, three more draft board actions took place: one in Pasadena, California, one in Silver Spring, Maryland, and a third major action with fifteen people destroying fifty thousand files on the south side of Chicago. And the flames of this movement raced across the country like wildfire. Draft boards were non-violently raided in Los Angeles, New York City (four different times), and Boston, and in Rochester, New York, FBI offices were hit for the first time by a group calling itself the Flower City Conspiracy. (I would later play an active role in organizing around their trial.) Women Against Daddy Warbucks, a group formed in response to the male domination of the Catholic Left, burgled a New York City draft board. An unidentified group raided the FBI offices in Media, Pennsylvania, which really raised the ire of the Bureau. After that J. Edgar Hoover intensified FBI pressure to crack what he saw as the "East Coast Conspiracy to Save Lives," the name taken by one of the groups.

Actions took place in Boston, Akron, Ohio; Auburn, New York; and Midland, Michigan—where raiders entered the Dow Chemical data center and erased its magnetic tapes that contained valuable information on biological and chemical weapons. There were raids in Providence, Rhode Island; Evanston, Indiana; Boston (by two teenagers called the Boston Two); and even a single raider on Christmas Eve 1970 in San Jose, California.

The one draft board action that I personally participated in was the Hoover Vacuum Conspiracy on the Sunday night of December 17, 1970, in Elizabeth, New Jersey.

Seven of us decided that the time had come to stop contributing good men and women to the federal and state penal colonies. It was still possible to slow down the grinding of the cruel draft board mills without the noble witness of waiting for the police and FBI to lead us away in cuffs after a moment of prayer. We felt that this stage had passed and the time had come for a new level of direct action.

The participants, beside myself, were gutsy former Sister of Charity Judy Peluso and Dick Scaine and Bill Gibbons, both married priests-to-be. Dr. Gene Monick, Jungian psychiatrist, and Mel Madden (who left us much too early)—also a married priest.

On the night in question, a group of us in a nearby car were awaiting a flashlight signal from Gene Monick in the railroad station signaling that a police patrol had passed and that the coast was clear. Then Mel Madden used his carpentry skills to pick the lock so that we could enter the premises, a tiny room containing the draft records. We estimated that we only had between 5 and 7 a.m. before the next police patrol would come by. We worked feverishly filling the garbage bags with thousands of 1-A files. I must confess to being frightened out of my wits with my heart beating like a trip hammer and close to peeing in my pants.

We filled our cars with many garbage bags of looted booty and thus made our (we hoped) sacred contribution to stopping the ruthless war machine in the name of the boys of Elizabeth, New Jersey. The next day Bill Gibbons and Dick Scaine took the files up to Dick's father's little summer cottage in elegant Lake Mohawk, New Jersey. There they burned them for many hours in the cabin's fireplace. Later a group of three hundred signed a public statement taking responsibility for the Hoover Vacuum Conspiracy.

The final drama of the draft board raids was somewhat embarrassing, but ultimately uplifting. Titled the Camden twenty-eight, it took place in August 1971 and was early on infiltrated by an FBI informer. The feds allowed the peacemakers to burgle the place for two hours and to destroy draft files. Then agents moved in for the arrest. The group was composed of many good people and dear longtime friends.

Father Mick Doyle, an Irish priest who worked in inner-city Camden, was one of the participants. One of his parishioners, Marine veteran Robert Hardy, had been recruited to be an informer for the FBI. He became a member of the group because of the FBI's promise that they would halt the action before it took place and no harm would come to his pastor or anyone else. Hardy supplied the group with burglary tools and training in carpentry and acted as an agent provocateur—and, of course, the FBI broke its word to him.

During the trial, Hardy's nine-year-old son was killed in a tragic accident and Mick came to comfort the family and later celebrated the funeral Mass. Hardy was so moved by this act of Christ-like love and forgiveness that he changed his mind and turned into a defense witness. As a result of Hardy's new affidavit, the government case was destroyed and all the defendants were acquitted. The judge remarkably allowed the eloquent defendants to speak and the real issues of the war to surface, practically unique among all the anti-war trials.

Thus the draft board actions essentially reached their end and climax with the Camden twenty-eight. It was a teaching about courage as well as about the occasional naiveté and gullibility of good people committed to good causes. It was surely just a matter of time before our movement would be infiltrated even more deeply—as future developments would show.

Above all, the Camden twenty-eight community demonstrated the transformative power of non-violent love and forgiveness of one's enemies, which is ultimately the heart of Christ's teaching and must remain at the heart of even the most radical actions of resistance against war and injustice.

"Be not overcome by evil but overcome evil with good" (Romans 12:20–21).*

During the time following Dan's capture, both he and Phil were eventually transported to the so-called medium-security prison in Danbury, Connecticut. The only thing "medium" about it was that they didn't hang the prisoners by their thumbs. Actually, they did have more mobility than in the full hard-time maximum security federal prison in Lewisburg, Pennsylvania. Phil Berrigan was at Lewisburg for a longer period and it even became too much for tough Phil.

The prison authorities there (at FBI instructions) kept him under special surveillance, occasional isolation lockup, and minimum family and other visits as long as Dan was an underground fugitive. This was the government's mean-spirited form of retaliation and of seeking clues for Dan's whereabouts. Finally, through the intervention of Dr. Robert Coles, the prominent psychiatrist and author and other influential allies, Phil was moved to Danbury.

I was on the official visitation list and drove up to Danbury every two weeks or so. It was always a joyful reunion and one could not help but be inspired by the positive outlook of the two. The daily prison grind must have been taking its toll, especially on Dan, the more sensitive and physically delicate brother. They both exercised a quietly influential prison ministry for their fellow inmates, especially for some of the young draft resisters and COs who were doing time in Danbury. The brothers would lead Bible study groups, occasional Eucharistic celebrations and as many other activities as the hawkish Catholic prison chaplain would allow. Later on, Dan received an almost fatal Novocain overdose while in the dental clinic where he also worked, which further weakened his health.

Still, when I came to visit, they would put on their best faces, and we always had a good time as well as doing some quiet strategizing. I skirted the prison rules by occasionally slipping in some small bottles

---

* The Camden action resulted in the production of one of the best films on the Catholic Resistance and perhaps even on the US peace movement called *The Camden 28*, directed by first-time producer Anthony Giacchino.

of scotch or brandy to make our time together even more spirited. They were always hungry for the latest news of the peace struggles as well as the accurate reports from Vietnam.

One of the highlights of our visits was one around Christmastime in 1970 involving Puerto Rican Jesuit Bishop Antulio Parrilla-Bonilla. Bishop Parrilla was a rare soul and it was hard to believe that he had been consecrated a bishop under the conservative Puerto Rican hierarchy. I had the idea of inviting him to visit the US mainland during the Christmas season when Cardinal Spellman (the military vicar and chief chaplain of the US Armed Forces) paid a visit to "our boys" in Vietnam. We announced that we were inviting our own bishop to also visit "our boys" in the military prisons, stockades and lockups—especially those who were military deserters, resisters or conscientious objectors, as well as those in federal prisons. The bishop was not welcomed in most facilities, and we even had a non-violent sit-in together at the Stockades in Ft. Dix, New Jersey, when we were refused access by the Catholic chaplain.

By some benign miscalculation the bishop did receive permission to visit Phil and Dan at Danbury and what a beautiful Christmas visit it was. Daniel, of course, was especially thrilled that a fellow Jesuit—and a bishop at that—should be visiting him in his peculiar Christmas crib. It was a wonderful Christmas and we regaled each other with stories of how the good work of the Prince of Peace was growing here and in southern climes.

CHAPTER 13

THE HARRISBURG CONSPIRACY CASE
Peace Activists as Kidnappers and Bombers

"WHAT THE HELL IS WRONG with this phone?" It was January 12, 1971, and I and my family had recently moved into our new community home on Park Avenue. Ray Sheenan (formerly Father Mark) had helped me with a day's painting of our new kitchen—a springlike yellow in the midst of a drab winter—and I had planned to make and receive some important phone calls that evening. The phone was completely dead for about an hour and the phone company was unable to be of assistance.

Then just as suddenly the phone came on again and rang with a stunning incoming call. It was an Associated Press reporter who insisted that I had been named as an unindicted co-conspirator in an alleged conspiracy plot to kidnap Henry Kissinger and place bombs in the heating tunnels underneath the US Capitol in Washington, DC. It was a story that came to be known as the Harrisburg Conspiracy case, and it was to make front-page news for some time to come. Only then did I realize that the dead phone was the beginning of a campaign of telephone tapping. This would be corroborated much later when I checked my Freedom of Information files, of which there were an incredible ten thousand pages coming from a broad menu of "intelligence" agencies.

The US government had indicted Phil, Sister Elizabeth (Liz) McCallister, Eqbal Ahmad (a brilliant Pakistani scholar and activist) and three priests: Neil McLaughlin, Joseph Wenderoth and Anthony Scoblick. The other unindicted co-conspirators besides myself were Dan Berrigan (still in prison), Mother Jogues Egan (provincial superior of the Marymount nuns), Marjorie Shuman, Bill Davidon and Tom Davidson. What these alleged criminals had in common was that we were all devoted to the cause of peacemaking and up to that time not guilty of violent criminal activity. Most of us were Catholics.

It had all begun on the previous November when no less than FBI Director J. Edgar Hoover appeared before the Senate Supplemental and Deficiencies Committee during the Thanksgiving recess with only a few senators present to request an additional $14 million for extra personnel. He denounced the fantastic scheme that supposedly masterminded a monstrous nationwide "conspiracy of anarchists," calling itself the East Coast Conspiracy to Save Lives to kidnap a highly placed government official and plant bombs in electrical and steam conduits underneath the Capitol Building. This conspiracy was, of course, being led by "the Berrigans." Later, even high-level associates of Hoover agreed that these were far-fetched charges that he used in his strategy to personalize evil-doing on the radical Left and thus support his case for increased funding.

The indictments went ahead and even in the White House a spirit of optimism reigned over this case. John Ehrlichman reported to President Nixon, who was working with the Internal Security Division of the Justice Department to amass a file known as the "White House Enemies List," that the "Berrigan investigation is going very well."

We, the accused, took the offensive by releasing a statement in which we asked: "Who are the true kidnappers and bombers?" all at the height of the Vietnam War. We would come to learn that the US-sponsored Phoenix Program in South Vietnam was actually kidnapping village leaders.

Meanwhile in the peace movement, especially in the circle of the indicted, it became clear that these were charges of the gravest seriousness and could bring even life sentences with a conviction. Some comfort came from a new superseding indictment three months later adding conspiracy charges to destroy Selective Service records, implicitly admitting that the government lacked confidence in the solidity of the kidnapping and bombing charges. The government also added two defendants, Ted Glick, a former draft file destroyer and draft resister, and Mary Cain Scoblick, a former nun and recent wife of defendant Father Tony Scoblick. Also mysteriously Dan Berrigan and I and others were dropped as unindicted co-conspirators. This was indeed strange since Dan had been named by Hoover as one of the evil geniuses behind this plot (all admissions of how flimsy their evidence was).

I was one of the coordinators for the Harrisburg Defense Committee (so called because the trial would later take place there), which operated in New York until we moved it to Harrisburg. Smaller defense committees sprouted all over the country to respond to this most recent vicious attack against the anti-war movement. The high-powered legal staff consisted of some of the great luminaries of the period: former US Attorney General (under LBJ) Ramsey Clark, Leonard Boudin, Father William Cunningham, Charles Glackin, Paul O'Dwyer (brother of New York's former mayor), Tom Menaker, Terry Lenzner, William Bender and Diane Schulder.

Our activities were kept under close FBI observation. FBI files that we obtained later indicated that I was (falsely) accused of being in Cuba to collect funds, and the FBI further recommended that my tax returns be scrutinized "for the past three years, possibility exists that a good income tax evasion case can be made." (I was to find out later from a friendly IRS agent that such an illegal audit of my tax returns did in fact take place.) Our New York City offices were even broken into and records were stolen and returned, probably after being copied.

I spent the next months traveling around the country speaking to large sympathetic student and community groups and religious audiences such as the General Assembly of the United Presbyterian Church USA. The outrageous charges and the cynicism of the government's strategy provided a bully pulpit to talk about the real crime—the immoral and illegal bloody war in Vietnam.

My lengthy stay of several months in Harrisburg was not an easy one. Naomi had generously agreed to join me there along with Peter and

Maria, our recently adopted daughter, and the move was not easy on them. There was no longer an open spirit of camaraderie between those of us on the staff and the defendants as had been the case in the past. It was clear that they were no longer interested in consulting and strategizing together, which I felt to be a contribution I could make. Of course, the defendants did face serious prison sentences. The reasoning behind all this, right or wrong, began to emerge as we learned more about the facts of the case, which were not doled out in generous helpings.

It seems that there had, indeed, been some indiscreet secret correspondence between Phil and Liz in which she, in a sincere attempt to encourage a despondent prisoner, reported some far-fetched theoretical brainstorming about non-violent kidnapping and even bombing of government property—all rejected as immoral and naive by the great majority of the discussants. There were even reports that Phil had naively made a "reconnaissance" visit to the tunnels in question. Of course, none of this amounted to a conspiracy but perhaps pointed to the grandiose (even a little silly) imaginings and feelings of deep frustration at the relative powerlessness of our movement in the face of the ruthless war machine. A good example of how even otherwise brilliant and dedicated souls can be carried away in the heat of struggle.

The letters in question were carried by one of Phil's fellow prisoners at Lewisburg, one Boyd Douglas, who Phil naively thought to be a newly converted disciple of his but turned out to be a key government informer and double agent.

It was these letters that Hoover had referred to in his leaked Senate testimony and on which the government would base its flimsy case. The letters were also, in part, love letters between Phil and Liz, who would later marry, have a beautiful family and found Jonah House, a peace community in Baltimore. In fact, I would perform one of their several wedding ceremonies.

The bottom line was this: Some or all of the defendants felt that because of the seriousness of the charges, the decisions should be made by those in jeopardy and not by their hotshot lawyers, who were all brilliant but not necessarily weighed down by excessive modesty (not a requirement for this time-honored profession).

The usual circle of friends and colleagues was also not invited to be part of the idealized consensus-building process. But in the meantime, what of this community, that central fulcrum of the Catholic Resistance of which Phil and Dan, and later Liz, had spoken and written extensively?

Were we all there simply to raise funds and recruit fresh-faced seminarians, nuns and clergy as well as movement activists to support and even come to Harrisburg? It was not an easy call.

Nevertheless, the national peace movement saw the impending trial as an important organizing moment against the war and the growing political repression. Politically constituted grand juries and other conspiracy trials were increasing. We had a large demonstration of ten thousand people with national celebrities and musicians on the weekend before the trial. On the night before the trial itself on January 24, 1972, hundreds of people kept vigil outside of the Dauphin County jail in support of Phil, who was locked up inside. (Dan was to be released from Danbury exactly a month later on early parole because of public pressure and poor health and arrived in Harrisburg in the middle of the trial.)

Judge R. Dixon Herman, a balding sixty-two, was as conservative as his community. A World War II navy veteran and a Sunday school teacher, he did not prove to be a brilliant jurist. The US attorney was William S. Lynch, one of the government's brightest and a Catholic, who had once served under Ramsey Clark at the Justice Department.

The informer, Boyd Douglas, took the stand for two full weeks with six days of them under the non-stop grilling of the defense lawyers. He was at first the smooth, good-looking, self-confident conman, but as the trial went on, he was exposed as a pathetic liar and manipulator.

When it came time for the defense case, Ramsey Clark, who had been the attorney general under LBJ when the Catonsville and Baltimore cases were first prosecuted, rose to begin. Much to everyone's surprise he declared: "The defendants proclaim their innocence, and state they will continue working for peace. The defense rests."

This strategy had been reached after much controversy. No one wanted to put Phil or Liz on the stand with possible embarrassment about their relationship. There was also fear about interrogation concerning the details of Dan's underground support network. Most of all, the majority had decided that a political defense, the preference of Phil, Liz and Eqbal, might alienate the jury further.

The judge was taken off guard and disappointed. The only next step was to send the case to the jury. After a less-than-coherent charge to them by the judge and after sixty hours of intense deliberation, the jury returned with the shocking news that they could not reach a verdict and the judge was reluctantly forced to declare a mistrial.

Hence even twelve good, reliable citizens of this ultra-conservative community could not reach consensus and ten of the twelve had voted against the conspiracy charges. They were not persuaded by Boyd Douglas (the informer and double agent) and could not believe that these priests and nuns, with whom they disagreed on many points, could be kidnappers and bombers.

Phil was delighted, as we all were. His chestnuts had been pulled out of the fire. He declared: "It was a tribute to people, to that cautious group of mid-Pennsylvanians, who wouldn't be finessed out by outrageous bullshit." Phil and Liz did receive a light sentence for smuggling letters into a federal prison, a conviction that was later overturned by a higher court.

The verdict was a humiliating setback to Hoover, Attorney General Mitchell and the Nixon administration. It was one of the few major antiwar cases that the government had lost.

The trial had taken its toll on what journalist Francine Grey had named "the ultra-resistance." Friendships had been damaged. It was the end of the draft board actions, except for a less-than-visible attempt in Harvard.

For me it became clearer that we had accomplished something very important. The draft board actions had deepened and radicalized the meaning of non-violence. They had inspired the larger peace movement. But now the time had come to move on. It seemed to me that we needed to return to the larger essential vision of King and Gandhi of building a mass movement for non-violence and non-cooperation. Small acts of conscience will always have their place, but we needed to build a serious movement that saw the general strike, Gandhi's great Salt March or the Black Southern campaign for civil rights in Birmingham as the most authentic vision of *Satyagraha* and as our ultimate goal.

Also, dare I say it—we had enough people in jail voluntarily. There will always be actions for which we must be willing to pay a price as in that inspiring annual campaign, now growing into the thousands, against the evil School of the Americas in Fort Benning, Georgia, where the torturers and assassins of Latin America are trained. Certainly one is grateful for the many years that Philip Berrigan and many others courageously served in prison. But I was happy to read an article written shortly before his death in which Phil extolled the primacy of mass civil disobedience.

And so the Harrisburg Eight conspiracy case, with all of its courage as well as its shadow sides, seemed to offer a natural line of demarcation for something new to begin. Some tried to hold on to this style of peace-making through the Plowshare actions, which were non-violent attempts to "beat nuclear warheads into plowshares" at major nuclear missile sites.

These were courageous and generous actions that generated some public support including my own, but I sometimes guiltily wondered whether the time had come to create new imaginative modes of resistance. Others also saw the need to leave this noble tradition behind with deep gratitude and to move on to address the challenge of building the larger mass movement for peace and social and economic justice.

If we take a hard look at this political moment [in 2010], what do we see? We are in the midst of interminable wars in Iraq and Afghanistan. We are being confronted by dangerous strategies, originally concocted by Dick Cheney and his minions, that promote unilateral war making supported by the development of new nuclear weapons systems and their possible use against Iran and other countries. We are also facing the impact of rapidly advancing global warming. The social change community—and all of us—are threatened with the suspension of civil liberties and blatant violations of the sacred right to privacy. In this moment today, after the illusions of the promise of the Obama presidency have dissipated, we need to actively seek and work for the creation of fresh approaches that offer real solutions

The God of history is summoning us to build a community much broader and more diverse than ever before. We must reach out to constituencies we have not connected with previously to create activities and campaigns born out of a fresh political imagination that is willing to transcend old models.

Let us return to the sources that gave birth to Catonsville and its children:

> And then I saw a new heaven and a new earth, for the first heaven and the first earth had vanished . . . I saw the holy city, the new Jerusalem, coming down out of heaven from God, made ready like a bride adorned for her husband. I heard a loud voice proclaiming from the throne: "Now at last God has His dwelling among people! He will dwell among them and they shall be His people, God Himself will be with them. He will wipe every tear from the eyes, there shall be an end to death and to mourning and crying and pain, for the old order has passed away!"
>
> Then He who sat on the throne said: "Behold! I am making all things new!" (Revelations 21)

CHAPTER 14

FBI Wet Dreams

My Public Information Files

I was in the midst of working on this literary adventure when I received two large cardboard boxes in the mail. Much to my surprise they were gifts from the FBI—my Freedom of Information (FOIA) files—about three hundred pages, only a small part of some ten thousand pages (as I had been informed by my attorney) covering all of US "intelligence" agencies' records of my nefarious past. I had applied for them so long ago that I had given up all hopes of their ever arriving.

The FOIA, administered in the most uncooperative if not hostile manner by our government, provides the only means for US citizens to discover how that same government has been spying on them.

This intensive campaign of spying and careful record keeping served the purpose of reminding me of activities I had long forgotten. Apparently on April 1, 1972 "at a rally held in Harrisburg . . . .Paul Mayer read 8 names of persons claiming responsibility for the York sabotage" where "313 casings for 500 pound bombs ready for shipment were damaged by a group referring to itself as 'Citizens Committee to Demilitarize Industry. While it is recognized that Mayer will be uncooperative when contacted . . . every investigative venue must be pursued to its logical conclusion."

The files engage in a fascinating analysis of my views on non-violence and violence. "Subject states that violence does not apply to things, such as draft files, but to people, such as napalmed children in Vietnam . . . .And subject states that 'the day may come when to be non-violent may be more violent than to be violent.'" This is a position once hinted at by Gandhi. But then a synopsis states that: "He believes that violence which applies to people is sometimes justified."

One analyst almost comes to my defense with: "Advise in detail where this is supported?" and concludes that "in no instances do the details indicate subject has stated (or believes) violence to people is sometimes justified." They were trying to determine just how dangerous I was. My day-and-night observers were also troubled that "he has expressed brotherhood with the Black Panthers and Weatherman while disagreeing with their tactics."

Hoover's G-Men seemed to listen to every rally speech, monitor my sermons and read every op-ed piece. Of course they also used phone taps and informers. I later realized that we had one living right in our East Orange, New Jersey, community house (a single mother with a child.). Through letters between the defendants (probably Phil and Liz) they accused me of traveling to Cuba in 1970 to raise money—a far-fetched and fictitious charge because this was many years before my first visit to Cuba.

Through this correspondence they discovered that I was "organizing minor sabotage among employees at Picattiny Arsenal." This charge was true and the leak scuttled a potentially powerful and profound action. I had met a group of devout Catholic laymen who worked as engineers and technicians in one of the biggest bomb plants in the country in Dover, New Jersey. They were seriously and prayerfully contemplating non-violent action against these instruments of death. Before receiving my files, I thought that their or my phones had been tapped. It was apparently through this same leak that the protectors of our First Amendment also discovered that "he assisted in harboring fugitive _____ ." (Name blanked out but undoubtedly that of Dan Berrigan.)

The files also report that "Paul Mayer led 15 persons in a sit-in at the Archdiocese of NY offices to protest the RC Church's position regarding demands made by [James Foreman in the Black Manifesto] for reparation to negroes [sic]."

Finally "due to his anarchistic [sic] beliefs, including his views of violence and his involvement at least in the defense of those who have participated in the destruction of Government property in opposition to the Vietnam War; and due to his frequent travels throughout the country making speeches supporting his views to obtain funds and muster support both for his cause and the cause of PCPJ [the People's Coalition for Peace & Justice], it is recommended that Mayer be placed on Priority II of the Security Index."

It's nice to get a promotion somewhere.

Would that US military, police, prison and intelligence agencies be held to such scrutiny, high standards and moral delicacy about their views on and use of violence.

CHAPTER 15

PROJECT SHARE

A New Community and Family Life

ON JULY 24, 1969, OUR son Peter Daniel was born in Roosevelt Hospital in New York. Naomi, who was a seasoned nurse-midwife, had midwives assisting the birth as well as a progressive MD. I attended some natural childbirth classes for prospective fathers but remember missing a few because of the intense peace activities of the period. Our son was three weeks overdue. Instead of on July 4, United States Independence Day, he chose to arrive on July 24, the birthday of Simon Bolivar, the Great Liberator of the Americas.

We had settled in a little apartment that was one side of a beautiful old house in Edgewater, New Jersey, in the shadow of the George Washington Bridge—a landmark of my Washington Heights childhood and adolescence directly on the other side of the Hudson River. Our tiny apartment consisted of two floors connected by a wooden winding staircase, giving one the illusion of living in a real house. The staircase soon became a source of danger and adventure for young Peter. The other half of the house was inhabited by Trude Rittmann, a prominent Broadway music arranger and an old friend of my parents from Germany. Trude soon took our little family under her nurturing wing.

Our house, along with similar handsome Victorian homes in the area, have since fallen victim to the demolition ball and have been replaced by many ugly and far more profitable "on the river" high-rise monsters. This area is now a ghetto of over-priced, high-rise habitations for upscale commuters to New York.

Naomi, always courageous, was not daunted by the considerable drive which we would have to take across the river to midtown Manhattan's Roosevelt Hospital at the expected coming of labor pains. She reassured me that first babies are usually born after protracted labor. Sure enough, the big day came and happily labor did not begin during the New York/New Jersey commuter rush hour.

It proved to be a long, difficult labor and Naomi responded with heroic perseverance and little—probably too little—complaint! I'm convinced that if we men had to bear the children and endure labor pains, the global overpopulation problem would be solved and the number of births reduced by half. She will never let me forget—and rightfully so—how I had to run out for a tuna fish salad sandwich in the middle of her travail.

I was there for the dramatic moment of birth and delivery and what a profound and overwhelming experience it was. I wept as I saw the mysterious appearance of our son and was the first one to hold him. What a sacred moment. Little did I know then that this homely infant would morph into an unusually wonderful person, even good-looking. My parents, of course, were ecstatic beyond words at their first grandchild.

Little Peter seemed to enjoy his new house. I can still remember his favorite piece of music, the Beatles' "Sgt. Pepper's Lonely Hearts Club Band." Peter not only loved the music but also adored the beautiful and colorful record jacket (we still had vinyl in those days) so much so that he literally ate his way through half of the jacket. A true fan.

Peter Daniel was baptized by Dan Berrigan, his namesake, in a sweet fountain in our little garden. It was a profound and beautiful moment as we were surrounded by family (including the Jewish ones), friends and many members of the peace community. Together we all were again baptized into His death so that we could go forth and live the new life of the Risen One during these dark times for our nation and the world.

When I had returned from Latin America two years previously, I began meeting with a small circle of friends once a week to share our lives, search the Scriptures or other holy and inspiring texts and ask ourselves and each other how we must live today as individuals and families in the midst of the obscene and bloody war. We focused on what were the peculiar challenges to us as believers or, at least, as conscious humans and how to confront a culture that increasingly worships at the shrine of militarism, racial superiority and imperial power. We also asked ourselves how we could resist the blandishments and perks of consumerism which Caesar offers us as the tradeoff for selling our souls and even our children into his service. How could we become resisters to the rewards for conformism and silence before the Moloch of mass culture?

Many of us saw the advantage of actually living together to realize the ideal of true community as opposed to the isolation of the nuclear family, so I proposed that we begin some exploration in that adventurous direction. We had enough young couples, several of them married priests and nuns, and others whose lives were not yet so fixed as to exclude the possibility of something radically new.

We began searching in the general northern New Jersey area, where many people had jobs, to find a large house to rent. Our thinking from the start was to combine communal with private living so that, while there were common areas, families and individuals would have their own space. Too many of us had come from a rigid communitarian experience in the religious life and didn't want to repeat that pattern.

We looked in the Newark area and surrounding communities and found nothing to rent that fitted our needs. Then a small three-storied apartment house presented itself for sale in East Orange. It was a handsome building in quite good condition with six roomy apartments. The price was reasonable in 1970 (today it would be a major bargain) and with typical generosity Lorna Scheide, an elderly, vital, progressive, well-to-do Quaker and a longtime friend, offered to lend people who needed it the money to pay for a modest mortgage ($1,000 per unit). Naomi and I were among the beneficiaries, many times, of her goodness and spirit of sharing. She has now also passed to her reward, which should be great. Eventually, we would be joined by more kindred spirits and we purchased the similar adjacent building as well. Lorna herself, in a spirit of adventure, also moved in and joined the community.

Our building was located on 546 Park Avenue, one of the main thoroughfares of East Orange, and had a spacious backyard for our children to play in. At the time, in 1970, East Orange was still a relatively integrated community—predominantly African American of middle- and working-class with a generous sprinkling of low-income people. Its small white population also spanned the social classes. Since then, East Orange, where I still reside, has become almost exclusively African-American, predominantly made up of low income and welfare-receiving people. Some working- and middle-class Black folks remain. It has been called by someone, according to percentage, "the largest African-American city in the country." All of this is due to red-lining by the banks and by the white flight which hit the country during these years. Our new community took on the name of Project Share and we slowly began to move in.

Our community was composed largely of married priests and their spouses.

There were a few single, probably celibate, priests, all of whom eventually married.

Added to this we had a sprinkling of just regular folks, mostly couples. A few lay people and a few nuns did not live under our roof but were fellow travelers and occasionally shared meals and celebrations. Essential to this mix was a whole tribe of lively, beautiful and interesting children.

There was a genuine spirit of community and mutual support. In the beginning it was more significant for the women, many of whom stayed home to some degree and helped raise the children on a daily basis and so developed a great spirit of solidarity among themselves. There were a few like Naomi who also had jobs or professions. The greatest winners were the children, who had an abundance of built-in playmates and a roomy backyard when we connected those of both apartment houses.

We held weekly meetings and common potluck meals. Some of us celebrated Sunday Eucharist together. Each year there was the Christian-Jewish Seder celebration around Holy Thursday and Pesach (Passover), which I would lead.

Pat and Jerry Mische, who lived in the building next door, became prominent peace educators and founded Global Education Associates. The Misches, along with Jeff and Pat Brown and Lorna in her quiet way and their other housemates, helped make their building a true center of peace education.

Looking back, it was evident that we lacked diversity, although there was a sprinkling of people of color and some of the couples had adopted children of different racial backgrounds. After all, we lived in an increasingly predominantly Black community and we did not want to be a white island.

To spice things up, there were some infrequent romantic affairs across the marital lines. A few led to breakups and regrouping with real heartbreaks involved.

All in all, it was an important, if imperfect, experiment. It enriched many of our lives, created deep and lasting friendships and did counteract some of those deadly feelings of isolation and the chilling of the heart which often become an integral part of suburban middle class- culture. It certainly enriched and often challenged the growing up experience of our children.

This brings me to the next adventure of our own family—the arrival of our beautiful daughter Maria in 1970. We had decided not to have another biological child. We did it once and felt there were enough children on the planet. Since we both spoke Spanish and had lived in Latin America, we decided to adopt a Latino child, if a child needed us.

We applied to the Foundling Hospital in New York and this proved to be an edifying, sometimes inspiring experience. It was wonderful to find a Catholic institution in the Archdiocese of New York that functioned in a truly humane fashion. This was probably due to the fact that it was run by the Sisters of Charity, a fine community of women in service to the greater good. We were especially fortunate in working with a young social worker who was completely committed to his children and parents, and who would occasionally bend the rules about how much information adoptive parents were "allowed" to have concerning their children's backgrounds.

Naomi and I were invited to the Foundling to meet some children. The first child we saw was behind a large glass window. She was a gorgeous little six-month-old girl with golden skin and curly black hair. We immediately said, "Search no further, this is our child-to-be!" And much to our joy, they agreed.

It took a little time—too long—to complete all the formalities and paperwork, but at last, the big day came. We were invited to come to New York to pick up our new baby, who was by then eight months old. We named her Maria, not only after the Blessed Virgin, but in honor of Mary Moylan of the Catonsville Nine. She did indeed turn out to have her feisty and combative spirit. More than we bargained for.

We did our best to prepare our firstborn son for the arrival of his new sister. There had been extensive conversation and dialogue as far as possible (Peter was two) and we even prepared him with a special gift. We bought a beautiful red toy fire truck—Peter loved cars and machines— and we said that it was a present from his new sister. Peter, who was still working on his diction, lovingly called it his "fuck." He quickly developed a love/hate relationship with Maria, and would alternately jump on her and hug her. Over the tumultuous years they have continued to be close friends.

Maria proved to be a challenging child. Her biological mother was Italian and her father a Black Puerto Rican/Dominican. And she has not let that Latin blood go to waste. She always expresses her feelings one way or the other.

Maria's temperament was a challenge to herself and to those around her. She was a child who thrived on love and respect. She had a very close relationship with my mother, who gave her unconditional love, and Maria loved her Oma. When she died, we were afraid to tell Maria. She was inconsolable and grieved her grandmother's death for months.

But fate did not always bring that same, unique grandmotherly quality of love into her life and this was hard for Maria to accept. She was often in conflict with her environment and had regular difficulties in school. At the age of eight, she socked her teacher, who had used some physical restraint and made a remark that Maria thought had a racial innuendo. Consequently, she was expelled from a very good alternative school.

At that point, Maria was already in weekly counseling and considered a "difficult child." She was beautiful with amazing curls, an irresistible smile and a large heart—and also a very sharp mind. For a while we sent both our children to the local public school with mainly African American children from the community in overcrowded classes. Peter, who was not a fighter by nature, did not last more than a year as the only white kid in his class. We eventually sneaked him into the Montclair Middle School. Maria ended up attending the well-integrated St. Venantius parochial school in nearby Orange, and neither she nor the school had an easy time of it.

Naomi worked as a nurse-midwife in inner-city Newark at what is now known as the University of Dentistry and Medicine of New Jersey. Most of her clients were the poor Black women of Newark and surroundings, predominantly teenage mothers. She served as a dedicated leader and instructor in the School of Midwifery and her skill and devotion played a key role in the development of generations of committed and competent nurse-midwives. She was also a pioneer in the still "underground" home delivery movement.

I tried to contribute to her professional life by caring for our children when Naomi had night duty at the hospital or in emergency situations. I was trying to move in the direction of sharing more household responsibilities even though I was still far from breaking the sexist mold. I did some cooking, took our children to school and picked them up and tried to be a good father. In retrospect, I see how my frequent absences for meetings, events and travels took me away and undoubtedly had some impact on Peter and Maria, even though I felt close to them.

This brings me to what was perhaps one of the greatest shortcomings of our little community (and also of our particular family)—the absence of open sharing of our feelings. It would also have been an invaluable tool or process in my earlier monastic community where there was very little space for the sharing of feelings, such as isolation, unless in some special friendship with another monk (officially frowned upon) or a dialogue with an unusual spiritual director. This is a wisdom I would learn many years later from working with young teenage survivors of the world's extreme war zones.

It was also only later in life that I understood how difficult it is for women to be in relationships with men who are unwilling or perhaps unable to communicate their feelings. Talking about her own feelings was not necessarily Naomi's strongest suit either, but maybe not doing so was another way of taking care of me. As for myself, I found the thought of revealing my real feelings, doubts, especially criticisms and fears, terrifying and something to be avoided and circumvented at any cost. Since then, in my counseling and group work with men, I have found this inability to identify and share feelings to be a chronic problem with many (if not most) men and, therefore, I feel it needs to be a central concern in the healing of our planet.

As community members began to move away, either to take care of aging parents or because they needed more ample space requirements or due to simple loss of enthusiasm for the effort, Project Share morphed into a friendly but less intimate co-op of people, some of whom hardly knew each other.

Finally, because some co-op members failed to pay their fees and the project suffered under the burden of cruel East Orange property taxes (a scandal of many inner-city communities), we almost lost the building and were saved only by the loan of a generous angel. I ended up being the sole unenthusiastic and unequipped caretaker of our once-beloved building until a-less-than-generous buyer delivered me from this fate. Thus I, as the founder of Project Share, would also become its terminator. Little did I understand then how the wheel of karma would deliver me with its always unerring accuracy to the next stage of my journey.

CHAPTER 16

"You Say You Wanna Revolution?"

The Anti-War Movement, the American Left and the Counterculture

ONE OF THE UNEXPECTED RESULTS of my work with the Harrisburg Defense Committee is that it propelled me into the larger mass peace movement. The anti-war movement regarded the Harrisburg Eight Conspiracy case and the ensuing trial as a major development in the United States Government's strategy to crush, vilify, repress and weaken the resistance to the war in Indochina. Along with the persecution of the Black Panther Party, the imprisonment of Angela Davis and the Pentagon Papers case,

Harrisburg was seen as a major moment in the Nixon strategy to silence all voices of dissent.

Accordingly, the Harrisburg Defense Committee (HDC) was invited to take part in the People's Coalition for Peace & Justice (PCPJ) which was, in the 1970s, the major network of national and local groups working in opposition to the war in Indochina and for the creation of a just society. I became the Harrisburg representative on the national coordinating committee, the principle decision-making body for the national anti-war movement—an intimidating undertaking, which surfaced deep feelings of inadequacy.

Suddenly, I found myself in the midst of an unfamiliar milieu. It was a quite different setting from the familiar religious, primarily Catholic peace community with its own values, symbols, language—even its own strategy. There I was, wet behind the ears, together with all of the national, sometimes venerable, peace organizations and leaders.

There were pacifist groups such as the Fellowship of Reconciliation, the American Friends Service Committee (both religious) and the War Resisters League (definitely not religious). Other participating groups were peace groups such as the Women's International League for Peace and Freedom, Clergy and Laity Concerned about the War in Vietnam and more. Even less familiar to me were the Communist Party, some Socialist groups and the radical, sometimes hippie youth groups such as Mayday.

I was in the presence of seasoned and experienced activists and strategists such as Dave Dellinger, Sid Peck and Norma Becker. We still had not achieved the goal of integrating our movement to any degree with people of color. But there was always Jim Haughton of Harlem Fightback, one of the great thinkers of the Black movement, who became a great friend—as did many of these people. There is nothing that so bonds people together as being engaged in the great life-and-death issues facing humanity. If we could only learn how to deal with the demon ego—but more on that later.

So in the presence of such luminaries, I listened and learned. Gradually, I began to realize that I and the community out of which I came also had a peculiarly important perspective to contribute to the greater good. I sometimes had the advantage of not coming from as doctrinaire a position as some of my colleagues did and so could look at issues and problems from a fresh point of view. Of course, the Catholic Resistance also brings its peculiar baggage and hang-ups to the table. Very slowly I developed the courage to make contributions before such an imposing and unfamiliar body of people. Also, it must be said, many of the committee members had never before worked with anything resembling a Catholic priest (or other religious people)—even someone as atypical as I was.

The members of the Communist Party presented a particular challenge. In spite of all my radical leanings, I had still been exposed to the anti-Communist propaganda of the Catholic Church and of the dominant culture over the years. Naturally, I found some of their rigid ideology, strict adhesion to party discipline and loyalty to the Stalinist Soviet Union to be a problem. At the same time, I developed some real friendships over the years.

Also, I always had a special affinity for the youth and student countercultural groups. Although they represented a large constituency (maybe the largest), they were often looked down upon by the more established (and sometimes stodgy) peace organization representatives. Their more radical politics were feared, as well as their commitment to tactics such as civil disobedience and, of course, their countercultural lifestyles with "sex, drugs and rock and roll." The traditionalists were even more freaked out by the dramatic actions of Abbie Hoffman and the Yippies such as throwing dollar bills from the balcony of the New York Stock Exchange or, God forbid, levitating the Pentagon.

I can still remember Rennie Davis, later one of the notorious Chicago Eight along with Jerry Rubin and Abbie Hoffman, taking me aside out in the hallway of a particularly long, boring movement meeting. We had many of those, which I faithfully attended. (I jokingly said that one day I would receive the Nobel Peace Prize for having attended more of these boring meetings than anyone else.) Rennie's motivation for rescuing me from the meeting was to offer me a few tokes from his special stash of marijuana to relieve the boredom. I would be introduced to that spiritual tradition much later.

In the spring of 1971, PCPJ decided to launch a major peace offensive in response to the weakened but unrelenting United States warfare in Indochina. We began in April with people visiting their own congressional representatives and senators in the United States Capitol. Where meetings were not agreed to or where the response was intransigent, some groups organized sit-ins right in the congressional offices.

Sid Peck, a political scientist from Boston and one of the leaders of PCPJ, received a strange call from I.F. Stone, the grand old journalist of progressive politics. He had received a call from Senator Barry Goldwater, the arch-Republican from Arizona, who had run for president in 1964. The senator complained that some of the young demonstrators who committed civil disobedience had behaved "rudely" in his office and would Izzie (Stone) convey his displeasure to the appropriate authorities. Sid offered to call Goldwater and did so. He explained to him that the young people "feel deeply about their views and sometimes get carried away. They do want to convey their heartfelt opposition." The senator apparently did not think that the US government was being rude by wanting "to bomb Vietnam back into the Stone Age" as General Curtis Lemay stated the government's objective.

On Saturday, April 25, a mass demonstration was held on the Washington Mall with 200,000 peace seekers. In a rare moment of unity on the always thorny issue of civil disobedience (when to use it, how, where, how radical, etc.) and because of the escalating crisis of the war, PCPJ had committed itself to some days of direct action six days later, beginning with Mayday, May 1. The young people's somewhat pretentious but idealistic slogan was: "If the government won't stop the war, we'll stop the government." The Mayday youth contingent played an active leadership role in designing a brilliant, rather complicated "battle plan" strategy for blocking the principal arteries, traffic circles and bridges during the morning Washington, DC, rush hour, employing non-violent actions in order to prevent government workers from reaching their desks.

Some of the more traditional peace leaders feared that the young people could not be trusted and would resort to violence, trashing cars and breaking windows. Dave Dellinger and I trusted the youth leadership and worked with them. Naturally there was always the danger of extreme actions, but as we have found out over the years, these are often instigated by police infiltrators and provocateurs.

The day came and on the first of May thousands of people jammed the avenues and byways of the Capital. The full strategy never came to fruition because the police illegally broke up a legal march across the 16th Street Bridge and began random arrests before any illegal sit down activity. But enough people were already on the streets to make the morning rush hour a disaster. Many government workers never made it and turned around (if they could) and went back home.

I was more than apprehensive at the prospect of facing arrest when I had one of my first encounters with police violence. I was maced directly in the face by a burly DC motorcycle cop wearing a menacing anonymous gas mask as I was walking peacefully on the sidewalk near DuPont

Circle. I experienced a terrible burning sensation and was temporarily all but completely blinded. Thank God that Naomi was nearby and led me to a fountain, where I tried to wash my burning face and eyes. By evening time my eyes were restored to normal, but it was a frightening experience.

The non-violent discipline of the young people had held up. In one case where a "renegade crew" (maybe police provocateurs) were running around flattening the car tires of government commuters, other young people were helping these people by pushing their cars to the side of the road and changing their tires. The day was a huge success for the non-violent movement and thousands of people were arrested. The city jails were so filled that the government had to use JFK Stadium to house the peace "criminals."

On May 2, our campaign continued with a sit-in of several thousand people outside of the Justice Department. We were coming to see the key role of this agency in trying to crush and discredit the peace and justice movement. The raids and unprovoked shootings of Black Panther leaders, the various conspiracy trials, the increase of surveillance and phone taps, and the growing White House list of opponents to the war were all being managed by the FBI and the ominous internal security division of this powerful arm of the government.

I remember sensing that the civil disobedience action was not well organized and urging Hosea Williams, one of the Black veterans of the civil rights movement, to motivate and direct the crowd made up mostly of young people. Hosea called on us in the fiery good old Church way to persevere and not to stand up or leave when the police moved in. I also remember looking up at the window and seeing some of the Justice Department honchos observing us, including none other than William Rehnquist, then deputy attorney general, later chief justice of the Supreme Court. They were not ignoring these days of action.

Finally, the police moved in and I was scared shitless as they began to handcuff us and lead (or carry some who refused to walk) us off to the waiting buses and we were transported to the already crowded JFK Stadium. There many of our friends and comrades greeted us with enthusiastic cheers and welcome. Also awaiting us were the delectable bologna sandwiches on white bread—the standard jail fare.

On the next day, May 3, there was a final event on the steps of the Capitol. A few anti-war members of Congress came out to address a crowd of several hundred people who were still "at large." When the rally finished and the crowd would not leave, the police moved in swiftly and carried people away, including some of the remaining PCPJ leadership.

Somewhere between seventeen and eighteen thousand peacemakers had been arrested over the course of the past four days, making this possibly the largest number of peace arrests in the history of Washington, DC. Some ingenious artist later designed a beautiful button for the JFK Stadium's temporary residents, saying: "I was a POW at Camp Nixon" against the background of a waving American flag. Our work was done for that week. Public opinion was shifting dramatically against the war and still the government continued its bloody campaign against the people of Southeast Asia.

In February of 1972, the Paris Peace Talks between the United States government and the Vietnamese had reached a new low. The international peace movement had been planning the Paris World Assembly to be held at Versailles (officially called the "World Assembly for Peace and Independence of the People of Indochina") for some time, but American participation looked like it would be small. That is until President Nixon's January 25 speech in which he pulled the rug from under any hopes of peace by adopting an even more bellicose stance towards the Vietnamese. The basic United States strategy was to bomb the Vietnamese into accepting their conditions at the conference table. The arrival of a third US aircraft carrier in the Gulf of Tonkin to reinforce the B-52 bombers already in the area was the United States' negotiating stance.

Nixon's cynical speech gave a vigorous shot in the arm to enrollment in the US delegation for the World Assembly. PCPJ asked me to attend, representing the Harrisburg Defense Committee, and become part of an impressive delegation. It included Al Hubbard, a black veteran from the Vietnam Veterans against the War, the Quaker Americans Friends Service Committee, the Southern Christian Leadership Conference from the Civil Rights Movement, labor unions and many others. The organizers seemed happy to have another religious delegate.

Ambassador William J. Porter, head of the United States delegation to the Paris peace talks, actually canceled the next meeting of the talks scheduled for February 17 on the grounds that our Versailles World Assembly conference was incompatible with the aims of the talks which were to reach a peaceful resolution of the Vietnam conflict.

It was hard to see how this peaceful, non-violent assembly of representatives from eighty countries and all five continents would or could impede the sincere work for peace. The presence of the Vietnamese representatives from the National Liberation Front from the South and the government in the North gave a quality of realism to the assembly, especially as they reported on the destruction of their countries and the suffering and losses of their people. There were also representatives from Laos and Cambodia who reported on those "hidden wars" affecting devastation in their countries.

For me, it was moving and exciting as well as a completely new experience to be in the midst of such a rich gathering of humanity from all over the world, all focused on the tragic plight of this tiny country in distant Southeast Asia that had become the latest political and military obsession of the giant from the North. In fact, next to the Vietnamese, it was the US delegation that received the most enthusiastic attention and applause. Our group of twenty or so began to appreciate the international perception of that subtle and yet profound distinction between the US government and the American people as never before. I was also elected to the steering committee to deal with the political and logistic decisions of the conference.

In this—for me—mysterious new world, there were many subcommissions working on different issues, drawing up position papers, and many meetings with the representatives of other countries, especially with the Vietnamese and other Indochinese delegates. It was surprising to discover that some of these veteran jungle revolutionaries were actually very gentle and even fun-loving people. I discovered and grew to love the soft-spoken, friendly and yet very determined Vietnamese. I wrote home that "the Indochinese were like a great breath of fresh air and a real incentive to keep struggling."

These meetings were reported in great detail in my illustrious FBI files, so there was an ever-present government informer in our midst.

On the next day Ambassador Porter continued to make disparaging statements about the assembly. He called us a "Communist claque" and termed us "agitators" and "scum." Actually, our very broad and diverse group represented many different cultures and political views as well as a variety of professional, trade, social and religious sectors. In response to this diatribe, the American delegation decided to issue its own statement at the end of the conference. The delegation chose actress Jane Fonda and me to read the final statement to the full assembly and to the news media. I guessed that I was the closest thing to a "respectable mainstream person" that they could come up with. My heart was beating like a trip hammer as I made my first foray into the public arena.

Some of the main points of our statement were:

- Each time the American ambassador has suspended the talks, this suspension has been a prelude to an escalation in the air war, sometimes called the third Indochina war.

- The tone of Mr. Porter's remarks shows a complete contempt for the serious purpose of these peace negotiations.

- The American delegation feels a great sense of shame at this travesty of statesmanship in the presence of distinguished representatives who have come together from around the world to work conscientiously to bring peace to the people of Indochina.

- We feel that these words are aimed at the growing American antiwar movement, because he knows that the Nixon government does not represent the American people in Paris and we do.

The Porter tirade had stimulated tremendous press interest in our statement and the story was carried internationally. Even my Israeli relatives sent a clipping of a photograph with Jane Fonda and a story in Hebrew.

On the last night, the People's Revolutionary Government Information Center hosted a party for the delegates to celebrate the Tet New Year with an abundance of delicious Vietnamese food, drink and music. It was a great farewell.

On the next morning, still exhausted, I was off to a six-day whirlwind speaking tour on behalf of the Harrisburg case to Germany, Holland and Austria. A new international phase of my work as a peace pilgrim was opening up, and I found that people all over the world wanted to hear about the struggle for peace right in "the belly of the beast."

We received a remarkable telegram just as the World Assembly ended:

"What can we say? In this war all is so clear. I can only say to those for Vietnam in America and elsewhere: I was always with them and I will always be with them."—Pablo Picasso

CHAPTER 17

Under the Bombs in Vietnam

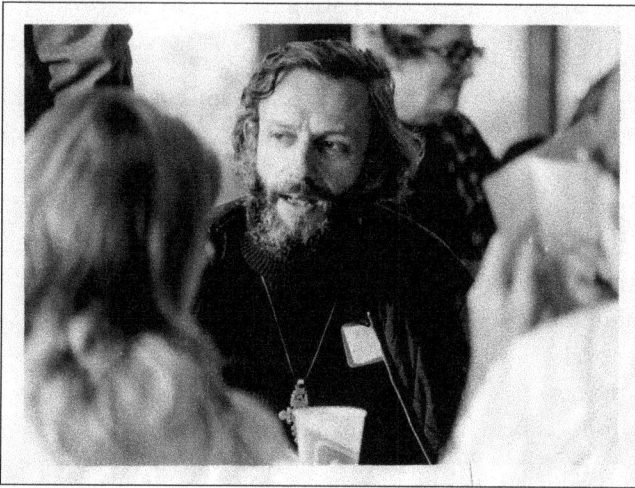

IN LATE APRIL OF 1972 I received an unexpected call from Cora Weiss, a doyenne of sorts of the American peace movement, extending me an invitation from the North Vietnamese government to join a small PCPJ (People's Coalition for Peace & Justice) delegation to visit North Vietnam in late May. I was overwhelmed by mixed feelings. I felt a sense of honor in being invited to visit these courageous people in their own homeland—the object of my daily work and struggle—up close. I was also a little frightened at the prospect of suddenly being in the middle of a bloody war zone. The invitation, Cora told me, was the North Vietnamese response to the April 20th resumption of the Nixon-Kissinger strategy of bombing the cities and mining the harbor of Haiphong.

This was a shocking development for the North Vietnamese and they were concerned with good reason. Daniel Ellsberg, who released the secret Pentagon Papers to *The New York Times*, reported possible plans to bomb the country's dikes, which would cause the flooding of the rice fields and possible extensive famine, or even the possibility of using nuclear weapons.

With good reason the North Vietnamese government called on its "American friends," as they liked to call us, to step up peace movement activities. It was a humbling responsibility because, after all, our movement was so inadequate, our commitment, courage and generosity were so weak in comparison with the extraordinary endurance and perseverance of the people of Indochina.

The Vietnamese devised a strategy of three delegations at two-week intervals beginning in early May. The first was Ramsey Clark, former US attorney general under President Johnson and a prestigious lawyer and an outspoken social critic. The final delegation, in early June, included Jane Fonda. And our PCPJ, four-person delegation would be the middle one during the last week of May.

The Vietnamese wanted Americans to hear firsthand reports of the civilian toll that the Nixon bombing campaign was exacting from the flesh of the Vietnamese people, since they didn't have much confidence in the US news media and with good reason. The main direct news reports from the North came from the Agence France-Presse, a first-rate, highly respected news agency, which was rarely quoted in our free and open society. Anthony Lewis of *The New York Times* was the only American journalist we met in North Vietnam and I was surprised to see him there.

We were a fairly solid group:

- Dr. Bill Zimmerman, a psychologist and former University of Chicago professor, representing the Medical Aid for Indochina Committee, an articulate and gifted intellectual.

- Margery Tabankin, president of the National Student Association, a very significant student leader, a dynamic and powerful woman and since then a very effective organizer in the Hollywood and philanthropic community and beyond.

- Rev. Robert Lecky, editor of *American Report*, the publication of Clergy and Laity Concerned about Vietnam, a slightly built Australian clergyman with a deep religious commitment to social issues.

↝ And myself, at that time an adjunct faculty member of New York Theological Seminary.

On the day before my departure, there was a loud knocking at our East Orange front and back doors simultaneously. It was the IRS turning on the heat because of our refusal to pay the three percent telephone excise tax, directed to specifically military expenditures by President Johnson. I whispered to my little family to lie on the floor and be very quiet and maybe these "bad guys" will go away, and after a while they did.

Then, after hurriedly packing, I embraced Naomi, Peter and Maria as I set off on this possibly dangerous journey. Peter, my three-year old, asked, "Dad, are you really taking me to Vietnam in your heart?" I choked up a little, said "Yes," and kissed everybody once more with a final "good-bye" and then I was out the door.

Our plans were to travel to Paris, then to Laos and Cambodia and finally to Hanoi via a Soviet Aeroflot flight. Our first stop in Indochina was Vientiane, the capital city of Laos. It looked like a peaceful small town to me and I took pleasure in strolling around the market square. The colorful vegetable stalls and the friendly rural farmers richly symbolized the spirit of the country. I wanted to try all the gorgeous produce but satisfied myself with a few beautiful souvenirs of Laotian weaving art.

We visited the DRV (Democratic Republic of Vietnam) Embassy and were welcomed by Pham Tam, the first secretary. He reported that Hanoi was bombed yesterday, but all was tranquil and optimistic. We went through the formality of obtaining a visa to North Vietnam without being asked for our US passports.

Early the next morning we boarded a Soviet Aeroflot airliner and, after a short rocky flight, landed in Hanoi, the ancient capital city of North Vietnam. Here Mr. Tram Minh Quoc, one of our chief guides and interpreters, welcomed us with warm handshakes. Then, along with our baggage, we seemed to be quickly brought to our awaiting car, an old Czech model.

Suddenly, without any explanation, our driver did a rather good imitation of a New York taxi driver high on something and hurtled through what seemed to be broad, elegant city avenues at literally breakneck speed. It took us a few minutes to figure out that we were about to be welcomed to Hanoi by our first air raid, compliments of Uncle Sam. Our loyal chauffeur, who we were going to befriend during the next few days, was merely trying to get us to our hotel without getting us killed.

As soon as we arrived at the hotel, a venerable and slightly worn building from colonial times, we were rushed into a subterranean air raid shelter. A number of people were already there, regarding this as part of a normal way of life. There was a young woman there, who was the hotel barmaid also served as a nurse taking care of sick people in the shelter.

Before the day was over there was another air raid. Then we gathered in the dining room for a pleasant dinner. Much to my embarrassment I had to request a fork because I had never mastered the use of chopsticks. Before the trip was over I had developed a new culinary skill, which I shared with my children upon my return.

We had lunch with Tony Lewis of *The New York Times* who told us that he was planning to stay another week. He reported that, in spite of the intensive bombing, he was impressed at "the amazing spirit of the people." Lunch was then interrupted by another air raid. In the shelter we met Joel Henri of *Le Monde* and he believed that "anyone who thinks that the Vietnamese will leave their position on South Vietnam is mistaken."

In the afternoon we were briefed by Mr. Tram Trong Quat, who was a colonel in the DRV army and our principle host. He was an older man, formal but friendly. His placid face was lined by suffering from the hard things he had seen and perhaps had to do. He laid out a rough itinerary and explained the emphasis on our security because of the constant bombing danger, which was also one of the reasons for the relative brevity of our stay. Ironically, in the midst of our meeting, we were interrupted no less than three times by our fellow Americans (it was still hard for the imagination to grasp) dropping their lethal baggage on the countryside and on us (patriotic Americans, as we thought ourselves to be).

Once again we were hustled into an air raid shelter, very crowded due to the nearby housing complex. Bill confided to me that he hoped that our hosts would introduce us to the crowd as Russian visitors, rather than as fellow countrymen and women of the bombers. But no, with full integrity we were introduced as honored American guests, whereupon an elderly gentleman stood up to welcome us with a large venerable smile. Even as he spoke, the shelter shook with the bombs and dust was falling from the ceiling. He said that he and his people were honored to have us here and that they clearly understood the distinction between the American government and the American people. He further praised our bravery—now we were really embarrassed—for struggling for peace right under the oppression of the Nixon government in the belly of the beast.

That night we drove to Haiphong, Vietnam's major port city. We did most of our traveling at night for fear of being detected by our bombers. We arrived in Haiphong, late at night, a city of bombed-out buildings. On Tuesday morning we were awakened at five in the morning for a hasty breakfast and then a meeting with Mr. Thieu and two other officials from the Foreign Relations section of the Haiphong municipal government, who were to be our guides to Phuc Loc.

We were taken to the village of Phuc Loc, about seven miles outside of Haiphong. What we were about to see must be prefaced by the claims of the Pentagon that through the use of "sophisticated" laser-guided bombs and missiles, the United States Air Force had an accuracy of within six feet of its target. If this was so, what we were about to see was evidence that the United State was intentionally bombing civilian targets in large numbers in North Vietnam.

The agricultural village of Phuc Loc was carpet bombed by B-52s at 2:30 a.m. on April 16, 1972. The results of the raid: sixty-three dead, sixty-one seriously injured, one hundred slightly injured. The dead include twenty-six women, sixteen old people and ten infants. We inspected many of the 142 bomb craters in the half square mile village. Among the peasants we interviewed, there was Mr. Thuc (aged seventy), who had lost ten members of his family, nine of them dismembered beyond recognition, and Tran Van Khoang, a thin fifteen-year old boy, who had lost eight family members, including his two parents, two grandmothers, an aunt, and three brothers. He told us his story as we sat together in an air raid shelter. The observation of this widespread civilian damage was further confirmed by conversations in Hanoi with foreign journalists and diplomats who had visited regions other than those that we were to visit.

There had been thirty bombing sorties that day. Often they were surprise attacks because the planes flew out of the sun to confuse the gunners. The area of Thuong Ly near a bridge we crossed the previous night had been hit, with two injured. Cong My village had been struck and we saw the flames of burning houses. The planes also fired rockets into the Ming Hai state farm. The Vietnamese had no official figures yet but they estimated eight American planes had been shot down over the three major cities. None of this was a source of joy but one does get a sense of the cost of the war to our own people.

During these days, we witnessed hour by hour the crucifixion of the Vietnamese people. Our rigorous discipline of little sleep, early awakening, late returning and constant travel, sometimes along rough roads, was such that we did not have the luxury of time to grieve, time to weep nor even time to reflect and pray as one would have liked to. Strong feelings of grief and compassion were our constant companions. Perhaps we were sharing deeply the experience of the people of Vietnam themselves who manifested such incredible courage, even optimism, and tried to live a normal life in the midst of the intensity of bombing, suffering and loss.

We now returned to the residential districts of Haiphong city itself, many of which were extensively damaged and destroyed. Most of them were more than a mile from the harbor, the only conceivable "military target" in sight. We saw a housing project and an adjacent senior high school that had been almost leveled. Before the inspection ended, the air raid sirens sounded and we were driven at high speed through the city streets back to our quarters in an effort to beat the US bombers. As we entered the air raid shelters, the phantom jets could be seen in the clear, blue sky dive-bombing into the already battered city.

In an act of bravery, Bill and Marj, wearing the incongruous helmets supplied by our protectors, ran out of the shelter across an open field to get clear camera shots of the dive-bombing. Our hosts were a little nervous about these "crazy Americans," but such was the dedication of those people to get the most accurate footage of the Vietnamese reality.

The suffering of frail ten-year-old Wa Ti Tong was a bitter commentary on the Vietnamese experience. He was wounded in a 2 a.m. bombing of the Cho Li quarter of Haiphong on April 16, 1972, a month before our visit. He was wounded again at 10 a.m. of the same day as he lay on the operating table of the Vietnam-Czechoslovakia Friendship Hospital, whose surgical ward and operating room were hit by many bombs and rocket fragments. Wa Ti's spirits were remarkably good as we visited him in another ward of the still partially demolished hospital. The sweetness of the beautiful children of Vietnam was a tragic and wonderful part of our pilgrimage.

Each day the front pages of the American press repeated with a kind of evangelical certainty the government's claims that their bombing targets in North Vietnam have been "railroad bridges, fuel dumps, trucks and SAM missile sites." This may indeed have been the primary intent of the Pentagon but does not square with the numerous destroyed civilian targets we saw, often not in the vicinity of any of the above mentioned. These assurances by our military would ring familiar decades later when we received similar pronouncements about the accuracy of the drone bombers in Afghanistan and Pakistan, often followed by similar heartbreaking reports about civilian casualties. Needless to say, the Defense Department vigorously denied the findings of our delegation, as if our one-week investigation was the chimera of a deluded imagination.

We left Haiphong after a banquet and warm farewells from our hosts there and marveled that they could organize such hospitality even amidst extreme social disruption. Now we set out for a bumpy night ride to Nam Din, Vietnam's third-largest city. We traveled via three ferries, presumably because the bridges had been bombed.

As we arrived at a handsome country villa, we heard that Nam Din was bombed—as was Haiphong during our stay (three alarms and one close shave). In fact, the house in which we were sleeping was hit and there was no water or electricity. We were admonished by our new hosts not to walk around the building for fear of unexploded anti-personnel ordinance. Then we retired by candlelight after a welcome by the local leaders who appeared quite nervous about our safety. Paranoia might have led us to suspect that "our boys" were dogging our steps—but that would have overstated our importance. We were told to be up the next day for a 6 a.m. departure.

We were the first foreigners, including journalists, to receive permission to visit Nam Din, the capital of the Non Ha province, since the recent increased bombings. Hang Sat Street was a heavily populated workers' residential area in this textile-producing city. This area was hit by anti-personnel bombs on May 23, 1972 (the day of our visit) at midnight and several blocks of houses were destroyed and many persons were killed. On the same day large areas of the city were bombed and strafed by several groups of planes. The damage included a high school, kindergarten, social club, the Von Cung pagoda, a textile mill and many other street quarters. We saw the fragments of US bombs being taken out of a destroyed church.

Our request for a meeting with American POWs was granted and we were scheduled to meet that day with eight captured US pilots. They were all mid- to high-level officers of the Navy, Air Force and Marine Corps captured between 1968 and 1972. This was to be, for me, one of the most painful of our encounters in Vietnam. It was not a matter of sitting in judgment of them. I would leave that to higher authority. Our meeting was certainly colored by some mixed feelings about their lack of freedom, including their lack of freedom to speak freely. I had fought against the idea of prisons and incarceration much of my life. Would it not have been possible to put them to work rebuilding Vietnam, sharing the very same lifestyle of the average peasant under this state of total war? Yet these were the outwardly attractive American young men who shared some major responsibility for this vicious and immoral attack against the infrastructure and civilian population of Vietnam, which we had witnessed during the previous days.

I was asked to chair the meeting and began by presenting the pilots with some basic questions we had prepared. We met in a formal meeting room, tea was served to all and the eight men entered and we shook hands.

They were typically fairly young and good looking, probably the cream of American manhood, our officers' corps. Perhaps they were a little pale but otherwise did not appear too much the worse for wear physically. Ho Chi Minh, the great leader of Vietnam, supposedly had the good sense to stop all torture and gross mistreatment in 1968, which of course should never have been used in the first place. He decided that it was not a good idea. The Vietnamese did acknowledge that there were incidents of beatings by local people when a shot-down pilot landed near the village he had been bombing. Before beginning the questions, I gave them a brief resumé of the suffering and the pilots' destruction we had witnessed in the past days. I invited them to introduce themselves and give their date of capture and hometown.

Then I inquired about their health and well-being and suggested that this had some of the elements of a pastoral visit as far as I was concerned. The pilots said that they were receiving adequate food, housing, medical care and recreational facilities. In response to our questions, they expressed strong dissent from President Nixon's recent decision to mine the harbors and increase the bombing. The bombing put them in danger (they probably were housed in the famous "Hanoi Hilton" prison in the city) and put off the day of their release. They expressed skepticism about whether Nixon has been honest with the American people and called on all Americans inside and outside the peace movement to end the war by all means, including election. Finally, the pilots handed us an anti-war statement they had written, addressed to Congress and the American people.

In the discussion the pilots, like average Americans, had a typically broad range of opinions as well as probably the same apathy. I was struck again by their ordinariness—they are not monsters—and could not help thinking about Hannah Arendt's words (reflecting on Adolf Eichmann) about "the banality of evil." I regret not ending the visit with a prayer, even though our delegation was not a religious one.

About a year later in February 1973, when the prisoners were freed, all but two retracted their statement and claimed that it was coerced. They were probably looking out for their careers, which was, after all, the highest spiritual value in American society. The two highest-ranking officers stuck to their statement: Commander US Navy David Hoffman and Lt. Col. Marine Corps Edison W. Miller. Ed Miller even began to quietly support peace activities in California.

Le Duc Tho reminded the Paris peace talks of Kissinger's cynical statement concerning the POWs: "Don't think that we will withdraw our troops just for some POWs." The cynical use of this issue continues even up to today, as if the Vietnamese were still withholding prisoners of those missing in action even after the resumption of diplomatic relations.

In July of 1972, right-wing Senator Hugh Scott (R-PA) tried to muddy the water by claiming that the Vietnamese never released all the French POWs. At that time the first secretary of the French Embassy unequivocally declared that all prisoners from the French war in Indochina had been returned less than three months after the conclusion of the Geneva agreement.

We were invited to participate in a radio interview with Radio Hanoi, which would be carried throughout Vietnam but might be transmitted to the United States troops in the South. Our interview basically described what we had seen, our feeling about it, the courage and determination of the Vietnamese people and an admonition to US troops not to engage in atrocities of any kind. There was no great outcry from our government concerning "treason." When Jane Fonda recorded a very similar interview two weeks later, the government and the (right-wing) media unleashed the wrath of God against her. They defamed her as "Hanoi Jane" and called her a traitor.

On the last day our delegation met with Vice Premier Nguyen Duy Trinh, a quiet, intelligent but relatively unimposing political leader, and shared some questions and concerns of the American public. He told us again that the mining and bombing were signs of weakness and would in no way undermine the determination of "the Vietnamese people who, united as one man, are ready to face sacrifice and hardships," that the seven-point Paris peace plan of the PRG was "just and fair," but he also expressed the readiness of his side to participate in substantive discussions.

Mr. Quat, the Army colonel, told us that he was going back to his home village for five days "to reconnect with his roots." Bill asked him how a colonel could take off that much time in the midst of this intensive war. The colonel replied, "We have been at war for thirty years and may be at war for another thirty years. We have to take care of ourselves." It seemed like sage advice for many a burned-out American peace activist.

We said our heartfelt farewells to our hosts that we had grown so close to. We had been bombed seventeen times and had survived. We wished the same protection for our friends and for all Vietnamese.

We had documented our journey in depth by footage of the destruction as well as interviews of victims, officials and POWs. It was the first time that an American group had been allowed to take color film without having it developed prior to leaving the country.

One of our members had a connection with Palmer Williams, a producer of CBS's 60 *Minutes*. (He recently played a minor role in *Good Night and Good Luck*, the brilliant docudrama on Edward R. Murrow.) Williams offered to look at our film and was particularly interested in what proved to be one of the first interviews of American POWs. Our peace pilgrimage ended up being a rather good nine-minute segment on 60 *Minutes*, hosted by Mike Wallace. Their payment for our footage was enough to fully cover the expenses of our trip.

After our press release, I received a call from the Associated Press. Would I come in to talk about our trip? They immediately brought me in to be interviewed by a fairly high-level editor. I remember a tough New York Irishman who debriefed me in such hostile detail that I felt sure that I was being interviewed for, if not by, the CIA. (AP had a rather conservative, pro-war stance at the time), but I figured that the government might as well know the true situation. The interview did finally result in a less than enthusiastic AP national story.

We all carried our Vietnam experience home with heavy hearts. I can still remember the details of the final briefing on how the United States was bombing the same targets in consecutive raids, how one sixth of Haiphong was already destroyed and how Hanoi would be destroyed within the next few days.

All of these possible threats, as well as the recent news of bombings of the dikes and greater repression, imprisonments and assassinations under the Thieu regime in the South, continued to up the political ante. I felt that these new developments and what I had seen and experienced in Vietnam called for a more serious response.

I unexpectedly came up with the idea of an open-ended fast for life. I wanted to reach back to that ancient biblical tradition when the people began to fast as a sign of repentance and purification, just as Jesus had fasted for forty days and forty nights before he began his public ministry. Mahatma Gandhi had also used the fast during moments of political turmoil and violence. His spiritual influence was so powerful that often the people repented from negative activity such as the Hindu-Muslim riots just to get him to stop fasting.

I began to share this idea with some of my peace comrades and gradually a community of fourteen generous and hardy folks began to form. Some of us were peace veterans like Dave Dellinger, Ted Glick and Anne Walsh, a campus minister from Boston University, and Father Tom Lumpkin, a tax resister from Detroit. All the rest were young people in their early twenties.

We decided to have a retreat together at the Paulist Novitiate in Oak Ridge, New Jersey. In the meantime, Dick Gregory, the charismatic African-American comedian and radical activist, had heard of our plans and was very excited about our project. He was a veteran faster and had profound religious faith in the power of the fast. He literally believed that a group of dedicated fasters like us could end the war in Vietnam, so much so that he offered to fly in Dr. Alvena Fulton, his personal fast physician and one of the leading experts in the field, to come to our retreat in order to brief us on the secrets of the long fast.

Dr. Fulton, an African American woman, went to great pains to instruct us on how to last as long as possible. These secrets consisted of careful preparation by a juice fast and colonic flush leading up to the real fast and then daily enemas and Epsom salt baths to detoxify the body and the consumption of at least a gallon of water a day. Not all of us would follow these prescriptions but all would drink a lot of water.

We had decided after prayer and dialogue to choose a water-only fast. Furthermore, it would be an open-ended fast without any time limits. If we reached a life-threatening point, we would reevaluate. This decision made many of our families and friends uneasy and some tried to dissuade us. But we had put our cause in God's hands, most of us were religious or spiritual people, and we would trust for a good outcome on behalf of the suffering people of Vietnam. Also we were a strong-willed bunch, including yours truly.

We drew up a one-page statement and put forward the seemingly impossible demands that would end our fast and, hopefully, end the war:

1. An end to all US bombing and shelling of Vietnam, Laos and Cambodia.

2. A firm date for complete withdrawal of all American military personnel from Indochina.

3. An end to all military and financial aid to the Thieu regime of South Vietnam.

Our statement emphasized:

The aims of our fast are concrete and political. We believe this is in the tradition of the Hebrew prophets, Jesus and Gandhi and others who fasted in times of national calamity similar in nature to our own. As fasters, we have no power beyond the power of those who agree with our basic demands and dedicate themselves to seeing that those demands are met.

Our fast is not a gesture of despair but rather an act of hope and faith in the basic decency of the American people.

On August 6, 1972, the fourteen of us gathered at New York Theological Seminary where I was teaching at the time. Through the good offices of President Bill Webber, the seminary had agreed to house our fasting community for the duration. August 6th was made sacred as the anniversary of the atomic bombing of Hiroshima, and we called on those hundreds of thousands of innocent souls to stand at our side. For Christians it is also the feast of the Transfiguration on Mount Tabor, when the Spirit that possessed Jesus became visible to others. We released our statement and set off on our journey of faith.

In the meantime, we had heard that a group of prisoners at Danbury Prison—mainly conscientious objectors and draft resisters—were planning to join us in our fast. Each day our group of fasters met to check in with each other, share a meditation and make sure that we got our gallon of water for the day. The seminary was on East 49th Street, not far from the United Nations. Dick Gregory had stressed the value of the fasters lying on the earth and absorbing that healing energy. We played a little cat-and-mouse game with the UN security guards. Each day some of us would sneak on to one of the spacious lawns and lie on the soft green of Mother Earth until we were discovered and escorted off the premises.

As the filia, the little hairs in the digestive tract, shut down, one's desire for food disappears. So after a week or so there was no great temptation when passing the lovely New York restaurants of Second and Third avenues. On the physical plane, one of the greatest challenges was to actually consume our daily gallon of water, no easy task. Even as I got weaker, my daily meditation became clearer and my yoga practice more flexible and intense.

But our task was not only on the physical realm. We let it be known that we would remain politically active and available for speaking engagements. So we were busy meeting with groups, writing letters and articles and involving ourselves in peace demonstrations and actions when possible. Rabbi David Saperstein, now one of the nation's leading rabbis in the Reform tradition, at that time ministered to a congregation on the East Side. He invited me in to talk about the ways his flock could get involved and hopefully inspire them and, indeed, they were receptive.

As the hot New York summer dragged on, it was taking its toll on our community. The heat seemed to have little impact on me, since as the fast went on, I felt chilly even in August. At night I would sleep under five blankets to keep warm.

One of our most dramatic moments was our decision to participate in the Republican convention in Miami, Florida. Traveling was hard but we were a determined crew. We organized a dramatic street theater event outside of the Miami Offices of the Committee to Reelect Nixon. One of our number organized a service in which we fasters stood outside together holding begging bowls, symbolizing the growing famine of the Indochinese people caused by the war. We also met with news people including Anthony Lewis, our Hanoi acquaintance, who wrote a good column in *The New York Times*.

The highlight of our stay was our participation in a mass march against the convention. It was a large, dramatic march of thousands down the main avenue in Miami leading to the convention center. The demonstration had attracted even more marchers than expected because of the growing opposition to the war and the outrage at the Nixon administration. The Miami police were brutal in breaking up our peaceful, legal march. We were all tear-gassed and it was especially hard to inhale the acrid fumes while fasting and several of us even ended up spending the night in the Dade County jail. Somehow we survived it all, in spite of our weakened condition.

When we returned to New York, we could begin to see the toll of the fast one another. We were losing about a pound a day so by mid-August our weight was dropping, especially for some like myself who were thin to begin with. My poor parents did not even want to visit me. "Too many remembrances of Dachau," my mother said. Naomi also found it difficult.

In the meantime, our numbers were falling. Dave Dellinger had to leave to join a delegation to Vietnam. He tried to continue the fast on his flight but it was too difficult. Others simply got too weak or became discouraged. As we got thinner, we kept vigil outside of St. Patrick's Cathedral to pray and dramatize the ever-escalating war before the passive, if not complicit, religious authorities of the archdiocese.

Many well-meaning comrades from the peace movement discreetly tried to discourage us. We had not calculated that we would make some friends feel guilty (on our behalf) for not stopping the war. A wonderful physician and peace activist came in to examine us every day. We were getting weaker, with our group now down to five members. But we remained spiritually strong and persevering.

Finally, Father Tom Lumpkin, a diocesan priest from Detroit, just eight years ordained and a deep, prayerful man, was beginning to falter and show symptoms of chronic weakness. He was already of slight build and his face was taking on a skull-like appearance. Tom's breathing was labored and our doctor was worried about his heartbeat. He was a man of great faith and commitment, and we knew that he would not end his fast voluntarily. So the remaining fasters conferred together and decided in a spirit of prayer and solidarity that Tom would only stop his fast if we all stopped together.

So on the symbolically powerful fortieth day we ended our fast for life. I had lost forty pounds and now weighed exactly ninety-seven pounds. My appearance was haggard, but my spirits were good. I was physically weak and was not able to participate in longer future fasts. But I had survived and would be back in shape after a little rest and relaxation. We broke our fast with some vegetable soup, as suggested by Dr. Fulton.

A few days later Naomi, Peter, Maria and I had a wonderful picnic in a little park in Teaneck, New Jersey. I had just visited my primary healer, the great chiropractor and all around genius Dr. Angelo Rose. He found me in perfect shape, if a little ragged around the edges. In quiet gratitude I ate a delicious raw vegetable salad that Naomi had prepared—my first solid meal.

We felt that we had achieved something. Only God knew the spiritual and political impact of our sacrifice.

Some time after the war I met Dick Gregory at a conference. He descended upon me with his beautiful African face beaming. He was so excited and said, "Hey, man, I told you that you guys would do it." He was firmly convinced that it was our fast that had ended the war. We pray that it made a difference.

CHAPTER 18

USSR: A Peace Journey with Grace Paley

Meetings with Dr. Andrei Sakharov and the Dissenters

The National Alliance against Racial & Political Repression, a predominantly Black- and Communist-affiliated coalition, appreciated my work in the campaign to free Angela Davis and my writing the Amnesty International report that helped free the Rev. Ben Chavis & the Wilmington ten from prison. It was through this connection that I was invited to serve as co-chairperson of the US delegation to the Moscow World Peace Congress in October of 1973. When I accepted this invitation, I did not realize that it would lead to one of the more dramatic experiences of my life.

The Moscow Peace Congress was to be a gathering of thousands of peace activists from all over the world at a time when the Vietnam War was at its height. Ultimately we felt that, in spite of differences with some of the Communist participants, we still shared a commitment to the many great efforts for world peace.

In April of 1973, I traveled to Moscow as part of the preparatory committee to plan for the World Congress later in October. Before, in New York, I had been approached by a young man who was deeply devoted to bringing to light the political persecution and imprisonment, professional ostracism, social silencing and sometimes execution being experienced by political dissenters in the Soviet Union. He provided me with irrefutable documentation and contacts in Moscow and prevailed on me to get firsthand information about the situation and possibly meet with some of those most affected.

So instead of a placid tourist sojourn, my conscience obliged me to find time during our busy (at times boring) deliberations to seek out some of these recipients of "special attention" from the Soviet government. It was not easy, since I had the impression that, while we were warmly welcomed by our Russian hosts, our movements were also being carefully monitored. I had been briefed on how to use pay phones and anonymous taxies (rather that the official ones at the hotel) and not to have sensitive discussions in our rooms, which were probably bugged.

I decided to begin by visiting Alexander Galich and Vladimir Maximov, two of the leading dissenters, at Galich's apartment. It quickly became clear to me that both the elderly woman in the babushka at the front door and the elevator operator were more than disinterested spectators or building employees. They were there to monitor the arrival and departure of guests. I was given more than a casual once-over.

Maximov, who had the blond, rugged appearance of a Russian peasant, had been a prominent novelist, author of *Seven Days of Creation*, at that time translated into German but not yet into English. He was a devout Russian Orthodox Christian and a political conservative. He spoke of a Russian spiritual reawakening going on and that tens of thousands of believers were worshiping in secret chapels. We hit it off personally but we were poles apart ideologically and probably theologically.

You can imagine that we did not see eye to eye on everything. On top of it all, it was Lent and Maximov was fasting and I, the former priest, was not. All of this led to fierce discussions, especially as I expressed my views on the state of the world. Yet I had compassion for his suffering and affectionate feelings for this man with whom I had such deep differences.

Alexander Galich was born a Jew (his family name was Ginsburg) and had recently converted to the Russian Orthodox Church. He felt strongly about his newfound faith although I noted, but did not belabor, the reactionary role that Russian Orthodoxy had played in the nation's history. Galich had been a popular film scriptwriter, playwright, actor, songwriter and balladeer. He had been expelled from the Writers and Cinematographers Union in 1971. His literary and artistic life had been reduced to communicating through the *samizdat*, the underground literary communications. His popular songs only existed on *magnitizdat*—copies of underground tapes—all forbidden by the government. He had, for all intents and purposes, become an artistic and cultural "non-person" with no outlet for any of his creative works and energy.

I had some strong political differences with Maximov and Galich since they automatically assumed that any positions espoused or supported by their government was more Communist propaganda, which was often the case. Unfortunately, these sometimes included issues that the Soviets were right on, such as the war in Indochina. And yet I was moved by their sincerity, their courage and willingness to suffer for their beliefs.

I was especially moved by Galich's difficult life and his health seemed frail as well. In a moment of inspiration, I took the beautiful, round, heavy Jesus medallion that Dan Berrigan had given me on the occasion of my son Peter's baptism, and which I really loved, off my neck. I was just beginning to give it to him as a gift when his warm and wonderful wife, Galina, came into the room. She had in her hand one of the most exquisite, large, bronze Byzantine crosses I had ever seen. The figure of Jesus was a most remarkable synthesis of love, surrender, suffering and transfiguration. She said that it had been in her family for centuries and she wanted me to have it. I was moved beyond words at the beauty and grace of the moment and I embraced them both amidst tears.

This was my first encounter with this community of suffering and contradictions. In the meantime, the planning process for the World Congress was in full swing. In my absence, I had been elected co-chair of the US delegation to the congress and I accepted the decision.

When we returned to New York I became involved in supporting the case of Martin Sostre, a Black Puerto Rican political prisoner. Marie Runyon, a spunky progressive member of the state assembly, asked me to join the defense committee. Martin had been a political activist in upstate Buffalo, New York, where he owned a small radical bookstore with the aim of conscientizing the largely Black and Latino youth of the Buffalo ghetto. There were good books, classes and discussion groups available for the young people and the store became an organizing center for the community.

The local police, who enjoyed a well-deserved reputation for right-wing politics and open racism, did not look kindly upon the idea of having the local youth awakened by the ideas of José Martí and Malcolm X. So in a classical maneuver of political subversion, they planted a large amount of heroin in Martin's store and arrested him under heavy drug charges of possession with intent to use and distribute.

I became involved in the New York City defense committee, a small committed group of people including Dan Berrigan, and took on the job of being its coordinator. Eventually, his case was adopted by Amnesty International and this helped our defense work.

I first met Martin in the old Tombs jail on West Street right next to the Hudson River. He was an imposing figure—tall, well-built, with dark skin, intense brown eyes and a shaven head not yet fashionable at the time. He was a compelling combination of streetwise toughness with a spiritual core.

Martin had been convicted—it's hard to defend oneself against a police frame-up—and was awaiting transportation to the upstate gulags which constitute the New York State prison system. They are known, first of all, for their extreme remoteness and for the practically all-white prison guards (poetically named correction officers), many of whom were notorious for their violence and racism. More than a few actually belonged to the Ku Klux Klan and other openly racist organizations.

During his time in the prison system, Martin became a thorn in the sides of the authorities in his own quiet way. First of all, he was an irrepressible organizer, helping other prisoners with their legal cases. In addition, Martin refused to submit to the humiliating strip and rectal searches that some of the guards delighted in. As a result, he spent years in solitary confinement as his captors waited for his reform. (The use of extended solitary torture has increasingly become a tool of the prison system.) In the process, he became a devoted disciple of the spiritual life, read voraciously and used the solitude and isolation to become a deep practitioner of yoga and meditation. We would spend a good part of our visits sharing our experiences of yoga and the spiritual life. My later participation in the Moscow World Peace Congress would have a mysterious and unexpected impact on his life.

In October of 1973 I returned to Moscow as part of the US delegation for the Peace Congress itself. One of my closest companions on this journey was my already longtime dear friend, the acclaimed writer Grace Paley, who we tragically lost in August 2007 after a long battle with cancer. She attended representing the War Resisters League along with Maris Cakars, another old comrade, now also departed. Grace was not only one of our contemporary literary treasures with the perfect blend of New York Jewish ironic humor and loving compassion for suffering humanity but was also someone with a serious political commitment to a peaceful and just world.

Fate would make us co-conspirators in the drafting of a statement prior to our departure which would later send shock waves through the Moscow World Congress of Peace Forces. Grace and I had decided that the public release of a statement on the Soviet dissidents at the Peace Congress would be a clandestine priority of our visit. It was signed by a group of well-known peace activists: David McReynolds, Sidney Peck, Dave Dellinger, Noam Chomsky, Dan Berrigan, Grace Paley and myself. I was chosen to read the statement publicly in Moscow.

The signers were all American dissenters of US policies who were using the occasion of this conference to condemn the Soviet government for its harsh and unjust treatment of the political dissidents in their society. But we also called upon these same dissidents to speak out against the political murders of tens of thousands in Chile and against the cruel imprisonment of hundreds of thousands in the "tiger c ages" of South Vietnam.

Grace and I both felt that it would be appropriate to meet two of the dissenters and some of their friends and colleagues before we issued our statement criticizing them.

Once again we sought out one of the "independent" taxis. This time we were greeted at the Galich family table like old friends. They were happy to meet Grace and immediately accepted her. We were plied with apples, sardines, tomatoes, and good Georgian wine, all from their very meager store. Galina Galich shouted "hello's!" from the bedroom because she was not feeling well. Later we found out that Galich himself had heart problems.

He spoke to us about Maximov and his struggles. Then we gave him a copy of our statement. He liked the words of support and solidarity. He did not like some of the next paragraphs, which he considered an attack even though there was nothing untrue in the statement. How could they know the true situation in Chile? They couldn't tell when the Soviet press was writing the truth, since they were lied to most of the time.

Finally, he objected to Sakharov being the only one mentioned by name. Andrei Sakharov was the famous physicist who was known as the father of the Soviet hydrogen bomb, although he later became a strong opponent of nuclear war. Galich said, "But you see, it was not Sakharov alone. Maximov and I at least were involved. We issued the statement together—you must put down our names. Always because he's the famous one, he has to bear it all." We added both their names to our statement.

Grace wrote beautifully in an essay about our visits to the Galiches's home: "When we visited the second time, the house was so full of saucers and chairs and voices speaking and sighing in Russian that it was as though I was at home. Angelina [Galina] said it, in case I hadn't noticed. 'Here you and Paul are at home.'"

This time, besides the Galiches and Andrei and Yelena Sakharov, another physicist Alexander Voronel and his wife Nellie were also present. Voronel gave us a petition asking for the release of fourteen Jews who had been picked up during the World Congress. We took it back to the congress and gave a copy to the representative of Amnesty International. Happily, we were able to call our friends back a few days later with the news that the fourteen had been released.

Andrei Sakharov had a beautiful, placid, intelligent Russian face. He listened intently. His wife Yelena was Jewish, intense and anxious to communicate the seriousness of these situations to us. They all regarded him as a saint who could be peaceful in the midst of turmoil. He allowed himself, because of his international recognition, to serve as the foil for much of the governmental pressure and repression.

We passed around a *New York Times* article describing the training of 170 military officers by the US military in Latin America. They were interested and kept the clipping.

Yelena thought we were naive. "You can't really understand what is happening here. Besides, maybe the ones in Chile were killed because they didn't want to live under socialism." Grace was furious; she had recently spent two months in Chile and knew the price that was being paid after the bloody right-wing military coup and the assassination of their legitimate president Allende.

Galich, Sakharov and I were speaking in German. I told them about a leftist friend in America who said, "Why bother with ten to twenty thousand Russians imprisoned when there are two hundred thousand in Saigon? Forget the Russians." But I told them, "We can't think like that!" Sakharov sipped his tea from his saucer and continued to listen.

Before departing, we asked whether our making this statement would jeopardize the three referred to by name and their families. Sakharov assured us it would have no effect on him. In his own way he understood what we were trying to say.

After our departure, the pressure on our friends continued. Yelena Sakharov was called in several times by the KGB and her husband and family threatened. But this did not stop Andrei Sakharov from his courageous, independent thinking. (His analysis later influenced Gorbachev and the *perestroika* process.) After our encounter, he published a long essay called "Why I Dissent," which indicated that he took our visit and statement to heart and wrote quite openly about the influence of some recent Western visitors.

It also gave one pause about the presumptuousness of people like us who live in safe situations lecturing people living in jeopardy, but it seemed necessary. His essay was significant because in it he separated himself from right-wing demagogues, even including the brilliant Alexander Solzhenitsyn. He wrote: "A part of the Russian opposition intelligentsia is beginning to manifest a paradoxical closeness to the secret Party-State doctrine of nationalism." A longer excerpt indicated the difficult position of people such as Sakharov as well as his basic honesty and decency.

Back at the Rossiya Hotel and the great conference center where the Peace Congress was taking place, the time came for me to read our statement. Grace and I stood at the podium of the human rights commission, a large well-attended gathering as this issue is such a desperate one all around the world. It was the last day of the commission meetings. My heart was in my mouth since I knew that in a moment my image as a respected religious leader from the American peace movement was about to change. Our statement spoke of our concerns about the repression of dissenters by the Soviet government but then moved into a more nuanced position, also criticizing the silence of the dissenters on injustice and persecution elsewhere.

Our critique of Soviet policy towards free political dissent caused quite a stir. The chair of the commission hearing tried to gavel me into silence, claiming that my allotted five minutes were up, but I plodded ahead determinedly because many other presenters had exceeded their five minutes. At the end, I noted that most of our statement signers had themselves spent time in prison for political offenses and one of our members (Dave Dellinger) was presently under indictment. And so we had earned the right to be heard.

Many of the congress participants were, of course, uncritical supporters of the Soviet Union, if not members of Communist parties from around the world. One could not overlook the fact that small third world countries living under the heel of Uncle Sam must look for support where they can get it. Attacks of this kind would not be popular anywhere but especially not in the heart of the Soviet Empire.

The first to respond was a Russian official, who criticized our statement in a fairly restrained, objective tone. Then came an avalanche of condemnations from Americans, Asians, Africans and Europeans. An emergency meeting of the US Steering Committee was called that night in which I, who had served as co-chair of the American delegation, was called a liar, a deceiver and even by implication a CIA agent. We later found that there was a sizable minority that actually agreed with our statement and others who just didn't care.

The critical majority feared that our statement would be seen as coming from the whole delegation. I resigned from my leadership position in order to prevent further divisiveness. I might have been expelled anyway. I also didn't want to divert attention from the other important issues which the congress was addressing, such as the war in Vietnam, poverty and social injustice, especially in the developing countries in Latin America, Asia and Africa. There were, of course, many important discussions of serious human rights violations in other parts of the world, although not of those in Soviet Bloc countries such as Czechoslovakia, Hungary or Poland—never mind China's oppression of Tibet and silencing of dissidents.

The next day I was taken to lunch by a few members of the Russian leadership who did not seem to agree with some of the more extreme name calling by our delegation members. They wanted to reason with me and bring me around to a better understanding of their situation.

The day before our departure, at Grace's suggestion, we arranged a private meeting with Alexei Nicolaevitch Stepunin, secretary general of the Institute of Soviet-American Relations, in his bedroom suite. We went together with our courageous friend Maris, who had since been arrested once for handing out the *New York Times* ad in Russian in GUM, the Macy's-type department store of Moscow. Stepunin was tall with short gray hair and was good looking in a rough sort of way. He reminded Grace of an old cop who had seen everything.

He asked why we had to do this and cause such uproar. He was especially surprised at me. "Paul," he said, "you know we are not a democracy but a dictatorship of the proletariat. We have no choice but to follow the will of the proletariat. The proletariat doesn't want us to publish all these bourgeois poets—especially Solzhenitsyn."

Yes, we agreed with some of these ideas, and disagreed with others. But our main point was how could we honorably protest the treatment of political prisoners all over the world and not include the generals in insane asylums, the difficult poets, the unOrthodox Marxists and some of the troublesome religious leaders here who were being silenced and imprisoned?

After an intense discussion, our dear Grace—in keeping with her name—left them with the coup de grace. She suggested they should have confidence in their own strength—their society was strong enough to tolerate underground papers, free *samizdat* and a little free speech. Look at the US, she told him, where we can have a half million people in front of the White House screaming and chanting and government leaders ignore them and still do what they want. Alexei Nicolaevitch looked at her with genuine surprise and then gave her a big Russian laugh, "What will these Americanskis think of next?" Grace immediately added that, of course, none of this would stop us from opposing the evil human rights policies of our own government.

We survived all this acrimony and made sure to meet with our Vietnamese friends and also some Palestinian representatives so they could receive our statement firsthand and hear the explanation of our action. Of course we, and especially Grace, handed out our statement to all who were interested in seeing it—and there were many.

And so we left our newfound friends, beautiful Moscow and holy Mother Russia to return to our homeland. We arrived exhausted at JFK Airport at four in the morning, New York time, and hailed a cab. We engaged our driver in conversation and, much to our surprise, he was what Grace called "our final Russian." He was a bearded, Jewish refugee from the Ukraine who has been here for ten years. He eagerly asked us for any news: "How are things in Moscow? What is happening there?"

He was glad that he came over but still missed many things: free healthcare, education and social services. Life in New York was a constant struggle for survival, he said, but here he could shape his own life. Working as a cabbie was not easy but there was also a freedom he never had.

Grace wrote about this encounter with her own lovely insight (with excessive generosity towards yours truly): "We had come to West 11th Street, my destination, and I couldn't speak to him anymore. It seemed certain, however, that we had fallen into his cab for several reasons: the first is that Paul is a holy person, whose life deserves an occasional selective revelation. The second, because I'm a storyteller; therefore, He probably moved in this unmysterious way (as He has many times) to offer to the beginning and middle of my experience an appropriate and moral end."

The New York Times enthusiastically ran two consecutive stories headlined "Peace Activists Hear Attacks on Soviet Policies by US Delegates" and "US Delegates in Soviet Oust Leader Over Statement." It was never easy for the peace movement to get the "paper of record's" attention but this was their political cup of tea—trashing the Commies. Needless to say, there was no mention of our critique of the dissidents' reactionary political views. A corrective Letter to the Editor was accepted but their one-sided story was out there.

The next "attack" from the right was the news that William F. Buckley Jr., the arch-conservative pundit and editor of the *National Review,* had written a laudatory column about our Moscow statement and me in the *New York Post.* It ran: "I do not know the background of the Rev. Paul Mayer, but I rejoice in him. He is truly the man who remarked that the emperor had no clothes, and his fate threatens to be the fate of those who tell the truth in a truth-denying world. Imagine, in Moscow addressing a chamber full of delegates to a Communist enterprise—The World Peace Congress—and giving a speech in behalf of seven (out of 150) Americans [none of which were Mr. Buckley's favorite heroes] complaining of the absence of freedom in the Soviet Union! This Father Mayer did and he wasn't a CIA plant."

Mr. Buckley waxed even more enthusiastic, speaking of "the brave words of Father Mayer within the hornet's nest in Moscow." Again there was no mention of our critique of the dissidents. Not surprisingly there was instant outrage from my critics in Moscow, now transplanted to the pages of the *Daily World*, the New York-based Communist paper.

I immediately phoned Bill Buckley complaining that he had only reported half the story. He was most gracious and agreed to send a letter that I would write clarifying the record to the editors of every paper which syndicated his column. He was true to his word and my corrective letter was carried all over the country. In contrast to the "Tea Party" bullies, he was, perhaps, one of the last genteel conservatives.

The final drama of our adventure in Moscow took an unexpected form. Shortly after our return to New York, the case of our own US political prisoner, Martin Sostre, who was still suffering the indignities and oppression of the New York State prison system, came into public light again. Our defense committee had been working hard. Christmas was approaching and the governor could grant Christmas parole for a few prisoners, if he chose to. We had appealed his case to Governor Hugh Carey, a fairly decent politician by today's sad standards, who passed away in 2011 at the age of ninety.

At approximately the same time, our beloved Andrei Sakharov was awarded the Nobel Peace Prize. We decided to send him background information on the Sostre case with an appeal to support the parole. Much to our delight, we learned that on the basis of our friendship and of Amnesty International's adoption of Sostre, Sakharov had agreed to write an eloquent letter of appeal to Governor Carey seeking the Christmas parole of Sostre. *The New York Times* also carried an editorial supporting his parole.

To our further surprise and joy, on Christmas Day, Carey announced the parole of Martin Sostre. Thus was the mysterious circle from Moscow to the Green Haven, New York Prison closed, fulfilling these words of Jesus, the Liberator:

> Blessed are those who hunger and thirst for justice, for they shall
> not be sent away empty" (Mt. 5:6). Amen, amen!

CHAPTER 19

A Journey to the Bloody Land of Milk and Honey

Israel and Palestine; Meetings with Yasser Arafat and Israeli Peacemakers

On October 19, 1973, Daniel Berrigan delivered a speech on Israel and the Palestinians to the Association of Arab-American University Graduates meeting in Washington. The speech literally ignited a storm of protest, indignation and rage from the American Jewish community that would muddy the waters of this necessary debate as few incidents had before. He was called an anti-Semite, a traitor, one who lacked sensitivity for the suffering of the Holocaust and worse.

Speaking as a poet, Dan had described himself as ". . . a Catholic priest in resistance against Rome . . . an American in resistance against Nixon," and then went on to say symbolically, "And I am a Jew in resistance against Israel." In the midst of so many powerful truths enunciated, he also alluded to but perhaps did not sufficiently acknowledge the courage of the peace community in Israel, which was much larger then than today, nor did he acknowledge the importance and role of the Jewish community in the US peace movement. Dan was also unsparing in criticizing the Arab countries for their wealth, opportunistic oil politics, dishonesty and contempt for their own poor. But all of this was to no avail because they were not the beneficiaries of the American Israel Public Affairs Committee (AIPAC), perhaps one of the most powerful and influential lobbies in Washington, then and now.

I had no essential philosophical disagreement with his speech. My first reaction to Dan's speech was wishing he had shown it to me first. I'm no expert on Middle East politics, but there are certain things that my big Jewish nose would have sniffed out. Certainly the allusions to Dan's "Jewishness" might have been eliminated or at least downplayed and clarified. (I speculate that if he had identified himself as a Jew because of his support for Israel, there would have been no such outcry.) Also a few innuendoes should have been softened about Israel's similarities to Nazism, though he never used that word per se. One might not need to be as careful today as things have so deteriorated there.

In essence, I believe his speech was valid then and is even more applicable today. I didn't question Dan's sincerity or the accuracy of his points, but, unfortunately, it was and still is considered unacceptable for anyone outside the Jewish community to criticize Israel so harshly.

Even sharp critiques of Israeli/US policy by Jews such as Norman Finklestein draw angry reactions and the charge that the critic is a "self-hating Jew." Similar observations that I have made, albeit more tactfully, have never been received well by B'nai Brith and others who once honored me with the label "anti-Semite." Happily, rabbi friends have come to my defense.

My good Jewish parents—longtime Zionists and no intellectual slouches—were outraged at their beloved Daniel being called an anti-Semite. "That boy doesn't have an anti-Semitic bone in his body," my father commented, after the flurry of attacks and charges.

But Dan was devastated. The criticism came from all sides, even the liberal Rabbis Arthur Waskow, Arthur Hertzberg and Balfour Brickner. All could have made their necessary critiques—in my opinion—short of charges of or even allusions to anti-Semitism. Then there were the Christians, often clergy, who make a cult of doing the necessary work of repairing ancient Christian anti-Semitism, but in a misguided way, by uncritical support of the state of Israel. Their counterproductive efforts include free trips to "the Holy Land" on which few ever visit a Palestinian or Arab community. Dan appreciated my words of comfort and would later write the beautiful tribute to me: "Peacemaker, Jewish Catholic, priest, monk, friend."

He was even turned down for the Gandhi Peace Award. People returned their tickets for the award ceremony. It was a dark moment in the life of a good man who had a sensitive ego and had made some miscalculations.

Dan, in what I consider a brilliant move, decided to travel to the Middle East to experience the reality there for himself and get away from all that undeserved craziness and abuse. I was pleased and excited to accept his invitation to accompany him on what would be my first visit to the region. I had unconsciously avoided going there for years. I had been raised with a love for the land of my people (Could it belong to other people as well?), a land where much of the family I have left resides. Although I thought I knew that I would have to face many contradictions, I had no idea of the firestorm of conflicting feelings that awaited me.

What was the true nature of this Jewish state so idealized in my childhood? What of my own Jewish identity? And what of these other mysterious people—our mirror image—who also claim nationhood, ownership and sovereignty over the land which they also call sacred, yet has become such a locus of bitter hatred and bloodshed? This would be an important pilgrimage home and not-home for me. I longed to experience what it is that makes this the Holy Land, the earth that bears the roots of my spiritual heritage.

I met Dan in Paris where he had gone (fled) to get some distance, and seek some comfort with the great Vietnamese monk, meditation teacher, poet and peacemaker Thich Nhat Hanh and other Buddhist friends. It was a grace to be in this peaceful, mindful community. Nhat Hanh and the nuns were quiet, gentle and filled with the spirit of suffering of their Vietnamese people. Sister Hung had been wounded, Sister Fung had been imprisoned and Nhat Hanh himself had been through the fires of persecution, imprisonment and now this bitter exile from his homeland. It was almost as if this quiet visit was a mindful counterpoint to the intensity of our impending journey.

Dan, one of the nuns and I were taking a leisurely walk through an old, still authentic Parisian neighborhood one evening. We found ourselves outside an interesting house with a plaque that stated: "This is where Theodore Herzl wrote *The Jewish State* in 1896." Herzl's work would contain the almost ironic Zionist description of that state, with a fiercely disputed description over how much blood would be shed and much suffering endured: "A land without people for a people without land."

We left Paris the next morning on Tuesday, April 16, and landed five hours later at Ben Gurion Airport in Tel Aviv. We were filled with mixed apprehension and anticipation of our adventure and later learned that Israeli airport security police were aware of our arrival. Perhaps they had been planning to interrogate us about the motives of our visit. But we were such a ragtag pair—Dan in jeans and long haircut, I with a beard and an old windbreaker—that we slipped through their security cordon. They were, no doubt, expecting two learned clerics, attired in modest stark black.

I had a strange reaction to all the young soldiers (men and women) in the airport, either on guard duty or merely passing through, all carrying automatic weapons. I felt at once repulsed by them yet proud, given my heritage, of being in a powerful Jewish nation—an unfamiliar experience. But I would soon learn how such sentiments could also be the seedbed of much tragedy and suffering.

There were hundreds of Greeks in the airport on the way home from their Easter pilgrimage. It was also immediately apparent how differently Arabs and Jews or other non-Arabs were treated by the military customs officials. The Palestinians were handled with greater aggression, suspicion and what Americans would recognize as "ethnic profiling" or old-fashioned racism.

We sat next to a young soldier on the airport bus and asked him about the political situation. He hoped for a less rigid government and called Prime Minister Golda Meir, whom the BBC labeled the "Iron Lady" of Israeli politics, "a stone, unfeeling and unthinking."

We took the bus to the home of my cousin Naomi Kaplinsky and her husband Elieser, both physicians. Naomi and her four beautiful sisters—all physicians or dentists—were the daughters of my aunt Ruth, my mother's younger sister. They were all Orthodox Jews but have always accepted me with love and affection as true *mishpucha* (family), a little *meshugah* (a little crazy), but their nephew and cousin whom they love. I treasure them first of all because they really are dear, loving people and also because they represented practically the only family I have. (Naomi was killed along with her daughter's husband in a tragic auto accident in 2005.)

They had a bunch of delightful kids and received Dan and me as honored guests. Elieser, slender and very bright, was a respected surgeon and also an exceptional violinist.

On the following day, we met with Peretz Kidron, a progressive reporter, a refusenik to the military and an astute observer of the Israeli political scene. I had long followed his accurate radio reportage on WBAI, the Pacifica Network station in New York. He reported a general state of demoralization in the government and among the population. Perhaps this might also be a new moment of openness concerning the Palestinians. He gave us some valuable contacts. (It was a more optimistic time.)

We took the bus to Jerusalem, where we had a meeting with Israel Shahak, the champion of human rights. A university professor, he was an older man, not in good health, a little bedraggled, but absolutely on fire with an almost biblical outrage. Few Israelis had spoken as clearly as he did concerning the cruelty and oppressiveness of the military occupation of the West Bank and Gaza. The lack of civil liberties, destruction of Palestinian houses, arbitrary arrests and even the torture of prisoners were described in his reports with great detail and accuracy. He came close to speaking of the new fascism. Since he himself was a survivor of Auschwitz, it became difficult to write him off as another "self-hating Jew," although he was despised and feared by the establishment.

But he did not spare his anger for the Palestinian leadership: "Perhaps even more terrible than the Kiryat Shmonah terrorist attack has been the Palestinian refusal to meet with Israelis—unforgivable and stupid. The most important task is to encourage some kind of meetings. But they must be public and not secret. I will not meet under the appearance of espionage or subversion."

His final words to us were moving and certainly reflected his own bitter experiences. They were like a mandate for the journey ahead: "Fear not!" (He spoke the same words Jesus used in the Gospel.) "You may receive criticism from both sides. Remember that no one can hurt you as much as you can hurt yourselves by keeping silent."

A brief conversation with a bright, young Palestinian student on the street was intense and troubling and confirmed much of what we had just heard. He did not see any quick solution for himself and his peers. As if to corroborate his feelings, on the next morning we visited two Palestinian refugee camps, Kalandia and Dheshia, together with two UNRA (United Nations Refugee Agency) officials. One was Palestinian and the other French. They struck me as dedicated social workers. UNRA helped to keep the schools and clinics and other social services running. The material situation was perhaps barely adequate, but the social and cultural life of the people especially had a peculiar feeling of confinement and frustration, especially for the youth. As we talked to people, I was struck by the beauty and spontaneity of the children—and wondered about their future.

We spent Shabbat, the day of rest and peace, with my family, Ruth and Ernst Wertheimer. In tactfully discussing the problems of the area, my uncle Ernst told the story of the Nazi professor who went to Vienna to check on the "Jewish situation." When he returned, he was flabbergasted: "I don't understand these people." Ernst then explained, "And this is why it is so difficult to come up with a solution to the Middle East crisis."

Later my cousin Ayalah's husband, Schmuel, a super-Orthodox Jew and university professor in a scientific field, kindly took these two strange American visitors ("Priests? What do I know priests?") to visit the Old City. It is at once magnificent, exotic, sacred and depressing. We saw the intrusion of the Israeli presence into what is really in part Palestinian territory.

Sunday Dan and I returned to the Old City, specifically to visit the Church of the Holy Sepulchre. A strange and wonderful place, the ancient Byzantine structure had been carved up between Constantinople and Rome like a piece of sacred real estate. Still, one is moved by the mystery of the place: *Resurexit sicut dixit*—"He has risen as He said." I prayed for the resurrection of this wounded land and for myself.

On the next day we had a troubling visit to the occupied West Bank near Nablus and saw the "other face" of all these discussions. A Palestinian family had been dispossessed the night before because an Israeli bulldozer demolished their little house. Their fourteen-year-old son was seen throwing stones at an Israeli patrol. The family of ten, including a baby and the eighty-year-old grandfather, were living under the stars and set up a campsite with a temporary tarpaulin and their raggedy furniture right next to the ruins of what was once their home. This represented what the government considered equitable military justice. It is not administered by any Israeli court of law but was rather the harsh regulations of military occupation inherited from the British, who exercised "justice" in the most arbitrary fashion.

We had been given the name of a Palestinian reporter to speak with. When we knocked on his door, he practically slammed it in our face, saying that he could not talk to foreigners. Later on our tour, he furtively caught up with us and offered a short conversation in the back of a little cigarette shop. The middle-aged and obviously knowledgeable journalist reported the brutality of the military occupation, not only the house demolitions but also the arbitrary arrests, humiliating beatings of young and old—sometimes in front of family members. Palestinian institutions, such as the highly respected Birzeit University, were barely tolerated and closely supervised and virtually no meetings of a cultural, social—to say nothing of a political—nature were permitted. One must add that the situation as I write today is even harsher. He then disappeared into the street and was gone.

Several people urged us to visit Ran Cohen, a Sephardic Jew and a highly decorated officer in the Israeli Defense Force who looked the part. He was also a champion for peace from a soldier's perspective. Later, he became a member of the Knesset and a cabinet minister. We visited him at Kibbutz Gan Shmuel, where he was an active member. We had a stimulating conversation and, as we left, he held my hand and almost pleaded: "Do everything you can to initiate some meetings with the Palestinians." His words began to evoke in me a sense of the potential seriousness of our trip.

Later that night the Hebrew University hosted a wonderful evening of a talk and poetry readings by Dan, who was at his best. He read from Merton's *The Way of Chuang Tzu* and some of his own poetry, including a touching one about Thich Nhat Hanh's sleepless nights.

On Monday morning, we had a meeting with Yitzah Ben-Aharon, a dovish Labor MP at the Knesset. There was elaborate security and we were thoroughly frisked. Special permission was required to tape our conversation. The discussion was good and he was hopeful for the future. However, we touched a raw nerve when we raised the question of US/Israeli relations, especially Israeli economic dependence and uncritical US military support. Yigal Allon graciously stopped by for a conversation during critical discussions on Labor's choice of him for the new prime minister. He was impressive, very bright and frank. It was important to hear these official Israeli voices for true peace, especially as we prepared ourselves for our sojourn in to the Occupied Territories and Arab lands.

We also had conversation with Amos Kenan, the Israeli writer and longtime peace advocate. He spoke about the awful quality of television, symbolic of the growing vulgarization of Israeli life. He alluded to the displays in the photo shops and the objectification of women. Women were almost invisible in our conversations with these men, and things did not appear to be much better in the Arab world.

The final meeting of our first week in Israel fittingly concluded with an inspiring conversation with Uri Avnery, editor of the *New Outlook*, a decorated hero, a three-term member of the Knesset who today, already on in years, still remains one of Israel's clearest, most courageous thinkers and a persistent thorn in the side of the establishment. His views corroborated everything we had seen and heard, and he had even more horrors to report. He fervently hoped that the post-war period could create some self-criticism and openness to new possibilities.

Father Joe Ryan, a Jesuit friend of Dan's, greeted us at the Beirut airport. He served in the Middle East for many years and was considered something of an expert. He was delighted to see us and drove us to the Embassy Hotel. On the way, we passed the US Embassy, guarded by forty soldiers and four tanks. These were all there to protect the new US Ambassador G. McMurtrie Godley, formerly ambassador to Laos, where he probably coordinated the secret US bombing of Laos and other clandestine military activity. This controversial appointment had already ignited student disturbances at the University of Beirut, quite a politically active campus.

At our hotel, we had an unexpected visit from Jubran Majdalany, the Palestine Liberation Organization (PLO) attorney, and a Syrian Baath member. He had come to discuss meetings with the PLO leadership, maybe with Chairman Arafat. In 1973, the PLO structure was centered in Beirut along with a large refugee population. Apparently, our visit had been expected and was being taken seriously.

Our first meeting with the Palestinian leadership took place the next morning with Nayef Hawatmeh, leader of the Democratic Front for the Liberation of Palestine (DFLP), a Marxist group, although he wanted us to know of his Greek Orthodox origins. They represented a major subgrouping within the PLO. He was young, articulate, militant and filled with mistrust of the US role in Middle East negotiations. He did not regard the Americans as "honest brokers" but rather as Israeli partisans dressed up in sheep's clothing. In our discussion on terrorism and violence, which his group had been involved in, he made a major disclaimer and pledged that the DFLP would desist from future violence, against civilians—a significant concession. We sensed that he took our meeting quite seriously. It would later play a significant role in our peace journey.

In the afternoon, we were driven to the PLO Research Center to meet Sabri Jyres, a young Israeli-Palestinian lawyer, imprisoned and expelled from Israel. He had finely chiseled features and a quiet, almost monastic bearing and a measured style of speaking. He preferred not to be taped and was friendly but reserved. He did not immediately perceive us as allies, although he warmed up a little as we conversed. Jyres had been a strong voice of conscience in the community of Israeli Arabs, often an unacceptable stance there.

We drove to the refugee camp, Tel al-Zaatar, one of the worst in Lebanon, with Dr. Nabil Shaat, later foreign minister of the Palestinian National Authority (PNA). It was originally built for five thousand people and now had a population of fourteen thousand Palestinians. Dr. Shaat was especially concerned about changing the behavior of the youth. He said, "We must prepare the young to live together with Jews and Muslims in a secular democratic society." That was one Palestinian political perspective. Since then even this vision has been overwhelmed by the disintegrating situation.

On our visit to the camp's youth club we found the young people listening to music. One third of the camp population is originally from the Palestinian village of Chalsa and calls that part of the camp "Chalsa" to keep the memory alive. The original village is near Kiryat Shmonah, an Israeli community and the site of a recent terrorist raid. Four hundred other villages have disappeared from the face of the map. On our return to Israel later we met with a young Israeli pacifist draft resister whose work was rediscovering the sites of these "lost villages" from old maps and personal research and keeping their memory alive.

Mohammed, one of the young men, invited us to his house—better to say shanty—still with the original water drainage system built decades ago for temporary use. He offered us tea and an orange and then proudly showed us his gun. Dan said that he "liked Mohammed but not his gun." We indirectly raised the idea of a non-violent struggle without much response. It was heartrending to see the hope in these young people amidst their hopeless circumstances.

The next day, Saturday, we visited a Palestinian hospital. Dr. Habib, a tall, thin, very bright man originally from Haifa and Jerusalem, looked just like one of my Israeli *mishpucha*—relatives. A primitive, sixty-bed facility supported with the help of the Lebanese Red Crescent, the hospital was another effort at self-help and established a sense of self-worth and self-determination. It provided for the needs of the Palestinian people, although anyone was welcome. Some patients were victims of the Israeli bombings and shelling in the South. Daily one heard sonic booms in Beirut as a grim reminder of the war in South Lebanon.

Sunday was a day off and we celebrated the liturgy with the Jesuits. It was the third Sunday after Easter, and in the Gospel reading the Risen Christ appears to the disciples with the Shalom greeting, "My peace I give to you, My peace I leave with you. Not as the world gives do I give" (John 14:27). It was a poignant message of Easter hope in the midst of so much despair.

Early on Monday we visited Camp Baalbek, located on the Sohar plain near a magnificent ancient temple site. The first population wave in 1948 was three thousand people. The camp had since grown to four thousand more, all located on an abandoned French military garrison measuring eighteen thousand square meters. Health conditions were deplorable and life hard, with snow six months of the year from November through late April, and only the most primitive kerosene heating available. Only seasonal employment for two to three months as farm or construction workers was available.

A heavyset man spoke to us with passion: "The hope of the imperial powers is that we will be absorbed into the Lebanese population and lose our identity. On the contrary, people in the camps cultivate a national identity among their children. Each section of the camp is named after the village from which we fled in 1948."

Just before our departure, we met for a meal with the leadership council of the camp who were suspicious at first "of all foreigners." So in this little shack we broke the bread of the poor and recalled the Easter Monday Gospel of Luke, recounting how "They knew him in the breaking of the bread" (Lk 24:35).

Someone arranged an unplanned meeting with Dr. George Habash, head of the Popular Front for the Liberation of Palestine, a radical revolutionary group. This was the organization that coordinated the hijacking of a number of civilian airliners beginning in 1968. He was a slight man with a small mustache and a quiet, courteous manner. Born into a Christian family, he and his family were refugees expelled by the Israeli military from the village of Lydda—a childhood memory that shaped his life. Later he became a respected physician until he decided that his people needed him for more radical action and he founded PFLP.

We spoke about violence and non-violence. Non-violence seemed to be quite absent from the cultural or spiritual (or political) vocabulary of the region. Since our visit, there have been several important efforts to build a non-violent movement. My dear friend Judith Thompson has been involved in some of them. Even the first Intifadah—although it involved some youths throwing stones—was still in essence an unarmed population confronting a mighty military power.

Habash insisted that they came up with the hijacking idea as a last desperate resort. "We tried every method of getting the issue of Palestinian rights before the international public: publications, strikes, demonstration. But we remained the invisible people. So we decided to do something that the world could not ignore, even if it meant taking on a negative image for some." He said that they were now committed to not striking at civilian targets and had put a halt to the hijacking strategy.

Our next journey was to Damascus, Syria, by car. We found ourselves on the "Street called Straight" near the gate of St. Paul's arrival into the city after he had a dramatic conversion experience and was transformed from being a key persecutor of the Christian community into a great apostle. (So there is still hope for his namesake—although I was named for my Orthodox Jewish grandfather.) Then we visited the Church of Ananias, named for the man who received Paul, still blinded from his conversion experience as recounted in the "Acts of the Apostles." Was there any hope for "conversion" (change of heart—*metanoia*) on this troubled piece of earth?

As if in response to our reflection, suddenly we received an urgent phone call. Yasser Arafat, chairman of the PLO, had agreed to see us. Apparently he was constantly on the move to avoid detection and possible bombing or assassination. It was said that he never slept in the same bed twice and rarely saw his family. So meetings of this kind were set up at the last minute.

We were taken, blindfolded, to meet him in an innocuous-looking apartment building in Beirut, not far from the camps. The security and well-oiled process of secrecy were intimidating. We were led into an empty meeting room and were served the traditional heavily sweetened tea. Then, as if on signal, Arafat appeared. His manner was gracious, his appearance the usual three-day beard and Palestinian Keffiyeh, his eyes very shrewd and observant. We spoke through an interpreter. His politics seemed pragmatic and moderate.

Arafat spoke of his people with what I could only discern as genuine feeling for them. He certainly had accepted a very rough, uncertain and probably uncomfortable life on their behalf at that time. We spoke of the state of the struggle, and he made it clear that the PLO supported a two-state solution with a Palestinian state on the Gaza Strip and the West Bank and gave us permission to quote him publicly on this relatively unknown development. For the more radical Palestinian factions the ultimate objective was still a democratic and secular state, thereby leaving room for individual religious expression for Christians, Muslims and Jews. Obviously, this latter formulation is unacceptable to the Zionist ideal of a Jewish state, although this was more or less the vision of Martin Buber.

What had been troubling since then was Arafat's increasingly opportunistic role as head of the Palestinian Authority, including the misuse of funds and his embracing of "the good life" while millions rotted in the camps. At the same time, it seemed like an act of arrogance by Israel and the US not to want to negotiate with a leader clearly supported by the people ("There is no one to talk to").

As we prepared to leave Lebanon, what struck me most were the similarities between the Israeli and Palestinian peoples. How often in the wretchedness of the camps we heard the recurrent feelings of deep yearning to return to their homeland. It suddenly became clear to me how, in some ironic way, the Palestinians had become the Jews of the Middle East. Their condemnation to a state of diaspora and exile evoked so many memories of Jewish history and suffering, memories of my own childhood growing up in a Zionist household in Frankfurt, and the dreams we were given.

One young Palestinian recounted how he had once heard, from an Israeli, that the Palestinian "refugees" would eventually be "absorbed" into the societies of their Arab host countries. First of all he noted the lack of welcome in Lebanon—even to the point of the Lebanese bombing the camps (and the later Lebanese/Israeli massacre of the Sabra and Chatila refugee camp). But above all he asked, "They have not forgotten their homeland in two thousand years and do they think that we will forget ours in twenty-five?"

Early the next morning we were sad to leave the suffering and human beauty of Lebanon for a flight to the capital of Egypt, the land from which the Hebrews escaped slavery in their Exodus three thousand years ago. We encountered security concerns at the Cairo airport, but some of Dan's friends met us to smooth our way and drive us to the Jesuit College in Cairo. On the way I was amazed by the crowded city—people hanging off buses by their fingertips and streets jammed with vehicles, animals and pedestrians.

In spite of some travel-related illness, we managed to have a few useful meetings. Then we left for Cyprus, since at that time there were no direct flights from Egypt to Israel.

There we met with Gaby Habib, who worked with the Middle East Council of churches and was one of the most knowledgeable and well-connected people in the Middle East. Now after some discussion with him and others on his staff, we decided not to bring the many tapes of interviews we had made back into Israel lest they be confiscated or meddled with by the Israeli authorities. So in what seemed to be a brilliant stroke, we had our tapes carefully packaged and shipped back home to await us there.

This decision would result in one of the minor tragedies of our trip because our package never arrived in the US, at least not into our hands. No amount of checking or tracing resulted in any clues about the tapes. So this collection of extraordinary conversations with some of the key players as well as some unusual "ordinary people" in the Israeli-Palestinian conflict would never result in the promising book that Dan and I had planned to co-author upon our return. We concluded that our package had been stolen by the CIA or Israeli intelligence agencies (or both), either to obtain information or to subvert our "subversive" mission for peace.

Many of our dovish Israeli friends were heartened by Arafat's willingness to support open meetings between Israelis and Palestinians to discuss new options for peace. At the time many considered this a major breakthrough. Today the strategy of the Sharon, Olmert and Netanyahu regimes, with their increasing repression and the use of "the Wall," has literally suffocated life in Palestinian society, cutting off communications through road and travel restrictions, preventing people from getting to work and even to emergency medical aid as well as encroaching on agricultural property. All of this is reinforced through new settlements, oppressive and humiliating checkpoints as well as the construction of highway networks only for the use of the Israeli settlers, even when peace talks were in process.

Perhaps the massive youth-led Israeli demonstration in August 2011 against the social inequities in Israeli society made the Netanyahu government uneasy. There has been no talk yet of the Palestinian conflict but some protest against the heavy use of public funds for the settlements.

It was after a peaceful meal at the Tel Aviv home of my cousins Naomi and Elieser that the terrible news reached us. Palestinian terrorists had struck in Ma'alot, a town in West Galilee in northern Israel, killing twenty-one grade school children and wounding sixty other youngsters. Nayef Hawatmeh's group, the DFLP, had taken responsibility.

Dan and I were struck by grief and anger and immediately called a well-attended press conference in Tel Aviv. In our opening statement we said:

"We condemn the taking of children as war hostages. No possible grievances can justify such an act. At the same time, it must be insisted that the indiscriminate bombing of refugee camps is in effect an equally barbarous assault on children and non-combatants. (. . .)

"It has been well said that in war truth is the first casualty . . . (Hawatmeh) said in response to our questions about the morality of certain Palestinian acts that his group had opposed terrorism publicly since 1969. May we not be justified in expecting a high standard of truth from our leaders? Mr. Hawatmeh, in other words, cannot have it both ways; either he opposes terrorism or he continues to wage a war on children.

"If we denounce the latest wave of terrorism of both sides, we wish, at the same time, to affirm our support for the Palestinian people in Israel and elsewhere. Their demand for a law of return that will apply to them is just and must be met. Such a solution moreover is late by some twenty-six years."

Dan added some thoughts of his own in addition to the statement:

"I felt personally betrayed by this whole Hawatmeh thing. I felt we had not gone in there as news people—we had gone in there as very serious people, accepted as such, and were given this view of life and violence. I've been very shaken by this."

We both had been badly shaken by this betrayal of trust. Surely there was no excuse. Perhaps Hawatmeh's change of heart could be attributed to the growing fears among Palestinians of US Secretary of State Kissinger's bartering away the future of the Palestinians in the negotiating process. His devious role in the Paris peace talks with the Vietnamese has since been well documented. But nothing could justify such a brutal action. It was another example of how a noble people with high ideals could be betrayed by unprincipled leadership.

Even in his pain and disappointment, Dan had been moved and even transformed by the trip, as had I. He wrote that he could see the Jews of Israel more as a nation still in shock from the great losses of the war, "still mourning the dead, still furious over recent Palestinian terrorism on a village apartment house." Moreover he was moved by the many Israelis anxious to find a just and peaceful solution to the conflict. Also years later he would write: "I am no longer angry at Israel. I reserve my anger for mythmakers and kingmakers, Israelis and Americans who shuttle like voracious locusts between Washington and Tel Aviv, bargaining away the lives of people, upping the military ante, fanning the fires of mythology and fear."

Shortly before our departure, one of our Israeli guides drove us through the night to Nazareth and beyond it to the little Arab village of Ibbelin, where we met with Father Elias Chacour, the Palestinian village priest. He was, alas, one of those rare phenomena in this world—a real Christian. Father Chacour was of medium stature, barrel-chested, with twinkling dark eyes and a black beard already streaked with gray.

He told us he was tortured by his inability to take sides clearly and simply: "I am stretched on the cross of having no real identity." He was a brilliant man, spoke eleven languages and had a degree from the Hebrew University in the study of the Hebrew Bible and the Talmud. But he was also a modest man of the people. When he first came to the village, he slept in his car for six months until residents insisted on building him a house. Now in a ministry of reconciliation, he invited young Jewish students and intellectuals to spend time in the village living in Palestinian homes.

Father Chacour is a native of the village of Biram in Galilee, one of three villages in the area systematically depopulated and then destroyed by the Israeli military. He was driven out of the village with his entire family, almost breaking the heart of his father who had tilled the fields, especially the fertile fig groves, with a nurturing love. They were never allowed to return to their village.

Father Chacour's own father was a devout Christian and as they were walking along the dusty road with a few rescued possessions on their back, he spoke these unforgettable words to his son: "Elias, the Jews have driven us out of our home and we must leave. I don't understand why. When you get older I want you to try to find out why. But above all do not learn to hate!"

On the day before our departure as we were packing, we heard that the Israelis in retaliation for the attack on Ma'alot had bombed the refugee camp Tel al-Zaater in Lebanon, which we had visited just ten days before. Dan's words as we left were "God help us all." And so He must, because no one else can.

As for me, I left this allegedly holy land with a heavy heart, hope wrestling with despair, in the realization that perhaps we Jews had lost our innocence and some of our vision as well. Or as my sainted Jewish Zionist mother put it, "I always knew that when Israel got its army that the dream of the Prophets was over."

CHAPTER 20

INTERFAITH PEACE WORK
Founding the Religious Task Force

THE PHONE RANG. IT WAS Norma Becker, one of my closest friends and chairperson of the War Resisters League. Norma was a feisty, Jewish New York City schoolteacher and a veteran peace activist and leader (whom we recently lost to cancer). "Paul, a group of us is getting together in DC to talk about starting up the nuclear disarmament movement again."

It was the spring of 1977 and the American peace movement had decided once again to confront the greatest threat to humanity—nuclear annihilation. It was Terry Provance, Leslie Cagan, Cora Weiss and others, all leaders of the Vietnam peace movement, who were getting together. The war in Vietnam was over, although its tragic effects would continue to fester for decades in Indochina through the hundreds of thousands dead and maimed, as well as a devastated and poisoned ecosphere in a land once known for its great beauty. Here at home we not only had tens of thousands of our youth come home in body bags, but also the walking dead—our veterans returned not only with battlefield wounds, but also with psychological trauma, heroin and alcohol addiction and genetic poisoning by Agent Orange. Even deeper was the spiritual wounding of the unrepented national sin of that "dirty little war."

Yet in some ironic way, the monstrous war had been a distraction from the ultimate global danger of nuclear holocaust with its threat of ending the human experiment as we know it. (Similarly, the wars in Iraq and Afghanistan have represented a certain diversion from this global life-and-death issue.) The cold war and the cynical nuclear arms race had continued to grind on and had even used the Indochina war as an excuse to up the ante.

Some elements of the international community seemed to recognize this danger and so the United Nations announced the convening of the first UN Special Session on Disarmament (UNSSD I) in May 1978. The main conveners were the poor and unaligned nations (neither pro-US nor pro-Soviet) who felt that their survival resources were being squandered in the out-of-control global arms race.

This announcement also became a major catalyst for the creation of a new US national peace and justice coalition called the Mobilization for Survival (MFS). Another catalyst for this new anti-nuclear consciousness was the dramatic and successful non-violent occupation of the Seabrook Nuclear Power Plant in New Hampshire by two thousand activists organized by the Clamshell Alliance of New Hampshire. It was a powerful, almost spontaneous outpouring of conscience against the growing specter of alleged "safe clean energy" derived from the same atomic source that had incinerated and irradiated the cities of Hiroshima and Nagasaki.

The "Mobe"—affectionately named after the major Vietnam coalitions—made Zero Nuclear Weapons its primary goal but also it added three others: Ban Nuclear Power, End the Arms Race, and Fund Human Needs.

Our simple initial strategy was to use the UN Special Sessions on Disarmament to be held in 1978 as an organizing forum for the coming period. Most UN conferences had not proven to be very exciting, effective or even visible events. But the hope was that national and even international citizens' activity through the NGOs (non-governmental organizations) would put the issue and perhaps even the special session itself on the map and thereby create a global momentum around the burning issue of disarmament.

In those days I was the closest thing to a religious figure to be found in the ranks of the new coalition initiators. Most of the leading participants came from leftist secular organizations and perspectives—although there was the pacifist interfaith Fellowship of Reconciliation (FOR), the Quaker-affiliated American Friends Service Committee (AFSC) and Clergy & Laity Concerned (CALC). I think that it was Leslie Cagan, a veteran organizer and friend, who approached me with the idea of convening a religious working group to support the ambitious goal of nuclear abolition and the MFS plans for the coming year, which were beginning to take shape. The apparently utopian goal of Zero Nuclear Weapons had actually been taken from the 1977 inaugural speech of President Jimmy Carter. It really seemed like the greatest moral challenge facing humanity and one which should gather the support of the communities of faith.

I—with what felt like presumption—convened a meeting of the major religious peace groups at the Washington Square Methodist Church, one of the leading New York City peace congregations, located on West 4th Street in Greenwich Village—unhappily since disbanded. At that point the participation of the mainline religious denominations was still minimal at best, but some of them would gradually join our ranks.

Of course, MFS was planning a mass demonstration at the UN during the special session and that was appropriate, but how could the faith communities make their own distinctive contribution to creating deeper disarmament consciousness? Could we organize three days of exciting and creative activity prior to the big demonstration to involve the communities of faith? Those were the questions our newly formed interfaith group was asking. We called ourselves the Religious Task Force (not the most poetic of names) and saw it as an ad hoc working group, never dreaming that it would gradually evolve into a major interfaith peace and justice network.

I immediately raised an issue that I had been wrestling with for years. How could Blacks, Latinos and other so-called "minority" people play a greater—even leadership—role in our largely white, middle-class peace movement?

People of color and poor people had always been the greatest victims of war. Witness Hiroshima and note that the atomic bomb was not dropped on the blond and blue-eyed citizens of Hamburg or Berlin, but rather on the non-white people of Japan who had been chosen as the first guinea pigs of nuclear war.

At that time I was an adjunct professor at New York Theological Seminary (NYTS) under the presidency of Dr. George William Webber, one of the truly visionary Church leaders of our time. I approached Bill with our still emerging plan for the UNSSD I and proposed that he use his and the seminary's good name to convene a meeting of Black, Latino and Asian clergy leaders to hear about our plan and get their input. Bill, who was always committed to peace and social justice, agreed and a month or so later there was an impressive and representative gathering of these leaders at NYTS.

He introduced me and I proceeded to give the white boy's version of our plans and why they and their communities might (read should) be interested in this important international gathering that was coming to New York City. The participants listened politely. I felt that I had given quite a clear and eloquent presentation and then I invited questions.

The first respondent was the Rev. Timothy P. Mitchell, the Black Baptist pastor of Ebenezer Baptist Church in Queens. He was a big man, impeccably dressed with a small goatee and an imposing Afro hairstyle. He was one of the most consistently courageous and outspoken religious leaders on behalf of the rights of poor African Americans in New York City.

Rev. Mitchell's response was direct and uncensored. In his polite but powerful way he gave me an instant education in Black/White relations in the Church and in progressive political movements and organizations.

"The White peace movement either doesn't understand or doesn't care about poor Black folks' concerns. You talk about nuclear holocaust and destruction. Our communities have already been hit by a bomb, we are already devastated. Our housing in Harlem or Bedford-Stuyvesant often looks like bombed-out areas. Our schools are disaster zones. Our hospitals are wretched. Our young men have no jobs and no hope. And you talk to us about future destruction. How about doing something on your special session in *our community* and under *our leadership*? Then we'll believe that you want to work together with us."

His colleagues were too polite to applaud, but you could see vigorous affirmative shaking of heads around the room. The rev. had struck a nerve and I was in a minor state of shock.

I took the message of this difficult but valuable meeting back to the RTFO. As a result of that meeting at NYTS, an event called Witness for Survival was planned in cooperation with the South Bronx clergy and took place on May 25. It initiated two days of religious activities preceding the march in support of the UN Special Session on Saturday, May 27. These two days were solemnly designated as the International Religious Convocation for Human Survival.

Our first celebration occurred in one of the most devastated communities of New York City, Charlotte Street in the South Bronx. At that time, this virtually deserted wasteland symbolized the price of militarism and the arms race. It had even been visited once by President Carter.

Charlotte Street looked like the end of the earth with its shells of burnt-out buildings, their missing windows like eyes gone blind from seeing so much suffering and poverty. Life had pretty well ground to a desperate halt within a three- or four-block radius. There were no inhabited buildings, no bodegas, not even the omnipresent exploitative liquor store.

Perhaps Charlotte Street offered a refuge for some of the neighborhood junkies and the most wretched of the local prostitutes to ply their desperate trade in the anonymity of an urban no-man's land. Not even the local police dared to patrol this kingdom of the hopeless.

It was an audacious decision by the South Bronx clergy and the RTF to hold the Witness for Survival in this place, which could compete with the favelas of Rio de Janeiro, the hillside shanty towns of Caracas and the sewer communities of Calcutta for the designation of "godforsaken." So we brought together religious people from around the planet to repeat the ancient question of the prophet Ezekiel: "Can these dry bones live again?"

At two o'clock in the afternoon on Thursday, May 25 (the twenty-first anniversary of my priestly ordination), a caravan of yellow school buses lined up in Manhattan in front of the Church of St. Paul the Apostle on West 59th Street to ferry religious participants, including many international guests, across the invisible River Styx separating two radically different worlds comprising New York City. The buses deliberately drove up Eighth Avenue, along Central Park and through Harlem. On each bus there were ministers and lay people from these communities to serve as guides for the pilgrimage to the South Bronx and the land of the forgotten. By the time we arrived in the South Bronx, we had driven down some of the mean side streets of Harlem as well to prepare us for the experience ahead.

The buses were greeted by South Bronx clergy and their communities at the Tried Stone Baptist Church on Boston Road. These communities of faith often represented one of the few resources of hope in these traumatized neighborhoods. We left the buses and walked in procession to the corner of Seabury Place and Charlotte Street, where some community people had cleared a site for our celebration amidst the weeds, the broken glass and the garbage.

Rev. Wendell Foster, a local African American Baptist pastor who was also a member of the New York City Council, welcomed us warmly into "this our neighborhood." He opened a well-worn Bible to the passage in Luke's Gospel where Jesus weeps over Jerusalem as if to remind us to love our city, lest other Jerusalem-like disasters befall us.

Then Ms. Fumiko Amano responded to those words of welcome in the name of the international delegation. Her small, stooped figure was made even smaller by the towering shells of the buildings surrounding her. On August 6, 1945, as a twelve-year-old girl, Fumiko was at the epicenter of the blast in Hiroshima that burnt off most of her skin and irradiated her with nuclear poisoning.

She said that she had come to give witness to that experience that changed her life forever and to pray that the sin would not be repeated "anywhere and anytime." She said that she was astounded at how much this urban scene reminded her of her own city's destruction and that it replicated her bombed-out city. Fumiko stood in awe of this place as she prayed her prayer for global liberation from such suffering and destruction, including poverty and deprivation.

Rabbi Marc Tannenbaum, of the American Jewish Committee and an indefatigable worker for religious unity, then read the ancient prophecy of how the day will come when: "They will hammer their swords into plowshares and their spears into sickles. Nation will not lift sword against nation, there will be no more training for war. Each man [and woman] will sit under their vine and fig tree, with no one to trouble them" (Micah 3:3–4).

What would it mean to take the billions offered to the insatiable Moloch idol of militarism and place them instead before the altar of life for schools, hospitals and jobs for the good people of the South Bronx and for their counterparts all over the world? Yes, every family could spend Sunday afternoons under their own fig tree at peace with the world.

Then a Diné (Navajo) medicine man stepped into the circle. He prayed in his ancient language and sprinkled sacred white corn meal on this fallow, seemingly unpromising piece of earth in the hope that something new might blossom forth.

For our closing ritual each participant came forward and picked up a piece of stone rubble and carefully placed it in the center of our circle, one on top of the other, in a kind of abstract motif. Together we created a Monument to Life. As we did so, there was a reading from the book of Joshua, chapter 24, verses 25–28: "Then Joshua took a great stone and set it up there, under the oak in the sanctuary of Yahweh, and Joshua said to the people: 'See! This stone shall be a witness against us because it has heard all the words that Yahweh has spoken to us, it shall be a witness against you in case you deny your God.'"

And so our Monument to Life would be a witness against us, the participants of that sacred ritual on Charlotte Street and against our entire peace community, if we forgot the people of Charlotte Street and all the poor people of the favelas, the barrios, the arid savannas and our own ghettos—and still claim to be peacemakers.

This historic visit to the South Bronx signaled an auspicious beginning to this three-day International Religious Convocation for Human Survival. It was perhaps one of the first times that the white US religious peace movement had connected in such a concrete way with poor religious communities of color.

Our visit was followed on the next day by the interfaith service at a noontime celebration at St. Paul the Apostle Church. The celebration moved powerfully from the *adhan*—the Islamic call to prayer—to the blessing by Chief Noble Red Man of the Lakota Nation, to the chanting of the Jewish Kaddish for the victims of all wars, to the final community affirmation proclaimed so loudly by the congregation that the old stone Church vibrated. Then the entire community followed the delegation of children through the Gothic portals of the Church in preparation for the religious procession to the United Nations.

As the procession carrying the banner with the Exodus text "Choose Life So Your Children May Live" stepped out onto Ninth Avenue, we were stopped by the police. My slight figure looked up at the burly, tall, Irish captain who held up his forbidding hand and informed us, "Sorry, Father, but you'll have to walk on the sidewalk," even though we had been assured that the streets were ours for our procession through the city. At that point I placed my diminutive self in front of the police officer—my head coming up to his chest—and said, "Captain, we are going to walk on the streets and if you want to arrest two thousand people, including bishops, rabbis and patriarchs, that's your responsibility." The police lines parted before us like the waters of the Red Sea before the Israelites.

We walked slowly through the streets of our beloved city singing, chanting, praying that we would never experience the nuclear mushroom cloud. When we arrived at the UN we were addressed by one of the great peace preachers of our times, Dr. William Sloane Coffin, Jr. The resounding community affirmation (composed by the good Father Tony Mullaney, formerly of the Milwaukee Fourteen) that we had proclaimed together at St. Paul's rang in our ears and hearts:

> "We, who live in the shadow of the mushroom cloud,
>
> We, whose very bones and lungs are threatened even now by radioactivity,
>
> Today declare our hope in the future.
>
> Before us today are set life and death.
>
> We choose life
>
> That we and our children may live.
>
> Let it be so.

The mass rally of the next day in all of its power almost seemed like an anti-climax to the preceding days of sacredness. Our international religious convocation set a tone that permeated the march and demonstration.

On the day of the rally, immediately after powerful words of witness by the Hiroshima atom bomb survivor from the speakers' platform, a siren sounded and many thousands fell slowly to the ground in a powerful symbolic die-in for survival simulating the bombed and irradiated dead.

After twenty minutes of silence the chimes rang. People rose and joined hands. Folksingers Pete Seeger and Rev. Kirkpatrick led all present in "Woke Up This Morning with My Mind Stayed on Freedom." We were still alive and there was much work left to be done.

In this spirit, on the last day of the "sit-in for survival" and in front of the UN where over a thousand participants were arrested the failure of the US government to come up with concrete disarmament proposals at UNSSD was highlighted. Once again I was led away in handcuffs.

Still, our worldwide movement had left its mark on the Reagans and Gorbachevs and their decisions regarding nuclear disarmament, and it slowly raised the bar of political discourse and moral vision on the issue of nuclear energy. Perhaps we were actually moving from settling for mere survival to embracing the hope for a human future.

In March of 1979, the Mobe and the whole country were faced with a potentially serious disaster—the nuclear accident at the Three Mile Island (TMI) power plant near Harrisburg, Pennsylvania. This was the most serious nuclear accident in American history, although by no means the first.

The water-cooling system of Unit 2 had failed, releasing a radioactive cloud into the atmosphere as well as contaminated water into the beautiful Susquehanna River. Rev. Bob Moore, executive secretary of the Mobe, in keeping with our second goal to ban nuclear power, called an emergency press conference in Harrisburg. The speakers included Dr. Ernest Sternglass, professor of Radiology at the University of Pittsburgh, one of the leading experts on the effects of nuclear radiation and Nobel Laureate in Biology, Dr. George Wald of Harvard.

Dr. Ernest Sternglass had a way of using his expertise to make a dramatic point. In this case, he came with his own Geiger counter. Consequently, he was able to report very high radiation readings taken when his plane flew directly over the nuclear plant and from his taxi driving through downtown Harrisburg.

These dramatic statements coming from such scientific authorities warning of the disaster's potential dangers to the local population and beyond provided the backdrop for the MFS to challenge the governor of Pennsylvania to evacuate the area's pregnant mothers and children. Significantly and surprisingly enough, Governor Dick Thornburgh responded by organizing an emergency plan for the ten surrounding miles and acceded to our demands.

Subsequently, tests showed a significant increase in radiation symptoms in the local population and in farm animals. Later on, according to studies by Dr. Sternglass, there were also substantial increases of cancer in the area as well as miscarriages by humans and animals.

In response to the accident, the No Nukes Coalition called a demonstration in Washington on May 3. The principal speakers among a long list of luminaries included Ralph Nader with Governor Jerry Brown of California, who was running for president at the time.

I was invited to open the rally with an invocation. I remember wrestling with the dilemma of honoring everyone's religious sensibilities. Finally, I chose a blessing based on the Native American Mother Earth spiritual tradition. The large crowd fell silent as I ended my prayer in the words of the holy man Black Elk of the Lakota Nation: "Great Spirit, Great Spirit, my Grandfather, all over the earth the faces of living things are alike. With tenderness have these come up out of the ground. Look upon the faces of these children without number and with children in their arms, that they may face the winds and walk the good road to the day of quiet."

Then the thousands broke into a great cheerlike "amen" to begin this historic event in a sacred way.

In 1986, the greatest nuclear accident in power plant history occurred at Chernobyl in the Ukraine and Belarus territories of the Soviet Union. It was an event of terrifying proportions with scores of immediate deaths and countless more predicted from the widespread radiation release.

One would have thought that this terrible tragedy for the earth would have been enough to end this foolish experiment in the "energy too cheap to meter" forever. But not so. The Bush administration tried to revive this source of "clean energy," and even some "pragmatic" climate environmentalists jumped aboard. Unfortunately President Obama has also thrown in his lot with these supporters of nuclear power, pledging thirty billion dollars towards nuclear development since Wall Street now considers the nuclear industry a bad investment.

Once again the US of A is completely out of step with the rest of the world. After the terrifying Japanese Fukushima accident—possibly even more dangerous than Chernobyl—German Chancellor Angela Merkel announced in 2011 an immediate ban on construction and the shutdown of all nuclear plants by 2022 together with a strategy to have fifty percent of Germany's energy come from renewable sources. The Italian electorate in a plebiscite overwhelmingly banned nuclear power and a majority of the Swedish Parliament followed suit. And where is the American government and public?

On the side of hope, a new anti-nuclear movement is beginning to emerge here and internationally—a movement that is determined that the memory of the victims of Hiroshima, Chernobyl, Harrisburg and now Fukushima will not be forgotten.

CHAPTER 21

BLESSED ARE THE FEET OF THOSE
WHO BRING GOOD NEWS OF PEACE

Travel to Japan and Meetings
with Atom Bomb Survivors

DURING THE ACTIVITIES SURROUNDING THE First United Nations Special Session on Disarmament (UNSSD I) in 1978, I got to know a young man named Chihara, an interpreter with the Japanese peace delegation. He was a graduate of the Peace Studies Program at Bradford University in England and had also been a high school teacher in his home city of Otaru. Chihara had the reserved bearing of many Japanese, but underneath there lay a passionate commitment to the task of nuclear abolition and a hope of educating people, especially the young about the urgency of disarmament and stopping nuclear proliferation.

We became good friends and he seemed impressed with my work in the peace movement. Much to my surprise, he invited me to consider a one-month speaking tour in Japan on nuclear disarmament during the coming year. He particularly wanted me to tour his home island of Hokkaido, which he felt was a neglected part of Japan, and also one of its most beautiful areas.

I was moved and excited by the invitation. Japan was a country of such physical beauty and ancient culture, and was, above all, the only nation ever to have been attacked with nuclear weaponry—and by my own country, at that. What a dubious distinction. After some consultation, we agreed on May 1979 for my tour.

Little did we know at that time that it would follow immediately after the March accident at Three Mile Island. TMI was a nuclear tragedy that would link the fate of our two peoples in a new, profound way—albeit our experiences were of a very different nature and magnitude. In fact, it would transform the major focus of my speaking tour into that of the inseparable link between nuclear weapons and nuclear power. Three Mile Island would definitely be on the mind of my Japanese listeners.

When Chihara returned to Japan after UNSSD I, I began to hear from him regularly. He was obviously a skilled organizer and seemed to enjoy the trust and respect of many major Japanese peace and religious groups, both local and national. He was promoting me as much more of a major American peace movement leader than I perceived myself to be.

My flight to Japan left Los Angeles on May 9, just a few days after the big anti-nuclear demonstration on TMI outside the US Capitol on May 3, where I had led a prayer. All of this heightened my sense that things were moving very quickly.

Chihara met me at the airport, bubbling over with enthusiasm (as far as that is permissible in the restrained Japanese culture). We took a bus and a train to a Tokyo suburb where we stayed with the Katsuragawas. Staying in people's homes was unusual because of the modest size and close living arrangements in the typical Japanese home, e.g., the sleeping mat is unrolled every night in the living room. Hence, other arrangements were usually made for overnight guests. I would learn to appreciate this privilege that Chihara had graciously arranged.

Mr. Katsuragawa was a nuclear physicist and activist and his wife loved Sherlock Holmes. Theirs was a beautiful home—a marvelous blend of the traditional and contemporary style. Mrs. Katsuragawa had been preparing an exquisite traditional meal all day. I stayed in a lovely,

Zen-like room with a woven mat floor, rice paper windows and subtle olive green walls. I was to experience more of this elegant hospitality, shared in this gracious matter-of-fact way.

The next morning, Mr. Katsuragawa drove us to a train to Center City, where we met with one of the senior editors of *Asahi*, a leading national daily. He was a perceptive, politically sympathetic interviewer and journalist. Chihara wanted to launch the tour with a significant story. The interview was so intense that we almost missed our flight to Hokkaido. The traffic was nightmarish—bumper-to-bumper all the way. Tokyo was already one of the world's most polluted cities, and traffic police and others wore protective face masks.

We barely made our plane to Kushiro in Hokkaido. The bus ride to the city from the airport was through a drab landscape—no signs of spring yet. It was a rather ugly, ordinary industrialized seaport town. We were met by two activist/teachers, former students of Chihara's. I spoke to a group of fifty to seventy teachers and local people.

Early the next morning we boarded the train to Asahikawa. The lovely scenery was now revealing the first signs of spring with distant snow-covered mountains, a blue-green shore line and the gorgeous cherry blossoms in early bloom. Hokkaido was beginning to deliver its promise and reputation for exquisite beauty. Not many Europeans visited here and I would only see and meet Japanese for almost my entire one-month journey.

We were met at the station by two veteran peace activists—Mr. Omida and Mr. Takahashi, both outgoing and enthusiastic. The next morning we stopped in for the monthly meeting of the local teachers' union.

After a three-hour train ride we arrived in Otaru, Chihara's hometown, and he was proud of it with good reason. It was a beautiful city located on the coast with majestic mountains in the background. They were covered with cherry blossoms, and from Chihara's little house we had a wonderful view of the valley dotted with red and blue rooftops with the ocean on the left and the mountains on the right.

In the afternoon we took a magnificent bus ride through the landscape of mountains, cherry orchards and the ocean to the coastal town of Iwanai, the proposed site of a future nuclear power plant. It was an ominous experience in the midst of such intense natural beauty. In the evening we met with fishermen and local citizens at a fishing cooperative who listened attentively to my presentation. Dr. Watanabe, a soft-spoken nuclear physicist, was the other speaker who painted a grim picture of the potential dangers of a nuclear facility at this vulnerable and beautiful site.

This "nuke" would be only six kilometers from a population center of twenty thousand people. Further, the potential threat to the fishing industry and the ocean was dire. The local activists had been at it for ten years, trying to change the site to a less dangerous one and had succeeded once. Alas, in the end the reactor would be built in nearby Tomari, in spite of these courageous people. Since the Fukushima nuclear accident, popular opposition has revived.

In a land like Japan with little oil of its own, nuclear energy was a very tempting option. And yet, what a candidate this small island was, with wind, sun, water and wave power for clean energy.*

Footnote: It grieves me to say that in 2011 the Japanese people acquired an entirely new and horrendous set of nuclear statistics. As I write these words, an apocalyptic tsunami and a powerful earthquake that has actually moved parts of Japan thirteen miles eastward and even shifted the earth's axis were accompanied by a historic nuclear accident that may approximate or even exceed the nuclear trauma of Chernobyl.

At this writing, three reactors at the Fukushima plant are in partial meltdown and over eighty tons of the "spent" partially exposed and highly radioactive fuel rods in outdoor holding pools are burning and spewing poisonous radiation into the atmosphere. Once again, as after the atomic bombings of Hiroshima and Nagasaki—in spite of reassurances by Japanese energy and government officials—radiation is spreading to food, water and human flesh, especially to the susceptible thyroid glands of children. These assurances are being outstripped only by those of US nuclear officials to the American people about their immunity to this radiation and the safety of similar American plants. In the end, the twin-headed monster of military and "peaceful" nuclear technology under the apt patronage of Pluto, the god of the Underworld, continues to be the bitter patrimony of the people of Japan.

Next came the most important, inspiring and painful part of this pilgrimage, my encounter with the *hibakusha*, the community of atom bomb survivors. Our flight was to Osaka, where we were met by Mr. Hiratsuka and Mr. Akaji of the local *hibakusha* organization. Their modest bearing was all the more shattering when I realized that I was in the presence of the surviving witnesses of the most disastrous form of modern warfare yet conceived by man's bellicose—dare one say diseased—imagination. With age their numbers are dwindling.

One out of every three hundred Japanese was a certified *hibakusha* (the word means "explosion-affected people"), a total of some 370,000 with ID cards. Actually, there are more uncertified who do not wish to be identified. In the last sixty years, the number of the certified has increased because the organized *hibakusha* movement encouraged the anonymous ones to "come out" and because of less stringent ID requirements. The social rejection was greater in the earlier years. In Japan's rigidly stratified society, being a *hibakusha* carried a social stigma that affected employment, desirability as a marriage partner and problems in the healthcare system.

One of the most moving experiences was our meeting with the *hibakusha* Women's Group in Osaka. They came together after many years of sorrow and isolation to develop a community of mutual support and compassion. Mrs. Shizuko Tagaki, the secretary general of the group, welcomed us warmly. At one point she still spoke with emotion of her wedding day. All of her husband's family opposed and boycotted the wedding. It was a day of joy mingled with heartbreak.

Fumiko Nonaka, a diminutive woman with the marks of her suffering upon her, was sweeping on Matsukawa-Cho Street in Hiroshima the morning of August 6, 1945. She recalled that after the bomb hit, "intense beams pierced my face. I felt my body shrink as if it were a dried squid which had been cooked on a fire. After I regained consciousness from the impact and began to walk, I realized that my skin had pulled completely off my body. The burnt flesh of my arms, hands and fingers was hanging out of my tattered sleeves and drooped down to my fingertips."

After years of suffering, poverty, desertion by her husband and social ostracism because of her disfigured appearance, Mrs. Nonaka eventually found a new life opening for her. Her suffering took on a new meaning as together with other women atom bomb survivors, she began working for the abolition of nuclear weapons and for world peace. Her face took on a new liveliness as she pleaded with me not to let her story be forgotten.

During the 1970s, second-generation problems came to the fore. Children of *hibakusha* teenagers were reaching their own teenage years with serious leukemia symptoms. Many died in their late teens or early twenties with a few dying as early as ten years of age.

Sumiko Mine survived the Nagasaki bombing and searched for her older brother at what later proved to be the epicenter of where the bomb fell. After a sickly childhood she grew up and married only to lose two teenage children to leukemia, probably a genetic effect of atomic radiation. Her oldest son, Kenicha, died at the age of seventeen on August 6, 1975, the thirtieth anniversary of Hiroshima. Her witness to peace was born out of her sorrow and despair.

Mrs. Mine was certified as a *hibakusha* only after her two children died. The women's group helped her apply for certification.

The Japanese government had previously released virtually no scientific information on the after effects of the radiation. For decades officials maintained that proof that leukemia and other rare cancers stemmed from radiation had not been "scientifically established." But most open-minded, progressive scientists called for greater study.

Right from the start, the Atom Bomb Casualty Commission (ABCC) had a shady history. It was allegedly set up for research at the urging of General Douglas MacArthur's military occupation government, but the commission only gave reluctant access to the Japanese victims to information concerning their own woundings. It did research, but appeared to be more interested in using the survivors as guinea pigs for planning future nuclear wars rather than finding cures and helping the victims.

Chihara said that "if President Carter or some other official had come to Osaka, these women wouldn't have spoken up. They told you their stories because you are their friend working for peace."

As I listened to the words of Mmes. Mine and Nonaka and these other noble women survivors, I was once again struck by the words of the prophet Isaiah in which he spoke of a mysterious sufferer: "Surely he has borne our infirmities and carried our diseases; yet we accounted him stricken, struck down by God, and afflicted. But he was wounded for our transgressions, crushed for our iniquities; Upon him was the punishment that made us whole, and by his bruises we are healed" (Isaiah 53: 5–6)

My original link with the impressive Japanese peace movement had been through the Buddhist monks and nuns of the Nipponzan Myohoji order, sometimes called the Japan Buddha Sangha. The order's original peace identity and inspiration came through their then one-hundred-year-old patriarch and founder—the Venerable Nichidatsu Fujii. As a young monk, he encountered Mahatma Gandhi and his non-violent philosophy in India. This experience so transformed the young Buddhist practitioner that he was eventually inspired to shape the spiritual work of the Japan Buddha Sangha to primarily follow the path of peacemaking.

The monks and nuns had a way of very humbly and unobtrusively appearing at peace events to drum and chant. They played a prominent role at the UNSSD II and would continue to do so throughout the years of my peace involvement.

Ven. Sato, my monk host, wanted me to meet a Buddhist abbot whom he considered one of the eminent sages and teachers on peace. We went to a monastery in the ancient temple city of Nara. We had an appointment and were asked to wait in a lovely guest area bordering on an extraordinary Zen garden and pond. It radiated such silence, simplicity and beauty and we were so drawn into the power of the present moment that we lost track of how long we had actually been waiting for the abbot—minutes, hours?

Finally, he appeared—an elderly man, dressed in the simple garb of an ordinary monk. He greeted us warmly and had tea brought to refresh us. We drank the fragrant libation and then sat there in the magical garden in complete silence. There was no media interview, no sound bites—just the power of the present moment, with the only commentary being sweet birdsong and more silence. Then the master arose, bowed deeply and yet warmly and left as quickly as he had come. Thus was this peace leader from the far-off West given the only teaching worth receiving.

One of the final highlights of the tour was a train trip to Hiroshima itself. It was truly a trail of tears except for a lovely reception by a class of schoolchildren at the station. They had garlands of multi-colored origami paper cranes to place around our necks.

These commemorated the story of Sadako, a little ten-year-old Japanese girl who had been irradiated by the bomb in Hiroshima on August 6, 1945. As she lay in her hospital bed, gravely ill from radiation poisoning, she feverishly made little paper cranes. She believed that if she could make a thousand, she would not die and the threat of nuclear war would end. Alas, she passed into eternity before the goal of one thousand was reached. But Japanese schoolchildren still make the cranes in memory of little Sadako and for the cause of world peace.

After this respite of color and joy, we proceeded to the Hiroshima Museum, which gives a stunningly accurate picture of this dark day in the history of humanity. The director of the museum, himself a *hibaku-sha*, gave us an intense and detailed tour. It was amazing how carefully the event has been documented photographically. Since then I have often been invited to speak at the annual anniversary celebration. It was moving to see how deeply this bitter day was remembered by all from political and religious leaders to the *hibakusha*s to ordinary citizens.

We had a touching evening meeting with the Survivors' Association and religious leaders at the YWCA. So many of the *hibakusha*s were of advanced age and were anxious that their story be told. As I write, I wonder how many of these precious witnesses of this heinous act are still alive.

Mr. Katsuragawa, our original host and a peace-loving nuclear physicist, met us at the airport with cooked bean rice balls filled with *umeboshi* sour plums prepared by Mrs. Katsuragawa. They represented the goodness and evolved humanity of the Japanese people. I embraced Chihara with gratitude, fearing that I had too often been the ugly American to this fine young man and his partner with too many requirements. We embraced—not a common gesture in this restrained society.

As we departed, I carried with me the burden of responsibility laid upon me by the stories and commitment of these unique noble survivors of the nuclear plague. These days it almost seems outrageous to call for a halt in the research, testing and production of these instruments of death. And yet these must continue to be the key demands of any peacemaking community.

Against this potential scenario of terror, the quiet but uncompromising voices of the *hibakusha* continue to cry out to the world leaders and to all people of conscience with the sacred words engraved on the Hiroshima memorial cenotaph as the only viable strategy: "The sin must never be repeated."

I had been so moved by this community of sufferers that I felt impelled to carry their precious witness to the world. Less than a year later my meetings and consultation with Japanese peace and religious leaders bore fruit in a remarkable project: the Japanese-US Nuclear Victims Tour. The tour, organized by the RTF, ran from March 26 to April 11, 1980, and visited sixty US cities in all four corners of the country.

A twenty-member Japanese delegation spearheaded the tour, including ten courageous atom bomb survivors who had made the long trip in spite of their frail and aging condition. Religious, peace and civic leaders accompanied them, serving as their spokespersons. The delegation also brought with them a stunning photographic exhibit—a bitterly incontrovertible testament to the nuclear reality.

The Japanese peace witnesses would be joined by US radiation victims, a suffering class unknown to the majority of the American public and media. In fact, they were intentionally kept invisible because their presence would reveal how deeply America had become a nuclear culture and how willing we were to make guinea pigs and unsuspecting victims out of some of our own citizens who had only desired to serve their country. These included soldiers, nuclear factory workers, Native uranium miners and others.

One of these unsung heroes was Harry Coppola. Harry had been a patriotic Marine—a photograph shows him young, handsome and dapper in his uniform—who had been sent into Nagasaki as part of a cleanup detail only a month after the dropping of the atomic bomb. After the war he moved to Florida with his family and worked as a house painter.

At the time of the tour he was already dying of multiple myeloma bone marrow cancer, prevalent among hundreds of other Hiroshima/Nagasaki veterans. Ironically it was one of the afflictions they had in common with many of the *hibakushas*. It was a classical disease of radiation sufferers.

Harry Coppola participated in limited parts of the tour with the last remnants of life energy that God granted him. He would soon succumb to this virulent form of cancer after a heroic struggle. Before his death, Harry and others like him tried in vain to secure medical and financial help from the Veterans Administration. As he spent his last dollars on chemotherapy and blood transfusions, Harry was also spending the last months of his life speaking out against the nuclear madness.

Another weaver of this tapestry of suffering and courage was Kitae Tomoyasu of Hiroshima. She was forty-four on August 6, 1945, the day of the atomic bombing of Hiroshima. That morning she was at home at 8:15 a.m. when the blinding flash of the bomb came. She went to look for her daughter and found her near the river dying, only able to whisper her good-byes.

Since then Mrs. Tomoyasu has suffered from breast cancer, liver diseases and many other maladies. At the time of the tour she lived in a nursing home for A-bomb survivors. She lived a lonely existence but continued to find meaning for her life by telling the story of her experience as a witness for all humanity. Mrs. Tomoyasu was part of that almost mystical sisterhood and brotherhood of the radiated.

This criminal disregard for human life and safety on the part of government agencies and nuclear corporations would also manifest itself in the culture of denial and refusal to accept any culpability and responsibility or make reparation for the deadly results of radiation poisoning.

It would often take surviving family members of the afflicted and their supporters, occasionally including courageous lawmakers or officials, over two decades of persistent effort, to win any modest compensation. Most never received any.

One possible candidate for our tour was Joe Harding, a worker at the Paducah, Kentucky, Gaseous Diffusion Plant for nearly twenty years. He wanted with all of his heart to participate in the tour and tell his story and that of thousands of co-workers in the nuclear industry to the American people. In a bitter stroke of irony Joe died of abdominal cancer in March of 1980 at the age of fifty-eight, just as the Japanese/ US Nuclear Victims Tour began. Before his death his bones were found to contain up to 34,000 times the medically permissible concentration of uranium.

He was denied compensation because official records showed that he was exposed to only small levels of radiation. Shortly before his death, Joe commented on his fight with the government: "It is absolutely futile, like fighting an elephant with a toothpick." After his death, his widow, Clara, and their daughter, Martha Alls, continued an unrelenting and courageous struggle for justice both for Joe and for all afflicted nuclear workers. On October 30, 2000, two decades after Harding's death, and after hearings, Congress finally passed a new law to compensate nuclear weapons employees of the Department of Energy and surviving dependents. On July 31, 2000, the Energy Employees Occupational Illness Compensation Program went into effect and Clara, knees trembling, was the first to receive the modest sum of $150,000 from the secretary of Labor for her years of suffering and loss. She vowed to continue to help other workers and their families.

The tour participants broke up into four subgroups, which included both Japanese and US representatives and traveled to some sixty cities in the Northeast, South, Midwest and the West. Enthusiastic audiences greeted them wherever they went. churches, synagogues and mosques organized evening events, special worship services on the theme of No More Hiroshimas Anywhere. The groups addressed young people in events at schools and participated in rallies and vigils across the country. The tour received extensive sympathetic news coverage.

One of the most impressive and moving tour participants was Ted Lombard. He had served as a GI at the Manhattan Project conducted in the laboratories at Los Alamos, New Mexico, where the final research leading up to the atomic bombing of Hiroshima and Nagasaki in 1945 was conducted.

Ted remembered that he and his condominium-workers often handled dangerous materials, including plutonium, with their bare hands and without proper monitoring. Wearing work gloves was a concession. "Contamination was rampant," he said. "In certain shops the fumes and dust were constantly in the air. The dust was on the floor. Uranium chips would be in your shoes. You went to eat with the same clothes and sat on the beds."

By the summer of 1945, Lombard was complaining of stomach problems—just before the bombing of Japan. In December, the Army gave him a medical discharge. His health was deteriorating with the tissue in his lungs becoming fibrous and his skin developing sores that would not heal. The worst of it, however, came with his children and grandchildren. He reflected, "I have a daughter, thirty-one, who appeared to be healthy until we looked back. .. .. It is a slow insidious process. Now she's in a wheelchair with neuromuscular, undiagnosed, multiple-type seizures, lack of antibodies, lack of digestive enzymes. . . . My youngest son is deaf/mute, subject to multiple seizures, blood conditions and other undiagnosed problems. He's mentally retarded too. Another son has migraine problems, . . . is aphasic and has blood problems. The two grandchildren are starting to show signs of digestive problems and blood conditions." Lombard filed a claim with the Veterans Administration, which acknowledged his exposures at Los Alamos but refused to provide his medical records.

Ted was a remarkable man who became a friend. He came from a working-class, military background and yet through his experiences developed a radical political perspective and analysis of how the government, the military and the corporate world function. He had a low-key, warm and open nature. I got to know him in the last years of his life and, in spite of severe stomach pains and other problems, he retained a friendly, positive outlook. No matter how he was doing, he rarely refused an invitation to speak at a rally or public event or to testify at a public hearing on the nuclear issue. Ted agreed to participate in the tour, which he thought was of the greatest importance. He was deeply moved by getting to know the Japanese *hibakushas* and experienced feelings of guilt. Ted died before he received the recognition and financial reparation that he struggled for during his last years.

I got to know his daughter Barbara, whose life had been devastated by all these problems. She suffered severe depression and other mental problems as well as extreme allergies to numerous chemical substances and muscular dysfunction. The similar plight of her little girl caused her great sorrow. I still regret how inadequate I was in responding to her myriad needs.

For me the tour was a shattering experience as it brought together the extremes of human suffering with the heights of courage and commitment.

I would like to report that this was the end of this shameful chapter of American history. Alas, there has been a continual attempt to develop "better" nuclear weapons—even for use in outerspace as in the Regan "Star Wars" strategy. Even further, while Clinton was in office, a Neo-Conservative think tank led by Dick Cheney, Paul Wolfowitz and Richard Perle (all future leaders of the Bush administration) privately crafted the Defense Planning Guide with a new strategy of "preemptive" war making, which included the offensive use of nuclear weapons. This unprecedented policy was considered unacceptable even during the cold war when nuclear weapons were still considered "deterrents." This frightening strategy was later officially embraced by the Bush administration and has not been rejected since. The nuclear issue surfaced again dramatically during the Iraq wars with the American use of allegedly harmless depleted uranium (DU) on the tips of missiles and other ordinance causing, according to a growing body of experts, the outbreak of radiation-type illnesses among US personnel and Iraqis.

And so it would seem that once the nuclear genie has been let out of the bottle, its demonic power will continue to manifest itself in many hydra-headed destructive forms until those in power admit to this reality and its dangers and take serious steps to control and reverse it. Some conversations between the Obama administration and Russia about nuclear arms reduction could be a beginning.

But in the end only a powerful popular movement can reverse this fearsome process. The cutting edge of such a movement will always be the voices of those who have themselves been personally effected by the nuclear culture—the victims, workers, miners, veterans and Japanese survivors.

"By [their] wounds we are healed" (Isaiah 53:5–6).

CHAPTER 22

UN SPECIAL SESSION ON DISARMAMENT II
A Season of Hope

WITH THE ANNOUNCEMENT OF THE convening of the Second UN Special Session on Disarmament in May 1982, the world community decided to move the disarmament process forward again.

The UNSSD II had been called by the third world and non-aligned (independent of both the US and the USSR) countries. This time they were looking for real changes from the rich nations.

Once again, the international peace community would take advantage of this historical moment to dramatize the disarmament issue and so strengthen and make visible the UN conference.

Rarely had the global peace community so creatively organized its resources, its members and involved new constituencies in a campaign that would have a powerful impact on world public opinion. At a time when the social movements seemed rather dormant, this would be a period of historic vitality.

A diverse, but often contentious coalition turned out a rally of a million people in Central Park in New York City on Saturday, June 12, 1982. The Nuclear Freeze Campaign in particular, the Mobilization for Survival and the many peace groups were expanding their membership and outreach.

There were African American groups that participated who had not always felt welcome in the traditional organized peace movement except for the Black Veterans after the Vietnam war.

A progressive/centrist mix had the makings of either a powerful coalition or of a political free-for-all. The latter model prevailed for the most part. Racial insensitivity persisted and Dave McReynolds of the War Resisters League wrote of one leader in a report that "he left puddles of racism wherever he sat."

The *Village Voice* had a front-page story called "Peace War." It was a literary attempt to shame the peace movement back to its senses and back to its mission—peacemaking.

Simultaneously, there was a major harmonious organizing and outreach effort by the religious community to people of all faiths, largely under the coordinating umbrella of the Religious Task Force.

Former co-worker Rick Boardman, a longtime peace activist who worked for the American Friends Service Committee (AFSC) and was a draft resister who served time in a federal prison, had this to say about my organizing style: "Paul was a consistent laborer in the field. Ninety percent of success consists in showing up and he showed up and could be depended on to show up. He was steady and reliable and knew a lot of people and had the gift of interacting with different types of people. He was also slightly quixotic and had an over-idealistic side."

We quickly decided to make June 11, 1982, the day before the Central Park rally, the occasion of a major international religious convocation for the Second UN Special Session on Disarmament. Bishop Paul Moore Jr., the late Episcopal bishop of New York, a great leader, peacemaker and friend, offered us the magnificent Cathedral Church of St. John the Divine as a venue, a project also supported by Dean James Parks Morton of the cathedral.

The talented and committed staff of the Religious Task Force made all of this possible. They included the visionary Maureen Roach, a former sister of St. Joseph, the untiring Esther Cassidy and Frank Panopulous.

I cannot exaggerate what an extraordinary "New Spring" of peace-making was blossoming all around us.

The Most Venerable Nijidatsu Fujii, founder of the Japanese Buddhist order Nipponzan Myohoji, launched the World Peace March led by the Japanese monks and nuns with these words spoken at the inauguration of the march in Japan in April of 1981: "The time has come! The time has come when we can no longer contain our inner urge to rush out of our abodes and do something! The time has come to look up to Heaven, prostrate ourselves on the earth and cry out! It is time to voice our grief and share it with everyone! This is what the World Peace March is all about . . . !"

Then a historic event took place in a New York City synagogue—a holy dialogue between Grandfather David, the one-hundred-year-old Hopi elder, and the Venerable Fujii, also in his one hundredth year.

These two ancient sages—one could have called them rabbis—taught us in the spirit of the ancient traditions. In fact, they said very little, but exchanged a few true jewels of wisdom. Venerable Fujii said simply: "Civilization is to hold one another in mutual affection and respect."

Grandfather David spoke mysteriously of the sacred trust for the Earth that the Hopi people carry: "By caring for our lands in the Hopi way, in accordance with instructions from the Great Spirit, we keep the rest of the world in balance. . . . The life of all people as well as the animal and plant life depend on the Hopi spiritual prayers and songs."

The climax of all of these months of spiritual efforts was the historic International Religious Convocation for the Second UN Special Sessions on Disarmament, consisting of ten thousand people, held June 11, 1982, at the Cathedral Church of St. John the Divine. Bishop Paul Moore in his warm words of welcome called it "the largest religious peace gathering in history." When the cathedral choir, accompanied by the magnificent organ, intoned, "Oh, God Our Help in Ages Past" and ten thousand fervent voices joined in that well-beloved Protestant hymn, the power and beauty of it brought tears streaming down my cheeks. We were also inspired by the Earth Jazz of Paul Winter and Radiance.

I summoned the huge community to worship with the assurance that "all this was the miraculous work of the Spirit." The presence of the

Divine was as palpable as I had ever experienced it in my so often imperfect search for the Holy.

Prominent world religious leaders—from Dr. Claire Randall, the general secretary of the National Council of churches to the Buddhist monk and courageous peacemaker Venerable Maha Ghosananda, sometimes called the Cambodian Gandhi, who recently left us for a full state of bliss—proclaimed words from the holy books of all the faith traditions.

"The Witness of the Children" were words of personal war testimony from Arn Chorn, and other children. He gave witness to the unforgettable Cambodian genocide.

A beautiful, multi-racial group of women dancers danced the earthen ceramic bowls of soil brought by all the participants from their home areas down the center aisle in sacred choreography to the front where it was received, blessed and healed by a group of elders from all the worldwide religious traditions.

Clan Mother Alice Papineau of the Turtle Clan of the Onondaga Nation of upstate New York along with other clan mothers led the procession and carried our seashell bowl of blessed earth to Central Park. Therein we planted a tree of life as Rabbi Lynn Gottlieb chanted and the Benedictine monks of Weston Priory, Vermont, surrounded it with a graceful circle of sacred dance.

On the morning of the next day, the city began to fill up early in the morning. People were arriving by bus and train from all over the country. The side streets around the UN were beginning to fill up, so much so that the march was forced to start even earlier than scheduled.

The historic rally of a million began with a dramatic reading by Orson Welles's "The War of the Worlds" radio play. The Performing Artists for Nuclear Disarmament had recruited some of the country's leading performers.

On Tuesday, June 14, the War Resisters League, Mobilization for Survival and assorted peace groups coordinated civil disobedience actions at the UN Missions of the five major nuclear weapon powers: the US, the USSR, China, Great Britain and France (we overlooked India and Israel), as if to remind the governments whose accomplishments were modest at best of the historic speech of President Dwight Eisenhower at the end of his presidency in 1959: "People want peace so much that one day governments had better get out of their way and let them have it."

Three hundred of us were arrested, and I was put into handcuffs at the French mission.

In 1983 as part of a US delegation to Europe to protest the new NATO medium-range missiles, I preached at an interfaith gathering in one of Stuttgart's largest Lutheran churches. I spoke in German and related my personal background and history as a Jewish refugee from the Nazi horrors. I said that it was of the greatest importance that, unlike during those darker earlier times, we stand up to the nuclear fascism that was threatening to take over the planet and even our souls. The role of the church was to stand up to "the principalities and powers," resist, take risks, speak truth to power and stand next to the victims—the poor and the powerless. I was given a long, standing ovation and was brought to tears by this moment of healing with what had once been my land, my culture and my people. Later I also visited a prospective missile site in Comiso, Sicily, along with Judith Thompson.

I have, alas, lost touch with some of these exceptional peacemakers whom I encountered in Japan, Germany and Italy. But they have left an indelible imprint on my peacemaking and my life. Together their faces have become part of that ancient dream for me of "beating swords into plowshares," a dream that transcends borders, cultures and even ideologies, and that is the only acceptable replacement for the nightmarish xenophobic, militaristic aspirations of the Empire that is today reaching new heights of aggressive war in Iraq, Afghanistan, Libya and beyond. It is a dream that continues to be inspired by the ancient teaching of Jesus, the Hebrew prophets and the Gandhis and Martin Luther Kings of history: "Blessed are the peacemakers for they will be called the children of God" (Mt. 5:9).

CHAPTER 23

"YO SOY UN HOMBRE SINCERO"
Visiting Cuba, Meeting Fidel

MY PHONE RANG. THAT SOUND signaled the beginning of so many of my adventures—and troubles. Arthur Kinoy, one of my oldest and dearest friends and one of the great radical constitutional lawyers of our times, was on the line. There is a wonderful picture of him, a man of diminutive stature, being carried out of a hearing of the House Un-American Activities Committee (HUAC) in 1966 by four burly marshals. He refused to be silenced by the chairman who was interrogating him.

Arthur, since deceased and widely mourned, got right to the point. "Hey, Paul, the Cubans want you and Norma Becker to go over there to visit." It seems that people in the Cuban government, especially those I would call the USA watchers, had been impressed by the news reports of our growing disarmament movement and especially by the million-person demonstration of June 12, 1982, in Central Park.

They wanted to meet with some of the organizers of that movement in order to have conversations about the state of the world and to introduce them to Cuba and the Cuban revolution. The Cubans have always been good students of US movements for social change and have maintained relations with them because right from the start the Cuban revolution had been snubbed (and worse) by our government.

The majority of the small island's population, especially the poor and many sophisticated sectors of the world community, were excited in 1959 at the prospect of this new experiment in social transformation in Latin America. Castro had come to New York to make contact with the US and possibly meet with President Eisenhower. He extended the hand of friendship and of possible future cooperation, but there was nobody there to clasp it. In one of the more "brilliant" moves of US foreign policy, our government, surprised that Castro did not come to ask for dollars, refused to talk to him. Eisenhower did begin a cozy relationship with the largely

upper-class Cuban exile community in Miami, who still enjoy a disproportionate voice in shaping US-Cuban policy.

It was a decision for which we—and the Cuban people—would pay dearly in terms of (negative) political energy, expenditures, loss of billions of dollars in trade and decades of political paranoia. It was undoubtedly a decision that drove Cuba more firmly into the arms of the Soviet Union and into a more rigid style of Marxism instead of the more tropical Socialism that was emerging.

After Castro's rejection by the White House, the African American community of Harlem under the leadership of Malcolm X, in a savvy political move, invited Fidel to be its guest. He was warmly welcomed by the Black community and took up temporary residence in the Hotel Theresa, Harlem's finest at that time. And so, Fidel became an honorary citizen of Harlem.

Immediately after Arthur's phone call, I contacted Norma Becker, a friend with whom I had worked for many years. As the Coordinator of the Fifth Avenue Vietnam Peace Parade Committee and again for the June 12th demonstration events, she had played a central organizing role in the American peace movement. We were both excited at the prospect of visiting Cuba, which historically and symbolically had played a role in the process of liberation, especially in Latin America. Neither of us had been there before—although I had wrongly been accused by the FBI of visiting Cuba to raise funds for the Harrisburg Eight case.

At that time, the US State Department forbade direct travel to Cuba—a policy still in force under Obama—so we connected to an Air Cubana flight in Montréal.

Our plane landed in Havana as "Guantanamera" (the well-known song by José Martí—"Yo soy un hombre sincero") played over the intercom, Hence the title of this chapter taken from that lovely tropical song and poem by the great Cuban Jose Marti: "I am a sincere man from the land where the palm trees grow . . . and I want to cast my lot with the poor of the earth." I was deeply moved by the music, even though I was not one of your starry-eyed, naive, uncritical Fidelistas. Yet anyone who has lived and worked in Latin America knows what that musical symbol of the Cuban revolution represents for the ordinary man and woman on the street, especially for the poor who are always in the majority and especially loved by God, as Abe Lincoln observed.

With its many imperfections—and we were to experience all sides of the Cuban reality—this little island represented a glimmer of hope that the lives of the world's poor and those of their children might one day be better. This is something that many smart and even well-meaning North Americans leave out of their critique of Cuba.

The people of Cuba bring to the typical Latin *joie de vivre* a great sense of humor and a sharp intelligence. Cuban art and creativity is celebrated worldwide, but it's probably their music that is closest to my heart. Its impact on jazz is just one example of the seminal power of these extraordinary Cuban sounds.

We were met at the airport by our hosts, including Georgina Cebau of the North American Interest Section of the Cuban government, whom I had befriended in New York at the UN. She was a sophisticated woman who had a nuanced understanding of the American progressive community, including our excesses and occasional nuttiness. We were treated like honored official guests of state (which occasionally felt a little uncomfortable in a developing society where life is still hard for many). Our delegation was housed at the Habana Libre, an elegant hotel, which, in pre-Revolutionary Batista days as the Hilton, was the hangout of the Mafia and show business celebrities who made Cuba their Caribbean playground.

The basic experience of Cuba is one of amazement, especially for someone who has lived and worked in Latin American as I had in

Panama. The people looked the same except you didn't see children with swollen bellies, the constant beggars, the abundance of prostitutes and the desperation.

Unfortunately, since our 1982 visit, daily life, already simple but adequate, became much harder for the ordinary Cuban. This was due in large part to the decades-long US economic blockade and to the demise of the economic aid from the former Soviet Union. Also the Cuban government has made some serious economic missteps.

The mean-spirited and self-defeating US embargo has contributed to severe food and medicine shortages and a much tougher life, including power outages and gasoline shortages. The embargo is opposed by the Cuban Catholic and Protestant churches, the overwhelming majority of the UN community of nations and the Vatican. Today it is also disheartening to see the return of prostitution and begging near the tourist areas. In 1992-'93 there was a near epidemic of severe eye diseases because of nutritional deficiencies and shortages of appropriate medications.

Over the next ten days, we visited housing developments where the system of microbrigades allowed workers at a particular factory, agricultural farm or even government office time off to build apartment complexes that they would later themselves inhabit. The Cuban health system, a model in the developing world, provides free healthcare for all, and the family doctor system makes a doctor personally responsible for one thousand families of a particular area. Many of the doctors are women and are relatively young since the majority of the established medical professionals left Cuba after the revolution.

We visited several neighborhood polyclinics and some rural ones as well as larger hospitals. It was refreshing to meet these dedicated young doctors. They are also trained in acupuncture and make extensive use of *medicina verde* (green medicine)—herbal medicine and other traditional protocols probably used by their grandmothers. We met Dr. Elena Gonzalez in a Havana neighborhood, and one could sense the informal rapport between her and her inner-city patients. She took patients with more complex needs to the specialized hospital for surgery or other procedures.

Prior to the revolution almost all the doctors were concentrated in the Havana area—almost none practiced in the countryside—and these were able to charge exorbitant fees. It is no wonder that most of the established doctors deprived of their prestige, comfort and income took off for Miami.

Cuba now has one of the lowest infant mortality rates in the world, much lower than in the US. Cubans are also proud of the many doctors that they have sent to other countries in times of earthquakes, floods or other crises, or simply to serve underdeveloped countries. Over a thousand doctors and medical volunteers attended victims of the disastrous January 2010 earthquake in Haiti, causing NPR (National Public Radio) to call them "Haiti's unsung heroes." Several thousand Cuban doctors have been sent to Venezuela, where they work with the poorest and train new health professionals in exchange for Venezuelan oil. After Katrina, the Cubans offered to send doctors and supplies to the devastated Delta region—an offer which was ignored by the state and federal governments of the US.

Norma was especially moved by our visits to Cuban schools, where she saw the same population as in her Harlem school but without the problems present in her students. The focus on education in Cuban society and its encouragement of young people have given Cuba one of the highest literacy rates in Latin America.

People at that time had jobs and most had housing, even though some of the buildings in Havana were in disrepair and quarters were sometimes cramped. Life was simple, sometimes rigorous, but I had the impression that people had enough to eat (although that has gotten tougher) and a roof over their heads. It was not life on the edge of misery that is common in most Latin American societies. And, of course, healthcare and education are guaranteed.

This was to be the first of many visits to Cuba in varying contexts and with different projects. Over the years, the friends I made in government circles and beyond at the UN Cuban Mission in New York or in Havana often sought me out for my insights, such as they were, on the US political situation, the world scene and even on the complexities of our own crazy movements. I like to think that they sought me out as a real friend to Cuba, but not an uncritical one. After all, what kind of real friend wouldn't tell you your tie is on crooked or you've got spinach in your teeth?

I never became such an admirer of the Cuban revolution or a fan of Fidel that I wouldn't tell the truth. On our first visit, Norma and I raised the issue of the treatment of gay people in Cuba. We had to bring it up because Cuban authorities had recently un-invited our good friend, Holly Near, still one of the most wonderful folksinger-songwriters, because she was a lesbian. We had also noted that in the lovely park in downtown

Havana, where people stand in long lines for the delicious Coppelia ice cream and which was also a homosexual gathering place, the police were harassing gay people.

We told Georgina and Felipe and others that we had worked our way through this issue in the US progressive community and now took the position that gay rights were human rights as much as the rights of Blacks, women, Latinos and the poor, and had to be honored and protected. Much to their credit, it seems that this point of view was taken to heart and over the years the Cuban position has opened up somewhat on the issue of homosexual rights (surely not due merely to our intervention). I did not observe the previous kind of harassment in that Havana park on subsequent visits and even Raul Castro's daughter has become an advocate for gay rights.

Any discussion about Cuba needs to address the issues of human rights violations, political prisoners and the arguments that use these issues to justify the decades-long economic blockade. Without excusing any violations against even a single human being—even those with awful reactionary views—we must understand how the US has contributed to this Cuban fortress mentality.

Right from the failed Bay of Pigs invasion in 1961 under John F. Kennedy to myriad documented acts of sabotage to numerous foiled assassination attempts against President Castro, the Cubans have felt themselves under siege.

Even the US court system collaborates by setting aside and manipulating US law for the purpose of persecuting Cuba. Luis Posada Carriles, self-confessed anti-Castro terrorist, killer, bomber and CIA- and FBI-collaborator (he is also charged with the 1976 bombing of a civilian Cuban airliner causing seventy-three civilian deaths), has only received a slap on the wrist by US courts. Yet in contrast, the so-called Cuban Five, whose non–violent "crimes" consisted of trying to spy on potentially dangerous groups in Miami planning to harm Cuba, were sentenced to maximum prison terms.

Still, even in the face of internal and external threats, one could ask: Is the Cuban society not strong enough today to open itself up to an initial free internal social dialogue about its future with the involvement of its well-educated and sophisticated population?

Our delegation had come with the sub-agenda of dissuading the authorities from construction of the first Cuban nuclear power plant in Cienfuegos. Accordingly, Australian pediatrician Dr. Helen Caldicott, an anti-nuclear expert, and her husband, Bill, were included in our delegation. Helen, Bill, Norma and I were part of that growing American national consensus that nuclear energy was neither "too cheap to meter" nor safe, as the apocalyptic Chernobyl accident in Ukraine in 1986 and the tragic Japanese Fukushima disaster in 2011 would demonstrate.

Norma and I, because of our longtime involvement with the issues of third world underdevelopment, were also deeply aware of the dilemmas facing Cuba. They would have liked to explore their environmentally perilous offshore oil supply. Cuba had been dependent for its survival on Soviet oil until that source dried up in 1991. The Cubans had, generally speaking, followed the Soviet industrial model of development, so for them their logical energy source would be nuclear, a direction that Castro was proud of.

The challenge of persuading our Cuban friends about the advantage of clean energy was daunting. But we were determined to give it a try since the prospect of a nuclear accident, whether a minor one or a meltdown on this relatively small island, was indeed harrowing. According to expert calculations it could kill tens of thousands and have serious health and environmental consequences for decades. The 2011 accident at the Japanese Fukushima nuclear plant demonstrates the extreme vulnerability of a small island population to nuclear disaster.

Our hosts took our concerns seriously because they set up a meeting for us with the Atomic Energy Commission of Cuba, housed in the Central Committee Building of the Communist Party. The commission consisted of a nuclear physicist, a biophysicist, two engineers and a mathematician—two of these were women. They were obviously a competent, forthcoming, likable group of mostly young people. (Standards of Cuban university and scientific training are highly regarded around the world, it should be noted.)

It was not an easy encounter. The Cubans would have been pained to hear how very similar their arguments and general *Weltanschauung* were to those of their capitalist counterparts. Despite what many leftist intellectuals preach, the crisis of the planet does not ultimately rest on the opposition between capitalism and socialism (although their differences are of grave consequence). Rather, this historic showdown is the fierce, historically decisive confrontation between the worldviews of the industrial culture of the Empire and that of the Earth Community, all brilliantly discussed in David Korten's groundbreaking book *The Great Turning: From Empire to Earth Community*.

The commission members got right to the point. The biophysicist and the woman engineer, all very bright and articulate, began by saying, "This is our first opportunity to have a conversation with a group such as yours and we are very interested and impressed."

The thrust of their argument was the severe energy challenges of their little island, and their confidence that the risks were calculated and worth taking, and that they could construct an almost failure-proof nuclear facility.

We were fortunate to have feisty Dr. Caldicott with us. She used all of her scientific wiles and voluminous health impact data to challenge the commission members, who were charming in that uniquely Cuban way but ultimately unyielding.

In retrospect, I wish we had had more specific data on clean energy sources and technology, though much less was available back in the early 1980s. I still feel guilt for not putting them in touch later with some US experts in the field. Yet they were clearly interested in this issue despite the lack of concrete information. Little did they know that history would eventually turn Cuba in a more sustainable, even organic, direction almost against its will, with the demise of the Soviet Union and cheap oil.

How tragic that Cuba, an island of sun, sea and wind in abundance with such potential for solar, wind and ocean-hydro power, cannot readily develop these at the moment without foreign technology and technical assistance.

The proposed site of the nuclear reactor at Cienfuegos (fittingly translated as "a hundred fires") was a few hours' drive from Havana. It was near the lovely harbor and so followed the pattern of locating these monstrous facilities near beautiful bodies of water to service the plant cooling system.

On arriving, we were greeted by Domingo, head of the Industrial Department of the Cienfuegos Province Communist Party. He was a convinced, ideologically oriented, charming and good-hearted party bureaucrat.

Domingo tried to help us understand the survival challenges facing his tiny, poor island nation that had virtually no fossil fuel resources while we sought to diplomatically—except for our militant Dr. Helen—underscore the dangers of this course. The Cubans seemed willing to strike this nuclear Faustian bargain and take the risks of accident or radiation in order to create this miracle of technology. In the end, the plant construction was put on indefinite hold, mainly out of fiscal constraints.

In the early 1990s Cubans were hit hard by the dissolution of the So-viet Union and the concomitant loss of Soviet-supplied oil. It hurt them on many levels and caused frequent electricity outages, severe gasoline shortages with drastic rationing and hopelessly long lines for buses.

Interestingly enough, this situation has forced Cuba to become a more environmentally sane society. It was recently rated as one the most sustainable societies in the world. Thousands of bicycles are on the roads. Hydroelectric power is being used wherever possible. Traditional *me-dicina verde* is used more than ever before, since petroleum for drugs is not available. Oxen are pulling the plows and farm machinery again. But the most dramatic effects are in food production.

Cuba has become one of the world's leaders in organic and semi-organic food production. Without petroleum for fertilizers, herbicides, pesticides and for machinery, the Cubans are using the resources of the plant and insect world to feed people. In the city of Havana, with 20 percent of the population (2.5 million), there are over eight thousand officially recognized organic gardens covering 30 percent of the available land.

Non-toxic microbial pesticides and fertilizers are used along with earthworm culture, and since 1993 over 80 percent of the farmland has been privatized—a radical departure from the strict Soviet-style model of government-owned and administered-state farms.

There are still conservative elements in the government who see organic farming as only a temporary measure until things return to normal, instead of recognizing the global significance of this pioneering test of large-scale sustainable agriculture. The Swedish Parliament pre-sented the Cuban Organic Farming Association (Grupo de Agricultura Orgánica—GAO) the Right Livelihood Award (known as the Alternative Nobel Peace Prize) for what some have called the Cuban organic revolu-tion of 1989.

The day before our departure, we received the dramatic news that a meeting had been arranged for our delegation with President Fidel Castro—a sign that they were taking our visit seriously. We drove to the Plaza de la Revolución in the center of Havana for a meeting. His well-guarded offices are located behind the José Martí memorial.

Dressed in his olive green fatigues, Fidel entered—a big bear of a man exuding energy and presence. He had an excellent interpreter, al-though it is said that he understands English. He seemed interested in us and our mission and began educating and questioning us, demonstrating an amazing encyclopedic knowledge right down to precise statistics. As Cuba's pre-eminent teacher, he often gave three-hour speeches and, from what I have observed, people actually listened to him.

Unexpectedly, he began his conversation by asking us about the "Moonies." Fidel seemed surprised that such a small, rather eccentric cult (the Unification Church was founded in 1954 in South Korea by Sun Myung Moon) could exert so much political influence. (He seemed more concerned about this than many progressive Americans.) He wanted to know how this could happen in such a religiously sophisticated country. He went on to other religious matters as I politely reminded him that I was the only religious person in the delegation.

He clearly has a hold on the psyche of this nation. Yes, you will run across some who hate him or are disillusioned or oppose apparently brutal decisions or the restrictions on civil liberties and holding political prisoners. They are rightfully critical of mistakes in policy—especially on economic issues such as decentralization and private ownership. His critics include supporters of the revolution. But it seems to me, from my numerous visits, that those who think some remnants of loyalty to the egalitarian ideal of the revolution and even to El Viejo himself no longer exist are mistaken. Many Cubans long for a better and different life, but whether they are ready to turn their country over to dreams of Disney and Big Mac capitalism is questionable.

Today Cuba is on the front pages again. Fidel Castro seems to be failing and the vultures are circling in anticipation of Cuba's collapse. His brother Raul, in his succession, has shown some flexibility and there have been no signs of an uprising. I suspect that these obituaries are premature. Fidel has made many mistakes and he will eventually die. He is a great figure with whom I have large differences on issues like political prisoners and an open, free society. Nevertheless, those who think that there will be an instant return to a pre-revolutionary value system may be surprised about the love many Cubans have for their own history and development.

There are many unknowns. Certainly Cubans are looking for a less difficult existence and they deserve a freer and more abundant life. I pray that the religion of corporate capitalism and the seduction of consumerism will not replace what was noble and valid about their revolution and the framework of an egalitarian society. Only they, not a few super-wealthy Floridians who primarily want their wealth back and more, can decide. May the saner elements in Miami be a responsible part of the process.

Raul Castro, less charismatic than his brother, has said that some *rapprochement* is possible and has already made economic life a little more tolerable for Cubans. In his relatively short tenure, the government has for the first time increased the latitude for private business enterprises, international travel for Cubans and access to the Internet.

The State Department has imposed pre-conditions to negotiations: the release of all political prisoners, change to a multi-party system with free elections and the creation of a free market economy. (Couldn't these demands provoke some soul searching into the state of our own democracy?)

What would happen if instead the US ended its economic embargo and opened a diplomatic dialogue with Cuba? This change in the political climate would certainly make such discussions about these issues more feasible and possibly more effective.

I look forward to an easing of the hardships of daily life for the noble people of Cuba. One can only pray that the tourist onslaught might be controlled, so that the rich culture, the egalitarian values, magnificent ecosystems and natural beauty of the beaches and deep sea splendor of this pearl of the Caribbean could be protected. In short, that some relationship of openness and respect be created without this small but dignified island being devoured by the insatiable giant from the North.

In the meantime, I continue to feel called by the God of justice to work for the protection of the right of self-determination for this extraordinary yet still imperfect *nuestra querida Cuba*—our beloved Cuba.

CHAPTER 24

RELIGION IN CUBA, PASTORS FOR PEACE

I WAS INTERESTED IN LEARNING about the Cuban religious scene and began to make contacts over several visits. I contacted Rev. Raul Suarez, who together with his wonderful, now deceased wife Clara was pastor of the Ebenezer Baptist Church in Havana and director of the Martin Luther King Center—a locus for much peace and justice activity. He was also one of the leaders of the Cuban Council of churches, which the Catholic Church did not join. Raul had obviously decided to work closely with the government and later became one of the first Christians accepted into the Communist Party and the first Christian member of the National Assembly, the parliament. The background on religious life in Cuba that he provided me helped in my later conversation with Castro.

During a later meeting with Castro when I served as the organizer of a religious delegation he launched into a discussion of religious themes.

He said he wanted to understand more about Liberation Theology, a movement that is based on caring about the poor.

He acknowledged that they had made many mistakes regarding religion and the Church, taking Marx's idea of religion as an opiate of the people too literally. Meeting Christian groups from Chile and Jamaica with social awareness changed his view. He also noted that it was primarily the Church in Chile that kept records of atrocities under Pinochet after the fall of the Allende regime.

Castro said they had discussed the possibility of cooperation between Christian and Socialist groups and had even spoken of an alliance that would be "not merely a tactical alliance but a strategic alliance, to work together for the social changes our people need."

The next day I visited the Catholic Seminary of San Carlos y San Ambrosio in Old Havana, all of which has been magnificently restored by UNESCO as a world art treasure, as has the classic Caribbean baroque cathedral. Attached to the cathedral is the seminary where I spoke with a priest member of the faculty, who was quite candid in our conversation.

He believed that some of the tensions between the Church and the Party were not so much a lack of good will as a lack of communication between the more enlightened position of the national leadership to the lower echelon leadership at the grassroots. Often there was little support and understanding of the new *rapprochement* by local leaders. The priest emphasized the difficulty of preserving the positive ideals of the revolution among the youth, noting that alienated teenagers listened to Radio Martí from Miami and were seduced by consumerism when their families came to visit from the US.

He concluded by saying, "Frankly, it's not easy being a Christian here. We are rarely admitted to a psychology department as professors and are almost never allowed to assume leadership roles in anything. But as Christians we must be part of the important task of building a new society."

After my first visit I had returned home with the idea of putting together a delegation of religious leaders for next April. The RTF organized a high- to mid-level leadership delegation to experience the fascinating Cuban reality and to foster the new religious opening that seemed to be simmering there.

We would come to see ourselves, along with later religious delegations, as part of the process of encouraging an incipient dialogue between the Cuban religious community—especially some of the less conservative

Protestant churches, and more reluctantly the Catholic Church—with the Cuban Communist Party.

One other important catalyst of the process was a visit in 1988 to Cuba by Rev. Jesse Jackson. On that visit he invited President Castro to accompany him to a large interfaith event held at one of Havana's largest Protestant churches in honor of Dr. Martin Luther King, Jr., for which Jackson was to be the keynote preacher. ("Bringing Fidel to church," as Jesse put it.) Castro was also invited to say a few words—not an easy feat for Fidel—who said he was very moved and surprised by the experience and the warm reception he received.

Soon after this came the publication of *Fidel and Religion*, a marathon twenty-three-hour interview of Castro by Frei Betto, a Brazilian Dominican-order friar and liberation theologian. The book was a sensation in Cuba and an instant bestseller because the Cubans were stunned by the leader of the revolution talking about religion and in such a personal way. The book is a brilliant work, occasionally a little dogmatic and self-serving, but on the whole a candid, self-revealing account of Fidel's religious background, school experience and views about the genuine possibilities, not only of tolerance, but of authentic *rapprochement*, especially between Christians and Marxists.

In the meantime, an Office of Religious Affairs (ORA) had been established by the government under the leadership of the genial Dr. Luis Carneados. Later called "the Red Pope" by some, Dr. Carneados was a highly respected law professor at the University of Havana. Our delegation had a frank and fruitful meeting with Carneados and several key Protestant Cuban religious leaders. We felt obliged to raise the thorny questions of the practical exclusion of Christians (and probably religious Jews) from full participation in Cuban society. Carneados seemed open to our concerns and later we were to witness some gradual loosening up of government policy.

Dr. Carneados—now deceased—seemed to be well respected by the Cuban religious leadership, both Christian and Jewish, as a fair-minded and decent person. His office included responsibility for such practical matters as providing construction material for the repair and building of religious structures, which had been halted for many years. Under his leadership there was the beginning of conversation about Christians being allowed to join the Communist Party.

We had some private meetings with important Catholics, but the Catholic Church, as such, was uneasy about public association with us, perhaps because of my checkered career (which they may or may not have been aware of), but especially because they may have perceived us as too sympathetic to the government. Some of the Catholics in our delegation, though, did have some frank, unofficial discussions with key Cuban Catholic Church leaders.

A process of self-reflection on the role of the Catholic Church in Cuba raised high hopes that it would usher in a new period of harmony and dialogue between Church and state. These hopes would not be fully realized from either side, but an important statement had been made and the symbolic power of this process could not be missed.

I had always pursued an interest in the non-Christian religions of Cuba, especially Santería, which was originally a kind of underground religion of the African slaves. Many Cubans, even Christians (and perhaps some Party members), were secretly practitioners at the time of our visit. All of this became more open later on. With the help of Natalia Bolivar Arostegui (a descendant of Simon Bolivar) and one of the great experts in this field, we visited Ibrahim, a *santero* and a Yoruba priest, for a blessing and a reading on our journey.

Later, in 1985, Father René David, a French theologian also teaching at the Seminary of San Carlos y San Ambrosio in Havana, wrote a brilliant document titled, "Towards a Theology and Pastoral Practice of Reconciliation in Cuba," probably the most important Catholic theological contribution at the time to come from Cuba since the revolution.

His thesis was that Liberation Theology does not seem to apply to Cuba "where the Revolution has already eliminated private ownership of the means of production and distribution . . . and has instituted free education and healthcare . . . " It called instead for a theology of reconciliation and self-criticism where Communists would transcend dogmatic ideological atheism almost turned into a pseudoreligion. Then Christians, in the same spirit, would recognize that the reconciliation of all people with one another to build a classless society is in accord with the spiritual demands of the faith that "there are neither Jew nor Greek, slave nor free, male nor female but all are one in Christ Jesus" (Galatians 3:28).

It was interesting to note how many similarities there were between his ideas and some of our conversations with Castro and even more with passages from *Fidel and Religion*. Alas, this compelling vision still seems far from realization on either side.

I did also meet some impressive Protestant theologians who were doing original thinking, among whom I remember Obed Gorrin. Adolfo

Ham, a progressive Presbyterian theologian and church leader (and yoga practitioner), was always a reliable interpreter of the Cuban intricacies for me.

On my first visit, I had initiated contact with the small Jewish community, which I pursued with some of the people of faith. I was very disappointed by our failure to have a rabbi in our delegation. (One had canceled at the last minute because of a family emergency.) Our Jewish friends who lived a relatively isolated existence were even pleased by my Jewish ancestry, since living in Cuba had given them a certain flexibility in outlook.

There had always been a very small Cuban Jewish community, which grew considerably by the influx of European Jews during the Nazi period. A high percentage of the community left Cuba after the revolution for economic reasons. My primary contact was Moises Asis who was not a rabbi, but because of his knowledge and the respect he enjoyed, served as the de facto spiritual head of the community. The last time I saw Moises I had a beautiful visit with his family, and he was sadly pessimistic about the political situation. He and his family have subsequently immigrated to "the States."

In the ensuing years I was invited to several international theological dialogues and some conferences on sociology and religion, where I was invited to lecture. It was fascinating how in an officially atheistic society, religion was studied with great seriousness like any other science. I often felt like I was having a serious dialogue with very knowledgeable fellow believers.

In 1992, my friend Rev. Lucius Walker, a charismatic African American Baptist minister, was at it again. He had once been an associate secretary general of the National Council of churches, but his advanced views on issues such as the liberation struggles in Africa seemed to be out of sync with that august body at the time. Lucius, or Lu as he was known to his friends, left the NCC and eventually started an effective organization of his own—IFCO (the Interreligious Foundation for Community Organizing) on 145th Street in Harlem—which addressed local issues such as housing and police violence, as well as international struggles such as apartheid in South Africa and peace in Central America.

Lu and I had become friends over the years because we recognized each other as kindred spirits who took the message of Jesus about justice and compassion literally. I was immediately intrigued when he invited me to join a project for Cuba called Pastors for Peace. I learned that IFCO had already organized humanitarian aid caravans of trucks, cars and buses carrying food, medicine, bicycles and other similar "subversive" goods into places like Mexico and Guatemala to help the poor and suffering people there.

Now, he was going to extend the Pastors for Peace caravans into Cuba and asked if I would like to participate. This project would be more complicated than their previous ventures because it was not possible to reach Cuba overland. And then there was the small matter of an official US embargo prohibiting the bringing of goods (even food and medicine) to this dangerous little island across the Florida straits.

What could I say but "yes!" I realized that Cuba was going through one of its "special periods," which meant a national tightening of the belt. The greatest democracy in the world was strengthen the embargo more through the Torricelli Bill, which would even prevent other countries from doing any kind of business with Cuba under threat of economic and diplomatic retaliations. It didn't seem to matter to our masters in Washington that these decisions caused malnutrition in children and serious epidemics of eye diseases.

So I packed my backpack and participated in a moving religious sendoff in New York. On the day before our departure, we had a press conference at the office of our New Jersey right-wing anti-Castro Representative Torricelli (later as senator, he was forcibly retired because of suspicions of financial irregularities). We were part of a caravan of dozens of vehicles coming from the Northeast and our segment would eventually rendezvous with five or six other branches of the humanitarian aid caravan, converging from all four corners of our beautiful country. The participants reflected a wide and diverse spectrum of generous humanity.

We traveled through many states stopping in cities, towns and villages. Sometimes we would be guests at evening gatherings at local churches or community centers, occasionally with music or theater but all opportunities for the "caravanistas," so called, to talk about our journey, our vision, our motivation, the goods we were carrying and to ask for further donations of material aid or money to further our work. In this way, we reached many new people about the true situation of Cuba.

I slept on many a Church or living room floor on the journey. Occasionally I was even blessed with a bed. One day it was peanut butter sandwiches and, on others, gourmet vegetarian meals. I had the honor of sharing the driving with Rev. Walker in his sometimes challenging Church van from Brooklyn. We got to be even better friends talking about the deeper things of life as we traveled north to south. I felt a little uneasy in a few of the Southern states, remembering my frightening experiences of the civil rights movement, but we met lots of fine people and some even responded to the signs on our cars about US-Cuban friendship.

We finally arrived in Laredo, Texas, on the Mexican border. It was here that we intended to enter Mexico and make our way to the port of Tampico where our aid cargo would be loaded onto Cuban freighters and we caravanistas would board an Air Cubana plane for Havana to spend a week distributing goods and meeting the people of Cuba.

But it was not to be that simple. At the Laredo US-Mexico Bridge, we were greeted by US Treasury police who had only one thing on their mind—yes, the Torricelli Bill and the economic blockade. There was some support in that little town, especially from some of the local clergy, and we were ready to meet the opposition.

The police stopped us to check our caravan of trucks, cars, vans and buses and to deny us departure across the border. Our confrontation shut down all traffic across the bridge. Tom Hansen, an organizer from Minnesota and the coordinator of the caravan, decided that we should hand carry as much of our aid as possible across the bridge, since we doubted that the government would want to close down all pedestrian bridge traffic as well.

So we began unloading our cargo and carrying boxes of medicine and containers of food across the bridge on foot. I was wearing my clergy collar for the occasion so Tom decided to have me carry some Spanish Bibles across the bridge, which we were bringing to Cuba because of the acute paper shortage there.

"Not so fast, my friend." Several husky Treasury police officers blocked my way. "You'll have to hand those over to us, sir," they said, reaching for my Bibles.

I pulled back and explained that I could not possibly give them these books because "these are Bibles that I have been commissioned to carry to the churches of Cuba." One big cop grabbed my Bibles and when I held on, he twisted my arm and literally flipped me over onto the ground. I continued to hold on and one officer grabbed me on each side with the Bibles under my arm and dragged me away. I asked whether I was under arrest. They ignored my question and said that they would have to hold me for a while.

In the meantime, several of our other key people had been apprehended including Rev. Walker. They interrogated us about our intentions, our organization, et cetera. Of course, they knew exactly who we were since we had previously applied for an export permit, which they had refused. I tried to engage one of the police officers who looked like a Chicano in conversation about the Bible, Jesus, the Cuban people and the unity of all Latino people. He remained silent but seemed to be listening.

In the meantime, our supporters nationwide were deluging the offices of the Department of the Interior with calls about our situation. The news media arrived and our story was carried nationally and internationally. The next day the front page of the second section of *The New York Times* had a large photo of me being dragged off by two cops with the Bibles under my arm.

We were preparing ourselves to dig in for the long haul when suddenly, much to our surprise, orders came from Washington to let us through. They had received a flood of calls from Church leaders, ordinary citizens and even a few congresspeople. (This was before the George W. Bush administration and 9/11, when the government was still concerned about appearances.)

However, we had to leave all computers behind, since there was fear that the Cubans might use these antiquated Mickey Mouse PCs for some nefarious plots, perhaps launching "weapons of mass destruction."

We drove off through the barriers and across the bridge, where we were met with tremendous jubilation from some Mexicans and even a few Cubans. It seems that we were seen as the first ones to ever have broken the US embargo. It was a small step, but symbolically significant. People applauded us as we drove along the Mexican roads and through towns. They loved the signs on our cars and trucks. People in the US don't understand what a powerful symbol Cuba is through all of Latin America. Everybody wanted to shake our hands.

Finally, we made it to Tampico, where our aid shipment was loaded onto Cuban freighters, and then we drove on to the airport. After a few hours, an Air Cubana plane bound for Havana landed. It's hard to believe that everybody in the world is not as crazy as the US is about the "evils" of traveling to Cuba.

We arrived in Havana. Driving our vans along the streets, we saw that many people had come out to welcome us. People went wild. Everybody was overwhelmed by the idea that the blockade had been broken and by a group of North Americans at that. Our fame preceded us on TV and even anti-government people wanted to welcome us.

That night the caravanistas were welcomed at an event at the biggest Methodist Church in Havana, and Fidel unexpectedly showed up. The Church was packed to capacity.

After hymns of thanksgiving, Rev. Walker gave a beautiful speech expressing our love and admiration of the Cuban people. He presented President Castro with a Bible—it was amons the ones I had tried to carry across the border. He told the story of the Bible. We could see that Fidel was deeply moved, and he asked, "Where is that heroic priest that wanted to bring us the Bible?" Hardly a description that fitted me. They pointed me out in the congregation and Fidel came down from the stage, waded into the audience and gave me a big *abrazo*—a hug. It was a very moving moment for all of us, since our whole caravan was "heroic" on that day at the border. It symbolized the unity of our two peoples in a sacred way.

Fidel then gave an amazing "homily" on the meaning of our caravan and the Bible. Speaking like a liberation theologian, he said that the Bible is a book that is not finished yet. Then he added quite movingly that by our mission here and by our work we were writing a new page of the Bible. It was a profound moment.

A few days later, the ships with our material aid arrived from Mexico and there were thousands at the dock, including Fidel and other dignitaries to greet them. We never dreamt that it would be of such import.

We all worked at unloading the trucks at the Martin Luther King Center under the supervision of Rev. Raul Suarez. We intentionally wanted the churches to handle the distribution in order to avoid all charges of government corruption. It was interesting to see how Fidel came back numerous times to "hang out" with us as we were unloading. He seemed to be quite interested in talking about the spirituality of our struggle and about our common goals and work.

During those days in Havana, I was recognized on the street by people from the TV news as *el hombre de la Biblia*—"the man with the Bible." Would that I could live up to such a titles for what else is there except to be a man of God, to really wield "the sword of the Spirit which is the word of God"? (Ephesians 6:17).

CHAPTER 25

JESSE JACKSON'S 1984 PRESIDENTIAL CAMPAIGN AND THE RAINBOW COALITION

IN THE FALL OF 1983 I was attending a New York clergy meeting. During a recess I was quietly resting on a corner bench. I observed a small group of Black clergy caucusing and overheard them discussing the Rev. Jesse Jackson's recent announcement to run for president. Suddenly, the group moved in my direction and stood right in front of me. One of them addressed me.

The speaker was Rev. Timothy Mitchell, the over-six-foot-tall formidable shepherd of the Ebenezer Baptist Church in Queens, made all the more so by his impressive Afro hairstyle. Tim got right to the point: "Paul, we need you to get involved in this campaign for Jesse. It's really important to us."

Now I did not turn down an invitation from Tim Mitchell lightly. In my book he was one of the great champions for justice in the Black church and increasingly a good friend. His causes were usually my causes as well. But he caught me off balance. "Tim," I responded, "believe it or not, I have never participated in an electoral campaign in my life." Not only did I have grave misgivings about our alleged two-party system—it was getting harder all the time to tell the two parties apart—I, like the majority of young and minority Americans, felt profoundly alienated from electoral politics. At the time only 33 percent of Americans voted. I felt a little like Abbie Hoffman: "Don't vote! It only encourages the bastards."

In the early 1980s, a large segment of the liberal left community (rightly or wrongly) still disdained elections. We didn't think that the outcome made any differences and often it hadn't. Apparently, a liberal Democrat like Lyndon B. Johnson could also become the principal architect of the war in Vietnam.

"Tim, you're talking to the wrong guy. Even voting is a big stretch for me, but working for a candidate seems like going to the moon."

Tim Mitchell and friends were not to be easily deterred. He said, "Paul, this campaign is different. You can't sit this one out. It's going to be really important for the Black community. We need you, your talents, and your movement involved in this one." He was probably recalling the million peace demonstrators that had gathered in Central Park on June 12, 1982. "Think about it, pray about it and we'll talk some more." With that the recess was over. We returned to the conference hall and I was left with some very conflicting thoughts and feelings.

I went home and spent the next weeks in intense prayer asking God for guidance. It felt like this would be a major divergence from my path. I liked to think of my path as a "radical" one that took me to the roots of the great issues.

At that time, there were not that many white activists who were both committed to building a multi-racial movement and were also trusted by others—Blacks, Hispanics and the poor. Since I had been given the gift of both, maybe this campaign was God's calling for me at that moment. Once again, I would have to surrender the luxury of "being sure" in the name of holy uncertainty.

At the time, I was working on a Doctor of Ministry degree at New York Theological Seminary, where I had previously taught for several years as a member of the adjunct faculty. It was an intensive program that I had undertaken with mixed feelings stemming from the competing demands of my political involvement and my ambivalence about the academic world of certification and degrees. I had gathered a team of advisors. The theme of my dissertation was to be multi-racial coalition building, a subject close to my heart.

As I gradually came to understand the import and demands of the presidential campaign of a Black candidate, the Rainbow Coalition and the significance of this precise historical and political moment with its possible opportunities, it became clear to me that I would have to choose between the two. Demands on my time precluded doing both.

It was with mixed feelings and some reluctance that I decided in favor of this new involvement in the presidential campaign of the Rev. Jesse Jackson and of commitment to the still nascent Rainbow Coalition. Recognition in academia would have to wait for another time, another lifetime, or maybe never.

The Rev. Jesse Jackson was an imposing figure no matter from what angle you approached him. He was handsome, well over six feet tall with an athlete's build. In his younger days he was a college football star. Jesse oozed charisma. He had an irresistibly charming personality, almost seductively persuasive gifts and a laser-like intelligence, all contained within a disarming self-assurance. Perhaps above all, he was one of the most powerful preacher-orators of our time, right up there with his mentor, Martin Luther King Jr. Let it also be said up front that his powerful ego was at once his greatest asset and—like most of us—his tragic Achilles' heel.

Jackson had grown up in grinding Southern rural poverty in Greenville, South Carolina, where he had been born out of wedlock and never acknowledged until his forties by his biological father, Noah Robinson. In other words, his life had followed the same Calvary path of so many other poor African American males in this great Jeffersonian democracy.

By dint of an ironclad will, he had made his way through the University of Illinois into the ministry, eventually becoming a key player in the Southern Christian Leadership Conference, the original organizational home of Dr. King and the mainstream Southern Freedom Movement. He had been present at the Lorraine Motel in Memphis, Tennessee, on that cruel and fateful day, April 4, 1968, when King was murdered. He then went on to become part of the inner leadership circle of the more centrist wing of the civil rights movement, as opposed to the more radical Black Power youth movement of the Student Non-violent Coordinating Committee (SNCC) led by Stokely Carmichael and others.

With his extraordinary gifts, he navigated the shoals of Chicago city and Black Church politics to become the founder of Operation PUSH (People United to Save Humanity), an influential and often controversial focus of community organizing in the mean streets of the Chicago South Side, the Black ghetto. It made major gains in the area of equal opportunity and jobs for the poor. Through the rough and tumble political intricacies of the Southern civil rights movement after Dr. King's death, Jackson had, over the years, become a significant figure in that community and was recognized by many Black ministers as a leader and acclaimed preacher.

Jackson was about to enter a political moment that would probably become the apotheosis of his career—nothing less than a contender for the office of president of the United States of America. However unlikely it was that such a candidate would be taken seriously by the political establishment of racist America and by a jaded and controlled news media, he was poised to give those "principalities and powers" a run for their money. He had heard the increasing urging of the Black community to "Run, Jesse, run!" and run he did.

At that time, in the fall of 1983, Rev. John Collins and I had become the principal point persons in the campaign to reach out to the constituency of the white religious and peace and justice communities for the historic tasks of building a true Rainbow Coalition. John and I had been friends, colleagues and sometimes amicable competitors because of his role as director of Clergy and Laity Concerned and mine as director of the Religious Task Force.

We had both been invited to participate because of our personal histories in the civil rights movement and because of the respect we enjoyed as brothers who "walked the talk" as allies of Black folks and other people of color. This is a badge I wear with honor. It is not an easy one to acquire because the poor and people of color have learned to not easily trust themselves and their futures to white people—and with good reason.

Ironically, the first challenge to my transformation into this new role would prove to be sartorial. "The Rev," as Jackson was affectionately known, always wore some of the most elegant suits I have ever seen, and this was also true to a lesser extent of many of his Black clergy retinue and supporters. In this setting I showed up skinny, white, with a beard and a Jewish profile, wearing an elegant (or so I thought) Chairman Mao jacket as a symbol of evangelical simplicity and revolutionary fervor.

Although not a word was ever said to me, I got the message. I slowly began to change my public persona with suit and tie or at least a fashionable black turtleneck sweater. My more counterculture friends were surprised, if not shocked, but I quickly concluded that to do otherwise would have been a lack of respect to my newly acquired comrades and mission. So I trimmed by beard, got a haircut and acquired some upscale suits and sport jackets from my favorite thrift shop.

The task of involving the religious community and the peace movement groups in the campaign could not be regarded as a shoo-in. Many of these groups did not see themselves as participants in an electoral campaign and certainly not one that had a Black candidate and was led by African American clergy and organizers. Even the most progressive among us have prejudicial and sometimes even unspoken subconscious racist attitudes and judgments.

Further, it was difficult to communicate to friends, comrades, colleagues and other potential allies that building this Rainbow Coalition was to be much more than one more electoral campaign, even in the best sense of the word. The self-understanding of the Jesse Jackson campaign was that it was really about building a social movement and coalition—a new political community—in a style and with a vision that had never been attempted before in precisely this fashion.

Jackson himself had laid it out in language that was both simple and visionary:

> "My commitment as a presidential candidate is to focus on and lift those boats stuck on the bottom full of unpolished pearls. For if the boats on the bottom rise, all boats above will rise—my views in this regard are the exact opposite of the 'trickle-down' views of President Reagan. The way I propose to do this is to build a new functional 'Rainbow Coalition of the Rejected' spanning lines of color, sex, age, religion, race, region and national origin. The old minorities—Blacks, Hispanics, women, peace activists, environmentalists, youth, the elderly, small farmers, business persons, poor people, gays and lesbians—if we remain apart, we will continue to be a minority. But, if we come together, the old minorities constitute a new majority. That is how I propose to be nominated and elected president."

This was the vision of the Jackson presidential campaign at its finest, and when it deviated from this ideal, it would lose what was most precious, profound and socially transformative about this politically magical moment.

This—at first sight—utopian strategy was actually based on a pragmatic analysis of the previous political period of the 1970s and '80s, the assault of the New Right. This period had followed the heady, even intoxicating '60s when a mass movement had been built around opposition to the war in Vietnam and the civil rights movement, when a countercultural mystique of freedom was in the air, and when many serious political people believed that we might be on the threshold of the birth of a new society characterized by political and personal freedom.

The neo-conservative spirit of the '70s and '80s reached its fullest expression in the presidency of Ronald Reagan. The Black civil rights movement had lost its momentum after the death of Dr. King for a variety of complex reasons. The white peace and progressive movement was focusing on nuclear disarmament and nuclear energy issues and had lost its ideal of uniting with the Black struggles as it had in past dramatic historical moments, such as the Selma voters' registration campaign. The nation was in the grips of an officially sponsored cold war obsession and the demonizing of the Soviet Union and the Communist threat.

It was against this background that Jesse Jackson appeared and presented his political vision of a new kind of unity. It was not the traditional unity engendered by the Marxist ideal of class warfare or by the workers' relationship to the means of production. Rather this new unity would be created by the "boats" apparently forever stuck to the bottom, a unity of those "rejected and locked out" whether because of race, national origin, gender, and even sexual orientation or age. It would be the almost biblical mission of this campaign to reconnect the biblical Anawim—the weak, forgotten ones—to their inherent dignity and sense of purpose.

The initial core followers of this campaign were predominantly African American—many of those clergy—and a sprinkling of Latinos, Arab Americans, Asians, gays, progressive Jews and others. John Collins and I were among the first white clergy peace activists. We were joined shortly by Sheila Collins, John's wife, a college professor of political science and dedicated activist who was to play a major role in the campaign as a key staff person. Dr. Barry Commoner, the brilliant environmental scientist and academic, was among the other white activists who joined the Rainbow Campaign.

As a result, either John or I or both of us and representatives of other constituencies would often help create the visual image of the rainbow on the speakers' platform behind "the Rev" during his whirlwind campaign of public presentations. This was no ordinary electoral barnstorming.

In fact, the Jackson campaign was probably unique in American campaign history. It was conducted with practically no financial resources and only a skeleton staff that was strong on commitment but weak on experience. In fact, there was virtually no one on the national staff who had ever been even close to a presidential campaign before.

The campaign began with $50,000 and a vision. Representatives from the peace, farmer, environmentalist, Native American, Arab American, Latino and other non-Black constituencies gradually came on board—at first as volunteers and then as modestly paid staffers. They often represented the cream of those respective groupings. Along with the networks of Black Church and political groups, representatives of Jackson's own Operation Push and, at first disorganized supporters of a more progressive America, slowly congealed into a modest, somewhat inexperienced and sometimes amateurish political machine. What the campaign of the Rainbow Coalition eventually achieved was nothing short of miraculous. It was all motivated and energetically infused by the dream of a new America based on an authentic moral vision as stated in Jackson's announcement speech: "Running for the presidency gives me the opportunity to serve this nation on a level where I can help restore a high moral tone, reestablish a sense of idealism and common decency in the national discussion of public issues, offer a redemptive spirit to the nation and rekindle a sensitivity to the poor and dispossessed in our country."

It was a campaign based on Black leadership, on the experience and struggle of Black people, on the goal of lifting up and liberating Black people but it was not a Black campaign. It authentically sought to transcend and build on these realities, to create something new—a multiracial, multi-ethnic rainbow insurgency against the sterile two-party system that manifestly no longer served the majority of the American people, if it ever had.

One of these "miraculous" aspects was its ability to overcome the liability of not having the resources to run television ads. That component—the apparent lifeblood of today's electoral campaigns—is a sterile substitute for genuine human contact. The response to this liability was to develop a grassroots, on-the-ground, door-to-door campaign, the likes of which our country has rarely witnessed. At its core was Jesse Jackson,

who drove himself mercilessly across the American landscape like a political evangelist with a message burning to be heard.

From dawn to dusk, he appeared before audiences of every hue and
social background in every kind of setting announcing the Rainbow Coalition message of human rights for all, respect for the earth, economic
justice, a place in the sun for the most disenfranchised members of our
society, and a foreign policy based on peace and sanity. Sometimes he
racked up an unbelievable twelve events a day. I had the privilege of accompanying him on some of those journeys in the New York/New Jersey
area, New Hampshire, New Mexico and beyond.

These were often moments of incomparable inspiration, not only
because of his eloquence (his speeches made electoral history through
their quality, brilliance and content) but especially because of the impact
they had on their audiences. I found this to be especially true in some of
the poorest communities of Black people. I can still remember a campaign visit to Camden—arguably the poorest Black urban ghetto in New
Jersey or even the country. Its industrial base had eroded. The famous
Campbell Soup plant had been long gone and, with the abandonment
of most of the white working-class population, the remaining Black and
Latino ghettos were concentrations of misery and sheer despair. There
Jackson addressed a surprisingly large crowd—a cross-section of the African American community in terms of age—in what essentially was a
vacant lot trying to look like some kind of park.

The crowd was made up of the lumpen of the lumpen in this desperately poor community. I looked out at the wretched and the broken
people dressed in just this side of rags, mothers who had dragged along
a brood of children, a smattering of the local homeboys, old people in
fragile condition with canes and crutches, a delegation of the local junkies and winos, along with the masses of the struggling, working poor.

It was through this community that Jesse's words traveled like electricity. As he proclaimed his message of new possibilities, a movement
was founded based on the experience of the rejected and locked out, a
movement that called for a society with full employment, respect and
new possibilities. His message was "God don't make no ugly!" Jackson is a
master of mass psychology, but not a demagogue—rather a Pied Piper of
hope. His gift of firing up his Black audience, in this case for the political
struggle ahead, made use of the traditional call and response of African
culture to transform his listeners' experiences of suffering and rejection
of into a source of hope. He chanted: "Repeat after me: 'I am somebody. I

may be poor, but I am somebody. I may be on welfare, I may be unskilled, but I am somebody. Respect me! Say that I am more than what you see. I am God's child. I am somebody."

It was mesmerizing to see this collection of the wretched and the ragged turn into a community of the hopeful and potentially empowered. This was no longer merely a desolate Camden ghetto, but a people with promise, faces transfixed with smiles of hope. It looked and felt like a moment of new beginnings. These experiences were especially important to me as someone who has lived in a similar community in East Orange, New Jersey—perhaps not quite as depressed—for over forty years. At that time, I still hoped that my people there might have their place in the sun some day.

Jackson often stayed overnight in those communities, the guest of a family in the housing projects. These experiences helped to deepen his own understanding and compassion—whether it was in Camden, a farm community or in a white factory worker's home in Ohio. His gift in all of these settings was to intuitively connect with the energy of his audiences—not only their enthusiasm but also the needs, hopes and aspirations of the "boats stuck to the bottom."

Time and time again I saw him proclaim his message with its deep understanding, intelligence and passion and watched as he connected with the specific needs, sufferings and issues of a particular group of people before him. He studied the challenges of Latinos, farmers, the Native American community down to what pieces of legislation or strategy might serve to ameliorate the suffering of this segment of the rainbow before him at the moment. His gift was also to weave these different needs and hopes together into one brilliant rainbow banner of hope and redemption—political and spiritual—for all.

At times I experienced the excitement (and, to be truthful, a sense of elitism) as part of the official entourage. In spite of all of my anti-establishment ideology, I felt the allure and illusion of power as I traveled with the Secret Service protection accorded to a presidential candidate (no matter how despised by the establishment) and occasionally rode in the official limousine. Secret Service protection was no idle gesture. Jackson had received three hundred and eleven death threats in the course of one week—more than almost any other presidential candidate. Nothing so provokes racist America as the threat of a Black man taking power for himself and for his (and all) people—a reality demonstrated all too clearly during the Obama administration.

It would be a mistake, however, to perceive the strong African American character of the Jackson campaign and the Rainbow Coalition as simply a racial issue. Race played a major role, but there was something more profound, more powerful and more significant at work.

The heart of this mysterious dimension was brilliantly captured by Black historian Lerone Williams, who is quoted in a lecture by John David Maguire, "The Necessity of Thinking Black" (delivered to Student YWCA at the University of Maryland, May 1978): "By the grace of God and the whip of history, Black people, in the main, have not completely assimilated those values that are driving Western man to social and spiritual suicide: acquisitiveness, for example, numbness of heart and machine idolatry . . . . To the extent that these things are foreign to the Black experience, to that extent the Black man is uniquely qualified to take the lead in recasting the human values of our civilization."

This dimension has also long been recognized by a small but enlightened sector of white progressive movements for social change. I had often heard esteemed colleagues like the late civil rights lawyer Arthur Kinoy enunciate this point with clarity and deep conviction. Such a vision implied that an authentic movement for justice, peace and social transformation must be led by Black people. I must confess that this perspective took me some years to grasp and internalize and that at first I perceived it as a form of some political mysticism. I gradually came to understand this as an analysis that stemmed neither from white guilt nor from some reverse cult of racial superiority but rather from an understanding of the consciousness and history of the Black soul.

I dwell on this insight because of its ultimate role in persuading me to put other commitments and even personal lifestyle aside to join the Jackson campaign. I had a strong intuition that this vision was about to take flesh in a new historic manner that could transform the American political landscape. This understanding is based on the unique character of the Black experience in America and the nature of the culture from which it has emerged. Granted, there have been deviations and betrayals (as in any group), but in the meantime this mysterious, silver thread of its vision and mission has run faithfully through Black history.

In spite of the bitter Black history of slavery and oppression, there had emerged instead of an attitude of despair, hatred and pessimism a mystique of hope in the future, an innate sense of solidarity with other oppressed groups, a strong sensitivity to injustice in all forms, and a determination not to forget this painful history—very much in the similar spirit of the Jews who had vowed never to forget the bitter experience and lessons of the European Holocaust. The primacy of the values of community and personal relationships has often been carried over into public life along with an emphasis on integrity and good example.

This consciousness allowed Jackson to announce that his campaign would definitely not be for "Blacks only" but that it would emerge out of the "Black experience and be seen through the eyes of a Black perspective . . . " Jesse Jackson had undoubtedly been encouraged by the impressive victory of Harold Washington as the first Black mayor of Chicago, Jackson's home base. Washington, a charismatic leader, had been elected with the support of progressive whites.

Thus, however imperfectly, these ideals would be realized in the Jackson campaign, in the end it remained an invaluable example of the principle of the centrality of Black leadership that must continue to be a guiding light for the work of authentic social change. In this respect, both the successes and failure of this period will remain a template for the ever present challenge to build a civilized, humanitarian and just society—a goal that in some way appears to be more remote than ever today.

The New Hampshire primary contest in Keene was a pivotal moment for the Jackson campaign. It was here in a state with practically no Black voters that the Rainbow Coalition could come with an image and a message. Here was an opportunity to address the issues of the environment and of nuclear disarmament from a fresh perspective. The US and NATO were deploying cruise missiles in Western Europe and threatening the delicate nuclear balance between the Soviet Union and the US.

John Collins and I had decided to go to New Hampshire during this critical period. His wife, Sheila, who had begun to volunteer for the Jackson campaign, called John to ask him if he would like to write a speech for Jackson on the dangers of deploying the "Euromissiles." He agreed and invited me to join him in creating the document. This was an important opportunity for Jackson to speak out on an issue that was not regarded by the general public and news media as a "Black issue."

Together we crafted a solid statement and then drove up to New Hampshire. We met some of the organizers at a diner in Keene. Rev. William Sloane Coffin Jr., pastor of Riverside Church in New York and a leading peace spokesperson, was there as well as Sheila, who had joined the campaign staff and became the chief biographer of the 1984 Rainbow campaign.

Jackson arrived a little later and immediately asked us for the speech. It was very much on his mind and he was looking forward to bringing this issue into the campaign. We joined in an intense conversation on the cruise missiles and the opportunity of making a major statement in New Hampshire during the primaries. He checked with one of his aides about the official position of the campaign on the deployment of these dangerous, medium-sized and relatively invisible missiles. They would make parts of Italy, Holland and Germany targets for Soviet retaliation and European protests were growing. His advisor agreed that this was a correct position.

Later that night, a huge crowd of close to a thousand people gathered at the Keene junior high school. To all appearances "the Rev" was prepared to deliver our/his statement. We were up on the stage along with local dignitaries and representatives. Jackson asked John and me to come backstage to consult one more time on the connections between the cruise missiles and US strategic policy and about the level of European popular dissent. He used our text but freely adlibbed and edited as he went along in the traditional Black preaching style.

It was a powerful and significant speech warmly received by the crowd. Above all, it put forward a vision of foreign policy that was not being supported by any of the other "liberal" candidates. It spoke about reducing and freezing the arms race, not building new weapons systems. Jackson also made the unavoidable link between military spending and the plight of the poor, a connection that seems unavoidable, except for the Reagan administration and for most of the other Democratic candidates who did not want to appear too liberal.

Heartened by the response to this emphasis on peace and disarmament, Jackson began to see the importance of lifting up other related issues. He asked us about the idea of a visit to Central America in order to highlight the immorality of US involvement and support in the murderous wars taking place in Nicaragua, El Salvador and Guatemala. He had been invited by the Sandinistas to be an observer at the upcoming elections in Nicaragua. Jackson asked whether we would be willing to be part of such a delegation, and both John and I responded with enthusiasm. This was clearly one of the major foreign policy issues of that period that was beginning to gain support in the religious community and beyond.

That weekend John and I would receive frenzied calls from Bill Howard (the Rev. H. William Howard), one of Jackson's key advisors and counselors. One minute the trip was on, the next minute it was off. Finally, a Sunday talk show had won out and the trip was definitely off.

Unfortunately, Jackson did not follow through on this inspired idea because of more secondary considerations. It was a bad decision on every count. Had he followed through on his plan, he would have been "safely" (in a major war zone) out of the country instead of granting a newspaper interview that would almost sabotage and certainly wound his blossoming campaign.

The fatal interview was an off-the-record discussion between Jackson and a group of Black reporters. In it he referred to Jews as "Hymies" and to New York as "Hymietown." His remarks were not publicized until two months later in an article by a white reporter (by chance?) immediately before the crucial New Hampshire primaries. The article evoked charges of anti-Semitism, which the white media capitalized on, and gave the organized Jewish community a field day savaging the candidate and the campaign. After that there was no press appearance that did not open with questions about the Hymie remark and it became the overriding issue of the campaign. The situation was exacerbated by the instant support of Minister Louis Farrakhan of the Nation of Islam, who added openly anti-Jewish remarks to his defense of Jackson.

As a Jew, I did not take this development lightly. I never accepted the explanation that Jesse did not really mean what he said or that he was unaware of his statement's implications. I would not have accepted these excuses for Jimmy Carter's remarks about "ethnic purity," Nixon's (later revealed) anti-Semitic slurs, Kennedy's use of the word "nigger," and Reagan's sympathy for the Ku Klux Klan. Incidentally, none of these were ever so widely chastised as was Jesse Jackson—and most of them not at all.

It is no great surprise that two groups with long histories of genocide and suffering should be very sensitive to attacks. Black culture has, undoubtedly, absorbed some of the stereotypes about Jews, and the American Jewish community has often not been responsive enough to Black sensibilities, especially with growing Black criticism of Israeli policies. There has been a cooling of relationships between the two communities after the more cordial and supportive period of the civil rights movement.

Jackson was wrong to have made the insensitive remarks and he should have apologized immediately. Instead he waited two weeks before he apologized on two separate occasions—one before a synagogue congregation and the second in a beautiful statement on the natural unity of Blacks and Jews based on their similar experiences, their historic ties as well as on their common use of the Hebrew Bible, given before the B'nai Brith in Framingham, Massachusetts.

I remember a long, intense conversation with David Dinkins, then borough president of Manhattan and later mayor of New York, urging him to use his influence to get Jesse to apologize immediately. No doubt he tried, but Jackson was getting opposite pressure from other advisors and Black public opinion. This was the predictable phenomenon of closing ranks around the aggrieved Black leader, so brilliantly critiqued by Black theologian and social critic Cornel West in his invaluable book *Race Matters,* where he uses the image of "gathering the wagons" in a protective circle around Jackson.

He should also have separated himself completely from Louis Farrakhan, but for similar reasons, Jackson was reluctant to do so. He expressed some distancing but never repudiated him completely, a position that could be understood as "principled" but proved to be severely damaging in the long run.

Nevertheless, for all of his demagoguery and misanthropic attitudes to women, Farrakhan's powerful attraction, manifested in his mega gatherings, should not be misunderstood. It would be a mistake to assume that these crowds all shared his jaundiced views on Jews, women, gays and other issues. Rather, the symbol of a Black leader standing up unapologetically to white racist America was and remains a powerfully attractive catalyst for many disenfranchised Blacks.

The anger among some elements in the Jackson campaign, even to the point of counseling against an apology for the Hymietown remarks, did not serve the greater good but was not without some justification. Attacks against Jackson by conservative Jewish elements antedated not only Hymietown, but also his presidential announcement.

Even prior to the announcement of his candidacy, the Anti-Defamation League of B'Nai Brith (ADL) circulated a nineteen-page confidential memorandum with the clear intent of discrediting Jackson. It was a compilation of his statements, often taken quite out of context. It focused on his position since 1973 on the Middle East crisis and implied that he was anti-Semitic, anti-Israel, pro-PLO and sympathetic to terrorism. The document ignored the fact that his position was increasingly in favor of a two-state solution, defending Israel's right to exist alongside a Palestinian state. Would that leaders of the stature of Rabbi Abraham

Joshua Heschel and Rev. Martin Luther King had been around to pour the oil of wisdom on these troubled waters.

The release of these damaging Hymie remarks came shortly after Jackson's dramatic peace mission to Damascus to rescue pilot Lieutenant Goodman from Syrian imprisonment. It had the significant impact of freeing Jackson from the media caricature of "a Black candidate" engaged in a "protest" campaign. Even *Newsweek* was forced to admit that Jackson had put Reagan on the defensive and had exposed the weakness of his diplomatic position on Lebanon, had overshadowed all of his seven Democratic rivals including Mondale, solidified his Black support and had broken down the communication impasse between the US and Syria. A presidential aide was quoted, "He knocked one out of four ball parks at the same time."

Nevertheless, from the moment of the announcement of the gaffe, the white media seized on every opportunity to repeat the quote and to pick up on every kind of racial tension to connect to Jackson's alleged anti-Semitism. One Black reporter working for a major newspaper confided to a friend that he had been taken off covering the Jackson campaign because he was not including enough references to the "Hymie" remark in his stories.

The mainstream media consistently avoided opportunities to cover Jackson's growing appeal to white voters under the assumption that he was only supported by the Black community. Major multi-racial rallies and support events were either ignored or misrepresented.

A classical exchange of this kind took place on NBC's *Meet the Press* shortly after Jackson won 26 percent of the vote in the New York primary, just one percent behind Senator Gary Hart:

> Mr. Lewis: Reverend Jackson, you've created great interest and consciousness among Black voters. I wonder if you think this interest will be sustained beyond this current campaign?
> Rev. Jackson: Number one, we just keep saying "among Black voters." I would have you know that we began to pick up votes in different communities. In New Hampshire there were eight candidates running, I came in number four. We began to pick up votes there. You don't win number two in New York City over Hart by almost one hundred thousand votes, just with Black votes alone. The Rainbow continues to grow, it continues to flourish (Transcript, April 8, 1984).

Jackson continued to forge ahead in spite of all obstacles and to drive himself and his staff mercilessly in the process. He seemed to be driven by a combination of enormous personal ambition and a genuine vision of a new kind of America. In the process he often pushed himself beyond the point of exhaustion.

One especially poignant personal moment came one evening after a long day of a brutal schedule when a few of us gathered in his hotel suite before a major evening event. Jesse suddenly asked me to come into his bedroom, "Come in here for a second, Doc," using the familiar address of Black clergy among themselves. He motioned me to a chair and then stretched out on his bed. I thought that he might want to unburden himself or have a personal conversation. But before he could speak, he fell into an exhausted sleep to which I was called to be the sole witness.

I was both deeply moved and a little saddened by the experience because I always felt that there seemed to be very few (even of his closest circle) to whom "the Rev" really unburdened himself. This was a heavy load for anyone to carry, especially the man on whose shoulders so much of the future rested at that critical moment of historical opportunity. And so in silent vigil at his bedside, I sent him good wishes and prayers. I never found out what was really on his mind for that mysterious moment.

In the end, "Hymietown" and Farrakhan missteps notwithstanding, Jackson racked up a historic number of votes in the primary. Even one of the key democratic strategists admitted that if he had been a white man, he would surely have been the presidential candidate of his party. The core secret of this phenomenon was that he was making the Rainbow Coalition a reality.

Besides the traditional Democratic constituencies such as labor, Jews, Hispanics, farmers and progressive women, there were groups who felt empowered for the first time by the Jackson campaign, such as Asian Americans, Arab Americans, Native Americans, gays and lesbians and the disabled. Jackson physically reached out to them, went into their communities, met with their leadership and actually addressed their issues.

Jackson was the only presidential candidate ever to visit the Navajo and Hopi Nations on their own land. It was here that the theft of Native land, the violation of land rights by the coal and uranium companies were perpetrated and whose legally binding treaties with the US government were broken.

It was Jackson's calculated gamble that the loyalty of the Black Church was such that it could either be won over or would overlook his enlightened defense of gay and lesbian rights. There is no doubt that in his skillful, respectful style he performed a major task of education around this issue so fraught with emotions of fear and prejudice. Unfortunately, much of this "conversion" to a more humanitarian (and even Christian) position in the Black Church community has not held fast. The George W. Bush administration, under the evil genius of the Carl Roves of the neo-con cabal, along with the Religious Right, wooed some important sectors of the Black Church into their camp by using the issues of gays and the "threat" of gay marriage.

In the end, the primary votes for Jackson made an unprecedented and incontrovertible political and moral statement for an America that was reluctant to either see or hear in spite of the connivance of the "bought-out" news media.

The campaign now began to set its sights on the Democratic Convention in San Francisco, scheduled for August. It was here that a number of significant dramas would play themselves out in the cruel light of stark reality. The first unavoidable overarching part of this scenario was the indomitable will of the ruling class, the Democratic Party and the Walter Mondale campaign to block the influence of and oppose any visible role for the Rainbow Coalition.

With good reason the Democratic leadership was apprehensive about this infiltration of the rainbow vision into the establishment stronghold of the National Convention. During the primaries, Jackson had made brilliant use of the media and his oratorical genius and had even made some traditionally thorny issues more accessible to the mainstream American public. Even those who would not vote for him still heard the eminent good sense of his message for a more peaceful and equitable society.

So by the time the amazing results of the primaries were in with the reports of Jackson's historic success, the Democratic Party honchos were bracing for an even more militant onslaught from the Rainbow Coalition at the convention itself. During the platform hearings, the Mondale delegates blocked every effort for a more progressive Jackson agenda. In the end, the Rainbow delegates came away with four "minority planks" that would be ignored in the end:

- Substantial real reductions in the military budget.
- Support for affirmative action with quotas. (Democratic Party regulars later took the teeth out of the concept with their withdrawal of support for quotas.)
- A No First Use of Nuclear Weapons pledge.
- The elimination of runoff primaries and all other impediments to the right to vote.

One of the most disappointing developments was the lack of support for the Jackson platform from progressive white women convention delegates, even including members of the National Organization of Women (NOW). With the shortsightedness of certain liberal forces, they were so elated at the imminent nomination of Geraldine Ferraro as the vice presidential candidate that they thought she would surely support a progressive agenda with or without Jackson, an expectation that was not to be fulfilled. In fact, Jackson's early support for a woman vice-presidential candidate had made her impending nomination possible.

The convention had one especially dramatic moment for me. I happened to be present at a strategy meeting of the Jackson brain trust. The issue on the table was the "no first use of nuclear weapons pledge," one of the four minority planks. An intense discussion was going on and there was some obvious confusion between the no first-use strategy and the no first-strike missile campaign. Apparently I gave such a clear explanation of the difference between the two that the late Ron Walters, one of Jackson's chief political advisors, came up to me afterwards and asked for a further analysis which I gladly gave him. Ron was one of the most impressive intellectuals in the campaign and a scholar of political science in the Black community. Then Ron asked whether I might be up to addressing the convention on the "No First Use" plank. I was a little taken aback at the prospect, but I said that I was open to the idea. He said that he would check further with "the Rev."

The next day the surprising word came back that Jackson wanted me to address the convention on the issue. I was both elated and frightened to death. This was not my world. Would I be up to the task of making the case for halting nuclear madness before this sophisticated, even jaded audience? It would be comprised of both slick professional politicos as well as many ordinary good folks—undoubtedly some of them with a progressive perspective, besides the Jackson delegates. I was intimidated at the prospect. All my past history had taken place outside of (literally) political presidential conventions, either alienated from them and therefore simply absent or out there demonstrating on the streets where my participation in the political process consisted of being tear-gassed, clubbed and arrested by the police, who were charged with dissuading dissent at both Republican and Democratic conventions.

The prospect of actually delivering a statement for a grudgingly doled-out five minutes was formidable to someone like myself who was accustomed to speaking in a somewhat spontaneous "off the cuff" style with no time limits. I decided to write out my speech in a disciplined and deliberate fashion. I was not accustomed to the high-tech world of the teleprompter and could barely type, so I stayed up into the night writing my text in longhand.

Tuesday, the 17th of August arrived and my heart was filled with uneasiness at the task that lay ahead. I walked from our hotel to the Convention Center by myself, deep in thought and prayer. Several of us were herded into a small side antechamber near the main stage, awaiting our turn on the program. The convention organizers had bunched all the Jackson minority plank presenters together in a mid-afternoon slot when they hoped that we would get minimal media attention, although CNN, at least, carried it all.

As I calmly sat there, it suddenly hit me like a blow to the gut—I had forgotten the text of my address in the hotel. After staying up into the wee hours, I had departed the hotel so anxious to be on time that I had left the inspired text behind. And now it was too late to retrieve it. I was thrown back onto my own personal speaking style of "winging it." And so with my heart in my mouth, I stepped out into the glaring lights, was ushered up to the podium to behold before me the sea of faces of thousands of delegates. I took a deep breath and began to speak from the heart:

> "Dear Friends! Today I'd like to speak in the name of the Rainbow Coalition which, under the leadership of Reverend Jesse Jackson, won more than three and a half million votes in the primary—votes of all colors of the rainbow. Twenty percent of them came from one million people in the white community and many from the peace community which I represent.
>
> "Today I want to appeal to this convention to support the No First Use of Nuclear Weapons plank. Not simply because it is one more plank in another political platform—the platforms come and go—but because this is a unique and significant

opportunity to send a message to our country, to the world and to the White House that we are introducing a new era of peace and disarmament.

"There is nothing more provocative, more destabilizing or more dangerous in United States military policy than the announced intention that, if American forces were threatened to be overrun by conventional forces of the enemy, we would be prepared to use nuclear weapons first.

"This policy is not only dangerous. It is morally and militarily insane. This is not merely a theory because if you read history, almost every single president since the dropping of the atomic bomb on Hiroshima and Nagasaki, perhaps with the exception of Gerald Ford, on one occasion or another seriously considered and even threatened to use nuclear weapons first.. . . This is a doctrine we must condemn and oppose.

"The Roman Catholic Bishops called No First Use a moral imperative. This is the imperative, sisters and brothers, which is before us today. I urge you to support it in the name of our children.

"During the Lebanese crisis, a Lebanese citizen was quoted in *The New York Times* as saying, 'There will be peace when we begin to love our children more than we hate our enemies.'

"For this convention, the time has come to make that statement!

"Thank you and God bless you."

Somehow it all came to me just as if I had a prepared script. Something might have stayed with me from my nocturnal preparation, but it was clearly the power of the Spirit who wanted me to bring this message against the nuclear madness to this great gathering. Much to my surprise and shock, I heard a roar of approval and applause from the crowd far beyond just the Jackson delegates.

It was a moment of elation but, in the end, the eminently sane idea of adopting this stopgap measure against nuclear holocaust could not gain the support of the supposedly more progressive of the two major parties. Such was the low level of political courage which could not stand up to the anti-Soviet paranoia and the Reagan administration's love affair with the Bomb.

This was part of the all-too-familiar Democratic strategy of trying to look more like the Republicans à la Gore in 2000 and Kerry in 2004 and Obama today. In 2006, the Democratic upset that won back the House and Senate was largely due to the outrage of ordinary people against the

Iraq War and not a strategy of the Democratic Party machine. We've seen that congressional follow-through has left much to be desired.

The high point of the convention (even for non-Rainbow delegates) was the historic speech delivered by Jesse Jackson himself on Tuesday evening, heard by thirty-three million people. It will go down as one of the great orations of American Convention history, even overshadowing a powerful presentation by Governor Mario Cuomo of New York on the first night of the convention.

The platform committee grudgingly allowed a group of Jackson supporters on the stage to stand behind Jesse, reflecting the diversity of the Rainbow Coalition. John Collins and I, representing white religious and peace leaders, had arrived late to the staging area, our hair and beards brushed and wearing our finest attire. The Secret Service was not letting people onstage without being vetted by John Bustamante, one of Jackson's key aides. The stage was already full so the Secret Service agents inquired about us. Bustamante answered, "Just these two rabbis," and so we ascended, half bent over in laughter.

Jesse delivered more than a speech, more than an oration. It was a spirit sermon in the best charismatic tradition of the Black Church. (Obama's famous campaign "unity speech" was in the same vein but Jackson's was extraordinary.) It was a historic summons to the Church, in this case the entire community of the American people, to rise to a new level of almost sacred unity, in spite of all the differences that have kept us apart:

> "Our flag is red, white and blue, but our nation is a rainbow—
> red, yellow, brown, black and white. We are all precious in God's
> sight! . . . . All of us count and all of us fit somewhere. We have
> proven that we can survive without each other, but we have not
> proven that we can win and progress without each other."

His speech was also a genuine eloquent mea culpa (although not the first one) for his Hymietown remarks, and many open-minded Jews were moved and some admitted that they had been excessive in their condemnation and rejections of Jackson and the Rainbow.

> "If in my low moments in word, deed or attitude, thought, some
> error of temper, taste, or tone, I have caused anyone discomfort,
> created pain, or revived someone's fears, that was not my truest
> self."

And later he declared:
"I am not a perfect servant. I am a public servant doing his best
against the odds. As I develop and serve, be patient. God is not
finished with me yet."

I wept through a good part of these extraordinary fifty minutes. As
I looked around, I could see that I was not alone. One Black Jackson delegate from a Deep Southern state reported: "I had nigger-hating crackers
standing next to me with tears running down their faces—grown white
Southern men, crying."

Then Governor (now Senator) Bob Graham of Florida commented:
"If you are a human being and weren't affected by what you just heard,
you may be beyond redemption."

In retrospect, history must recognize the contribution of this period
to the dramatic accession of Barack Obama to the White House in 2008.
The victory of an African-American as the forty-fourth president of the
United States grew directly out of the struggles that preceded him. The
seeds of this extraordinary, if still imperfect, event were sown, first of all,
on those hot dusty—sometimes bloody—streets of Selma, Alabama, during the noble campaign for the rights of Black people to vote.

But this process was further powerfully sustained and advanced
when Jesse Jackson and his Rainbow Coalition won seven million votes,
half of which were white, in the 1988 Democratic primaries. And let it be
noted, with all due respect, that unlike the Obama campaign, this electoral struggle consisted of a clearly undiluted progressive agenda outside
of the control of the Democratic Party.

One of the most touching moments of the historic November 4th
election evening in 2008 was the television shot of Jesse with tears in his
eyes as Obama gave his brilliant victory speech in Grant Park, Chicago.
They were surely tears of joy, but perhaps also tinged with disappointment at what might have been.

But in the end, the 1984 convention represented nothing but rejection and humiliation for the Rainbow Coalition. The Democrats could
have made room for some Rainbow interventions, if only out of respect
for the massive support of Black citizens that Jackson activated and of
whom the Democratic Party claims to be the champion. Even the Democratic promises of some key positions in the party structure for Black
Rainbow leaders were ultimately broken.

In the end, it was difficult for the Democratic Party not to recognize
the historic contribution of the Jackson campaign—not that it would ever

publicly acknowledge it. But the party machine ignored these contributions and continued its path of neo-conservative centralization of power through the alleged Democratic Leadership Council.

However, the greatest tragedy of this period came from within the Rainbow campaign and from within Jesse Jackson himself. It was the tragic failure to resolve the apparently irreconcilable conflict between Jesse's presidential ambitions (the tail that wagged the dog), as opposed to seizing the opportunity of building a powerful, ongoing, historically unique, independent, multi-racial, multi-issue people's Rainbow movement even after the elections. The latter could still have had some connections to the progressive wing of the Democratic Party and might (and this is an open question) consciously have worked towards the eventual option of a new authentic third party. This threat/possibility might also have gained it greater respect from and power within the Democratic Party itself.

This was not a decision or commitment that Jackson seemed capable of making. First of all, he generally rejected organizational and personal accountability to the still nascent Rainbow Coalition organization—and this in spite of some considerable pressures from and ultimatum meetings with members of the key Black leadership. Such meetings, and there were several, were called "taking Jesse to the woodshed." He was too gripped by the drive in his guts to continue to seek the sugarplum of the presidency as his priority rather than seeing it as a powerful leverage to what must always be our political priority: movement building and the creation of Martin Luther King's "beloved community."

Jackson was a driven man but in the end, the price was too high. That high price led me to drop out of the 1988 Jackson campaign along with Dr. H. William Howard, one of the intellectual and moral leaders of the Rainbow Coalition and a longtime friend and associate of mine who seemed to share this analysis.

Jesse wrestled with being a prophet speaking truth to power and being a player and actor within the power structure itself. After the extraordinary experience of his speech at the convention—never mind the Democratic slap in the face to the Rainbow Coalition—he must have felt himself under the seductive pull of an irresistible political aphrodisiac. Where else was there to go but to more of the same? As he heard so often from his supporters, "Run, Jesse, run."

I believe that this period represented one of the greatest tragic lost opportunities in the history of US progressive politics. It is a period that still breaks my heart when I think of it. Will we ever have such an opportunity again? Will we ever have the opportunity to create a multi-faceted, progressive movement that enjoys sufficient national popular support and wins significant primary votes in so many states, a movement that brings together the poor of the Camden ghettoes with the suburbanites of Beverly near Chicago and the farmers of Nebraska, forward-looking Arabs and Jews, the environmentalists of New Hampshire, the workers of the Rust Belt and Latinos of the Southwest and beyond?

This was a moment in which it seemed that much could have happened and it was lost to some extent because of the ego of one man. I grieve for us all and I grieve for him.

The last time I saw Jesse was at the march protesting President Bush and the Republican National Convention in front of Madison Square Garden in New York in August 2004. There he was in the frontline of the giant march, a little heavier, a little grayer, but still tall and imposing in a tan safari outfit. It was "the Rev" at his best. He was still one of the most eloquent leaders and spokespersons of our movement for peace and justice. Few could or can articulate the tragedy of the bloody hopelessness of Iraq and Afghanistan, the despair of our urban poor or the corporate roots of our financial collapse like Jesse. And there he was once again enchanted by the siren call of the TV cameras and reporters who were equally magnetized by this almost irresistibly attractive object of their attention.

In the meantime, our movement lumbered forward from one demonstration to the next, nobly striving to do good but still seeming to lack the vision, the focus, the political inspiration, the unity, which were once almost ours in those Rainbow months, so filled with promise, of 1984.

I have been assisted enormously in this chapter by the insights and analysis of my good friend Professor Sheila Collins and her book, *Rainbow Challenge: The Jackson Campaign and the Future of US Politics* (Monthly Review Press, 1986)

CHAPTER 26

"AND A LITTLE CHILD SHALL LEAD THEM"
Children of War

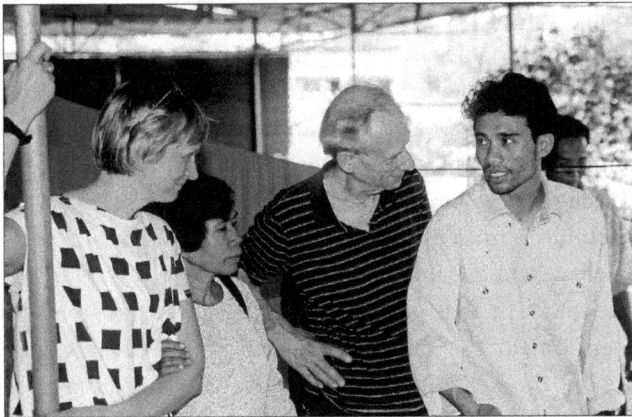

IT WAS A TRANSFORMATIVE MOMENT. The great nave of the Cathedral Church of St. John the Divine—the longest of all the world's cathedrals—was filled with ten thousand peace worshipers, even overflowing on to Amsterdam Avenue. Leaders of all the world's great religions in their magnificent regalia were storming the heavens for peace in a powerful ritual on behalf of the UN Special Session on Disarmament II. They ranged from Buddhist patriarchs in saffron robes to Iroquois clan mothers to Catholic bishops in their stately purple. The cathedral was rocking from the thunder of its organ along with the earth music of the great Paul Winter Jazz Ensemble.

But instead of focusing on this sacred splendor, all eyes, ears and hearts were riveted on the frail figure and quiet words in imperfect

English of a sixteen-year-old Cambodian boy, who was almost hard to find in the enormous vaulted cathedral. He looked more like thirteen, and he was part of the "Witness of the Children." This was at first glance a minor component of the Religious Task Force's International Religious Convocation of June 11, 1982. He spoke quietly into the microphone and the silence in that cavernous space was so complete that I could hear myself breathe.

"My name is Arn Chorn. Today a few of us here are representing all children who are victims of war and violence. There is a common ground of suffering among all of us. As for myself, I saw all of my family executed. In fact, I saw thousands die. In Cambodia one million children died. The smell and sight of blood decorated the walls of the children's killing center's house. The children were abandoned and made hostage of the madness of adults. Different countries sold my people guns, which then were used to kill children. The more guns, the more bombs, the more power to kill. When I saw babies being smashed, I died myself a million times. I thought it would be better to be born in another life, instead of living in a world where there was no love and compassion. So many children died. Often I held them while they were dying, but I could not help them. They were caught in the monster of violence. And for them we pray, and for all the children from everywhere around the world. Please, may our suffering help others to grow in peace."

In the midst of that great silence many were weeping, including myself. Even some of the TV crews and reporters had tears in their eyes. Little did we at the Religious Task Force realize that in the midst of this magnificent liturgy, it would be that modest ten-minute witness of this Cambodian boy that would transform our lives and the lives of many hundreds of thousands.

The following weeks, in response to Arn's powerful witness, the RTF office received letters and phone calls from people wanting to help and hear more of this remarkable witness by children. One of the most significant letters came from Father Joseph Towle, then the vice provincial of the New York Jesuit Province and a board member of the RTF. Joe had also been a great servant to the struggling people of the South Bronx. His letter stated: "The children had a compelling and touching effect on all who heard them that day—and this not for reasons of sentimentality, of which their witness was remarkably free, but for the artless truth and witness which came from their mouths. If other people around the country could only hear them, it will accomplish more than we can imagine."

Little did he or any of us at the RTF realize how prophetic these words would be. They became the seed from which a great tree would grow, a true Tree of Life, whose roots would extend far around our planet into those bloody regions where war was causing extreme suffering to the innocent, especially to children. And the fruits of that great tree would offer healing, enlightenment and transformation to many. This sacred tree would be called the "Children of War."

It was Judith Thompson who discovered Arn Chorn in 1980, just three days after he arrived in the US, adopted by Rev. Peter Pond, a Lutheran minister from New Hampshire who had originally encountered him in a desolate refugee camp in Thailand. Arn had miraculously escaped the clutches of the Khmer Rouge's children's killing camp where he had seen sights that no child should ever see, sights of torture, cruelty, murder and humiliation. Then his captors had forced him to become one of the world's child soldiers, to carry a gun against the Vietnamese. Through some miracle, he had escaped and made his way, half naked, through the Cambodian jungle where he was kept alive by fruit that the monkeys occasionally threw down to him from the treetops. He finally crossed the border into Thailand and ended up in the Sakeo Displaced Persons Camp with thousands of other Cambodians. An estimated 28,000 had been relocated to a bare three-acre site enclosed by barbed wire where they arrived in poor health, often suffering from hunger and malaria.

Rev. Peter Pond, a minister from Vermont, had been working in this camp for the Lutheran World Service's ministry in the late 1970s. He worked together with a Cambodian Buddhist monk, Maha Ghosananda (later known as the Cambodian Gandhi for his peace marches), trying to make the Buddhist temple a sanctuary for the refugees. Eventually, Reverend Pond would adopt twelve Cambodian children into his family to be raised by him and his generous wife, Shirley. As they raised their children in a Cambodian cultural setting, Peter would foster their—and especially Arn's—future vocation: "You are children of the Prince of Peace. You survived. There is a reason. You have a calling!"

It was out of this experience as a social worker with young refugees that Judith had begun thinking of the possibility of bringing some young Cambodians to New York during the United Nations Special Session on Disarmament in June 1982.

It was then that Providence led Judith to the RTF's International Religious Convocation as its press coordinator. The Witness for the

Children and especially Arn's testimony had a profound effect on all of us. And when Father Joe Towle came up with his brilliant insight, a collective light went on for us about the possibility of capturing that extraordinary moment and sharing it with many by an ongoing project such as a national tour of young people like Arn.

Finally, in December of 1983, I presented the idea of a national tour of young war survivors to the executive committee of the RTF. Somehow, out of the depth of our dream, I persuaded them that we could raise the money and that this project could be one of the most significant things that the RTF would ever do. And so this divinely inspired, guided and sustained effort began with this risk-taking act of faith, which we all took together. It was a decision that we would never regret, because my own, Judith's and Arn's vision would be fulfilled beyond our wildest imaginings. We were about to step into the realm of the magical and miraculous, and divine wonders awaited us. And so our newborn project was christened "Children of War."

We quickly put together an impressive advisory committee that also served as a board of directors, including Harry Belafonte, Coretta Scott King, Bishop Paul Moore Jr., Martin Sheen, Archbishop Raymond G. Hunthausen (later harassed by the Vatican for being too much of a Christian), Liv Ullman, Vali Rayah (a stellar high school student from a youth peace group), Dr. Benjamin Spock, Dr. M. William Howard (later the first Black president of the National Council of churches) and many more exceptional and loyal supporters.

When we first set out on this program, we saw it simply as an educational and inspiring speaking tour of a group of young war survivors, mostly international but some domestic as well, who would travel around the country sharing their experiences in schools and religious communities, primarily with other young people.

Joyfully but with considerable challenge, we discovered that not only were we creating new models of therapeutic war-trauma healing for young victims, but we were developing new forms of youth leadership for international and domestic peace and social justice movements. At the same time, our efforts contributed to raising awareness and compassion about the world's worst crisis situations through the simple dynamic of having the young people tell their stories.

The first stage of this extraordinary revelation came to us as we set out on the apparently prosaic task of finding adult tour guides to accompany the small youth groups on their journeys. To begin with, I had the good fortune of inviting John Bell's advice in identifying appropriate candidates.

I had known John primarily as a tall, enthusiastic folksinger and as something of an organizer who had helped in finding workshop leaders for an earlier venture.

After I explained our project to John, he suggested our tour guides perhaps should come from the RC community. This decision did more than we could ever have imagined to transform Children of War into the historical and magical entity that it became. John helped us find excellent tour guides who brought their co-counseling experience and their understanding of its theory as well as the ability to apply it to our unique group of young people. This was a unique counseling theory based on having people listen to each other respectfully and well rather than giving advice as a away of creating healing and self-understanding.

The importance of these extraordinary revelations and insights for Children of War cannot be overemphasized. Without them, the Children of War project would not have blossomed into the powerful force for good that it became.

The insights provided by John Bell and co-counseling awakened us to a better way of working with these young people who would soon come to us from the hellholes of the planet—from the killing fields of Cambodia, the violent townships of Soweto, the rural terrorism of the mountains of Central America and the mean streets of the hoods of our own urban battle zones. These would be our children—dare I call them that although some were young adults—whose fragile lives had witnessed and often experienced killing, kidnapping, torture and imprisonment.

In the meantime, we had begun to contact agencies such as the South African and Middle Eastern Councils of churches in the various conflict countries to help us select youth candidates to participate in the tour. The criteria used to screen candidates for the Children of War tour were that they be young people between fourteen and seventeen (although we were flexible) who had a strong desire to share their experiences about war, conflict and/or peace. They must be confident, assertive, cooperative and self-aware. We wanted an appropriate balance between boys and girls and we hoped that they could converse reasonably well in English. We asked that, ideally, there be two candidates from each region so that they could support each other in their journey to a strange land and upon their return home. On the whole, we were sent really exceptional young people, who made Children of War the historic event that it was.

People often asked us how we had gathered such a wonderful community of young people. I always believed that it was due to, in part, the good judgment of our international partner agencies. But ultimately the secret was the mysterious transformative chemistry that was created when these young leaders encountered a mirror image (occasionally their "enemies") of themselves from other areas of bloodshed. The other essential factor was the healing process that lifted the heavy weight of pain, anger, hopelessness and even self-loathing, and allowed their authentic radiant beings to emerge.

On the eve of Election Day, November 6, 1984, thirty-eight teenagers from fourteen war-ravaged countries arrived at the Queen of Peace (surely our patroness) Retreat House at St. Paul's Abbey in Newton, New Jersey. Yes, in another act of—some would say—outrageous chutzpah, I had enlisted the support and involvement of my old monastic community in this project, perhaps one of the most important of my life. Abbot Justin Dzikowicz, formerly one of my younger supporters during my days as a monk, and Father Basil Wallace, formerly one of my lay retreatants when I was retreat master, graciously let us use the old, beautiful retreat house at a generously reduced fee.

It was more than ironic that these young peace ambassadors should arrive on the eve of the re-election of Ronald Reagan due to the compromising and almost issueless campaign of Walter Mondale. (Remember the modest efforts of the Jackson campaign to change things?) Reagan's victory gave us four more years of nuclear buildup, war in Central America and cutbacks for the poor with giveaways for the rich. Unless one believed in such Biblical contradictions as "A little child shall lead them" (Isaiah 11:6), it would seem preposterous to take the arrival of this group of youths from the lands of global bloodletting with any degree of seriousness. And yet these victims, often of the wars of imperial expansion, would capture the hearts and minds of Americans in fifty-four cities.

Our tour participants were a remarkable gathering of representatives of the earth's pain and loss. They came from places whose very names evoked the ominous images of war: Belfast, Beirut, Israel, the West Bank, Uganda, South Africa, Namibia, El Salvador, Guatemala, Nicaragua, Cambodia, Vietnam, the Marshall Islands, and East Harlem. Their experiences had robbed most of them of a normal and safe childhood and now they would come together to transform their pain into wisdom, to become role models of courage, first of all to each other and then to the young people and many adults who they would encounter in the churches, synagogues, schools and community centers that they would visit across the breadth and width of our land. The excitement and anticipation of their arrival on that first evening will long live in our memories as the seeds of deep new friendships began to be planted.

But most of them could not anticipate the alchemy of the spirit that they would experience in the coming days. Often they were shy, apprehensive and not quite sure what lay ahead. The three young Israelis and three Palestinians actually arrived on the same El Al flight from Ben Gurion Airport in Tel Aviv. Arriving at JFK Airport in New York, they carefully sat apart as two separate groups at opposite ends of the airport lounge, never saying a word to each other as they waited for someone to pick them up. This would change in the most interesting way during the coming weeks.

The human quality of these future leaders and their growth and transformation in such a short time was remarkable as shown by a few of their stories. David Imbili, seventeen, of Namibia, lived under heavy military occupation and had often been caught in clashes of the war in Namibia—an overflow from the South African struggles. David had a beautiful, clear, deep-black African face and smile, and he was one of the candidates who practically stepped off the plane expressing himself in almost perfect oratory as if he had been thinking about these matters for a long time. His words spoke for all the participants: "Our suffering is your suffering because we are all inhabitants of this planet. I want to inspire other children—perhaps they are the leaders of tomorrow—not to do the same wrong things as our leaders of today are doing."

What more can one say?

Danny Kuttab was a fifteen-year-old Palestinian boy, one of our youngest participants, from East Jerusalem. His brother, Jonathan was a prominent human rights attorney in Ramallah and his father a Nazarene Church pastor in Jerusalem. He spoke with deep feeling of his solidarity with Ronnie Alroy, a dynamic sixteen-year-old girl who was working for peace and justice in Israel.

We had outstanding US participants, often from middle-class white communities, to represent the growing fear by the children of those communities of the menace of the escalating nuclear arms race. Also, there were representatives of the war at home in low-income, largely minority communities who lived under the shadow of gang violence along with the struggle against hunger, poverty and racial discrimination. Nancy

Vientidos from Harlem, a sixteen-year-old Puerto Rican girl with intense deep-black eyes, was one of these.

Marvyn Perez was a seven-year-old Guatemalan boy with a quiet, understated external demeanor that belied his burning commitment to justice and a sophisticated political analysis. Marvyn, who was involved in a student movement for which he was imprisoned and tortured by the government, was to become one of our strongest leaders.

This is the caliber of young human beings that the universe sent us to initiate this historic venture. These were the seeds of their witness of hope over despair that we would sow across the landscape of our country.

We had come to understand early on that the primary vehicle, the most fundamental catalyst, the distillation of the sacred mission that lay ahead was our message to the tour participants to "Tell Your Truth!" formulated by Judith. The young peace emissaries began by gathering in small circles and sharing their experiences with each other. They discovered the power contained in the straightforward act of telling their stories to each other.

This simple action moved and inspired their listeners, often to tears, as when little Donal Daly, a Catholic boy from Belfast, and at fourteen the youngest member of the group, told his heartbreaking story. At the age of ten in 1980, he had seen his mother assassinated in their home because she belonged to the H Block Committee working for political prisoners. He said, "I couldn't go out for revenge against those who killed my mother. I'm not that kind of person, but it puts anger into you."

In Donal's case, his story helped the members of his travel group to identify their own stories of pain and loss with his. For fifteen-year-old Mayson Ibrahim Abbad, a Palestinian girl, it connected to her life in the Dheishe refugee camp in Bethlehem.

Arn Chorn, a student advisor for the tour, served as a trainer and, on the first day of the orientation, encouraged others to share their pain with the students and adults they would meet. He said: "Give them your pain. It will educate them—you will see—they will love you for it. It is because you are the victim that you can be the healer."

Here was a profound theology of the mystery of Death and Resurrection. Arn's insight would be the energizing catalyst of the entire tour as it can become the source of vision and strength in all our lives.

Telling their stories was also a powerful and perhaps the most profound source of healing for these young storytellers themselves. First of all, it broke through the personal prison of feeling isolated and alone with the horrors of one's life and the bitter memories and the feeling that no one cared or was even interested. Once the young survivors had gotten up the courage and felt safe enough to tell their story—and this was sometimes for the first time—they had an extraordinary experience.

It was, first of all, the experience in a small group of being seen and carefully listened to with respect and compassion. It was there that the deep healing process began. The safety created in these circles was such that the young people allowed themselves to release or discharge deep emotions and even tears that in other settings could bring negative results. Arn Chorn once narrated how in the Khmer Rouge children's killing camps, when the Pol Pot cadre killed a child and another child cried, the second child was also murdered. So in many settings these young people had taught themselves to suppress these deep and awful feelings. Many suffered in silence for years from shame or survivor's guilt for not having been able to save family or friends.

Gradually, as part of our leadership training, we used the simple principles of RC and taught the young people how to support each other, by one-on-one mutual listening sessions or even with experienced adult assistance. In all of these, the primary source of healing was the simple experience of being listened to with complete, sincere and compassionate attention.

Finally, on November 8, 1984, the Children of War Tour was announced to the public at major press events, first at the United Nations together with Undersecretaries General Jan Martinsen and Robert Muller. We were welcomed in one of the large UN conference rooms with the tour participants seated at a large circular table (like the official government representatives they should have been recognized as) and from there, several told their dramatic stories.

Robert Muller who, after his retirement, continued on as a great international peace leader and founder of the University for Peace in Costa Rica, welcomed us warmly and was moved by their stories: "I grew up during wartime in Europe and I saw killings and horrors which compare to what you have told me. It has never left my memory. I've been here now for thirty-six years and I can tell you that I feel like crying when I see what the heads of state are doing. I want to give you a request. I wish you would write a Children's Charter, similar to the United Nations Charter which would start: 'We the children of the world!' Thank you for coming here and please help us."

In the afternoon there was another press briefing at General Theological Seminary with Archbishop Desmond Tutu of South Africa who had recently won the Nobel Peace Prize. The press turnout at both events was overwhelming and resulted in a huge barrage of media attention, leading off with an excellent front-page story in *The New York Times*. In fact, there would be few peace campaigns or projects that would attract the phenomenal news media coverage that the Children of War received.

I can still remember how radiant Archbishop Tutu was on that day, how thrilled he was with our young people, and the beauty of the message that he left with us:

> "Thank you for who you are. When you return home and are walking down the street and someone says, 'Who's that?' Remember the important things you are doing here and answer: 'I am a sign of hope.'"

And then with a big smile he simulated one of the young people walking down the street in a jaunty strut. (He would later become chair of our advisory board.)

In the comprehensive *New York Times* front-page article the stories of Marvyn and Arn were particularly highlighted. Part of Arn's statement made the Quotation of the Day: "We are less sure that we are absolutely right. Adults who are sure they are absolutely right, they make war over their absolute rightness."

This front page story in the *Times* with a photograph of myself with Archbishop Tutu represented an ironic and bittersweet moment, almost a parable, about the bond between myself and Judith. For me it seemed like a triumphant dream moment of recognition, healing my ancient childhood deprivation. So it came like a hammer blow to my blind, unschooled male consciousness that that morning's paper, so exciting for me, would be a source of deep sorrow and pain to one of the people closest to me. For Judith it dramatized how my male role, clerical title, dress and persona overshadowed and deprived her of her share of recognition for her equal, perhaps sometimes superior, work, all accentuated by Judith's own childhood pain. This dynamic would often haunt the deep feelings we had for each other and perhaps contribute to our eventual separation.

Now our little community of young peacemakers fanned out across the country in six groups by plane, train and van toward the fifty-four cities that eagerly awaited them. In preparation for their visits to schools,

Educators for Social Responsibility had prepared an excellent three-day curriculum about the world's conflict areas.

The Southwest regional travel group was made up of Danny Kuttab and Ronny Alroy; Carmen Aguirre, 15, the daughter of the director of the Nicaraguan Council of churches (CEPAD), who had lived under the bombs of the war there. Anna Maria Lopez, seventeen, of El Salvador had her life threatened for collecting money for a water pump in her school; Panha Psith Mao, 14, escaped from the hell of Cambodia with his mother after his father was taken away; Dao Tran, 14, a Vietnamese refugee lived through the war in Saigon; Annete Stevens, fifteen of South Africa, whose father, a minister, was imprisoned for his student ministry; and Hilary Whelan, seventeen, a dynamic high schooler from Los Angeles and an anti-nuclear activist were also in the group.

This rich gathering of youth suffering and youth courage had a profound impact even on cities like San Diego—a strong military and naval stronghold. When they visited San Diego State University, this was the response of a freshman who was too shy to even have her name used: "The Children of War Tour was the most amazing thing I have ever heard. I was never influenced by a lecture or visit from anyone, but to hear the children speak of their own experiences made me think of my views and my life. How selfish and uninterested I was with the world and with my own attitude. Now after hearing Children of War, I will pay more attention to what is going on around me."

After the presentations of the tour participants, there were always opportunities—sometimes in large but often in small groups—for the young listeners to ask questions but to also tap into their own stories and feelings.

A Jewish, strongly pro-Israeli teacher in a Los Angeles school heard one of our young Israelis tell how much he identified with the oppression of his Palestinian tour friends and was so disturbed that she reported Children of War to the B'nai Brith Anti-Defamation League (ADL) for anti-Israeli, perhaps anti-Semitic tendencies. Unfortunately, this report appeared in the California ADL newsletter and it took a letter from a rabbi supporter to come to my defense, but some damage had been done.

What the ADL leadership found difficult to grasp was that we did not instruct the young people on what to say, nor did we censor their presentations, or direct their feelings. This amazing metamorphosis of a young Israeli from a moderate peace activist still supportive of Israeli mainstream opinion to a proponent of Palestinian rights came from listening to the stories of the young Palestinians and getting to know them.

There were, of course, sometimes heated debates between the two sides as well along with changes in attitudes. I recall a bus trip home from an event in New York when we almost had to physically separate a young Protestant and a Catholic representative from Belfast.

The local organizers, teachers and students sent, wrote and called in their amazement, their joy and their gratitude for the tour. Rev. Alice Lane, a United Church of Christ minister from the First Parish in Concord, Maine, who served as Boston tour organizer, wrote eloquently: "Our experience with the Children of War Tour for everyone involved was extraordinary; people listened in breathless silence. No one could walk away untouched—unchanged—without receiving hope. I have been involved in the peace movement for twenty-one years, but this is the most powerful experience I've ever had—and the most hopeful. We are honored to have met these children and to have participated in this effort."

All through the tour we continued to receive unprecedented news media coverage. The tour was literally in every major newspaper, on every network news program and on most of the major TV talk shows such as *David Suskind, Merv Griffin, Phil Donahue* and others. *The Phil Donahue Show* with Harry Belafonte was particularly effective both because of Harry's eloquence, but especially because the young people were given generous time to tell their stories. The RTF national office was deluged with responses to the *Donahue Show*—three huge mailbags full.

Here's one from a US serviceman that left me speechless:

> It is beautiful what you are doing. I've been in the U.S. Navy for ten years and now I'm in the Reserves. In April, I'll be finishing my active naval career and would truly love to help your organization any way I can. I want so desperately to participate in helping your cause for peace throughout the world.
>
> Cal Thurmon, Chicago, IL

In addition, this powerful story was also carried in all of the major local newspapers, and radio and TV stations of every town and city visited, including the international media. At least twenty independent video productions resulted from the tour. Also an hour-long television documentary appeared on PBS and the video was used extensively around the country.

It was an historic moment when Danny Kuttab was interviewed on the *CBS Evening News*. It was the first time that I ever heard the Palestinian point of view put forward on US national network television. Danny spoke with great simplicity about the hardships of daily life for his family on the West Bank and his desire for a homeland for his people. He expressed the desire of the average Palestinian to live in peace with the people of Israel and his personal friendship with Ronny here on the tour.

In short, we took the country by storm. Everywhere we turned doors and hearts opened. We rarely heard a "no" response when we turned to people for help. Even on the phone people immediately fell in love with the vision.

Celebrities were eager to help. Harry Belafonte became one of our strongest friends and advocates. He, together with his wife, Julie, helped us with fund-raising, opened their home for several house benefits, brilliantly emceed a number of our major public gatherings and understood (as few people on the more traditional left had) that here was a rare wedding of the personal and the political without compromising either one. Harry constantly came up with new ideas to promote Children of War.

Martin and Janet Sheen were supporters. Mohammed and Veronica Ali invited us to use their luxury home in Los Angeles for a fund-raiser with the young people. Casey Kasem, at that time the most popular Top 40 disc jockey in the US and a prominent Arab American of Lebanese descent, became a great supporter and promoter of the tour. He and his wife, Jean, were the first to subscribe to our "Sponsor a Youth" program by sponsoring both an Israeli and a Palestinian young person for the tour.

As I look back, I am still in awe of the power of divine love and of our collective faith in enabling this extraordinary phenomenon to manifest on our planet against all human odds. To begin with, it is hard to believe that within approximately six short months with our small staff we were able to create a reality that involved organizing coalitions in fifty-four cities with as many local organizers, six regional organizers (all volunteers) and thirty-eight young people from fourteen war-torn countries, as well as from numerous domestic crisis areas. This was a project that had international ramifications: the South African and Middle East Councils of churches told us how much Children of War impacted their critical youth organizing.

Children of War was clearly an expression of the miraculous. There was a high level of inspiration that propelled us forward like a mighty wind, especially Judith and myself. Judith speaks about it as the first time in her life that she completely threw herself into something, and she recently spoke of the experience: "All this came about because of the presence of the Divine that took our still imperfect act of faith and inspiration and transformed it into a wondrous happening. For this I will always remain humbled and grateful. What a privilege to have been an instrument in the creation of a true manifestation of that Peaceable Kingdom we all dream of."

Early on in the tour Harry Belafonte had said to me, "Paul, what Children of War needs is an anthem of its own and I know the man who can write one." Harry was talking about Jake Holmes, sometimes known as the "King of the Jingles." Jake had, in fact, composed some of the famous advertising jingles that have become part of the cultural landscape. This was his inspired creation:

THE CHILDREN OF WAR

> *A song written from the words of participants in*
> *the* 1984 *Children of War Tour by Jake Holmes*
> We've been the hostages of madness
> We've been the prisoners of pain
> We've lived through storms of hatred
> We've seen our world go insane
> We've seen our street bloody rivers
> We've heard the screams of agony
> We've seen bodies smashed and broken
> We've seen what eyes should never see
> But now we're rising from the ashes
> And we're holding out our hand
> To touch inside you with our story
> See through our eyes and understand.
> Chorus:
> We have all kinds of peace inside us now
> We have all kinds of hope where no hope was before
> And with all kinds of love, we can stand together now
> We are the children of war
> From Beirut to Belfast to Soweto
> From the Holy Land to El Salvador
> We will make peace our only battle

It's time for us to say "no more"
There is no comfort, no shelter
There is no wrong, there is no right
There is no glory, no medals
Just the terror of the night
They play their games in the ruins
They carry wounds that never heal
For them there is no pretending
For them the killing is real
You say it's just a distant thunder
Look in your hearts and you will see
These are your sons and daughters
They are you, they are me
<u>Chorus</u>

The last three soulful days before the departure of the young people would be used to evaluate the tour, sharing the many experiences about their journeys and planning the future of the Children of War program, again at Queen of Peace Retreat.

Their insights and evaluation, as always, were brilliant, insightful and instructive. Rema Ellard was a vivacious sixteen-year-old high school junior from Seattle and a peace activist. She spoke movingly of her experience: "More than anything else this tour gave me hope. With every step I felt that we came closer to peace. I'll never forget that, as young people, we have an incredible amount of power."

Pransa Pisith Mao, fourteen, a rather shy young person, had really blossomed during the tour after his unspeakable sufferings and loss in Cambodia: "I didn't talk about all this before the tour because I thought no one cared. Now, I feel all those things I suffered I can share with people, and let them understand what's going on in the world. I have all kinds of peace in me now."

The final discussions made it clear that there was a unique power in peer-to-peer communication and teaching. Young people are infinitely more open, more willing and able to listen to the words of each other than the message coming even from an eloquent adult. What a great teaching! The community brainstorming during the debriefing surfaced a strong consensus to help the project to grow, to maintain the network and the contacts through newsletters, leadership training and more tours.

The returning Children of War participants began to organize in their home countries. The South African Council of churches planned an in-country youth tour of its own and the Israeli and Palestinian participants continued to meet. Speaker requests kept coming into the RTF office and a speaker bureau was formed.

These final days together were a time of joyful reunions and heart-breaking farewells. Remarkably deep friendships and genuine love had been created in such a short time. These feelings were based on the fine qualities of the young people but especially on the tragic and beautiful similarities of experience and background as well as the intensity of these weeks together.

On November 26, the Children of War Tour staged its farewell event before a full house at the Unitarian Community Church in New York City. It was a stunning evening hosted by Harry Belafonte and his daughter, Shari. Harry spoke with depth and heartfelt eloquence. His words were so brilliant and luminous that they bear repeating: "How naïve it was for the students during the Vietnam crisis to think that their presence in the streets, peacefully marching could end so horrendous a war. How naïve it must be for the Blacks and the few whites in South Africa to think that one day the struggle to end apartheid would succeed. How naïve it is for many people to think that it is possible to bring together Children of War; that they would walk the length and breadth of this nation at a time of such incredible cynicism and that perhaps doors could open up once again and that the hearts and minds of people in this nation could be filled with a righteousness that will lead us once again to truth."

Actor Mike Farrell, a strong Children of War supporter and another one of those truly principled and consistent people in the arts community, also left us with some deep thoughts: "I thought when we first sat down here, how sad it is that our leaders are not here. And then, when I was able to realize that there's another way to look at this, I realized how proud we can be that our leaders are here."

And so the Children of War all sang and wept together one last time before they packed their bags, embraced and went back to their homelands with hope renewed to continue that noble and difficult struggle for a peaceful world.

This transformative project also had a deep effect on my own life journey, resonant of the Prophet Ezekhiel's promise to "give them hearts of flesh for their hearts of stone." Not that I was a hard-hearted person but childhood fear had kept me from opening up to my emotions for most of my life.

It was during a Children of War Refugee Conference in Los Angeles, as I sat on the sidelines during a session, that I confided to Marvyn that I was myself a child refugee and had never told my story to anyone. Whereupon he, wise young leader that he was, insisted that I tell my story to the group. And so Paul Mayer, refugee and child of war, amidst healing tears and surrounded by much love, told his story and opened his heart.

We at the RTF did not have much time to rest on our laurels. A month or so after the tour, I received a call from Allegra Morelli, deputy director of UNICEF. She said that she had been following the Children of War Tour on the news media and was deeply touched and impressed. She said that UNICEF was about to take a major step into a new dimension of the crisis of the world's children beyond poverty, disease and the child refugee situation. It was the area of children in armed conflict and they planned to begin by a major study of this crisis.

Ms. Morelli wondered whether Judith and I and some of our youth leaders would be willing to meet with her leadership team to share our insights, opinions, perhaps even guidance—and so we did.

Eventually, UNICEF ended up sponsoring and funding the "Creating Our Future" Conference which immediately followed the second Children of War Tour in November 1986.

No sooner did we return from the 1984 tour than we began to plan the next tour in 1986. We had learned our lessons well in 1984 both from the great successes as well as from our weaknesses and shortcomings—especially the need for follow-up. There would be two additional tours—a mini-tour in 1987 and our final one in 1990.

Undoubtedly, one of the most impressive in this group was Victor Mavi from South Africa. At twenty, he was a little older than most of the other participants and he came to us already possessing some rare qualities of leadership. His deep-black eyes were set in a deceptively serious face because he had a smile that could light up a whole room and an even deeper laugh. He also had a deep voice, was a wonderful singer and already had oratorical gifts with a traditional African flavor, which became even more polished in his time with Children of War. Victor had served as the chair of the youth board of the South African Council of churches. He later attended Union Theological Seminary and was ordained to the ministry.

The South African participants brought a wonderful energy to the final tour in 1990. These latter were Children of War in the most literal sense. Many of them had already experienced being shot at, tortured, "detained" (a polite code word for "arrested and often tortured") and often had been living underground, separated from their families in flight from the brutal racist Apartheid regimes. It seemed that the very intensity of their struggle and the cruelty of their oppression had given birth to a joyful resistance culture of singing and dancing used at demonstrations and marches and chanting that was very powerful. These songs, chants and dances were now adopted by the young tour participants.

The mystery and grace of tears was revealed to us by a remarkable letter we received from South Africa written by a young man, Hlula Nkala. He was writing about a 1986 tour participant, Thami, a wonderful participant who had made a significant contribution to Children of War. The letter read:

> I am a very close friend of Thami Mpilo, and we have known each other from childhood. We are brothers, therefore.
>
> I want to thank you for making it possible for Thami to participate as well. He has changed suddenly. From being a feelingless young person who couldn't cry over the death of a friend simply because he had run out of tears. He cried till he couldn't. All because of Apartheid.
>
> Thami is full of love now. The experience has made him feel he has a place and that he has the power to bring peace and justice in the world. His spirit is very high.
>
> In great hope for the future,
> Hlula Nkala, South Africa

Early in 1987, we were approached by Harry Belafonte, who was chair of the Martin Luther King Jr. Commission of New York State, with the idea of a Children of War project around the anniversary of Dr. King's assassination. He came up with the idea that a few Children of War youth leaders would serve as resource people at a major conference for New York State educators on the "Roots of Racism," but it blossomed into something much more ambitious and exciting. At the end of the conference, the working group chaired by the state Commissioner of education recommended that the Children of War model of youth storytelling and leadership training be incorporated into the New York Public School system.

This tour would also include more inner-city schools. There was a remarkable exchange when Thami from South Africa and one of the Brooklyn students described the challenges of their daily lives to each other. One described the Apartheid society, the beatings, torture and life in hiding. Then the brother from Boys High in Brooklyn shared his life in the projects with poverty, drugs and gang life, drive-by shootings, sometimes with automatic weapons. To our amazement, the South African (from Soweto) participant's response was, "I'm glad I don't have to live there, because I'd never make it."

A heartfelt letter from Vernon Manley, assistant commissioner of the New York City Department of Probation said it all: "I cannot say what the organization is all about any better than Donovan McCoy himself—one of the participants—answering questions I posed to him regarding the leadership training provided by Children of War: 'I don't feel like Children of War trained me, but what they did was take what was already inside of me and help bring it out."

Another important development of the 1990 tour was that for the first time we included young people from the environmental war zones, places where a cruel and relentless warfare against the Earth herself was being carried on and having its impact on the youth there.

Most powerful and moving were the four children from the Chernobyl nuclear disaster. They struck one as particularly tragic—small and frail with their Slavic faces already pinched with suffering from the plague of radiation sickness through lymphatic cancer. They spoke quietly but powerfully in Russian with translation to mesmerized audiences, and their poignant message was all too clear. I am not sure how many of them made it to adulthood.

We had also included two wonderful Native American girls from the Diné (Navajo) Nation in the southwest on previous tours and they had brought the important perspective of their ancient tradition with its connection to their magnificent desert and mountain land. Now we expanded the Native American participation by including three young people from the Haudenosaunee nation (People of the Long House) of the Six Nation Confederation (commonly called the Iroquois) from upper New York State. All of these young Indian people represented true war zones, not only because their history was one of bloody warfare, as land theft and cultural genocide, but also because these realities were not ancient history.

In the end, Children of War left a profound imprint on the sacred work of peacemaking in our country and its power had been felt around the world. It had contributed to the creation of a unique model of healing the wounds of war and violence on a new level of empowerment and transformation. Our eyes had been blessed to see the fulfillment of the prophetic words: "And a little child shall lead them" (Isaiah).

CHAPTER 27

A SECOND FAMILY LIFE
Grandchildren in the Ghetto

IN THE MEANTIME, I had begun a love relationship with Judith Thompson. Naomi and I had agreed to have an open marriage, which allowed for other relationships when they made sense. Perhaps it was one of those ideas that made more sense in theory than in practice. I was probably more of an initiator and more enthusiastic about the idea than she was. Naomi had also explored the Women's Movement. It was the sixties, the time of the counterculture and experimentation was in the air.

As Judith and I worked closely together, a strong mutual attraction that was physical, political and spiritual developed. I did let Naomi know where I was heading. The ideal of openness never worked out perfectly, but maybe it made our relationship more honest, even though it also caused pain.

Our marriage, which eventually came to an end, had its strengths and weaknesses. The main point was that we loved each other, were good friends and shared a strong commitment to social justice and a peaceful world, and much of that is still true today. Sexually it was a mixed experience—never completely satisfactory for either of us, or so it seemed. I initially brought my raging hormones together with my celibate, adolescent inexperience to the marriage bed. I think that Naomi seemed to have some ambivalence towards sex. She also had an attraction for women—perhaps even a preference—something that I found both interesting and sometimes threatening.

As I grew up, I began to realize that my own father would sometimes stray from the marriage bed (with or without my mother's knowledge or approval). I believe that it often caused her great pain, although their marriage held. (Like father, like son.)

Our marriage ended, but Naomi was a deeply devoted daughter to my parents and would not separate while they were alive. I still regret the impact on our children and the pain that it caused Naomi, although there has been much good healing over the years. In retrospect, there were many things I would have done differently—especially demonstrating greater sensitivity on my part. But I believe that ultimately it was for the good.

My good mother left us in 1982 for her rewards, which must be great. In the last days of her illness, she was taken off her anti-Parkinson's medication because of resulting leukemia and thus suffered acute tremors. That last night as she moved into the final hours of her life, a well-meaning West Indian nurse, wanting to spare me from witnessing her extreme convulsions, urged me to go to sleep and said that she would rouse me in case of new developments. She woke me a few hours later to tell me that my mother had just died. I still deeply regret that I did not keep vigil at the side of my extraordinary mother who had stood at the side of so many suffering people.

My father died a few years later of colon cancer. He was hospitalized in Washington Height's Jewish Memorial Hospital, one of the many places where my mother had served as a nurse. Naomi and I were with him at his bedside when he had a fatal heart attack. It took so long for the emergency team to come to his room that he was already gone when they arrived, in my opinion, because of the understaffing and overwork of our healthcare workers. Perhaps we might have had him with us a little longer. I regretted never having a closer relationship with him. I did help him and support him, as did Naomi in his last years, and he once told me that he was proud of my work for a better world, but I think that towards the end I had just begun working up the courage to tell him that I loved him.

Today Naomi is in a happy relationship with her partner, Barbara, in San Francisco and we are friends. I often stay with them and on my last visit I taught them a yoga class each morning. Naomi has retired from her hospice work but continues on as an active volunteer. Both are teaching the Spiritual Exercises of St. Ignatius in their Jesuit parish and Barbara has become a leader in this tradition.

Judith and I stayed together for five years and then we separated, largely due to my difficulties in being emotionally open and vulnerable (not an unfamiliar challenge for the male of the species). These were skills that I was to develop—still imperfectly—much later in life. After the breakup of my marriage and the failure of a number of relationships with women, I began to suspect that perhaps love, romance and marriage were not my destiny. I experienced periods of loneliness and, in my typical style, tried to compensate mainly through my work and my connections to a few friends in the peace and environmental communities, but mostly I focused on work.

Then, thanks to my daughter, Maria, everything changed for me in my family life. My separation and divorce and Naomi's move back to her ancestral San Francisco had been a shock to my children, probably more than I admitted to myself. (We had decided that it made more sense for the children to stay with her.) In spite of some understandable resentments against my inadequacies as a traveling "peace movement father" often more intent on global conflict than on familial needs, my children and I had maintained a strong bond. But our divorce and their uprooting to the West Coast was a blow.

I think that my son, Peter, worked out his disappointment in part through a fierce adolescent encounter with a hard-drugs lifestyle from which he recovered by a courageous cold-turkey struggle to the light. He and I later had a touching healing moment when he surprised me by flying to New York to attend my graduation from the Advanced Lifespring Program, which had been a major emotional breakthrough for me. I had even been challenged to shave off my beard of decades during the weekend. (Perhaps I was hiding behind it?) Peter, who had never seen me without that beard, seemed delighted and we had a wonderful encounter.

I will never forget Peter's precious words: "Dad, I forgive you everything," as we embraced and kissed.

I was not going to get off that easy with my wonderful, troubled Maria. She had already gone through a difficult childhood: she punched her sixth grade teacher, was expelled from schools, had disciplinary challenges and made many trips to the child psychologist. I suspect that she had been deeply affected by her adoption experience. What child could escape the wounds of the profound trauma of losing one's mother in infancy and being handed off to several interim caretakers before she joined our family at the age of eight months?

Underneath, however, was our beautiful Maria, always a delightful and gorgeous Latina, with an incredible head of wild, jet-black curls and the olive skin and mestizo features of her Puerto Rican, Dominican and Italian ancestry. She was smart, funny and compassionate and an emotional volcano filled with repressed rage.

She had always had an ambivalent relationship with Naomi. Maria had a need to cling—"always up on my hip," Naomi would say. Perhaps Naomi had an unspoken fear of being suffocated by too much closeness. It was not a promising social contract.

At about age twelve Maria began to raise hell in St. Anne's, the local parochial school in San Francisco, and was eventually expelled. She began to experiment with drugs early, a premonition of her future path, and hung out with similarly troubled young people. In San Francisco Naomi undoubtedly put up with more than was required but ultimately let the state juvenile agencies take over Maria's case. Maria did not take kindly to the various youth facilities, group homes and therapeutic communities and eventually opted for the open road and what she hoped would be freedom.

She would periodically check in with me by phone from her adventures on the road. We had always maintained a close relationship and she sensed an unconditional acceptance from me—no matter the antisocial escapade of the day. When she found out that I would not fund her lifestyle, except perhaps at the most extreme moments, she gave up soliciting me for money. Nevertheless, she would call collect periodically from various questionable places all over the country (and from situations I would rather not know about in detail) to check in and inquire "about my welfare."

As I said, everything changed in my life when one day in 1987 she called me in East Orange. She was seventeen and was in Kansas City,

Missouri, and wanted to know whether she could "come home," that is, live with me. I almost fell off my chair but said that I would think about it. With my heart in my mouth, I thought, How can I say "no" to my own child?, even though I suspected that this decision could bring some considerable disorder to my life as well as connect me in a dramatic and real way with others—in this case, family.

So a new lifestyle began. I was no longer a solitary individual but had a family member to care for. What would this mean? I was to find out. Much later in February, after her eighteenth birthday, Maria discovered that she was pregnant. At the time, Maria was unstable, doing drugs and generally living an aimless life. I could not imagine this immature child herself having a child. Both of us were confused and frightened. She asked me what to do. I said that I did not know, but I would think and pray about it. As I recall, Maria said she had thought about abortion as an option. Although the idea troubled me, part of me wondered whether this might not be the most merciful solution all around.

Mysteriously, from some other dimension, the inspiration came to me: "Don't think of Maria as a problem child but rather as a woman of God." I reluctantly began to entertain that possibility and, through some process of grace, this unfamiliar vision of things began to grow upon me. Finally, from this mysterious place, Maria said: "Dad, I'm very scared, but I'm going to have this baby." And so the months passed and we began to reacquaint ourselves with each other again.

On Thursday, November 23, 1989 amidst a raging Thanksgiving Day snowstorm—at University Hospital in Newark, Brandon Paul Anthony Mayer, my first grandchild, saw the light of day and what a true day of Thanksgiving it was for all of us.

Brandon came onto this planet at around one in the morning on that blessed day and I was graced to be the first one to hold him. This was to be the beginning of a strong and sometimes challenging bond I have always had with my firstborn grandson who is twenty-two as I write. My profound birth experience with Brandon was repeated over the years as I accompanied Maria for the birth of four of my five subsequent wonderful Afro-Carribean grandchildren.

In rapid succession it was Shana, Kristopher, Tatiana, Imani and Mikey—each beautiful and bright in a unique way—and I like to think that this is not just Jewish grandfatherly pride.

With the birth of Brandon, a new generation of Mayers took up residence at 546 Park Avenue, once the home of Project Share. By that time, our original community had dispersed and we had morphed into a housing co-op. But there were still enough friendly folk to be of some support. In the end, it was Maria and the grandfather who were the primary caregivers of this newborn being.

Maria had decided, according to her lights, to be a good mother, which, in her heart of hearts, she always wanted to be—even in the midst of later dysfunction! For a while, she stopped all use of drugs, alcohol and tobacco and even tried to follow some of my vegetarian diet.

Our great immediate blessing was that Naomi flew east and gave some support to her daughter and grandchild. She spent a week or two cushioning the shock of the arrival of the newborn and preparing Maria—as far as possible—for her new role as caregiver. This turned out to be a double blessing for me, since I had to jump on a plane to lead a weeklong religious delegation to Cuba that I had organized.

And so, when I returned, our new family life began with its baby-dictated routine. "Dad, could you watch Brandon for a few hours this afternoon? I have to run some errands." The first hour would pass with Brandon looking at me with his serious eyes and cuddling against my chest. Then he needed his diapers changed. He might settle for a nap while I fielded phone calls from movement people I was working with to set up a national protest effort. Just as I'd get started on an article for a New York paper, Brandon would begin fussing for his supper, which meant I had to search to see if Maria had left food for the baby. Fortunately, my former family life skills quickly revived. But often I'd find myself soothing Brandon at two in the morning wondering what had happened to Maria.

On the one hand, I was relishing having this young family with me, but truthfully speaking, I sometimes resented being pressed into this service involuntarily. Juggling my new responsibilities with my work and movement obligations became the major challenge of this period of my life. We struggled to work things out, but after a reasonably peaceful interlude, a pattern appeared that was repeated with painful regularity with Maria's later children.

A key component of her negative pattern was the acquisition of a new male companion who might also become her drug partner or a dealer providing her with drugs. These would usually be young Black men, sometimes with good intentions, who often brought with them a history of drugs, prison, instability and the burden of being Black, young, male and poor in America. In the beginning, I naively welcomed these "family units" with my new grandchildren into my home until belongings began to walk, domestic violence and child abuse developed, and the urban drug culture incubated under my roof.

As Maria was more frequently "running the streets" of East Orange, mired in the use and pursuit of drugs, the children became my grandparental responsibility. Over the years I would play some significant role in the rearing, nurturing and protection of most of my six sweet "grands"— as the Black folks say. In the end, eventually the four younger children made new lives for themselves with caring family members and generous souls. I was blessed and challenged with the full-time task of raising my two oldest grandchildren, Brandon and Shana, the lovable little girl who arrived two years after her brother. I did my imperfect best to create a stable family life for them, and we grew even closer as the unique family which we still are.

In the meantime, the NJ Department of Youth and Family Services (DYFS)—itself later under investigation for abuse in its child welfare programs—had appeared on the scene and was threatening to place the children in foster care unless a family caretaker could be found. Thus, the court eventually made me their legal guardian. One snowy winter day I stood before a Black judge at the less than perfect Newark court system trying to explain why I, an elderly white man, was the best person around to raise these two Black children. I'm not sure which of the two of us was more perplexed.

In the course of the years I came to understand that Maria was trying to cover her pain, anger and fear with the self-medicating insulation of drugs. Once, at a moment of my criticizing her, she responded with the important insight: "Dad, you don't know what it's like." In truth, I am certain that I do not in any way comprehend the *via crucis* of despair that my beloved daughter walked each day and how desperately she attempted to mask that pain with drugs, all to no avail. Therefore, any critical-sounding narrative on these pages always comes from this dimension of deep respect and compassion.

Thus did I join the growing sorority—because in my community most were single grandmothers—of grandparent caretakers. I was fortunate in being able to assemble occasional childcare volunteers of friends and neighbors so that I was still able to carry on some of my peace work and other involvements. When this help was not available, I would sometimes take one or both children along with me to movement meetings and events, and so they received an occasional unsought education on the great issues of our times. Maria's children had already experienced a bigger slice of life in the urban reality than most Americans and so had a built-in sophistication and wisdom about social realities that most other children would not acquire in a lifetime.

Amidst much love, at times our mutual feelings of resentment would bubble to the surface. Theirs at feeling deprived of a normal childhood and their mother, mine at being pressed into partially involuntary service of having to carry the burden as a surrogate parent.

I also, accordingly, became educated in the realities of life in what Michael Harrington called "the other America" in his 1962 classic. This was the hidden America that very few members of mainstream society even knew existed, except in television caricature, racial stereotypes or in the demi-monde "showbizness" world of gangster rap or its approximations. (Here I'm not talking about that hip hop which is the raw authentic youth poetry of the ghetto.) We were living in the bitter reality of life in the midst of urban decay, rampant drug culture, regular random drive-by shootings, bare subsistence existence and even hunger—right here in the good old US of A.

The experience of all three of us being on food stamps—and Brandon and Shana on welfare—was an education in itself. I participated in the hour-long waits in the drab East Orange Welfare Office where I was usually the only male and generally the only white person. I developed solidarity with these mainly Black and a few Latina mothers who were struggling for the crumbs that would hopefully fall from the master's table for their children. In retrospect, I wish that I had expressed that solidarity more explicitly. It could have been a ministry and a deep soul learning experience. Maybe I was also feeling too overwhelmed and intimidated.

My long wait would finally lead to an encounter with a welfare worker, which was even more humiliating. There were occasional exceptions of workers (even one supervisor) who were compassionate or, at least, just. But they were often themselves oppressed people, sometimes people of color, underpaid, overworked and probably just a few steps away from the welfare rolls themselves. Instead of being in solidarity with their fellow strugglers for survival, they sometimes treated the poor women who were their clients with a lack of respect and with such punitive attitudes that one would have thought that it was their own money they were dispensing. My appearances there—an elderly white man in charge of two Black children—regularly perplexed both the other welfare clients and the social workers.

It is indeed a crime to have such a large part of our population waiting for its humiliating monthly dole, and we are in danger of creating a pitiful multi-generational system of dependency. But let's look at the reality. I had to deal with the inferior educational system for inner-city youth and the low level of expectations by teachers. This is what my grandkids were facing everyday. What was ahead for them—flipping hamburgers at McDonald's, if they even managed to graduate from high school, which prepared them for very little?

Is there a way out of this? Maybe this is the question: Is there the political and social will to forge another reality for inner -city kids and for all of America's poor children? As our economy deteriorates, are there any crumbs left over for these, "the least of my brothers and sisters"? In 2011 with the Republican "teabaggers" in the congressional saddle and many Democrats also bought out by the corporations, our poor people had fallen off the scale of national priorities.

My experience of the other America included periodic visits to the East Orange General Hospital's emergency room with Brandon or Shana or with Maria, when she lived with us. I suppose that one should be humbly grateful for its existence at all because in recent years the hospital in nearby Orange was simply closed down overnight—the only healthcare facility for miles—because it was no longer financially feasible. Since then two other hospitals in the area have closed. Thus has the high Hippocratic ideal of medicine as art and service been completely taken over by the captains of commerce, creating what Dwight Eisenhower might have called "the medical-industrial complex."

The emergency room of East Orange General (where Maria and I discovered recently one late night that their in-patient psychiatric unit had been shut down due to cost-cutting) was just one step away from the ante-chamber of the charnel house. The wait—sometimes even for grave emergencies—could be many hours. I must confess that on occasions I yielded to the temptation of white clericalism by donning my Roman collar when I seriously feared for the well-being of one of my little ones in the emergency room, but even this tactic did not always win them better care.

As with many families on the margins of society, housing was often a challenge. Once when Maria had the children in her care, she was living with a seemingly stable older couple. It took me a month or two to realize that this residence was really a glorified crackhouse right on our Park Avenue. The DYFS paid several investigational calls but did not seem to deduce this fact. It became clear to me that we had to get the children out immediately and this meant taking them under my roof in order to prevent DYFS from placing Brandon and Shana in foster care.

In the meantime, I was going through my own personal housing crisis. Since our home of over twenty years had shifted from being a community to becoming a legal co-op, interpersonal relationships and even legal and fiscal realities had changed. The chief of these was the failure of some co-op members to pay their monthly fees and the danger of eventually losing our building either to the tax collector, New Jersey Power & Light or the East Orange Water Department. After a dramatic sale of our building after a few years I eventually ended up in a local high-rise.

So began another mysterious phase of the journey. In the meantime, through the indirect intervention of retired Bishop Paul Moore Jr. of New York, I had succeeded in getting Brandon and Shana full scholarships to the Episcopalian St. Phillips Academy in Newark. The generous Headmaster Miguel Brito even provided them with uniforms.

This extraordinary institution created the possibility of a superb pre-high school education for mainly African-American students on the level of the academies and finishing schools from which they had always been excluded. It was a warm, nurturing community of staff, teachers, parents and students and they welcomed my grandchildren, who flourished there, at least in their earlier tenure.

Despite such support, my efforts at educating the children in private schools proved less than successful and they eventually re-entered the East Orange public schools. At the time, Brandon was fourteen or fifteen and Shana was eleven or twelve so I was the beneficiary of those often glorious adolescent years. For them this meant not only the "normal" stresses of hormones, puberty and "coming of age" eruptions but also, and perhaps especially, the cruel wounding of years of abuse, abandonment and unfulfilled longing for stability, a family and a mother and even a father.

This inner turmoil was to play itself out in their new school setting for Brandon in the middle school and for Shana in the lower school. They were now in the dysfunctional overcrowded reality of the urban inner-city school machine.

This was to be another phase of my education about the other America. I had seen some of it when my grandchildren were in the lower grades in East Orange, but now the whole pathology stood out in stark relief. It was not only the general neglect of education in America, where we would always prefer to fund a war as opposed to funding a school, but the application of these morally bankrupt priorities to poor children of the "wrong" pigmentation.

There was also a lower level of tolerance for my grandchildren acting out their distress than they would have experienced in a more friendly setting in suburbia. Both children were sitting on top of intense repressed anger that surfaced in inappropriate ways toward teachers or other students. As a result, I was often summoned to the principal's or disciplinarian's office for reports of suspensions, detentions or worse.

I became a well-recognized figure as I entered the almost traumatic chaos of my grandchildren's school building with its incredible noise level, outbreaks of violence and massively overcrowded and understaffed classes. I met with teachers, many of whom were in various stages of hopelessness and cynicism. I observed the children—often from single-parent welfare homes, who should have been our treasure and hope for the future—being prepared for despair and uncertainty.

Yes, there were occasional (usually inadequate) special programs, special classes and counseling for Brandon and Shana but nothing that went to the root of their issues. We did discover a few skilled and compassionate counselors at the Family Center in Orange, but little in-depth help was available within the school system, which was drowning from overload and lack of resources.

All of this would be exacerbated by my grandchildren finally having to move out of my apartment because of landlord pressure against having tenants not on the lease. One more painful displacement of these innocent children. We found what we hoped would be temporary housing with friends of the family in hard-core urban Newark in what might be called the low-rise version of "the projects." These were generous people who were already carrying their own economic and family burdens and were not immune to the cruel pressures of life in the urban wasteland. Now on top of this came two wonderful but difficult children who were themselves carrying the heavy burden of their lives.

In the end, in June of 2005, it seemed as if all the issues were coming to a head simultaneously. The East Orange school authorities had begun to notice that my grandchildren were no longer East Orange residents. This, in combination with their increasing behavior problems, inclined school authorities to use this as an excuse to push them out of the school system. At the same time, the domestic tensions between Brandon and

Shana and their temporary hosts in Newark also made their stay with them more tenuous.

It was a fearful moment of crisis with DYFS bureaucrats again threatening to place my grandchildren in foster care, but an unexpected window of grace opened up—surely created by a higher benign power. Members of Shana's father's family had moved from Jersey City to rural South Carolina. Her Aunt Zena had decided that she no longer wanted to raise her three children in the negative inner-city environment of Jersey City. She invited Shana and later Brandon to come down to live with them. We all jumped at the idea of getting them both out of East Orange and Newark, with its urban dangers and adolescent allurements, and they even liked the idea of being close to family and to Shana's father, who was living nearby.

How much there is to be learned from the generosity of the poor. Even though Zena lived in a trailer in Latta, South Carolina, on a meager income from her work in a chicken processing plant, there was always room for another hungry nephew and niece. And so they moved under the tent of this Southern extended family. Since then, Brandon and Shana have graduated from high school, one of the major accomplishments of their challenging lives.

Thus did my education proceed slowly but deliberately forward. Ironically, it concerned issues that I had been addressing in the macrocosm of social change movements for years, but what a difference between the abstractions of the macro and the flesh-and-blood experience of the micro. It is one thing to debate and demonstrate about issues such as racism, the shredding of the welfare net during the Clinton presidency, the pursuance of hopeless and bloody wars and an insane nuclear arms race supported by an astronomical defense budget. It is quite another to see these realities reflected in the innocent eyes of my grandchildren and my home community.

After years of struggle with her demons and almost a year in the cruel New Jersey state prison system, Maria has also courageously turned her life around. She is reaching out to reconnect with her children and is intensively pursuing the path of recovery from addiction, with many a stumble on the way.

In the meantime, my son Peter has, happily for me, moved from San Francisco to Brooklyn, where he continues to pursue his music and works as a production designer in the world of music, television, advertising and staged events.

In 2008 he volunteered a month of his time in Cambodia to construct a state-of-the-art recording studio in Phnom Penh and on another visit produced a highly regarded CD of Khmer music for the Cambodian Living Arts (CLA) Program. This is the brilliant program conceived by Arn Chorn of Children of War, which I had some role in launching, to preserve and protect the rich traditional music of his beloved Khmer people. Ninety percent of the great musicians of Cambodia were ruthlessly murdered by the Khmer Rouge. Now, through this visionary program, many surviving artists have been rehabilitated, returned to their dignity as the premier musicians of the land, had their great music recorded and have begun master classes to teach young Cambodians to play these ancient instruments.

In the meantime, Peter and his then-partner, April, have presented me with my gorgeous seventh grandchild, Alasdair—Celtic for "Defender of the People." Both Naomi, with her midwife's wisdom, and I were there for his gentle but dramatic arrival.

In this way, my state of aloneness and loss of family was more than compensated for by greater and wiser powers (perhaps possessing an ironic Jewish sense of humor). And so I continued to water the verdant tree of my children and grandchildren so that it might bring forth good fruit for themselves and for posterity.

CHAPTER 28

I Do! Marriage at the Crossroads

I HAVE CELEBRATED WEDDINGS ON small sailboats fighting the wind in New York Harbor, in tiny inner-city living rooms, in the sanctuaries of stately churches, on steep mountaintops and windy beaches, in deep forests and sumptuous ballrooms. I have performed ceremonies in English, Spanish, German and in sign language, with holy rabbis, exotically garbed Hindu priests and fervent Black Pentecostal ministers, or by myself in the ancient Catholic rite. In the end what made each experience an authentic wedding transcends psychology, legal contract or even romance, and takes us into the realm of mystery. In the Jewish tradition the heavens open for the couple, and for Christians the sacrament makes present the mystical union between the Christ and his beloved people—the Church.

It is no easy matter these days for a young couple to find their way through the maze of gourmet menus, florists, videographers and high-priced fashion consultants—and still maintain a clear focus on the priority of the sacred ceremony itself as the centerpiece and *raison d'etre* of the entire wedding experience. Certainly the ceremony of matrimony was always intended to be one of the few most significant and potentially transformative rites of passage in the lives of a young man and woman. But is this ancient ritual still discernable underneath all of these encrusted layers? Or is it destined to become what so many see it as: merely a formalistic, hurried preface to the party that will follow?

These were the questions that confronted me some years ago when I embarked on the new vocational path of a wedding ministry as a non-institutional Catholic priest. My most immediate experience was the enormous growing need couples had who did not fit into the traditional wedding mold and could not easily find a clergy person to serve these needs. Also I was struck by the number of couples that neither fit the pattern offered by traditional wedding resources and services, nor indeed wanted any of that at all.

They were, first of all, couples who desired a Catholic ceremony but had decided to marry outside of the Church building proper, in a banquet hall or hotel or even on a mountaintop or beach or some other site sacred or meaningful to them and would be turned away, sometimes harshly, from most Catholic rectories. The theological rationale for this was arcane. After all, Adam and Eve had not wedded in St. Patrick's Cathedral.

Then there were couples who could no longer identify with the religious institution of their birth and upbringing, whatever it might be, but still sought a spiritual experience for their public commitment to each other through a non-traditional ritual. Further, there were many divorced Catholic couples excluded from the official sacramental wedding solace of their Church who yet longed to express their love for each other in a sacred way blessed by God.

There were also growing numbers of Jewish-Catholic couples who experienced difficulty in finding enthusiastic clergy on either side to bless their union in a ritual that genuinely expressed and honored both traditions. I was also moved by the increasing number of gay and Lesbian couples who were trying to find a meaningful celebration of their commitment in an often unsympathetic religious world. Finally, there were the couples who didn't identify with any specific "religious" tradition but still have retained a sense of the spiritual and sacred nature of this ancient rite of passage. Together we sought to create an experience that was not part of any denomination but was part of that genetic intuition of the holiness of uniting two people in this ancient way.

Could I find a way of transforming this often rote and mechanical event into a profound and memorable experience, not only for the bride and groom, but also for their family and friends? Could weddings still express the power of that ancient rite of passage whereby a woman and a man leave their birth families to join their two destinies in the great journey of life, while still retaining their precious individualities? Could I assist them in making holy this major step of entering together the larger community on a new level of mature membership as families, parents and even as guardians of the future? How would I best be able to serve in the face of so many individualistic, privatized, trivialized and often isolating messages from popular media as well as the standardized and often untrue experiences of love, romance and marriage we are all barraged with in contemporary Western culture?

I experimented at the outset with the centrality of creating the sacred reality of this special event by involving not only the couple but all of the participants in that profoundly social and communal celebration that weddings have always represented among traditional peoples of all kinds. Antoine de Saint-Exupéry reminds us of this in *The Little Prince* by the lovely insight that "love is not about two people spending the rest of their lives looking into each other's eyes but rather spending their lives looking off into the same direction together." In this spirit, love and marriage are seen not as a flight from the world into a kind of romanticized privatism, but rather a deeper step into the world and the community. Accordingly, all the wedding guests are invited to join me in the act of marrying the bride and groom by focusing their spiritual heart energy on uniting these two people to each other. In this way they begin to step out of the typical passive spectator mode of wedding participant and enter into the community consciousness of engagement and commitment.

These weddings were always deeply fulfilling experiences for me. I felt fulfilled, not as the ritual custodian of the necessary mechanical even magical words, but rather as the privileged catalyst creating a circle community of love and support for our beloved couple.

Thus, for an instant, the whole wedding community is lifted above the ordinariness of their daily lives to enter the tribal realm of the mythic.

I was first struck by this when couples and their guests would share with me how they felt momentarily freed from the often separating experience of the urban beehive of apartment life or from what some even referred to as their "little boxes" of suburbia. I began to realize how, by the grace of the sacred ritual, they were all transformed into a holy community receiving these two members as a new family unit, now united and accountable not only to each other but to this very same community and to the greater common good.

I soon became aware that in the sacred act of bringing together these two souls in the bond of marriage, all present are momentarily transformed in that intimate experience of true community that all our hearts long for. Again and again, I would hear from brides and grooms and their loved ones how they "felt changed" from the flatness of daily existence as they were gathered up into an experience of the sacred and of a celebration that transfixed their hearts. Invited guests said they "no longer felt like mere onlookers." As I listened to their words, I came to recognize that they were experiencing the power of tribal intimacy and perhaps even that of the "beloved community," the dream of Martin Luther King Jr., an experience so often lost in our high-tech world.

The size or location of the ceremony does not seem to matter. I have celebrated marriages in simple homes with a dozen people standing in a candle-illuminated circle sharing their deepest thoughts and feelings. Then there have been weddings with two hundred people in a formal, elegant setting experiencing the power of the ancient traditional Catholic ritual. Ultimately it was the embrace of the community and the contact with the sacred that made the ritual both profound and transformative.

Now, in contrast to my early concern about marrying couples, I look forward to every experience of this most special rite of passage that leaves no one in attendance untouched. The bride and groom surely enter into sacred space and time as the ritual of joining their lives intersects with the direct intervention of the Creator Spirit, transforming that ordinary place into a sacred power vortex filled with holy energy, mystery and magic. It is this experience of the Holy that opens to all present an entranceway into a luminous sacred circle and even leads to the healing of their hearts. All those present, especially couples, are invited to participate in this powerful moment by renewing their own commitment to each other.

In the hundreds of weddings I have been privileged to perform over the years, I have come to see that the wedding ritual reconfigures and makes present again the ancient creation story found in Genesis and the other creation myths. It is the story of man and woman made in the divine image and placed in a pristine garden, a place of beauty and delight. Here the wedding transcends mere sentimental romanticism and instead powerfully charges the couple to again accept the original trust and responsibility for the earth garden and all living beings. In this responsibility they are reminded that the garden is no longer in its original pristine condition but has also become a locus of woundedness, including poverty, hunger, homelessness, injustice, war, violence and even the ecological devastation of our beautiful planet home.

In this way the new husband and wife are not only bonded with each other, but also with the larger community in their primal vocation of transforming the garden into a haven of harmony, peace, justice and love for their children and for future generations. They are reconnected to their sacred calling to be guardians, not only of home and children, but also caregivers and healers of their neighborhood, society and of the entire earth family.

So what initially appears to so many as yet another wedding they've been invited to, yet another potentially uninteresting, repetitive social event they've attended numerous times, is no longer that at all. Something shifts for all those in attendance, and I am continually surprised by joy when I see their faces change early on in the ceremony as they are all invited to participate in the marriage itself. The tired, age-worn event becomes truly memorable as it is lifted into the realm of the mythic and magical. Even the celebratory time of feasting, wine, music and dancing afterward takes on a deeper and more wonderful quality of dynamic community and closeness to each other, as well as a connection to the sacred cosmos.

Finally, for the couple itself, the wedding day represents a powerful new beginning of future life together. They are empowered to walk hand in hand on the road of life, which will be filled with joys, sorrow and the inspiring challenge to become full human beings. Their vows of "I do" have become filled with new depth, beauty and meaning as their wedding rings symbolize not only the presence of the Infinite One, but also of their entrance into the sacred circle of the community.

Weddings for me, then, and for the many people I have come to know during the exchange of vows, are at something of a crossroads in Western culture. To guide and serve such a profoundly awakening experience is more rewarding and humbling for me than anything I could have ever imagined. As for the many who come dressed in their finery, they are often filled with tedious dread of yet another typical wedding. Instead, we gather together with our "dearly beloveds" at the threshold of "I do" and express our commitment to the couple and to the new meaning their lives are invested with, as well as to the lives of children they will perhaps bring into this always new world.

CHAPTER 29

YOGA PRACTITIONER AND TEACHER

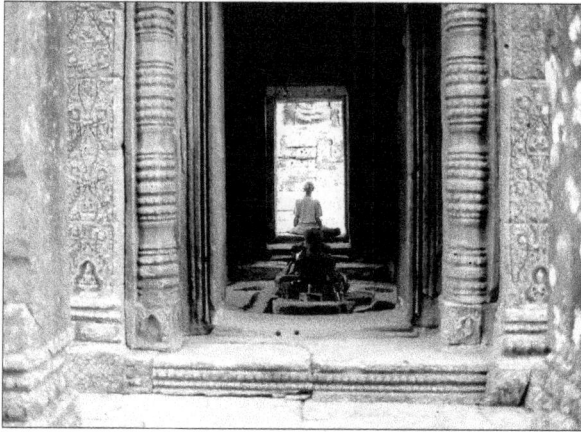

I WAS STILL YOUNG IN the practice of the monastic life when Father Augustine, the laconic librarian, handed me a thin book and said, "Father Elias, this just came in and I thought that it might interest you." He knew of my interest in strange and esoteric matters. It was called *Christian Yoga*, and I wasn't quite clear about the subject matter. It was written by Dom Jean-Marie Déchanet, a French Benedictine monk; we immediately had something in common.

The small book laid out, in the most elementary and clear language, what the original theory of yoga was, how it began, some general ideas of the practice and a section on the various poses with clear illustrations. It was this last part that fascinated me.

So after reading the book and being reassured that this was not some secret form of paganism (something that still might have troubled me in those days) and that, in fact, it was all quite peacefully compatible with Christianity and even compatible with the monastic life, I decided to dip my big toe into this intriguing pond of mystery and promise. Little did I know that it was, in fact, an infinite ocean and that this modest experiment would have a profound transformative impact on my life journey for decades to come.

The diagrams spoke to me because they were the closest thing to a teacher that I would have for many decades. And so, in the brashness of my youthful unschooled enthusiasm, I began to experiment, starting on that very day with the ancient practice of yoga asanas, or poses. I remember the one that spoke to me first was Sarvangasana, or the shoulder stand. I now know that I did it quite imperfectly, more in a boomerang shape than the elegant candle-straight pose that I still marvel at when executed by a trained practitioner. This would be true of my sophomoric version of the other poses, but it didn't matter. I had placed my foot on the sacred path of yoga, and only the world of spirit knew where it would lead.

From that moment forward, there was rarely a day that I did not pursue this practice, following the guidelines of this wonderful little book. I did not share this secret with most of the other monks, some of whom already regarded my ideas about Church, state and the monastic life as deviating from the prescribed straight and narrow. Each day, after our early 4:40 a.m. office of praise, I returned to my cell for a silent time of *lectio divina*, or monastic meditation, and would first spend a half hour or so practicing yoga asanas.

It grew on me. I loved it. I quickly began to experience its benefits, physical, mental/psychological and spiritual. The Sanskrit word *yoga* is derived from the word yoke, since it yokes together the world of the body, the mind and the spirit. In the beginning, I had no idea what that really meant and am still trying to excavate its deep significance today. But I intuited that I had stumbled upon, or had been led to, a reality whose secret hidden pearl would only reveal itself in the mysterious rhythm of the coming years.

In subsequent years, I would find myself in yoga poses on the floors of the strangest places, including community houses during clandestine meetings planning draft board raids, during our humanitarian aid caravan to Cuba, in people's living rooms or in the backs of churches. The beauty of the practice was that all that was required was a little piece of floor so that even a temporary jail cell would not frustrate my practice.

February 1991, the eve of my sixtieth birthday, a powerful and dramatic intervention in my life path awaited me. For some time, my friend Janice Rous, a gifted Alexander technique practitioner and yoga teacher, had been urging me to take a class with her own yoga teacher, Mary Dunn. She sealed her invitation with a birthday gift of two classes with her, so I gratefully accepted.

I arrived at the Jewish Community Center on West Eighty-sixth Street in Manhattan for class, where I was surprised by a small, pretty woman with an engaging smile and a welcoming spirit, who might have been taken for a Westchester housewife. She did, in fact, live in Westchester. Mary Dunn immediately made me feel at home and asked me about my yoga experience. I felt quite proud of myself when I could report that I had been practicing more than twenty years.

Her class was for beginner and intermediate students, so I assumed that I was probably in the right place. The experience that followed was surprising, destabilizing, wonderful and stunning. To sum it up, I felt as if I had never done yoga before. Mary's teaching was filled with such precision, such subtlety and nuance, such physical challenge in the mere duration of the poses, such energy that came out of this very focused practice that it defied explanation. To begin with, I was confronted with the relatively amateurish character of my yoga style, in spite of many years of practice; not a terrible thing, but definitely a blow to my ego.

What I had experienced in that first class of one-and-a-half hours was something that would still be revealing itself to me some eighteen years later as Mary's student. It was, first of all, her brilliant mastery of this form of yoga. It was also her finely honed skills as a communicator and teacher, often using very homey, down-to-earth examples. But it was, above all, her ability to weave the depth of spiritual wisdom and the training of the mind into the technical brilliance of her teaching that would lift yoga practice into a realm that I had not experienced thus far.

I left the Jewish Community Center and floated down eighty-sixth Street both exhilarated and exhausted, still not quite clear as to the nature of the experience. I knew that this class represented a turning point in my life. As soon as I got home, I sat down and wrote this letter:

> Dear Mary Dunn,
>   I just had the privilege and grace of participating in your class.
>   It was a peak experience for me and I am deeply grateful to you and the world of spirit.

I would like to tell you about my life vocation. I have attempted to be of service to the Earth and all living beings through working for peace, social justice, and our wounded environment. I would like to invite you to walk on the path with me by taking me on as a scholarship student, since my income is modest at present.

I know that this may seem like a presumptuous request, but I believe that it will strengthen my life of service and open up new doors for me on the spiritual path.

With deepest respect and gratitude and wishing you God's blessings,

Paul Mayer

This consummate act of chutzpah was inspired by the clear conviction that I had been led to Mary and to her teaching in spite of my slender financial circumstances at the time. I heard back from Mary almost immediately. She called to say, "Paul, I would be pleased and honored to have you in my class." She also told me that she came from a Quaker family so that peacemaking had always been an important part of her life. Mary loved the idea of Children of War, which I was involved with at the time.

In the course of time, I discovered that the particular form of yoga that we were practicing was called Iyengar yoga, the traditional yoga of India that has been suffused by the unique spirit and genius of B.K.S. Iyengar, whom the BBC once called "the Michelangelo of yoga." He studied under one of the traditional masters and scholars, his brother-in-law, Tirumala Krishnamacharya.

As a child and teenager, Iyengar suffered from malaria, typhoid and tuberculosis. He attained health and vigor through intense practice of yoga. His personal experience was the basis for developing this yoga form as a therapeutic tool not only for the sick, but also for people with limitations of inflexibility or old age. Through the use of props such as blankets, wooden blocks, straps and chairs, yoga became accessible to people with limitations. My personal experience showed me how this yoga form can help knees and back injuries—and even helped me recover from pneumonia.

Mary, it turned out, was one of the senior Iyengar teachers in North America. In fact, it was her mother, Mary Palmer, who introduced Mr. Iyengar to the US in 1973 to teach at the Ann Arbor Y. She was also a yoga teacher and had encountered Mr. Iyengar at his institute in Pune,

India. Her experience was so powerful that she decided to invite him to visit our country and lead classes here. It was the first of periodic visits.

That was over fifty years ago, and since then the Iyengar community has virtually exploded here and worldwide. In 2004 B.K.S. Iyengar was named one of the one hundred most influential people on the planet in a cover story in *Time* magazine.

I began to attend Mary's class twice a week and they were generally the high point of my day. I learned that her genius was making the mysterious and even apparently impenetrable accessible and even doable. Her devotion to her students was such that it seemed that she would settle for nothing less than pushing them to glory.

I also began to see that this practice was about more than mere physical proficiency and stamina, which are indeed demanded both because of the nuanced precision of the pose but also because of the sometimes challenging length for which the poses are held. But the depth of the teaching is sometimes hidden in the almost throwaway lines in which Mary communicates a rich spiritual wisdom and psychological insight as during a seemingly endless Trikonasana/Triangle pose: "Now, try to let go of the resentment toward the teacher or toward life or toward yourself or toward this pose—and instead embrace and extend even more fully and generously into the pose." For Mary, behind her apparently mainstream-American attractive appearance was, I believe, a great spiritual teacher even though she might have rejected the idea.

Yoga is science, art and philosophy subtly woven together. However, it is not sufficient to simply attend these classes, wonderful though they may be. Rather, it is through independent (ideally daily) practice that one begins to test the validity and power of the practice. Even a few minutes a day for a beginner can garner rich benefits.

I must say that I have always had some reservations about the cult and the culture of the guru. I have seen too many forms of spiritual elitism, other forms of manipulation, even guru abuse and a sense of hierarchy that I had fled from in the Catholic Church! But, in B.K.S. Iyengar, I found great clarity, integrity, simplicity and an authentic connection to his power without any artifice.

At eighty-six, "the father of modern yoga in the west" is still an elegant, powerful apparition with long white hair, erect posture, piercing black eyes, ready smile and always beautifully attired in the traditional white robe of the Indian teacher. He still practices yoga five hours a day, and his rendition of the asanas would challenge the average eighteen-year-old.

After ten years as Mary Dunn's student, one day, in a burst of enthusiasm and forwardness, I presumed to ask her how she felt about my studying to become a yoga teacher. Mary said that she would take it under consideration, so obviously it was not self-evident. After a few days of reflection, she agreed and suggested that I join her weekly teachers' training class in Greenwich, Connecticut. I was elated and intimidated simultaneously at the prospect of this lengthy and challenging process of certification.

The teacher's training process is a rigorous one, and many of the other students were already accomplished teachers who were advancing their certification level. But it was an opportunity to be part of a warm, accepting community of teachers, mainly women, who are devoted to this unique yoga path and whose level of proficiency and sophistication was both intimidating and inspiring. I was encouraged by Mr. Iyengar's insightful words: "Teaching is a difficult art, but it is the best service you can do to humanity."

I cannot overstate the brilliance of the Iyengar method as a therapeutic tool to deal with injuries and illness. I have used it often on my personal problems of sacroiliac, knee and ankle injuries, as well as problems with my digestive tract.

Over the past few years, I have also been teaching a weekly yoga class to elders in the building where I live in East Orange. Since I am not very connected to this seniors' residence in its daily activities and culture, I thought that this would be a good way of sharing one of my greatest treasures with the residents of "The Pavilion," as well as with any outside community people who would like to participate; there would be no fee.

I also saw it as a way of "giving back" to the predominantly African American, low-income community in which I have lived for forty years. As one of the few remaining white residents (after the white flight of the '60s and '70s), I have always felt it a privilege to live in East Orange and to have raised my family/families here. To have been accepted as belonging has been a great blessing and privilege for me. For all of its wounding in poverty, drugs, crime and dysfunction, there is the underlying rich vein of the precious metal of this ancient culture with its sense of tribal interconnection and spirit of community, its presence of the ancestors, its pulsating rhythms and its sense of the sacred. As Ibn, my grandson

Brandon's best friend, said during a discussion on racial identity, "Hey, Mr. Paul, you ain't no white man; you belong to us!" I was deeply moved.

So, every Monday morning at 10:15 our yoga class meets in the arts and crafts room. Somewhere between six and thirteen people participate. They are almost all African American women. I can only begin to imagine the hard lives they have had. They are the grandchildren of slaves, have survived daily racism, exploitative jobs, oppressive men, abuse, rape and more. They come in with their dignity, wisdom and humor; I am honored.

I use my own age, a modest eighty-two, and Mr. Iyengar's ninety-five, as an incentive for all. Our students range from the sixties up to the nineties and come with an assortment of canes, walkers, wheelchairs, oxygen tanks; some walk in upright or a little bent over. Erline, with terminal cancer, came in her wheelchair right up until the end. I proclaim that yoga might be the best antidote for scoliosis, osteoporosis, Alzheimer's, the blues and all the assorted infirmities and lies that the dominant culture inflicts on old people. And then we practice yoga. While I tailor it to people's conditions and limitations, I do not patronize my students. I challenge them to their edges. They begin by resenting me and occasionally grumbling, but then they usually end up rejoicing. They tell me about victories over high blood pressure, bursitis, sciatica, arthritis and more. And they look more erect each time.

When Mary Dunn's mother first went to India in 1968, Mr. Iyengar told her: "I will teach you to stand on your own two feet so that you can face whatever challenge life brings." Whether he was speaking about the beginning Tadasana/Mountain pose or of the whole body of yoga practice, he gave a simple vision of this ancient practice that reminds us that it all begins with our two feet—our bodies. And yet, it transcends a merely physical, athletic exercise because our bodies, as St. Paul reminds us, are "temples of the Holy Spirit" and therefore the sacred gateway to the inner journey to the mind and the core of the soul.

Mary wrote beautifully of yoga and of the role of the teacher and as I read her words I am heavy of heart. Mary died of cancer on September 4, 2008. Her death was one of the great losses of my life. She died as she had lived: conscious, practicing Yoga even on her sick bed, teaching her students when they visited, and never losing her humor and intelligence.

It is for all these reasons that yoga has a particular power and importance for those of us who identify as social change agents and peace activists. As we confront the daily realities of global warming, war, hunger and injustice, we need to nurture and sustain ourselves and each other. Yoga is one of those practices that Gandhi would have encouraged us to use and probably used himself. It can help us maintain balance and strength as we walk this sometimes challenging road to a transformed planet.

I still regret my last conversation with her. Instead of focusing on her—perhaps it was too much—I asked some self-centered questions about my teacher certification. Then on my way to her lovely memorial service at our institute, I was walking through one of the great halls of Penn Station, which happened to be relatively empty and quiet. The only sound was that of a young girl playing the guitar beautifully and singing poignantly the Beatles' song "Let It Be":

> When I find myself in times of trouble
> Mother Mary comes to me
> Speaking words of wisdom, let it be.
> And in my hour of darkness
> She is standing right in front of me
> Speaking words of wisdom, let it be.
> Let it be, let it be.
> Whisper words of wisdom, let it be.

It was my beloved Mary in her inimitable way, cheering me on with her radiant smile and assuring me that all was well.

CHAPTER 30

THE MAKING OF AN EARTH GUARDIAN

*Nature, Native American Legacy
and Other Influences*

MY LOVE FOR THE EARTH began to stir during my childhood in Nazi Germany. I had the good fortune of having a father who had a passion for nature. He had skied in the Vosges Mountains, hiked in the Swiss French Alps and had a strong affinity with the Taunus Mountains near Frankfurt where we lived. This love for nature was a point of connection with my father in our otherwise difficult relationship.

His poetic nature and romantic sensibilities gave him a remarkable connection to the earth, a love in which my mother also shared. On Sundays, the whole family would delight in wonderful weekend hiking excursions into the Taunus, sustained by my mother's lovingly made Kosher cold-cut sandwiches on good German rye bread. At that time, my father's often irascible and existentially insecure nature would be transformed into an expansive spirit as he rejoiced in the beauty of those magnificent mountains. So this would be a rare time when I experienced greater acceptance and inclusion.

Later, in my at times difficult childhood and stormy adolescence in Washington Heights, I became a very active and ambitious Boy Scout and often spent my summers at the Ten Mile River Scout Camp in upstate Narrowsburg, New York. I always attended Camp Ranachqua—the Kosher camp—located on glorious Lake Nianque. (I still remember anti-Semitic canoe forays by scouts from the other camps.) Although missing home, I developed the skills of hiking, camping and knowledge of the natural world.

Much to my surprise and pride, I was nominated for and accepted into the secret honor society of the Order of the Arrow. Scouts were elected on the basis of their "cheerful service" to others, and I still can't recall why I would have qualified. The inspiring and almost mystical (also quite rigorous) initiation ceremony was based on the ancient tradition of the Lenni Lenape Indians who once inhabited these gorgeous mountains, hills, lakes and woods. The ceremony took place outdoors during a dark night, with everyone seated around a blazing fire. Amidst Indian chants and drumming, canoes filled with older scouts, impressively dressed as painted braves and carrying torches, suddenly appeared on the lake gliding out of the dark.

We were told to bring nothing but a sleeping bag. As we all sat around the fire listening to the beating drums, I was suddenly tapped on the shoulder then half dragged into the dark woods to spend a night alone in the forest. For an impressionable fifteen-year-old, the combination of the mystery of a dark, starlit night with the half-naked painted braves dancing around the flickering fire along with the ancient chants accompanied by the drums made a deep impression. All of this was against a background of the Native American mystique of young warrior courage being tested in the face of adversity and became a kind of rite of passage into a new level of maturity and service to the community.

This introduction into the culture and spirit of the First Nations of our continent would stay with me and surface later in mysterious and unexpected ways. The ritual also bonded me more deeply with the earth in its beauty, its mystery and its power even as I lived out my daily adolescence in an urban setting.

Later our Scout troop would take the ten-mile hike across the George Washington Bridge to the beautiful Alpine Scout Camp, where my connection to the natural world deepened. I found myself focusing more and more on my emerging grief for the earth. At times, I would actually weep at the realization that species, ecosystems and the planet itself as we know it as life-giving could all be lost—and within the not-too-distant future. How could I feel equanimity in the face of this unprecedented tragedy that could eventually overshadow all other forms of suffering and loss?

As I grew up, I was gradually being guided into a deeper understanding and experience of the indigenous reality. It was graced to me most powerfully by reading *Black Elk Speaks* (edited by John G. Neihardt, one the great ethnologists and poets of the Plains region). This simple little book was to become one of the guiding lights of my spiritual journey.

Perhaps Black Elk, a medicine man of the Lakota people on the Pine Ridge Reservation in South Dakota, was so open to the white stranger, John Neihardt, who suddenly appeared at his isolated cabin door in 1931. Perhaps he was so willing to share the mystical vision bestowed on him as a nine-year-old boy because he sensed the dark times that lay ahead, not only for his people but for all peoples. Could it be that he wanted his vision and message about the "things of the other world" to be transcribed so that they would not be lost? Perhaps he realized that a planetary crisis was coming and that it was time for his message to be heard beyond the world of the Plains Indians.

From the age of five, Black Elk had heard voices calling to him. One day when he was nine he collapsed with swollen arms, legs and face and fell into a deep coma, which his parents did not think he would survive. In this deep state he experienced a mystical earth vision comparable in beauty and grandeur to the visions of the Prophet Ezekiel and the Book of Revelations. The six ancient Grandfathers handed over to him the flowering tree of life, the cup of sacred water, the four-branched herb, the daybreak star, the sacred hoop—all symbols of his new power and calling. The oldest grandfather spoke and encouraged him: "My boy, have courage, for my power shall be yours, and you shall need it, for your nation on the earth will have great troubles."

The vision and teaching of this slender volume have equipped me in some unique and powerful way for my vocation to be an Earth Guardian. It has led me into a new and mysterious realm of consciousness about the Earth as Mother and the reality of the interconnection of all living beings in "the sacred Web of Life." I owe more to Black Elk and his extraordinary revelation than words can express.

Throughout my life this modest volume continued to inspire me. In 1978 I came up with the rather presumptuous idea of teaching a course on Native American spirituality at New York Theological Seminary. At the beginning, my major qualification was my increasingly deep feelings about this spiritual path and an underlying conviction that this tradition of the Earth religion was mysteriously and inextricably connected to the survival of life on the planet. Nor did I ever feel for a minute that there was any conflict with my faith in the God of Moses and Abraham or with the Father (Mother) of whom Jesus speaks!

The other major influence in my life, and especially on my love for the Earth, was Thomas Berry, with whom I would share my teaching plans. Little did I expect that we would meet and that this influence would become even more profound. His book *The Dream of the Earth* became my environmental Bible, and its original insights, poetic language and lucid analysis of the ecological crisis impacted me profoundly, both on the level of understanding and feeling.

It was surely not by chance that I encountered Thomas Berry at a peace gathering. Dan Berrigan had sometimes spoken of this quiet, non-conventional, free-thinking priest, a member of the rather conservative Redemptorist order. Dan would sometimes meet him in the subway as both were on their way to Sunday parish assignments. They would share their common revulsion for the war in Vietnam and the silence of their church. When I met him before he became better known, Tom was already a scholar of Chinese and Indian philosophy and spoke those languages. He was also the founder of the society based on the thought of the visionary Pierre Teilhard de Chardin, the French Jesuit priest/paleontologist, once considered heretical.

Tom casually mentioned his connection to Native American thought, and when I told him of my ambitious teaching plans, he invited me to visit him at his home. I had no idea that he was an expert in this field as well. Tom received me as an honored guest at his house near the Hudson River in Riverdale. We began with a cup of herbal tea served underneath the massive grandfather oak that stood as the shamanic guardian of his little home and under which he channeled the Earth's energy into his luminous pages, surely some of the seminal ecological writings of our times.

After tea, Tom opened his generous heart and his abundant library on Native American literature and research to me. Most wonderful of all, he gifted me with boxes of his own brilliant monographs and articles—many still unpublished. These were a treasure trove of the most extraordinary insights into the life, history, spirituality and culture of indigenous peoples. Tom's deep conviction corroborated for me my growing intuition that the First Nations of the continent held in their hands and hearts—bruised and bloodied by centuries of suffering and genocide—the wisdom that was the key to the very survival of the Earth.

The writings and the teaching that he shared during subsequent visits under the grandfather oak opened for me the world of the traditions of the Elders, the sacred ceremonies and the writing of the great Indian thinkers, such as Vince Deloria and other wonderful writers and poets. I also consulted with some friends I had begun to make in the Native American world. Slowly, with trembling hands and heart at the presumption of it all but with much inner excitement at involvement in a reality that touched me so deeply, I began to formulate a rough syllabus for a course for the New York Theological Seminary students. Some surprises some challenges and much learning awaited me.

The uniqueness of NYTS was its interesting racially and culturally diverse student body. It could not have been more unlike the more typical white and middle class student bodies of Union, General and Jewish Theological Seminary. Under the courageous leadership of its president Bill Webber (whom we recently lost), a traditional, rather stodgy and conservative white Evangelical Protestant seminary had been transformed into a unique, progressive center of learning and academic certification for the clergy of the forgotten parts of the city. This implied a student body that was largely non-white—African American, Latino and some Asian—often less formally educated, older and already experienced in the ministry of the streets, ghettos and barrios. Some of the most authentic Gospel ministry in New York City came out of poor storefront churches instead of cathedrals.

I quickly discovered that most of the students were in my Native American spirituality and religion class primarily because it was the last course open and were there with mixed enthusiasm at best. Most of them came from Baptist AME (African Methodist/Episcopal), Pentecostal or other theologically conservative Church backgrounds and, therefore, probably regarded the objects of this course as pagans and the subject matter as concerning itself with a highly questionable form of religion. They also regarded the alleged teacher of such dangerous doctrine (clergy or not) as a dubious vehicle of divine doctrine. So this was the less-than-friendly audience that awaited me as I set out on this new adventure in the world of academia.

Together, and often reluctantly, we read and discussed *Black Elk Speaks*, *The Sacred Pipe* (also by Black Elk), some of the speeches of the great warriors and chiefs and other important analyses of the history and culture of the American Indian. We had the good fortune of having Chief Oren Lyons spend four enlightening and moving hours with us for one evening class. We also learned to our surprise that Black Elk himself served as a Catholic deacon and saw no contradiction between that role and his calling as a Lakota healer and medicine man.

In our readings and discussions, we slowly began to see Jesus Himself as deeply attached to the earth reality, often making use of images and parables taken from the world of nature. To my advantage, I was able to refer my primarily Black and Latino students to their own indigenous ancestors and traditions, which actually had much in common with the people and culture we were studying.

In the end, I witnessed a mysterious metamorphosis. On the last night of the course during an evaluation session, a prominent woman Pentecostal minister from Harlem stood up and gave a most remarkable testimony: "Dr. Mayer [in the Black church, the doctor title is generously assigned to all clergy], tonight I want to testify that the Indians are really the true Christians."

Thus was my first foray into the mysterious world of teaching and learning about the spiritual path of the tribal peoples of this continent.

In 2003 I led some workshops for educators together with a Diné (Navajo) Indian from the New Mexico Diné reservation, the largest in the country, which also includes large sections of Utah and Arizona. His name was Larry Emerson and he was to have a great influence on me. His manner of presentation was always soft-spoken and he proclaimed his indigenous teachings in a simple, intelligent and understated fashion. He was in his late thirties, of medium height with the handsome, open features of his people. Larry was a member of the medicine society, which was unusual for a person of his relative youth. I later found out that he was also a Vietnam veteran, had struggled with his own demons and had served as an assistant to the president of his nation. Now he was committed to working on different community projects with a special emphasis on addressing the problems of the young people at home who were facing the same grim challenge of most young Indians: alcohol, drugs, extreme poverty, despair and even suicide.

I was trying to deepen my understanding of indigenous tradition and we immediately hit it off. Larry was a gifted communicator, and I found the Diné way to be very subtle, with a complex, ancient cosmology and a very refined artistic and poetic sensibility. In this way it was different from many of the other indigenous cultures and religious forms that I had encountered. For example, in the Beauty Way Chant (one of the major prayer ceremonies of the Diné people), there is exquisite poetry and sensitivity to the shapes and colors of the natural world.

It occurred to me that perhaps we had been brought together so that I could gain experiential knowledge of this beautiful tradition. I casually asked Larry one day whether it would be possible for me to pay a visit to him in New Mexico and perhaps spend a few days with him. I was surprised to see that his response was very polite—as he always was—but also a little reserved. He said that he would have to think about it. And then he asked a very wise, but unexpected question: "What would you have to bring to my people?" His response at first took me aback until I realized how many white anthropology types and wannabe Indians probably came to the reservation only to subtly (or not so subtly) exploit and take from the culture and life of the people without a thought of what the people needed. I realized that I still had a great deal to learn about how to deal respectfully with this ancient culture.

I thought about it a little bit more and made the suggestion that I could do some youth work using the Children of War leadership development process and model to train young Diné people for leadership and empowerment. Larry, as an educator, seemed quite intrigued. He said that he would think about it all but did not extend an explicit invitation, although he gave me his address and phone number. Thus began my education about a new level of connection to Native American people.

Later that year, I was invited to speak at a seminar on peace education in Taos, New Mexico. So, on a lark, I called Larry Emerson and told him that I was visiting New Mexico and could I come out a few days early to visit him. To my delight he said that he would be pleased to see me, and so I prepared for one of the great spiritual adventures of my life.

As I drove out from Albuquerque, the New Mexican desert and landscape opened before me in its stark magnificence. The sage-covered earth, the red soil and, above all, the bluffs and mesas in their sculptured richness and majesty became more beautiful the farther I got from the populated centers. The towering mesas took on even more fantastic forms: limbs and appendages of huge primitive animals, temple-like shapes guarded by shamans, priests and saints and whole cities appeared in the red, gray and blue stone. It was as if these towering plateaus were the last fortress, the farthest outposts of the Native people who have survived and indeed were guarding the Earth herself against the final onslaught.

I opened the car window to take in the hot, sweet desert air. I experienced a deep longing in my heart, a stirring and a sense of having been here before, of coming home. I began to weep uncontrollably as I was overcome by the beauty and sacredness of this desert earth. So stark, so pure and stripped of all excess, of all superficiality. It was not hard to understand why it is the terrain of the Spirit, of sacred encounter and of the other world.

I also experienced a joyful anticipation, a sense that some great adventure of the Spirit, even a new phase of my life awaited me. I felt deeply blessed for having been invited into the great unknown.

Larry's directions seemed a little vague, but after some ten miles on the big, straight four-laned highway, there was an almost imperceptible opening in a fence where "the road and the high-voltage wires intersect" and I turned off onto a dirt road that appeared to go nowhere.

A few hundred yards down the road, I came to two houses which at first sight appeared a little rundown, even ramshackle. Later, on closer inspection, they turned out to be wonderfully comfortable, environmentally gentle on the Earth, beautiful and well designed and built by Larry.

He greeted me in his low-key way. (I was probably excessive in my embrace.) He was shy and reticent, especially when it came to Navajo culture and ceremony. I, the ever-searching Talmudic intellectual, was too inquisitive, too pushy—something which I gradually learned to restrain. It was not good manners to ask many questions, especially about sacred matters. Occasionally I slipped into the interrogative mode, which could probably be a sign of interest, respect and even caring in another culture. But not here.

Later in a moment of indiscreet enthusiasm, I asked Larry to do a healing ceremony on my leg, which had been giving me a lot of pain. He seemed somewhat open but pointed out that it was not about healing necessarily but about getting information and insight about the larger picture. Immediately, he noted that the problem was connected with my lower back and later said that it was part of the passage that I was going through. I also learned very quickly (although it was communicated with great politeness) that it was not appropriate for an elder like myself to walk around in shorts.

Later Larry shared with me his own remarkable journey: How he had grown up on the reservation and enlisted in the army during the early Vietnam War period, struggled with drugs and alcohol. He returned, became a leading activist in his area during the radical AIM period and then decided that his path was not one of anger and violence. It was then that he became more connected to the spiritual center of his Navajo people, which culminated in his initiation into their medicine society.

The next day we went out early to work on Larry's new hogan. The traditional hogan—a low, dome-shaped structure that originally was the Navajo family home—has now taken on more of a ceremonial and community function. We prayed together, with Larry praying in Diné, using the traditional sacred cornmeal, and then we began to work making the adobe for the hogan in the hot desert sun.

That day was Larry's forty-fourth birthday, so around one, after we washed up, we went over to his parents' house for a birthday lunch celebration. I felt privileged to be invited into the larger family circle. His parents were beautiful, traditional people with faces deeply lined like the furrows of the earth. Neither of them spoke English. I saw that underneath the rather reserved cultural demeanor of Larry and the family, there was also a great sense of humor and a spirit of fun. They were respectful but a little perplexed by my vegetarianism. Larry said that for his people survival has meant eating what is available, but the important thing was to pray before and after the hunt and ask permission of the spirit of the deer or antelope before killing them.

After a day or so of simply hanging out on this barren but beautiful, very hot desert landscape without asking too many questions, Larry invited me for a healing ceremony. I lay down on the earth and he prayed over me intensely with cedar smudging, tobacco offering and chanting. He told me that I should wear an eagle symbol next to the little green-glass cross around my neck because I was connected to this symbol of the Great Spirit.

I felt that I had stepped over some spiritual threshold because after the healing ceremony, Larry seemed much more open and began to share the rich teaching and tradition of his people with me. He seemed to accept me as someone serious about the spiritual path and also committed to the survival struggle of his people. I spent the next few days doing my yoga practice, meditating, writing in my journal and receiving teaching's from Larry.

Much of his teaching was about the sacredness of Mother Earth. I sensed the deep, intimate, mysterious and yet quite natural connection that his people have with the Earth and its creatures. I came to realize more clearly the perversion of Western dualism in which we consider ourselves separate from and superior to the natural world. By objectifying the Earth, we allow ourselves to use, exploit and devastate this supposedly separate reality. We must heal this alleged chasm. Oh, for that lucid insight of Tom Berry that "the universe is composed of subjects to be communed with, not primarily of objects to be used"*

I am repeatedly struck by the sophisticated yet simple Diné cosmology, psychology, healing philosophy and understanding of the origin of the universe. It is at once very beautiful (one of their ceremonies is even called the Beauty Way Chant), refined and yet grounded in the concrete realities of the earth. Most compelling and mysterious to me was the sense of the living, even intelligent nature of the material world—fire, earth, tobacco, water, plants and the animals—intimately connected to the world of the ancestors and spirit guides, all of which play an intimate role in our daily lives if we allow them to. I will always remember a conversation in which Larry emphasized the importance of communicating with and even listening to all the beings of the Earth—the plants, the animals, the tobacco and the wind. "And by the way," he emphasized, "these are not metaphors and this is not poetry, but objective reality."

On my last day, I reluctantly prepared for my departure. After consulting with his father, Larry told me he wanted to perform the eagle feather ceremony with me, a powerful blessing for someone going on a journey.

During the ceremony Larry gave me a small pouch of sacred white corn pollen, which medicine people pray with, and also a small pouch of tobacco used for offering and prayer. He told me that I am not a medicine man but both his father and he believe that I have a special calling to be a bridge between their people and the world of the white Europeans. He gave me these sacred objects to use and to pray with to strengthen me in

---

* *Evening Thoughts*, Sierra Club Book, 2006, p. 149.

this role. I was deeply moved and tears came to me eyes. I experienced the power of the ceremony and felt the sacredness of the moment and the Presence of the Great Spirit.

After I returned home, I kept in touch with Larry by phone and he periodically gave me supportive teaching, especially when he heard that I was attending the Rio Earth Summit. He has always been an enthusiastic supporter of my work for the environment.

On subsequent visits, Larry continued to share wisdom and ceremony with me in a spirit of great generosity and trust which moved me deeply. On these visits, I would sleep on the earth floor of the hogan which we had worked on together. This was also where we would meet for conversation, teaching and ceremony. The hogan was not only the traditional home of his people but is also a symbolic earth womb out of which new spiritual life and knowledge are born. May it be so!

Of the many teachings that Larry has shared with me, one sticks in my memory. "Your problem is that you think too much with your intellectual brain," he said. "That is the Western way. As an earth healer, you must learn to think from your solar plexus." And he pointed to my abdominal area. I was particularly struck when he told me that he has almost stopped reading books for the time being because he was living too much of his life "above the eyebrows." This was no small statement because Larry was a very sophisticated, well-read person. He is an artist and a writer and since then has completed his doctorate at UCLA on Diné ways of knowing, a fascinating field.

Over the years I have had the privilege of being invited to other Native American lands and of participating in many sacred ceremonies. One of such peak experiences was being invited to the Cheyenne River Reservation in South Dakota by Lakota, Dakota, Nakota Chief Arvol Looking Horse, the nineteenth generation pipe carrier of the White Buffalo Woman Pipe. The gathering was for the Mending of the Sacred Hoop ceremony and I made the long grueling journey by Greyhound bus.

It was one of the first times that religious leaders of other traditions had been invited for such an event. This gathering launched the annual celebration under Chief Arvol of a World Day of Prayer for Peace on June 21, the summer solstice. During my stay there I pitched my tent, without knowing it, in sight of the small building that housed the sacred pipe. It is jealously guarded, some say even by a battalion of fierce carpenter ants. I remember being kept awake several nights in prayer by deep feelings for the earth and by my proximity to what is like a holy sacrament for the Lakota people.

When it was time to begin the journey back home, I found it hard to leave the holy land filled with the power of Wakan Tanka, the Great Spirit. I also recognized that these lands are filled with much suffering and poverty and bitter memories of cruelty, oppression and racism. Yet I felt the sweet burden of taking the spiritual grace of these days back with me to try to become, more than ever, an advocate for the struggle and teachings of these noble and violated First Nations of our great Turtle Island continent. The Lakota prayer remains on my lips and in my heart: "Mitakuye oyasin—All my relations."

CHAPTER 31

EARTH SUMMITS / GLOBAL MOVEMENTS

IN THE LATE 80s and early 90s, after my painful separation from Children of War and simultaneously from my beloved Judith, there came a long hiatus of feeling useless. With Bob Dylan I felt "like a rolling stone, with no direction home, like a complete unknown." And yet it came both as a surprise and as no surprise when I received that unexpected phone call from Danny Martin inviting me to become involved in the planning activities for the UN Earth Summit (UNCED) in Rio in 1992.

Danny, a genial, charismatic Irish priest who later married, had convinced a group of mid- to high-level interfaith religious leaders under the umbrella of ICREE (International Coordinating Committee on Religion and the Earth) to explore the impact that the communities of faith could have on this historic gathering. It would be the first time that the UN would address the apparently opposing realities of environmental protection and development—the need for poor countries to progress economically and socially.

The key question was: Could we have both without one overwhelming the other? Would the creation of an environmentally sustainable world necessarily block the development of poor countries, especially if they followed the high-tech industrial model of the West? Does protecting rainforests, oceans, the atmosphere and water imply that underdeveloped countries will never be able to create societies that clothe, feed, educate and provide work for themselves? On the other hand, is this apparently insurmountable conflict between the environment and development real? It would seem that fulfilling the semi-official definition of sustainable development would be the self-evident path for all of "meeting the needs of the present without compromising the ability of future generations to meet their own needs."*

Whether it is the struggle between destruction of the Brazilian tropical rainforests along with their indigenous inhabitants and the logging companies or the demands of upstate New York residents that the greedy mining companies desist from poisoning their water supply through hydraulic fracturing ("fracking") of the shale, the unequal conflict between environment and development goes on. In the end, this apparent conflict seems to reluctantly make room for the natural world (and the poor), illustrating Thomas Berry's warning that you "can't negotiate with the earth."

In the end, the outcome of the Earth Summit would not be completely satisfactory to either party, especially because the rich, developed world would not let go of its privilege and wealth and fund poor developing countries for the clean energy technology necessary for them to become sustainable societies. This struggle would continue at each of the ensuing UN climate Change Conferences with the best outcome being inadequate pledges from the rich nations, which were usually not fulfilled. The general conviction of the poor countries that true development lay with the Western industrial model—instead of with a new sustainable path—brings to mind the words of James Baldwin that he was not so sure about whether Blacks wanted to be "integrated into a burning building."

The participants in the ICCRE meetings were a relatively open-minded group. They included Archbishop Sir Paul Reeves of New Zealand, who was the Anglican observer at the UN and was part Maori

---

* Brundtland Report, 1987.

himself. Then there was Rabbi Joseph Glaser of the Central Conference of American Rabbis, Dr. Eleanor Rae of the North American Conference on Religion and Ecology, Reverend "Skip" Vilas of the Episcopal Church and Danny Martin.

I may have seemed a little disruptive because it had become increasingly clear to me that the time had come for the indigenous voice to be heard at this upcoming UN Conference. I put forward the unusual, if not outrageous, proposition that at this unique moment of crisis in planetary history, the traditional Western and Eastern religions must take a sacred step backwards in holy humility to allow the spiritual traditions of the tribal peoples of the world to step forward into the center of the sacred circle with their earth wisdom. This powerful teaching held the key to resolving the crisis, which had been caused in part by the blindness of the Western religious traditions. This would not be an easy step and is still more of a dream than a reality.

One of the ICCRE projects was the creation of the First Earth Charter, which has since gone through many reincarnations and is now a popular document. I fought hard for the indigenous reality to be lifted up in this document and it was included in "the following changes necessary to stop the Earth's degradation and allow man to live in harmony with nature." One of these was promotion of "religious traditions that foster responsibility for the environment and challenging those that do not." It was here that further mention was made of indigenous religious tradition.

At that time, we naively believed that our Earth Charter might actually be incorporated into the final documents of the Earth Summit. In New York during the preparatory meetings of Rio at the UN, there seemed to be a rare unprecedented spirit of bonhomie and cooperation between the government delegates (especially a few of the environmentally attuned ones, like those from Scandinavia), the UN agencies involved and the citizens' groups (NGOs). We were allowed to have input into the official drafts and were welcomed into some closed meetings and so we expected that this spirit would prevail when we got to Rio.

But once we arrived in Brazil we quickly realized that we were in another world and that a great freeze had set in. First of all, the official UN meeting center was located at Rio Centro, an hour's drive away from the meeting and activity sites of the hundreds of NGO groups that had come to Rio, often at great expense and sacrifice. Rio Centro was also surrounded by barbed wire, armed guards and tight security, primarily to keep the scruffy non-official rabble away from the gates of the elect. This template would be replicated in subsequent UN environmental conferences allegedly convened so that "the voice of the world's people could be heard."

We assumed that some of the governments, probably led by the USA, had been threatened by the involvement and input of the NGOs during the New York City meetings. Some of these citizen's groups, led by brilliant, often knowledgeable, young leaders from developing countries, were especially threatening. Their detailed and well-documented analyses and recommendations were frequently insightful and compelling and were well received by some of the more open-minded government delegates. The NGO community had been persuaded that we could have substantial input and make a significant difference.

Some of the basic principles of our Earth Charter seemed to us rather fundamental, if not self-evident. These included promotion of environmental education as an integral and compulsory part of public education; promotion of food consumption that is lower on the food chain; revival of peaceful co-existence between people and wild animals; promotion of community as the basic unit for balanced environmental living; recognition of religious traditions that foster responsibility for the environment and a challenging of those that do not; and redistribution of land, wealth and natural resources "for the good of all." One can imagine that this last one would be seen as especially threatening by many governments and by the corporate delegates.

We quickly found out that the chances of having our Earth Charter incorporated into the UNCED (UN Conference on Environment and Development) final documents or having much impact on the proceedings was nil. Yet through some miracle, some language on the importance of indigenous traditional teaching for the environment did make it into the final official conference document.

At first glance, the choice of Brazil, with its poverty and rainforests and its jewel of Rio de Janeiro with the great Cristo statue overlooking the bay as the site of the summit seemed a brilliant one. But we discovered that while the Brazilian government had spent $200 million for an extravagant face-lift of this city composed of some of the world's most desperate slums (the favelas), local environmentalists complained that essential research institutes were denied basic funds to survive. There had also been a police sweep of thousands of street children and poor vagrants who had been rounded up into trucks and dumped into rural settings or other secure holding areas, lest the UN delegates and environmentalists see the true face of injustice and marginalization in Rio.

When I first arrived in Brazil, I felt a little like a fish out of water. There was so much going on: meetings, consultations, presentations and caucuses with which I could not connect. Thirty thousand NGO delegates had made their way and everyone was anxious to put forward their piece of "the environmental crisis."

At the site of NGO meetings and other activity, the Spirit soon showed me why I was in Rio. In the registration area across the large hall, I saw the handsome, aquiline profile of Chief Oren Lyons of the Six Nation Confederation in upper New York State, a friend with whom I had worked over the years, and he waved me over. After a warm greeting, he told me that he was with a group of indigenous representatives from all over the world. They had just returned from an all-indigenous meeting. However, they were either not registered for the conference, did not want to register under their country of origin but rather as members of their indigenous tribal nation or had no funds with which to register at all. Could I help? Many of them would be deeply disappointed because they had reluctantly left their often distant tribal lands at great hardship and expense and had come this long distance expecting to participate in the official conference.

I immediately went to work on behalf of the group. Of course, I naively imagined that the UN would welcome the participation of these tribal leaders and make special provisions for them. I found that the opposite was the case. In some way, they were a source of embarrassment because they might raise the delicate issue of Indian national sovereignty or land rights. This would confront nations such as the United States, Canada, Australia and others with the painful reality of appropriated indigenous land—land stolen over the centuries though bloodshed, genocide, plague-like diseases often spread intentionally by the invaders—and centuries of injustice and exploitation. Where there had been treaties, most of them had been observed in the breach. What these governments wanted least of all was to have these dark-skinned people, in strange regalia and speaking unfamiliar languages with long, accurate memories and sometimes even indicting documents, to raise embarrassing issues about their land rights or national sovereignty. Nor were they anxious to hear the principles, ethics and even rights of the Earth raised from an indigenous perspective.

In the end after much conflict and pressure, the official conference would allow only one indigenous speaker, Chief Oren Lyons, at the official Earth Summit and that only came about after pressure from many sides. In the meantime, even the effort to gain accreditation for some of these noble people from all over the world as NGOs seemed formidable. I immediately began to knock on doors, fight with the registration office and even made one long, frustrating trip to the official site at Rio Centro to twist some bureaucratic arms.

I naively tried to make the case that these people had more right to be at this "Earth" Summit than almost anybody else and that they should not have to pay (because often they could not). And further, that they must not be forced to register as citizens of the United States, Canada, Brazil, Colombia, et cetera, since they did not consider themselves citizens of those countries. They had their own national identity and sometimes their own passports, as Oren Lyons always carried.

Somehow, through a combination of the intervention of the Great Spirit and a few enlightened and concerned people I found in the UN system, we managed to get all the indigenous delegates accreditation, sometimes with fees waived and people looking the other way as to national designation. These were happy exceptions to the indifferent and hostile UN policies at the time. I had experienced this earlier when this attitude practically slammed the door in the face of the Hopi elder Grandfather David during the 1978 Special Session on Disarmament. When we did finally arrange for Thomas Benyaca, another Hopi leader, to address the general assembly in 1982, he spoke to a half-empty room. It is almost miraculous to report that in 2002, a UN Permanent Forum for Indigenous People was established where this important constituency can (almost) be recognized and occasionally have its voice heard within the UN community.

Then I helped this group of indigenous delegates find a welcoming pipe ceremony being held for all the indigenous people. They immediately joined the sacred circle and felt at home.

Many people found the networking and camaraderie of the NGO conference inspiring and informative, but it was not only an hour's drive but many political light-years away from the action of the official Earth Summit for which many of the thirty thousand had come. This caused much frustration. There was a dramatic march through the streets of Rio one afternoon, made up of a Brazilian group as well as international

NGOs, in protest against the lack of political courage and principles of the official UN conference proper.

I came up with the idea of having a religious event both of protest and support right within the precincts of the official conference center at Rio Centro. This seemed highly unlikely in light of the tight security and policy of separateness. We were stonewalled by the UN officials until I suggested that a non-violent sit-in of religious leaders might not be good publicity for the conference. So in the end we created an inspiring Witness for the Earth under United Church of Christ (UCC) sponsorship and they later produced a beautiful video.

In the end, a group of young delegates (often the most hopeful constituency) accused the conference of selling out to "transnational corporations, the United States, Japan, the World Bank and the IMF." After staging a non-violent sit-in in the lobby, they were stripped of their credentials and ejected from the hall. So much for intergenerational dialogue.

Each day makes it clearer that unless the Western corporate model ultimately supported by the Rio Conference is restrained, and industrialization and growth is mitigated and transformed, the future of our planet is in grave jeopardy. The great Thomas Berry puts it simply:

> "Will the human economy be accepted as a subsystem of the earth economy? The greatest folly of our times may be the setting of these two in opposition to each other when obviously any conflict between the two is a disaster for both . . . . The transnational corporations, with allegiances to no other power than themselves, now control almost every phase of human activity and have turned this power toward control of the earth process on a global scale."*

The Business Council for Sustainable Development, the newly born coalition of multi-national corporations touted as an NGO, called for self-regulation rather than government regulation. This position and the mostly toothless documents of UNCED did not set specific binding timelines or targets for the attending governments, even for the signatories of the respective protocols. The General Environmental Facility, run by the World Bank, has only minimally increased environmental aid to third world countries.

* Evening Thoughts: Reflecting on Earth as a Sacred Community Counterpoint, 2006.

In so many words, the message of President George H. W. Bush to the summit was: "The American way of life is non-negotiable." Other countries, especially those from the developing world, did not mistake his message.

In contrast, President Fidel Castro of Cuba delivered one of the most powerful and profound speeches of the Earth Summit. It was historic because it only lasted three minutes (instead of his usual three-hour lectures). Brilliant and eloquent, it was the only speech at the summit that received a long standing ovation. He said among other things:

> "An important biological species is in danger of disappearing due to the fast and progressive destruction of its natural living conditions: mankind. We have now become aware of this problem when it is almost too late to stop it. . . . Tomorrow it will be too late to do what we should have done a long time ago."

Sad to say, Earth Summit II, held ten years later (2002) in Johannesburg, South Africa, which I also attended, made the Rio conference look promising by comparison. Its only accomplishment was a plan of action, which was neither. The voluntary "partnership" between governments, corporations and even NGOs could not take the place of legally binding laws or treaties between governments. It lacked leadership, except for the negative leadership of the United States that was taking us all straight over the edge of the ecological cliff. This time the president of the United States did not even deign to attend the summit, although many world leaders came. His absence in South Africa was interpreted as a sign of contempt for the agenda of the world's poor.

I was personally disappointed by my first visit to South Africa after a long involvement in the anti-apartheid struggle and especially after my work with the extraordinary young South African leaders of Children of War. This time one of the sites of the NGO encampment, the Mbutu Village, was even more grossly co-opted by corporate exhibits, booths and presence. But even here among the many NGOs there were pinpoints of light, especially the Circle of Faith, organized by Tribal Link Foundation and others, which served as a sanctuary for silence and meditation amidst the political hubbub. The circle also hosted several interfaith gatherings, especially a powerful fire ceremony for the healing of the Earth, and of South Africa in particular, convened by indigenous spiritual leaders from all over the world.

The official UN conference site was the super-luxurious Sandston Convention Center located in an upscale suburb many miles removed from the NGO site and even more distant from the misery of the townships that are like so many running sores of beautiful "Joburg." It was guarded like an elegant armed fortress.

The official conference could have been on another planet. Some of the township people who were organizing themselves at their own meetings were not even allowed to march near the conference center in Sandston, which had become a militarized zone.

I had the bittersweet privilege of visiting some of the noble South African people in the destitute townships of Soweto and Alexandria. A large percentage of the population lives in these townships. I had learned to love the South African spirit through my encounters with some of our Children of War young leaders. Now that racial apartheid had been conquered, there still remained the cruel economic apartheid of unequal distribution of wealth, deprivation of water rights, wretched housing and unemployment.

I met courageous, critically ill HIV-positive mothers and their children, who sang us a moving welcome song, as well as inspiring members of religious communities living in the midst of much hardship who were personally and politically living out their faith in the Christ who had come to "preach good news to the poor."

The final draft of the summit could not even accept—due to American pressure—the setting of any targets and timetables for reducing the carbon emissions into the atmosphere and increasing even minimally the production of the world's energy from renewable sources. Similarly, no agreement was reached on significant financial support for the technical assistance so essential to the developing countries to help them move into a more sustainable economy and lifestyle.

Next I had the mixed experience of participating in the 2009 UN conference in Copenhagen where I was invited to give a presentation on "the Global Warming Crisis and the Prophetic Role of the Communities of Faith" to the educational caucus of the UN Commission on Sustainable Development, a small but impressive group, which gave me a sympathetic hearing. A total of forty thousand people attended the entire conference, most of them NGOs.

Access to the official Bella Center was once more severely restricted, even to accredited people; thousands of NGOs stood in the bitter cold and never got in (part of UN strategy?). Never mind the mainly youthful masses whose enthusiasm, courage and creativity never cease to inspire. Hundreds of the latter were brutally arrested and made to sit on the cold pavement for hours—often for just showing up—by the police of this allegedly progressive and sustainable city and country. The outcome of this conference was pathetic and devoid of substance—in spite of President Obama's brief cameo appearance and some mild political arm wrestling with the Chinese.

As a result of similar negative experiences over the years, I have mixed feelings about attending future conferences of this sort, unless there are serious indications promising substantive results. People much more knowledgeable than I believe that we must now place our hopes in the emergence of a new, powerful global popular social movement for climate change and on local and regional efforts. Such efforts include the World Mayors Council on Climate Change where 135 mayors agreed to serious environmental measures, the coalition of Northeastern US states (temporarily stalled because of the 2010 Republican ascendancy) and courageous efforts by California. Hans Joachim Schellnhuber, the German Chancellor Angela Merkel's chief climate advisor, is a strong proponent of this local and regional strategy as opposed to the hopeless international decision-making process at UN conferences.

I stuck to my ambivalent resolution and did not join the crowd for the December 2010 UN climate conference in Cancún, Mexico. Bill McKibben, dedicated climate activist of 350.org, commenting on the similar cast of characters—pro and con—from other UN gatherings observed that "it was like a family gathering on the *Titanic*."

Once again, there were no binding goals or timelines for carbon reduction and no clear, adequate and enforceable financial commitments from the rich world for the clean energy technology urgently needed by the developing countries. It was almost pathetic to see the post-mortems of Cancún desperately trying to extract any "accomplishments" from a menu of failures and compromises.

Fortuitously, during the weeks before, some of the leaked Wikileaks diplomatic documents revealed the cruel economic arm-twisting and bribery that the developed countries—especially the US government— applied to the poor countries to lower their voices and to conform to the goals and policies of the coal and oil companies. One of the few "future-looking" decisions of the conference was the plan for another UN conference in 2011, once again in South Africa. In the end there was little reason to regret my decision not to participate in the Climate Change Conference in Mexico.

It was only a little discouraging (little because we didn't expect much) to report about the next conference in Durban in December 2011. One wonders how they had the nerve to return to South Africa after the disappointment in Johannesburg in 2009.

A clear-eyed young policy analyst from Friends of the Earth brilliantly summed the conference up as having "lacked ambition, equity and justice." She described the conference as "one more milestone" of delayed action for five to ten years while awaiting a treaty, of shifting the burden of change primarily onto the backs of the developing nations, who did not cause the problem and, finally, of lacking fairness in not providing concrete funds (as opposed to promising them) to help poor countries become sustainable. One delegate summed it all up as: "Allow Africa to burn."

As always, the best news was the young people with the new energy of Occupy Wall Street and their "mike check" disruptions, who brought some life to the scene.

These disheartening developments (with the presence of the Republican/"Tea-bagger" caucus in the Congress, most of whom even deny the reality of global warming) and increasing reports of major environmental disasters in Russia, Pakistan, Brazil and Australia cast a pall over my spirits. It was a time to regroup, to strategize, to build community and to hunker down into those deep places where one reconnects to the roots of faith and prayer.

CHAPTER 32

CLIMATE CRISIS COALITION
Turning to the Future

IT WAS IN DECEMBER OF 2003 that I awoke in the middle of the night, sat up straight in my bed and said aloud to myself: "My God, it's global warming!" At that time I was deeply involved in the movement against the bloody, never-ending war in Iraq. The work for peace and justice in its many forms has always been my passion over the years. But that night it came to me with crystal clarity that I was now to make the issue of the climate crisis of the Earth the priority of my life's work.

I had gradually become more aware of this great danger to all living beings and I had increasingly been filled with grief and fear at its historic and unprecedented impact on the planet. The growing realities of record temperatures, melting glaciers, swelling oceans, the spread of climate-related diseases and the increasing disappearance of species were haunting my thoughts and breaking my heart. I had been shocked by the under-reported story of more than forty thousand deaths of mostly older people from the 2003 heat wave in Europe, accompanied by raging forest fires.

Now through this midnight epiphany the inspiration came to me that I should help form a new kind of coalition that would transcend the borders of the traditional environmental movement. The broad and inclusive composition of the new partnership must make the statement that no one will be immune to this plague of the industrial age. My vision was that this coalition would invite the peace movement, youth, labor unions, farmers, low-income communities, people of color, especially Native Americans, women, scientists, business-people, artists and many more. It was to be a vision of what Dr. King had called the "beloved community."

Over the next months of contacting people and organizations, I began to slowly and painfully realize just how ambitious this dream was and how unreasonable it appeared to many. This was only in 2003 and yet it was light-years ago in terms of a less-developed public consciousness and perception of the issue—even in politically enlightened circles. It's hard to believe how much has transpired during those brief years—inadequate to be sure—but suffice it to say that there was nothing in the air then about an Oscar-winning documentary by Al Gore, Nobel Prizes awarded to him and the UN Intergovernmental Panel on Climate Change (IPCC) nor cover stories in *Time* and *Forbes*, and major policy statements by the United Nations and the British government.

I hasten to add that after the 2010 mid-term congressional elections one feels less sanguine. Even with a Democratic majority, the less-than-courageous Senate was unable to pass a basically mediocre and toothless energy bill. Now with the new members, close to half of the Republicans newly elected to the Congress are members of the Flat Earth Club of global warming deniers.

Of course, I naively thought back then that my comrades in the peace and justice movement would be the natural constituency to accept this new idea. Not so fast, my good utopian buddy. I even presented the idea at a steering committee meeting of United for Peace and Justice

(UFPJ), the main peace coalition that I had helped to launch and had supported right from its inception, especially in the faith community. It seemed obvious to me that as long as the US continued its addiction to fossil fuel, it would also have to extend its ruthless wars and imperial ambitions into Iraq, the Middle East and other oil-rich parts of the planet. No one could disagree with the basic premise of my proposal. But the conclusion that the issue of global warming would, in the not-too-distant future, become a primary one, perhaps even overshadowing other major issues such as modern warfare, the economic crisis, poverty, hunger and disease, seemed completely farfetched to them. Instead of being welcomed like a respected comrade, I was benignly regarded as some kind of elderly eccentric Luddite—out of touch with the seriousness of the war in Iraq and other related issues.

After my failed appeal to the UFPJ steering committee, I was unexpectedly approached by Ted Glick, an old co-worker for peace, who was present at the meeting. I had performed the marriage ceremony for him and his wife, Jane, years ago. To my surprise, he expressed great interest in my ideas and said that he had been thinking along similar lines. Of course, I was delighted and we quickly set up a meeting to have an intensive discussion about devising a strategy and laying down some concrete plans to give flesh to our common vision. It was out of these discussions that the Climate Crisis Coalition (CCC) was born. Then Connie Hogarth, an old friend and laborer in the peace and justice vineyard, also expressed interest in our project. We were soon joined by Ross Gelbspan, one of the godfathers of global warming consciousness, a Pulitzer Prize-winning editor and author of the seminal book *The Boiling Point*. In it he implied his support of the CCC vision: "Any successful [climate change] movement must involve horizontal alliances with groups involved in international relief and development, campaign finance reform, public health, corporate accountability, labor, human rights, and environmental justice."

After that first dialogue, we decided to convene an organizing meeting in March 2004, which would reflect the vision and political breadth of the new and diverse coalition that we hoped to create. On the night before our meeting, filled with some trepidation about the ambitiousness of our plans, I called my Native American friend and mentor Larry Emerson in New Mexico. I still remember his enthusiasm and down-home response: "What you guys are doing is really neat." He assured me that his prayers at sunrise with the sacred corn pollen would be focused across the continent on the success of our venture. I slept peacefully that night.

We felt strongly about the importance of including African Americans, Latinos, Native Americans, labor and other constituencies not usually included as part of the environmental movement right from the ground floor. The late great Damu Smith, an old friend and a pioneer of the Black environmental justice movement, made the long trip from Washington to join us. The meeting opened with the moving traditional prayer and song of Clayton Thomas-Muller, a young Cree leader from Canada. So literally on a wing and a prayer we launched this ambitious venture for Mother Earth.

A great blessing was the acquisition of a staff person, the multi-talented Tom Stokes, who was to become the executive director of the CCC. The CCC set up its office in the beautiful Berkshire Mountains of western Massachusetts—a fitting site for our daunting task—and slowly assembled a small but competent staff. This was one more leap of faith in my journey. With almost no funds, relatively few tested allies and an issue that was almost invisible, we began that familiar and yet always intimidating challenge of walking on water.

Our first public action was such an act of faith—and also a humbling experience. The CCC organized an all-night vigil and fast outside the US Capitol in Washington to encourage strong congressional energy legislation. We had been promised support and attendance by the participants of a nearby green energy fair but our event was never announced or encouraged. So a small but hardy group of CCC staff, organizers, some board members and a few loyal friends gave witness that night. I can still remember wrapping myself in my sleeping bag as we stood in vigil and sat in our lawn chairs on that cold autumn night of September 18–19 in 2004. One of the inspirations of the evening was Sister Clare, a Buddhist nun from Massachusetts, deeply devoted to the international peace marches, who beat the prayer drum all night for the planet and to keep our raggedy movement awake. We were also joined by a sweet young man who had learned about us on the Internet and who symbolized hope for the future. Such was our modest beginning.

Our first major public action took place in December of 2005. The signers of the UN Kyoto Global Warming Protocol (along with some of the prominent embarrassing non-signers like our own government) were gathering in Montréal, and the world's slowly growing climate change movement was converging on the freezing Canadian city. The CCC helped to bring Americans to swell the ranks of tens of thousands of Canadians and led the presentation of our Peoples Ratification of the Kyoto Global Warming Treaty—"Kyoto and Beyond"—petitions (endorsed by Al Gore) along with other petitions to the US Embassy. Later we helped to inspire a national emergency email and phone campaign that helped to shame the US delegation to the conference from at least not abandoning the Kyoto process altogether.

In a few short years, the CCC has achieved an impressive list of accomplishments. In the beginning, we often provided the table around which a broad spectrum of organizations gathered for unified action—a proper role for a coalition. We raised the issue during the 2006 congressional elections and convened several well-attended strategy meetings hosted by United Health Care Union 1199 in New York, with racially and politically diverse participants. In its early years our coalition process had increasingly created a sense of confidence in the CCC and in its ability to serve as a trusted convener for projects, activities, and a collective response to significant political moments or events.

In November 2008, the CCC became one of the principal initiators along with other groups of the Price Carbon Campaign, a visionary effort to transform the controversial issue of a simple carbon tax into a strategic centerpiece of the movement to stop global warming. In the beginning there was some debate among the CCC leadership but I and others pushed for this important step as opposed to the cap and trade policy, soundly defeated in the Lieberman-Warner Energy Bill but still supported by "Big Green" the large, well-funded Washington-based environmental groups. Most of Congress still bristles at even the mention of the word "tax" although there are several good bills being proposed.

We took our new campaign to Washington and had briefings for House and Senate members and their staffs led by Dr. James Hansen of NASA, a strong supporter of the carbon tax along with other economic and scientific experts. A small group of us also had some good meetings with those few Representatives supporting this position. I especially recall the integrity and intelligence of Republican Bob Inglis of South Carolina, defeated by the "Teabaggers" in 2010 and accused of "satanic beliefs" for his recognition of climate change as a reality.

In November 2010, the CCC was one of the primary organizers of a highly successful national conference on pricing carbon at Weslyan University in Connecticut attended by an overflow crowd and watched by thirty thousand students on the Internet. The interest and enthusiasm of the young people was inspiring and plans were laid quickly for similar conferences in other parts of the country.

In the meantime, CCC has become less active. However, I became involved in 2011 in co-founding IMAC (Interfaith Moral Action on Climate). This reflected my deep conviction of the need for a prophetic interfaith network to confront climate change as the greatest moral challenge of our time.

The reality is that global warming is probably so far advanced that we will only have a short window of opportunity before its full impact is felt. We most likely cannot stop it, but we can still prevent some of its worst consequences through a crash program of clean energy and conservation. On a personal level, the burden of this knowledge sometimes made it painful to work on this issue on a daily basis.

The time has come to start talking seriously and candidly about our inability to fully reduce the amount of carbon in the atmosphere and fully reduce its impact because climate systems move so slowly. Climate systems change so slowly that even if we were to halt carbon production tomorrow and shift to clean energy, it might still take decades to return to a state of balance. Mark Hertsgaard, a leading climate journalist, has written, "the battle to prevent climate change, feeble as it was, is over. Now the race to survive it has begun." As we intensify our struggle against its most extreme consequences, we must teach our people—especially our youth who are the heirs of the future—how to practically, emotionally and spiritually survive and live in a world profoundly changed by global warming. This is also a primary pastoral task for the communities of faith.

The day is far advanced and the news is not good. We can take some modest hope from changes already taking place. They are an inadequate but a hopeful beginning. Even in the six short years since the inception of the CCC, impressive changes have taken place in which we have occasionally played a modest but valuable role. Much remains undone—specially the broadening of our movement, particularly to strengthen the leadership of poor people and people of color. Hundreds of thousands have seen Al Gore's film An Inconvenient Truth followed up by a creative program to train traveling activist educators. However, there is still a disastrous tendency to give—in the interest of "balance"—the same media time and respectful credence to the minority of skeptical scientists, many funded by corporations that have a stake in delaying action, as opposed to the majority scientific position. With the 2010 election of the new "Teabaggers," the movement to discredit climate scientists has intensified.

We are still lacking a mass climate change movement proportionate to the crisis. Consciousness is moderate at best, even in progressive circles. There have been numerous relatively small but significant civil disobedience actions across the country. On May 20, 2009, fifteen of us were arrested for peaceably blocking the door to the DC office of Representative Rick Boucher, at the time one of the major recipients of Big Coal money in West Virginia, who had received $176,000 for a recent election campaign. He had done almost more than anyone else to oppose and weaken a strong climate bill and we hoped that our action might dramatize the need for effective energy legislation.

The Capitol Police nearly kept me for a longer visit in the grim DC jail because I had been arrested twice for non-violent actions during the previous year—once for protesting the war in Afghanistan at the White House and once in Senator Joe Lieberman's office for his role in undermining a single payer health bill. Thankfully, a severe but thorough African American desk sergeant discovered late that night that I had no outstanding arrest warrants and I was allowed to go home.

While small acts of conscience are important, these critical times call for mass civil disobedience. It was heartening that in the summer of 2011, a powerful campaign was organized to stop the construction of the dangerous XL Pipeline designed to carry one of the dirtiest forms of petroleum extracted from the tar sand deposits of Alberta, Canada, to the Gulf of Mexico. It was inspired by Bill McKibben of 350.org and many young people and resulted in a two-week campaign of civil disobedience at the White House with over twelve hundred arrests. I was arrested on August 29 along with a religious group. We were joined in our arrest by James Hansen, the climate scientist who predicted that if the pipeline was constructed, it would be "game over" for the global warming crisis. (He has since resigned from NASA so that he can speak more freely.) On November 6, some twelve thousand people surrounded the White House and, much to our joy, on January 18, 2012 the Obama administration announced that it was denying permission for the construction of the XL pipeline. This decision is once again being "reconsidered" undoubtedly due to the corporate pressure of Big Oil and Big Coal.

NOTE: Up until March 11, 2011, I saw my work with the environment primarily driven by the global warming crisis. Now with the Japanese earthquake and tsunami and a nuclear disaster possibly approaching

Chernobyl-like proportions, the framework we operate in has been dramatically altered. Once again I must find ways of taking up the work of supporting the Japanese groups who are trying to alert their country and the world to the dangers of nuclear development and also connect to the nuclear perils within our own borders.

We must now fall in love with the Earth again and form the most powerful movement for social, political and cultural change in planetary history. Our coalition must literally include everybody: Evangelical Christians (who have come out with some excellent statements), soccer moms, hunters and fisherfolk, conservatives and liberals. This will not be an easy wedding but there is no other way. It will be a challenge to our social change movements to think "outside the box," to harness our collective creative imagination, to do something we have never done before—be politically principled even while we make room for unfamiliar bedfellows. The Earth will settle for nothing less. In this respect, it was encouraging to see Pope Benedict XVI speak out more frequently, depicting climate change as a moral issue along with even stronger statements by the Dalai Lama and other religious leaders. Most exemplary has been the courageous leadership of the Ecumenical "Green" Patriarch Bartholomew of Constantinople.

But the challenge transcends global warming. It goes to the most fundamental assumptions of our scientific-industrial culture. Even John Broder of the New York Times wrote after the Durban conference, expressing skepticism about these conferences: "Effectively addressing climate change will require over the coming decades a fundamental remaking of energy production, transportation and agriculture around the world—the sinews of modern life" (December 12, 2011).

This extremity of the earth crisis could create a moment of planetary awakening. David Korten, in his important book, The Great Turning: From Empire to Earth Community,* lays out a compelling vision. It entails a turning away from Empire with its strategy of "domination at all levels from relations among nations to relations among family members" and a turning towards Earth Community. This includes a world organized to guarantee the well-being of the many instead of ownership and profit by the few. The turning towards Earth Community "by contrast organizes by partnership, unleashes the human potential for creative cooperation and shares resources and surpluses for the good of all." This is a model that

---

* The Great Turning: From Empire to Earth Community, Berrett-Koehler Publishers 2007.

strangely enough both Karl Marx and Jesus would recognize, although it simply flows from the deepest aspirations of the human heart.

But, as I begin my eighty-second year and look back over my unpredictable life and look forward to a frighteningly uncertain future for our planet, I think of a technology even more ancient and more powerful than what the Internet offers us for communication—the technology of the human heart. It is what has guided my life at its best and what must now guide us all out of the seemingly hopeless dilemma that we have trapped ourselves into.

This is what Thomas Berry must have had in mind when, in his book *The Dream of the Earth*, he alluded to the "supreme pathology" of our present situation. The wisdom he offers us instead is that we must now embrace our original genetic coding that is connected to the earth rather than our cultural coding, which has created what is perhaps the greatest crisis for all species in planetary history.

This is what has always been one of the most hopeful insights in his writings for me because it suggests that the Earth herself can call forth from the depth of our being insights and actions that will show us the way to the light. How profoundly fitting that it should be the Earth as Mother who, with her love and wisdom, can still speak directly to our hearts, if we can once again learn this ancient heart-to-heart communication.

As I wrestle with the final pages of this tale (enough already!) and my desire to leave my readers who have made it this far—especially the young people—a few hints for the future, a remarkable book has come into my hands, surely brought by the Divine Muse. This treasure is entitled: *The Secret Teachings of Plants: The Intelligence of the Heart in the Direct Perception of Nature* by Stephen Harrod Buhner.

In it, Buhner, a wonderful poet as well as a brilliant herbalist researcher, teaches us that the most recent neurological findings have discovered that most of the heart is composed of neural cells, making it a brain in its own right with its own intelligence—not in the linear, rational, scientific mode of the cerebral brain but rather in a "holistic/intuitive/depth mode of cognition." Thus the heart as an organ of perception can communicate with and gather information from the plants and the entire natural world in a manner that is "extremely elegant, sophisticated and exact."

The role of brain and heart have taken on a new dramatic import for me as on February 7, 2013, I had a cancerous brain tumor removed ironically on the very day on which I should have appeared in criminal court for an Occupy Wall Street civil disobedience action. I am working on healing myself through holistic and natural means.

But back to the heart as "an organ of perception". Larry Emerson has taught me that the way indigenous and all ancient people have learned the uses of plants as medicines—and other teachings from the natural world—not by analysis and trial and error but by communication. "Talk to the tobacco when you pray with it, listen to the fire during the ceremony." They have learned from the heart of the world by using their own heart as "an organ of perception."

Buhner says that in order to save the planet—really to save ourselves—we must "come to our senses" and reclaim this ability that has been built into our being over evolutionary times. In this way, Berry offers us his pearl of wisdom that we must reconnect with our genetic coding to the earth. The primary challenge is to reclaim this power from its theft by the linear/analytical/reductionist/scientific culture and its way of knowing that sees the world as a machine and is destroying it. Any deep, effective, lasting ecological strategy and action must be rooted in this ancient and utterly modern way of perceiving the Earth and connecting to it/her in this way. Thus our falling in love with the Earth again is a very concrete and practical strategy.

I write these lines in Jamaica, where I am visiting at the very western tip of this glorious island right next to the old lighthouse. My little cabana is perched high above the blue-green Caribbean on top of the ancient cliffs. I am in awe of this towering volcanic rock formation and its primitive sculpting over the millennia by the powerful ocean. I marvel at the beauty of the crustacean fossils embedded in the stone, as if by clear artistic design.

Although linear Western scientific culture would have me regard all of this as lifeless and inanimate, the rich insights of this book and the experience of my heart open me to the intense aliveness of sea, cliffs, plants and sky. May they speak to me and I to them not as poetry but as that deep reality that can begin to lead us out of our planetary cul de sac to a new culture of hope.

"Surely goodness, goodness and mercy shall follow me all the days of my life."

"Psalm 23"

Epilogue

The day will come after harnessing the ether, the winds, the tides and gravity itself, we shall harness in God the energies of love, and on that day for the second time in the history of the world, humanity will have discovered fire.

—Pierre Teilhard de Chardin, *The Divine Milieu*

To those of you who have persevered this far, I offer congratulations and gratitude. I wish us all blessings and good fortune as we face the future. It could very well be the most challenging century of human history and it will require tremendous faith and steadfastness of purpose, not only to survive but even more to transform.

What history is calling for is nothing less than the creation of a new human being. We must literally reinvent ourselves through the alchemy of the Spirit or perish. We are being divinely summoned to climb another rung on the evolutionary ladder, to another level of human consciousness.

In the magnificent dinosaur exhibit of the American Museum of Natural History, we see how relatively minor evolutionary changes in the jaw joint of the Tenontosaurus dinosaur created amazing new possibilities of both nutrition and survival for this ancient creature. Can we also learn from the evolutionary wisdom of that first fish that had the audacity to emerge from the sea onto dry land to take that miraculous first step of becoming an amphibious creature? Can we now become the architects of "a new human" as in the vision of the great Pierre Teilhard de Chardin?

Let us envision a global citizens' movement of historic proportions and imagine a million green tendrils reaching into millions of local

343

communities connected to each other across planet Earth. We are speaking of a transformation in politics and institutions, in consciousness and values, as well as in personal and family relationships.

This will clearly require a revolution, hopefully non-violent, a confrontation with the principalities and powers of the corporate state with its anti-vision of Empire rather than the dream of global Earth Community. Could this be "the new heavens and the new earth" (Isaiah 65:17, Rev. 21:1) that have been prophesied? It is already happening in microcosm—in the midst of much darkness. We experience simultaneous bursts of light in the growing aspirations and vision, in the holy dissatisfaction with the status quo both of individuals and of communities, no matter where one travels on our beautiful planet. This miracle will require a historic act of faith in the divine powers, however we understand them, in ourselves and in each other.

It seems that the brilliant writings of Eckhart Tolle, spiritual teacher and trailblazer, offer some extraordinary insights into the path of planetary consciousness transformation. His challenge of "evolve or perish" is right on the mark. His teachings transcend denominational borders in a remarkably universal manner and are awakening millions across the Earth.

We must encounter the Divine in authentic prayer and deep humility as never before. All of this must transcend the suffocating and boring categories of so much that passes for religion. (Forgive me if I also dissent from the new fervent evangelism around atheism, much of which is as boring as its religious counterpart, although I concur with the revulsion against reactionary and dehumanizing forms of religion from which it stems. After all, what thoughtful human being is not part atheist? [Note the recent reports of Mother Teresa's struggle with unbelief and doubt.] But do we really need another fervent atheist "religion"?)

I especially have the shining eyes of all our youth before me as I write, eyes filled with the enthusiasm of their loving and open hearts. In testimony to them, may these pages be not just one more self-serving, narcissistic, pious tome, but rather a word of truth in lying times, to offer some guidance both through my victories and missteps and occasionally provide some entertainment.

I also write for all good people who might benefit from my eccentric roller-coaster life. It's been one hell of an interesting ride and I rejoice in the myriad people I have loved and who have loved me. Their name is legion and I want to thank them all. I also want to thank all those to whom I have been a pain in the ass and those who have reciprocated in kind by making my life difficult. Without them I might have stayed the same and never been forced to change. What a bore. No hard feelings, but with some of you, I would do it again and maybe I will still have to: the bishops, the FBI directors, the religious superiors, the Henry Kissingers and all the others at the top of the food chain.

Above all, I want to thank God for putting up with me, for never giving up on me in spite of my stupidities, betrayals and vanities. My life has been filled to overflowing with grace and blessings. May these pages in some small way give Her honor and thanks. I have been surrounded by the kingdom of the miraculous all the way. Even when the way seemed dark and uncertain, the God of love never deserted me, even for a moment.

May these pages be a testimony to this furnace of divine love that has continued to rage and roar within and without me all these many years. All gratitude to the Seraphic beings who have guided and guarded my journey.

> "Set me as a seal upon your heart, as a seal upon your arm, for love is strong as death, passions fierce as the grave. Its flashes are flashes of fire, a raging flame. Many waters cannot quench love, neither can floods drown it." (Song of Songs 8:6)

List of Images

CHAPTER 1   BERTEL MAYER WITH PAUL MICHAEL MAYER 1931

CHAPTER 2   1942

CHAPTER 3   1946

CHAPTER 4,5 ST PAULS ABBEY NEWTOWN NJ

CHAPTER 6   CIVIL RIGHTS EXHIBIT

CHAPTER 10   NAOMI MAYER W PARENTS BERTEL AND ERNEST MAYER 1968

CHAPTER 11   PAUL WITH DANIEL BERRIGAN

CHAPTER 13   PAUL WITH NAOMI MAYER

CHAPTER 14   PAUL WITH NAOMI AND CHILDREN, PETER AND MARIA, EAST ORANGE NJ

CHAPTER 21   PAUL WITH TOM DAVIDSON (PAULS R)

CHAPTER 23   PAUL RECEIVED BY FIDEL CASTRO

CHAPTER 25   SPEAKING AT DNC 1984

CHAPTER 26   (L-R) JUDITH THOMPSON, UNKNOWN, PAUL AND ARN CHORN-POND

CHAPTER 27   (L-R) GRANDCHILDREN BRANDON, KRISTOPHER, TATIANA AND SHANA

CHAPTER 32   WITH GRANDSON ALASDAIR

www.ingramcontent.com/pod-product-compliance
Lightning Source LLC
Chambersburg PA
CBHW060325100426

42812CB00003B/887